THE CONTEMPORARY SHAKESPEARE SERIES

VOLUME V

Antony and Cleopatra
*
Measure for Measure
*
The Merry Wives of Windsor
*
Troilus and Cressida
*
The Two Gentlemen of Verona

Edited by A. L. Rowse

Modern Text with Introduction

UNIVERSITY PRESS OF AMERICA

Copyright © 1986 by A.L. Rowse

University Press of America,® Inc.

4720 Boston Way
Lanham, MD 20706

3 Henrietta Street
London WC2E 8LU England

Library of Congress Cataloging-in-Publication Data
(Revised for vol. 5)

Shakespeare, William, 1564-1616.
  The contemporary Shakespeare series.

  Contents: v. 1. Hamlet. Julius Caesar. The merchant of
Venice. A Midsummer night's dream. Romeo and Juliet.
The tempest—[etc.]—v. 5. The merry wives of Windsor.
Measure for measure. Antony and Cleopatra. Troilus and
Cressida. The two gentlemen of Verona.
  I. Rowse, A.L. (Alfred Leslie), 1903-
I.Title.
PR2754.R67   1984b   822.3'3   84-5105
ISBN 0-8191-3934-3 (alk. paper)

The plays in this volume are also available individually in
paperbound editions from University Press of America.

Book design by Leon Bolognese

WHY A CONTEMPORARY SHAKESPEARE?

The starting point of my project was when I learned both from television and in education, that Shakespeare is being increasingly dropped in schools and colleges because of the difficulty of the language. In some cases, I gather, they are given just a synopsis of the play, then the teacher or professor embroiders from his notes.

This is deplorable. We do not want Shakespeare progressively dropped because of superfluous difficulties that can be removed, skilfully, conservatively, keeping to every line of the text. Nor must we look at the question statically, for this state of affairs will worsen as time goes on and we get further away from the language of 400 years ago—difficult enough in all conscience now.

We must begin by ridding our mind of prejudice, i.e. we must not pre-judge the matter. A friend of mine on New York radio said that he was 'appalled' at the very idea; but when he heard my exposition of what was proposed he found it reasonable and convincing.

3

Just remember, I do not need it myself: *I live in the Elizabethan age*, Shakespeare's time, and have done for years, and am familiar with its language, and his. But even for me there are still difficulties—still more for modern people, whom I am out to help.

Who, precisely?

Not only students at school and in college, but all readers of Shakespeare. Not only those, but all viewers of the plays, in the theatre, on radio and television—actors too, who increasingly find pronunciation of the words difficult, particularly obsolete ones—and there are many, besides the difficulty of accentuation.

The difficulties are naturally far greater for non-English-speaking peoples. We must remember that he is our greatest asset, and that other peoples use him a great deal in learning our language. There are no Iron Curtains for him—though, during Mao's Cultural Revolution in China, he was prohibited. Now that the ban has been lifted, I learn that the Chinese in thousands flock to his plays.

Now, a good deal that was grammatical four hundred years ago is positively ungrammatical today. We might begin by removing what is no longer good grammar.

For example: plural subjects with a verb in the singular:

'*Is* Bushy, Green and the earl of Wiltshire dead?' Any objection to replacing 'is' correctly by 'are'? Certainly not. I notice that some modern editions already correct—

These high wild hills and rough uneven ways
Draw*s* out our miles and make*s* them wearisome

to 'draw' and 'make', quite sensibly. Then, why not go further and regularise this Elizabethan usage to modern, consistently throughout?

Similarly with archaic double negatives—'Nor shall you not think neither'—and double comparatives: 'this is more worser than before.' There are hundreds of instances of what is now just bad grammar to begin with.

There must be a few thousand instances of superfluous subjunctives to reduce to simplicity and sense. Today we use the subjunctive occasionally after 'if', when we say 'if it be'. But we mostly say today 'if it is'. Now Shakespeare has hundreds of subjunctives, not only after if, but after though, although, unless, lest, whether, until, till, etc.

I see no point whatever in retaining them. They only add superfluous trouble in learning English, when the great appeal of our language as a world-language is precisely that it has less grammar to learn than almost any. Russian is unbelievably complicated. Inflected languages—German is like Latin in this respect—are really rather backward; it has been a great recommendation that English has been more progressive in this respect in simplifying itself.

Now we can go further along this line: keep a few subjunctives, if you must, but reduce them to a minimum.

Let us come to the verb. It is a great recommendation to modern English that our verbs are comparatively simple to conjugate — unlike even French, for example. In the Elizabethan age there was a great deal more of it, and some of it inconsistent in modern usage. Take Shakespeare's,

'Where is thy husband now? Where be thy brothers?'
Nothing is lost by rendering this as we should today:

Where is your husband now? Where are your brothers?

And so on.

The second and third person singular—all those shouldsts and wouldsts, wilts and shalts, haths and doths, have become completely obsolete. Here a vast simplification may be effected—with no loss as far as I can see, and with advantages from several points of view.

For example, 'st' at the end of a word is rather difficult to say, and more difficult even for us when it is succeeded by a word beginning with 'th'. Try saying, 'Why usurpedst thou this?' Foreigners have the greatest difficulty in pronouncing our 'th' anyway—many never succeed in getting it round their tongues. Many of these tongue-twisters even for us proliferate in Shakespeare, and I see no objection to getting rid of *superfluous* difficulties. Much easier for people to say, 'Why did you usurp this?'—the same number of syllables too.

This pre-supposes getting rid of almost all thous and thees and thines. I have no objection to keeping a few here and there, if needed for a rhyme—even then they are sometimes not necessary.

Some words in Shakespeare have changed their meaning into the exact opposite: we ought to remove that stumbling-block. When Hamlet says, 'By heaven, I'll make a ghost of him that *lets* me', he means *stops*; and we should replace it by stops, or holds me. Shakespeare regularly uses the word 'owe' where we should say own: the meaning has changed. Take a line like, 'Thou dost here usurp the name thou ow'st not': we should say, 'You do here usurp the name you own not', with the bonus of getting rid of two ugly 'sts'.

The word 'presently' in the Elizabethan age did not mean in a few minutes or so, but immediately—instantly has the same number of syllables. 'Prevent' then had its Latin meaning, to go before, or forestall. Shakespeare frequently uses the word 'still' for always or ever.

Let us take the case of many archaic forms of words, simple one-syllable words that can be replaced without the slightest difference to the scansion: 'sith' for since, 'wrack' for wreck, 'holp' for helped, 'writ' for wrote, 'brake' for broke, 'spake' for spoke, 'bare' for bore, etc.

These give no trouble, nor do a lot of other words that he uses: 'repeal' for recall, 'reproof' for disproof, 'decline' for incline. A few words do give more trouble. The linguistic scholar, C. T. Onions, notes that it is sometimes difficult to give the precise meaning Shakespeare attaches to the word 'conceit'; it usually means thought, or fancy, or concept. I do not know that it ever has our meaning; actually the word 'conceited' with him means ingenious or fantastic, as 'artificial' with Elizabethans meant artistic or ingenious.

There is a whole class of words that have completely gone out, of which moderns do not know the meaning. I find no harm in replacing the word 'coistrel' by rascal, which is what it means—actually it has much the same sound—or 'coil' by fuss; we find 'accite' for summon, 'indigest' for formless. Hamlet's word 'reechy', for the incestuous kisses of his mother and her brother-in-law, has gone out of use: the nearest word, I suppose, would be reeky, but filthy would be a suitable modern equivalent.

In many cases it is extraordinary how little one would need to change, how conservative one could be. Take Hamlet's famous soliloquy, 'To be or not to be.' I find only two words that moderns would not know the meaning of, and one of those we might guess:

> . . .When he himself might his *quietus* make
> With a bare bodkin? Who would *fardels* bear. . .

'Quietus' means put paid; Elizabethans wrote the Latin 'quietus est' at the bottom of a bill that was paid—when it was—to say that it was settled. So that you could replace 'quietus' by settlement, same number of syllables, though not the same accentuation; so I would prefer to use the word acquittance, which has both.

'Fardels' means burdens; I see no objection to rendering, 'Who would burdens bear'—same meaning, same number of syllables, same accent: quite simple. I expect all the ladies to know what a bodkin is: a long pin, or skewer.

Now let us take something really difficult—perhaps the most difficult passage to render in all Shakespeare. It is the virtuoso comic piece describing all the diseases that horseflesh is heir to, in *The Taming of the Shrew*. The horse is Petruchio's. President Reagan tells me that this is the one Shakespearean part that he played—and a very gallant one too. In Britain last year we saw a fine performance of his on horseback in Windsor Park alongside of Queen Elizabeth II—very familiar ground to William Shakespeare and Queen Elizabeth I, as we know from *The Merry Wives of Windsor*.

Here is a headache for us: Petruchio's horse (not President Reagan's steed) was 'possessed with the glanders, and like to mose in the chine; troubled with the lampass, infected with the fashions, full of windgalls, sped with spavins, rayed with the yellows, past cure of the fives, stark spoiled with the staggers, begnawn with the bots; swayed in the back, and shoulder-shotten; near-legged before, and with a half-cheeked bit, and a headstall of sheep's leather', etc.

What on earth are we to make of that? No doubt it raised a laugh with Elizabethans, much more familiarly acquainted with horseflesh than we are; but I doubt if Hollywood was able to produce a nag for Reagan that qualified in all these respects.

Now, even without his horsemanship, we can clear one fence at the outset: 'mose in the chine'. Pages of superfluous commentary have been devoted to that word 'mose'. There was no such Elizabethan word: it was simply a printer's misprint for 'mourn', meaning dripping or running; so it suggests a running sore. You would

need to consult the *Oxford English Dictionary*, compiled on historical lines, for some of the words, others like 'glanders' country folk know and we can guess.

So I would suggest a rendering something like this: 'possessed with glanders, and with a running sore in the back; troubled in the gums, and infected in the glands; full of galls in the fetlocks and swollen in the joints; yellow with jaundice, past cure of the strangles; stark spoiled with the staggers, and gnawed by worms; swayed in the back and shoulder put out; near-legged before, and with a half-cheeked bit and headgear of sheep's leather', etc. That at least makes it intelligible.

Oddly enough, one encounters the greatest difficulty with the least important words and phrases, Elizabethan expletives and malapropisms, or salutations like God 'ild you, Godden, for God shield you, Good-even, and so on. 'God's wounds' was Elizabeth I's favourite swearword; it appears frequently enough in Victorian novels as 'Zounds'— I have never heard anyone use it. The word 'Marry!', as in the phrase 'Marry come up!' has similarly gone out, though a very old gentleman at All Souls, Sir Charles Oman, had heard the phrase in the back-streets of Oxford just after the 1914-18 war. 'Whoreson' is frequent on the lips of coarse fellows in Shakespeare: the equivalent in Britain today would be bloody, in America (I suppose) s.o.b.

Relative pronouns, who and which: today we use who for persons, which for things. In Elizabethan times the two were hardly distinguished and were interchangeable. Provokingly Shakespeare used the personal relative 'who' more frequently for impersonal objects, rivers, buildings, towns; and then he no less frequently uses 'which' for persons. This calls out to be regularised for the modern reader.

Other usages are more confusing. The word 'cousin'

was used far more widely by the Elizabethans for their kin: it included nephews, for instance. Thus it is confusing in the English History plays to find a whole lot of nephews—like Richard III's, whom he had made away with in the Tower of London—referred to and addressed as cousins. That needs regularisation today, in the interests of historical accuracy and to get the relationship clear. The word 'niece' was sometimes used of a grandchild—in fact this is the word Shakespeare used in his will for his little grand-daughter Elizabeth, his eventual heiress who ended up as Lady Barnard, leaving money to her poor relations the Hathaways at Stratford. The Latin word *neptis*, from which niece comes also meant grandchild—Shakespeare's grammar-school education at Stratford was in Latin, and this shows you that he often thought of a word in terms of its Latin derivation.

Malapropisms, misuse of words, sometimes mistaking of meanings, are frequent with uneducated people, and sometimes not only with those. Shakespeare transcribed them from lower-class life to raise a laugh, more frequently than any writer for the purpose. They are an endearing feature of the talk of Mistress Quickly, hostess of the Boar's Inn in East Cheapside, and we have no difficulty in making out what she means. But in case some of us do, and for the benefit of non-native English speakers, I propose the correct word in brackets afterwards: 'You have brought her into such a canaries [quandary]. . .and she's as fartuous [virtuous] a civil, modest wife. . .'

Abbreviations: Shakespeare's text is starred—and in my view, marred—by innumerable abbreviations, which not only look ugly on the page but are sometimes difficult to pronounce. It is not easy to pronounce 'is't', or 'in't', or 'on't', and some others: if we cannot get rid of them altogether they should be drastically reduced. Similarly with 'i'th'', 'o'th'', with which the later plays are liberally bespattered, for "in the" or "of the."

We also have a quite unnecessary spattering of apostrophes in practically all editions of the plays—''d' for the past participle, e.g. 'gather'd'. Surely it is much better to regularise the past participle 'ed', e.g. gathered; and when the last syllable is, far less frequently, to be pronounced, then accent it, gatherèd.

This leads into the technical question of scansion, where a practising poet is necessary to get the accents right, to help the reader, and still more the actor. Most people will hardly notice that, very often, the frequent ending of words in 'ion', like reputation, has to be pronounced with two syllables at the end. So I propose to accent this when necessary, e.g. reputatiòn. I have noticed the word 'ocean' as tri-syllabic, so I accent it, to help, oceàn. A number of words which to us are monosyllables were pronounced as two: hour, fire, tired; I sometimes accent or give them a dieresis, either hoùr or fïre. In New England speech words like prayèr, thëre, are apt to be pronounced as two syllables—closer to Elizabethan usage (as with words like gotten) than is modern speech in Britain.

What I notice in practically all editions of Shakespeare's plays is that the editors cannot be relied on to put the accents in the right places. One play edited by a well known Shakespearean editor had, I observed, a dozen accents placed over the wrong syllables. This is understandable, for these people don't write poetry and do not know how to scan. William Shakespeare knew all about scanning, and you need to be both familiar with Elizabethan usage and a practising traditional poet to be able to follow him.

His earlier verse was fairly regular in scansion, mostly iambic pentameter with a great deal of rhyme. As time went on he loosened out, until there are numerous irregular lines—this leaves us much freer in the matter of modernising. Our equivalents should be rhythmically as

close as possible, but a strait-jacket need be no part of the
equipment. A good Shakespearean scholar tells us, 'there
is no necessity for Shakespeare's lines to scan absolutely.
He thought of his verse as spoken rather than written and
of his rhythmic units in terms of the voice rather than
the page.'

There is nothing exclusive or mandatory about my project. We can all read Shakespeare in any edition we like—
in the rebarbative olde Englishe spelling of the First
Folio, if we wish. Any number of conventional academic
editions exist, all weighed down with a burden of notes,
many of them superfluous. I propose to make most of
them unnecessary—only one occasionally at the foot of
very few pages. Let the text be freed of superfluous difficulties, remove obstacles to let it speak for itself, while
adhering conservatively to every line.

We really do not need any more editions of the Plays
on conventional lines—more than enough of those exist
already. But *A Contemporary Shakespeare* on these
lines—both revolutionary and conservative—should be a
help to everybody all round the world—though especially
for younger people, increasingly with time moving away
from the language of 400 years ago.

Antony and Cleopatra

INTRODUCTION

Sir Thomas North's translation of Plutarch's *Lives*—he translated not from the Greek but from the French—proved a gold-mine as a source for Shakespeare's classical plays. Not that *Antony and Cleopatra* of 1607 is a classic play, as *Julius Caesar* was, of eight years before. *Antony and Cleopatra* continues the story, but in a very different mode: it is brimming with romanticism and riotous colour, as befits the subject. Some of North's rich Elizabethan prose could be taken up into the play almost directly, for blank verse was very close to Elizabethan speech. (We may notice the phenomenon similarly with the speeches of Abraham Lincoln—no wonder, for he educated himself largely out of the Bible and Shakespeare.) A famous example is the voluptuous description of Cleopatra's visit to Antony, in which she laid herself out to ensnare his heart:

> The barge she sat in, like a burnished throne,
> Burned on the water. The poop was beaten gold;
> Purple the sails. . .   She did lie

In her pavilion, clotn-of-gold of tissue, etc. It is late Renaissance like Veronese or Titian.

But what is of prime significance is how much Shakespeare differs from Plutarch and history, in creating his own picture of Cleopatra. We shall see why. Professor C.J. Sisson well says, 'if Hamlet is

13

Shakespeare's greatest character among the men of his creation, Cleopatra is far the greatest in stature among his women, and in her own right.' In historic fact Cleopatra was essentially political, queen and ruler, intensely ambitious—like the Macedonian-Greek family she was descended from. She used her sex to the end of power with both Julius Caesar and Antony: she pursued her aim, ruthlessly and undeviatingly, of raising herself from a client-queen to partnership, even aiming at becoming mistress of the Roman world. This is why Rome hated her and—the only person besides Hannibal—feared her.

Though the political element is there, Shakespeare makes it all into a tragedy of love. He depicts her as an alien, changeable, inconstant, undependable. (Where have we met that before?) She is all moods, 'storms and tempests', and that is how she holds Antony. She exerts a spell over him, a 'charm'; she is a witch, treats him tyrannically—as Antony realises, but cannot help himself. It is a story of infatuation—of infatuation against reason and interest, against his own judgment, against circumstances, against everything. 'Would I had never seen her!', he admits; and describes her thus:

> Whom everything becomes, to chide, to laugh,
> To weep: whom every passion fully strives
> To make itself in thee.

She is the most passionate, the most erotic woman in Shakespeare—a unique creation, quite unlike the numerous women in love depicted in all the other plays. She is like no English woman. Agatha Christie, a good Shakespearean, who, though not a scholar, had more intuitive perception than most, thought that in his depiction of Cleopatra he was remembering someone. Whom but his Italianate mistress of some years before?—also half-alien, a creature of 'storms and tempests', who would create a scene—'create' in the vulgar sense of 'play up'— with her lover to hold him tyrannically (Shakespeare's word is 'tyrannous'.) Cleopatra exerts

her power over Antony by crossing him, varying from
mood to mood. When her waiting woman advises her to
give way, she knows better:

Thou teachest like a fool: the way to lose him.

Perhaps the Shakespearean word 'becoming', or 'becomes', is itself a pointer: 'whom everything becomes. . .' He had written years before of Emilia in the
Sonnets,

Whence hast thou this becoming of things ill?...
And

O, from what power hast thou this powerful
    might. . .

To make me give the lie to my true sight?
Or

Thou art as tyrannous, so as thou art.
His eyes, 'anchored in the bay where all men ride',
which his heart knows well is 'the wide world's
common place'—and yet, such strength and skill in 'the
very refuse of thy deeds. . .'
—It might be Antony speaking, after Cleopatra's deser-
tion of him at Actium: 'triple-turned whore'—

You have been a boggler [inconstant] ever. . .
    the wise gods seel [sew up] our eyes,
In our own filth drop our clear judgments, etc.

The political element in the play—the other half of it,
so to say—is more in keeping with Plutarch and history,
and has an interesting continuity with *Julius Caesar*,
references back to 'mad Brutus', Cassius and Philippi.
The strong scene of Antony's quarrel and reconciliation
with Octavius Caesar reminds us of that between
Brutus and Cassius before their final defeat in that
battle.

It is usual again for literary critics to find the political
type such as Octavius was, unattractive—since they do
not understand it. Octavius Caesar is in full control of
himself, as a ruler should be, but they prefer Antony,
more human through his weaknesses. But Octavius is
not inhuman: he is devoted to his sister, whom Antony

jilts. He is friendly disposed to Antony, and does not want a breach; he is reasonable, moderate, and just, ready to forget and forgive Antony's breach of trust, to renew friendship and keep the alliance firm. All the more remarkable in so young a man, whom Antony despises as a 'novice'. The more fool he: he finds that the young Caesar is no novice, besides the fact that he has inherited the charisma of the deified Caesar, who had adopted him. And Shakespeare gives the young Caesar a good press. We notice at every point at issue his practical sense and judgment in few words—none of Antony's romantic rhodomontade.

Of course Antony has his good qualities: generosity goes with warmheartedness. When Enobarbus foresees his fall and deserts his leader, Antony sends his possessions after him, in no vein of contempt either. It is just what Essex might have done with Francis Bacon, who went over to the other side when he saw Essex running blindly on to catastrophe:

> The loyalty well held to fools does make
> Our faith mere folly.

That was what, in historic fact, Bacon had thought; in the play it broke Enobarbus's heart to betray Antony. We find Shakespeare's own judgment, drawing the moral, in:

> I see men's judgments are
> A parcel of their fortunes, and things outward
> Do draw the inward quality after them.

We should expect little that reflects Shakespeare's personal background in this canvas of the gorgeous East. But his profession is there as always: Cleopatra foresees the ballad-makers rhyming upon her and Antony:

> the quick comedians
> Extemporally will stage us, and present
> Our Alexandrian revels: Antony
> Shall be brought drunken forth, and I shall see
> Some squeaking Cleopatra boy my greatness. . .

Actually, it serves to show how professional the

Shakespearean theatre had become that a boy actor
could perform Cleopatra, the most demanding woman's
part in all the Plays.

We notice traces of the countryman as always. Who
but a countryman would have likened Cleopatra's ship
hoisting sail in flight to 'a cow in June' stampeding from
the 'breese', the gadflies, upon her? His early familiarity
with hare-coursing comes back in—

> Let us score their backs
> And snatch them up, as we take hares, behind.

In Octavius Caesar's noble lament for Antony at the
end, their failure to co-operate is put in country terms:
'We could not stall together in the whole world.'

An earlier sympathy of mind existed between
Shakespeare and Samuel Daniel, besides their association through Southampton's Florio. In this year of the
play Daniel now revised his own *Cleopatra*, profiting
from Shakespeare's to make it more dramatic. Earlier he
had profited from Daniel's *Civil Wars* for his *Richard II*,
which Daniel then used in revising his account in his
own book. Only two or three years later Emilia Lanier
then drew on Daniel for the stanzas she devoted to
Antony and Cleopatra in her long poem *Salve Deus Rex
Judaeorum*.[1]

Many passages of splendid, often quoted poetry attest
the inspiration Shakespeare derived from his theme.
Antony contemplating death:

> Where souls do couch on flowers, we'll hand in
>   hand,
> And with our sprightly port, [bearing] make the
>   ghosts gaze:
> Dido and Aeneas shall want troops,
> And all the haunt be ours.

---

[1] v. my edition of *The Poems of Shakespeare's Dark Lady*.

Cleopatra dying:

> I am fire and air: my other elements
> I give to baser life.

Similarly the language is more oblique and elliptical than ever. Antony's 'Grates me. The sum.'—the news from Rome is unwelcome: tell it briefly. Drifting clouds suggest a series of pictures—Shakespeare's mind is intensely visual and one can almost see him scrutinising them; then, elliptically, 'the rack dislimns'—the pictures break up. Eros is described as 'windowed' in Rome with 'pleached' arms, watching Antony led in Caesar's triumph.

By the same token there are difficulties, which modernising can remove for the reader. The word 'modern' with Shakespeare means ordinary or normal, 'still' is often used for ever, 'scald' may be replaced by scurvy, etc. Difficulties not only for the reader, but for the actor: it is not easy to pronounce 'thou browsèd'st', for instance, or 'wot'st thou whom thou mov'st.' Why not, you browsèd; and know you whom you move? 'Shouldst thou' is difficult to say. And why retain 'woo't', for will you (wilt thou); 'disgested' for digested; 'droven' for driven; 'show's' for show us; 'it' for its; 'in's' for in his; 'ha't' for have it, 'y'have' for you have; 'becomed' for become; 'whiles' for while; 'enow' for enough? These and other usages have been regularised for easier reading; the rich vocabulary of the play is quite difficult enough in itself.

CHARACTERS

Mark ANTONY
Octavius CAESAR } triumvirs
LEPIDUS

DEMETRIUS
PHILO
ENOBARBUS
VENTIDIUS
SILIUS } Antony's friends and followers
EROS
CANIDIUS
SCARUS
DECRETAS

MAECENAS
AGRIPPA
TAURUS
DOLABELLA } Caesar's friends and followers
THIDIAS
GALLUS
PROCULEIUS

Sextus POMPEY
MENECRATES } Pompey's friends
MENAS
VARRIUS

CLEOPATRA,   Queen of Egypt

CHARMIAN
IRAS
ALEXAS } Cleopatra's attendants
MARDIAN
DIOMEDES
SELEUCUS

OCTAVIA,   Caesar's sister, Antony's wife

Messengers, A Soothsayer, Attendants, Soldiers, A Boy,
Antony's Ambassador, A Sentry and Watch, Guards, An
Egyptian, A Clown

Act I

SCENE I
Alexandria. Cleopatra's palace.

Enter Demetrius and Philo

PHILO
    Nay, but this dotage of our general's
    Overflows the measure. Those his goodly eyes,
    That over the files and musters of the war
    Have glowed like plated Mars, now bend, now turn—
    The office and devotion of their view
    Upon a tawny front. His captain's heart,
    Which in the scuffles of great fights has burst
    The buckles on his breast, reneges all temper,
    And has become the bellows and the fan
    To cool a gypsy's lust.

    Flourish. Enter Antony, Cleopatra, Charmian
    and Iras, attendants, with eunuchs fanning her

                      Look where they come.
    Take but good note, and you shall see in him
    The triple pillar of the world transformed
    Into a strumpet's fool. Behold and see.
CLEOPATRA
    If it is love indeed, tell me how much.
ANTONY
    There's beggary in the love that can be reckoned.
CLEOPATRA
    I'll set a bourn how far to be beloved.
ANTONY
    Then must you needs find out new heaven, new
        earth.

Enter a Messenger

MESSENGER
  News, my good lord, from Rome.
ANTONY   Grates me! The sum.
CLEOPATRA
  Nay, hear them Antony.
  Fulvia perchance is angry; or who knows
  If the scarce-bearded Caesar has not sent
  His powerful mandate to you: 'Do this, or this;
  Take in that kingdom, and enfranchise that.
  Perform it, or else we damn you.'
ANTONY   How, my love?
CLEOPATRA
  Perchance? Nay, most likely.
  You must not stay here longer. Your dismission
  Is come from Caesar. Therefore hear it, Antony.
  Where's Fulvia's process? Caesar's I would say! Both!
  Call in the messengers. As I am Egypt's Queen,
  You blush, Antony, and that blood of yours
  Is Caesar's homager; else so your cheek pays shame
  When shrill-tongued Fulvia scolds. The messengers!
ANTONY
  Let Rome in Tiber melt, and the wide arch
  Of the ranged empire fall! Here is my space.
  Kingdoms are clay. Our dungy earth alike
  Feeds beast as man. The nobleness of life
  Is to do thus—when such a mutual pair
  And such a twain can do it, in which I bind,
  On pain of punishment, the world to know
  We stand up peerless.
CLEOPATRA   Excellent falsehood!
  Why did he marry Fulvia, and not love her?
  I'll seem the fool I am not. Antony
  Will be himself.
ANTONY   But stirred by Cleopatra.
  Now for the love of Love and its soft hours,

Let's not confound the time with conference harsh.
There's not a minute of our lives should stretch
Without some pleasure now. What sport tonight?

CLEOPATRA

Hear the ambassadors.

ANTONY   Fie, wrangling queen!
Whom everything becomes—to chide, to laugh,
To weep; whose every passion fully strives
To make itself, in you, fair and admired.
No messenger but yours, and all alone
Tonight we'll wander through the streets and note
The qualities of people. Come, my queen;
Last night you did desire it. *(To the Messenger)* Speak
    not to us.

Exeunt Antony and Cleopatra with the attendants

DEMETRIUS

Is Caesar with Antonius prized so slight?

PHILO

Sir, sometimes, when he is not Antony,
He comes too short of that great property
Which still should go with Antony.

DEMETRIUS   I am full sorry
That he approves the common liar, who
Thus speaks of him at Rome; but I will hope
Of better deeds tomorrow. Rest you happy!

                                        Exeunt

SCENE II
The same.

Enter Charmian, Iras, and Alexas

CHARMIAN Lord Alexas, sweet Alexas, most anything
    Alexas, almost most absolute Alexas, where is the
    soothsayer that you praised so to the Queen? O that I
    knew this husband, who you say must charge his
    horns with garlands!

ALEXAS   Soothsayer!

Enter a Soothsayer

SOOTHSAYER   Your will?

CHARMIAN   Is this the man? Is it you, sir, that know
   things?

SOOTHSAYER

   In Nature's infinite book of secrecy
   A little I can read.

ALEXAS   Show him your hand.

Enter Enobarbus

ENOBARBUS

   Bring in the banquet quickly; wine enough
   Cleopatra's health to drink.

CHARMIAN   *(to Soothsayer)* Good sir, give me good
   fortune.

SOOTHSAYER   I make not, but foresee.

CHARMIAN   Pray then, foresee me one.

SOOTHSAYER

   You shall be yet far fairer than you are.

CHARMIAN   He means in flesh.

IRAS   No, you shall paint when you are old.

CHARMIAN   Wrinkles forbid!

ALEXAS   Vex not his prescience; be attentive.

CHARMIAN   Hush!

SOOTHSAYER

   You shall be more beloving than beloved.

CHARMIAN   I had rather heat my liver with drinking.

ALEXAS   Nay, hear him.

CHARMIAN   Good now, some excellent fortune! Let me
   be married to three kings in a forenoon and widow
   them all. Let me have a child at fifty, to whom Herod
   of Jewry may do homage. Find me to marry with
   Octavius Caesar, and companion me with my mistress.

SOOTHSAYER
  You shall outlive the lady whom you serve.

CHARMIAN   O, excellent! I love life better than figs.

SOOTHSAYER
  You have seen and proved a fairer former fortune
  Than that which is to approach.

CHARMIAN   Then perhaps my children shall have no names. Pray, how many boys and wenches must I have?

SOOTHSAYER
  If every of your wishes had a womb,
  And fertile every wish, a million.

CHARMIAN   Out, fool, I forgive you for a witch.

ALEXAS   You think none but your sheets are privy to your wishes.

CHARMIAN   Nay, come, tell Iras hers.

ALEXAS   We will know all our fortunes.

ENOBARBUS   Mine, and most of our fortunes, tonight shall be drunk to bed.

IRAS   There's a palm presages chastity, if nothing else.

CHARMIAN   Even as the overflowing Nile presages famine.

IRAS   *(to Charmian)* Go, you wild bedfellow, you cannot soothsay.

CHARMIAN   Nay, if an oily palm is not a fruitful prognostication, I cannot scratch my ear. Pray, tell her but a workaday fortune.

SOOTHSAYER   Your fortunes are alike.

IRAS   But how, but how? Give me particulars.

SOOTHSAYER   I have said.

IRAS   Am I not an inch of fortune better than she?

CHARMIAN   Well, if you were but an inch of fortune better than I, where would you choose it?

IRAS   Not in my husband's nose.

CHARMIAN   Our worse thoughts heavens mend! Alexas —come, his fortune, his fortune! O, let him marry a woman that cannot walk, sweet Isis, I beseech you;

you; and let her die too, and give him a worse. And let
worse follow worse till the worst of all follows him
laughing to his grave, fiftyfold a cuckold! Good Isis,
hear me this prayer, though you deny me a matter of
more weight; good Isis, I beseech you!

IRAS Amen. Dear goddess, hear that prayer of the
people! For, as it is a heart-breaking to see a handsome
man loose-wived, so it is a deadly sorrow to behold a
foul knave uncuckolded. Therefore, dear Isis, keep
decorum, and fortune him accordingly!

CHARMIAN Amen.

ALEXAS Lo now, if it lay in their hands to make me a
cuckold, they would make themselves whores but
they would do it.

ENOBARBUS
Hush! Here comes Antony.

CHARMIAN   Not he; the Queen.

Enter Cleopatra

CLEOPATRA
Saw you my lord?

ENOBARBUS   No, lady.

CLEOPATRA   Was he not here?

CHARMIAN
No, madam.

CLEOPATRA
He was disposed to mirth; but on the sudden
A Roman thought has struck him. Enobarbus!

ENOBARBUS
Madam?

CLEOPATRA
Seek him, and bring him hither. Where's Alexas?

ALEXAS
Here at your service. My lord approaches.

Enter Antony with Messenger and Attendants

CLEOPATRA
  We will not look upon him. Go with us.
  Exeunt all but Antony, Messenger and Attendants
MESSENGER
  Fulvia your wife came into the field.
ANTONY
  Against my brother Lucius?
MESSENGER
  Ay.
  But soon that war had end, and the time's state
  Made friends of them, joining their force against
        Caesar—
  Whose better issue in the war from Italy
  Upon the first encounter drove them.
ANTONY   Well, what worst?
MESSENGER
  The nature of bad news infects the teller.
ANTONY
  When it concerns the fool or coward. On.
  Things that are past are done. With me, it is thus:
  Who tells me true, though in his tale lies death,
  I hear him as if he flattered.
MESSENGER   Labienus—
  This is stiff news—has with his Parthian force
  Penetrated Asia; from Euphrates
  His conquering banner shook, from Syria
  To Lydia and to Ionia,
  While—
ANTONY   Antony, you would say—
MESSENGER   O, my lord.
ANTONY
  Speak to me home; mince not the general tongue.
  Name Cleopatra as she is called in Rome.
  Rail you in Fulvia's phrase, and taunt my faults
  With such full licence as both truth and malice
  Have power to utter. O, then we bring forth weeds
  When our quick winds lie still, and our ills told us
  Is as our ploughing. Fare you well awhile.

MESSENGER
   At your noble pleasure.   *Exit*
ANTONY
   From Sicyon, how the news? Speak there!
FIRST ATTENDANT
   The man from Sicyon—is there such a one?
SECOND ATTENDANT
   He stays upon your will.
ANTONY   Let him appear.
   (aside) These strong Egyptian fetters I must break,
   Or lose myself in dotage.

     Enter another Messenger, with a letter

                  What are you?
MESSENGER
   Fulvia your wife is dead.
ANTONY   Where died she?
MESSENGER
   In Sicyon.
   Her length of sickness, with what else more serious
   Imports you now to know, this bears.
ANTONY   Forbear me.
                  Exit Messenger
   There's a great spirit gone! Thus did I desire it.
   What our contempts do often hurl from us,
   We wish it ours again. The present pleasure,
   By revolution lowering, does become
   The opposite of itself. She is good, being gone;
   The hand could pluck her back that shoved her on.
   I must from this enchanting queen break off.
   Ten thousand harms, more than the ills I know,
   My idleness does hatch. How now, Enobarbus!

     Enter Enobarbus

ENOBARBUS   What's your pleasure, sir?

ANTONY   I must with haste from hence.

ENOBARBUS   Why, then we kill all our women. We see how mortal an unkindness is to them. If they suffer our departure, death is the word.

ANTONY   I must be gone.

ENOBARBUS   Under a compelling occasion, let women die. It were pity to cast them away for nothing, though between them and a great cause they should be esteemed nothing. Cleopatra, catching but the least noise of this, dies instantly. I have seen her die twenty times upon far poorer moment. I do think there is mettle in death, which commits some loving act upon her, she has such a celerity in dying.

ANTONY   She is cunning past man's thought.

ENOBARBUS   Alas, sir, no; her passions are made of nothing but the finest part of pure love. We cannot call her winds and waters sighs and tears; they are greater storms and tempests than almanacs can report. This cannot be cunning in her; if it is, she makes a shower of rain as well as Jove.

ANTONY   Would I had never seen her!

ENOBARBUS   O, sir, you had then left unseen a wonderful piece of work, which not to have been blessed with would have discredited your travel.

ANTONY   Fulvia is dead.

ENOBARBUS   Sir?

ANTONY   Fulvia is dead.

ENOBARBUS   Fulvia?

ANTONY   Dead.

ENOBARBUS   Why, sir, give the gods a thankful sacrifice. When it pleases their deities to take the wife of a man from him, it shows to man the tailors of the earth; comforting therein that when old robes are worn out there are members to make new. If there were no more women but Fulvia, then had you indeed a cut, and the case to be lamented. This grief is crowned with consolation: your old smock brings forth a new petticoat;

and indeed the tears live in an onion that should
water this sorrow.

ANTONY

The business she has broachèd in the state
Cannot endure my absence.

ENOBARBUS   And the business you have broached here
cannot be without you; especially that of Cleopatra's, which wholly depends on your abode.

ANTONY

No more light answers. Let our officers
Have notice what we purpose. I shall break
The cause of our parture to the Queen
And get her leave to part. For not alone
The death of Fulvia, with more urgent touches,
Does strongly speak to us, but the letters too
Of many our contriving friends in Rome
Petition us at home. Sextus Pompeius
Has given the dare to Caesar and commands
The empire of the sea. Our slippery people,
Whose love is never linked to the deserver
Till his deserts are past, begin to throw
Pompey the Great and all his dignities
Upon his son, Who, high in name and power,
Higher than both in blood and life, stands up
For the main soldier; whose quality, going on,
The frame of the world may danger. Much is breeding
Which, like the courser's hair, has yet but life
And not a serpent's poison. Say our pleasure,
To such whose place is under us, requires
Our quick remove from hence.

ENOBARBUS   I shall do it.   *Exeunt*

SCENE III
The same.

Enter Cleopatra, Charmian, Alexas, and Iras

CLEOPATRA
  Where is he?

CHARMIAN   I have not seen him of late.

CLEOPATRA   *(to Alexas)*
  See where he is, who's with him, what he does.
  I did not send you. If you find him sad,
  Say I am dancing; if in mirth, report
  That I am sudden sick. Quick, and return.

                             Exit Alexas

CHARMIAN
  Madam, I think, if you did love him dearly,
  You do not hold the method to enforce
  The like from him.

CLEOPATRA   What should I do I do not?

CHARMIAN
  In each thing give him way. Cross him in nothing.

CLEOPATRA
  You teach like a fool: the way to lose him.

CHARMIAN
  Tempt him not so too far. I would forbear.
  In time we hate that which we often fear.

    Enter Antony

  But here comes Antony.

CLEOPATRA   I am sick and sullen.

ANTONY
  I am sorry to give breathing to my purpose—

CLEOPATRA
  Help me away, dear Charmian! I shall fall.
  It cannot be thus long; the sides of nature
  Will not sustain it.

ANTONY   Now, my dearest queen—

CLEOPATRA
  Pray you, stand farther from me.

ANTONY   What's the matter?

CLEOPATRA
  I know by that same eye there's some good news.

What, says the married woman you may go?
Would she had never given you leave to come!
Let her not say 'tis I that keep you here.
I have no power upon you. Hers you are.

ANTONY
The gods best know—

CLEOPATRA   O, never was there queen
So mightily betrayed! Yet at the first
I saw the treasons planted.

ANTONY   Cleopatra—

CLEOPATRA
Why should I think you can be mine, and true—
Though you in swearing shake the thronèd gods—
Who have been false to Fulvia? Riotous madness,
To be entangled with those mouth-made vows
Which break themselves in swearing!

ANTONY   Most sweet queen—

CLEOPATRA
Nay, pray you seek no colour for your going,
But bid farewell, and go. When you sued staying,
Then was the time for words. No going then!
Eternity was in our lips and eyes,
Bliss in our brows' bent; none our parts so poor
But was a race of heaven. They are so still,
Or you, the greatest soldier of the world,
Are turned the greatest liar.

ANTONY   How now, lady!

CLEOPATRA
I would I had your inches. You should know
There was a heart in Egypt.

ANTONY   Hear me, Queen.
The strong necessity of time commands
Our services awhile; but my full heart
Remains in use with you. Our Italy
Shines over with civil swords. Sextus Pompeius
Makes his approaches to the port of Rome.
Equality of two domestic powers

Breeds scrupulous faction; the hated, grown to
    strength,
Are newly grown to love. The condemned Pompey,
Rich in his father's honour, creeps apace
Into the hearts of such as have not thrived
Upon the present state, whose numbers threaten;
And quietness, grown sick of rest, would purge
By any desperate change. My more particular,
And that which most with you should safe my going,
Is Fulvia's death.

CLEOPATRA
Though age from folly could not give me freedom,
It does from childishness. Can Fulvia die?

ANTONY
She's dead, my queen.
Look here, and at your sovereign leisure read
The troubles she awaked. At the last, best,
See when and where she died.

CLEOPATRA   O most false love!
Where are the sacred vials you should fill
With sorrowful water? Now I see, I see,
In Fulvia's death, how mine received shall be.

ANTONY
Quarrel no more, but be prepared to know
The purposes I bear; which are, or cease,
As you shall give the advice. By the fire
That quickens Niles of thick slime, I go from hence
Your soldier-servant, making peace or war
As you affect.

CLEOPATRA   Cut my lace, Charmian, come.
But let it be. I am quickly ill and well,
So Antony loves.

ANTONY   My precious queen, forbear,
And give true evidence to his love, which stands
An honourable trial.

CLEOPATRA   So Fulvia told me.
I pray you turn aside and weep for her;

Then bid adieu to me, and say the tears
Belong to Egypt. Good now, play one scene
Of excellent dissembling, and let it look
Like perfect honour.

ANTONY   You'll heat my blood; no more.

CLEOPATRA

You can do better yet; but this is pretty.

ANTONY

Now by my sword—

CLEOPATRA   And buckles. Still he improves.
But this is not the best. Look, pray, Charmian,
How this Herculean Roman does become
The carriage of his anger.

ANTONY   I'll leave you, lady.

CLEOPATRA

Courteous lord, one word.
Sir, you and I must part, but that's not it.
Sir, you and I have loved, but there's not it.
That you know well. Something it is I would—
O, my oblivion is a very Antony,
And I am all forgotten.

ANTONY   But that your royalty
Holds idleness your subject, I should take you
For idleness itself.

CLEOPATRA   'Tis sweating labour
To bear such idleness so near the heart
As Cleopatra this. But sir, forgive me,
Since my moods kill me when they do not
Eye well to you. Your honour calls you hence.
Therefore be deaf to my unpitied folly,
And all the gods go with you! Upon your sword
Sit laurel victory, and smooth success
Be strewed before your feet!

ANTONY   Let us go. Come.
Our separation so abides and flies
That you residing here goes yet with me,
And I hence fleeting here remain with thee.
Away!   *Exeunt*

SCENE IV
Rome. Caesar's house.

Enter Octavius Caesar, reading a letter, Lepidus,
and Attendants

CAESAR
You may see, Lepidus, and henceforth know
It is not Caesar's natural vice to hate
Our great competitor. From Alexandria
This is the news: he fishes, drinks, and wastes
The lamps of night in revel; is not more manlike
Than Cleopatra, nor the queen of Ptolemy
More womanly than he; hardly gave audience, or
Allowed to think he had partners, You shall find
      there
A man who is the abstract of all faults
That all men follow.
LEPIDUS   I must not think there are
Evils enough to darken all his goodness.
His faults, in him, seem as the spots of heaven,
More fiery by nights' blackness, hereditary
Rather than purchased, what he cannot change
Than what he chooses.
CAESAR
You are too indulgent. Let's grant it is not
Amiss to tumble on the bed of Ptolemy,
To give a kingdom for a mirth, to sit
And keep the turn of tippling with a slave,
To reel the streets at noon, and stand the buffet
With knaves that smell of sweat. Say this becomes
      him—
As his composure must be rare indeed
Whom these things cannot blemish—yet must
      Antony
No way excuse his faults when we do bear
So great weight in his lightness. If he filled

His vacancy with his voluptuousness,
Full surfeits and the dryness of his bones
Call on him for it. But to confound such time
That drums him from his sport and speaks as loud
As his own state and ours—it is to be chidden
As we rate boys who, being mature in knowledge,
Pawn their experience to their present pleasure
And so rebel to judgement.

Enter a Messenger

LEPIDUS   Here's more news.
MESSENGER
    Your biddings have been done; and every hour,
    Most noble Caesar, shall you have report
    How it is abroad. Pompey is strong at sea,
    And it appears he is beloved of those
    That only have feared Caesar; to the ports
    The discontents repair, and men's reports
    Hold him much wronged.
CAESAR   I should have known no less.
    It has been taught us from the primal state
    That he who is was wished until he were;
    The ebbed man, never loved till never worth love,
    Comes feared by being lacked. This common body,
    Like to a vagabond flag upon the stream,
    Goes to and back, licking the varying tide,
    To rot itself with motion.
MESSENGER   Caesar, I bring you word
    Menecrates and Menas, famous pirates,
    Make the sea serve them, which they plough and
        wound
    With keels of every kind. Many hot inroads
    They make in Italy. The borders maritime
    Lack blood to think of it and flush youth revolt.
    No vessel can peep forth but 'tis as soon
    Taken as seen; for Pompey's name strikes more
    Than could his war resisted.

CAESAR   Antony,
   Leave your lascivious wassails. When you once
   Were beaten from Modena, where you slew
   Hirtius and Pansa, consuls, at your heel
   Did famine follow which you fought against,
   Though daintily brought up, with patience more
   Than savages could suffer. You did drink
   The piss of horses and the gilded puddle
   Which beasts would cough at. Your palate then did
       take
   The roughest berry on the rudest hedge.
   Yea, like the stag when snow the pasture sheets,
   The barks of trees you browsèd. On the Alps
   It is reported you did eat strange flesh,
   Which some did die to look on. And all this—
   It wounds your honour that I speak it now—
   Was borne so like a soldier that your cheek
   So much as thinned not.
LEPIDUS   It is pity of him.
CAESAR
   Let his shames quickly
   Drive him to Rome. It is time we twain
   Did show ourselves in the field; and to that end
   Assemble we immediate council. Pompey
   Thrives in our idleness.
LEPIDUS   Tomorrow, Caesar,
   I shall be furnished to inform you rightly
   Both what by sea and land I can be able
   To confront this present time.
CAESAR   Till which encounter,
   It is my business too. Farewell.
LEPIDUS
   Farewell my lord. What you shall know meantime
   Of stirs abroad, I shall beseech you, sir,
   To let me be partaker.
CAESAR   Doubt not, sir;
   I knew it for my bond.   *Exeunt*

SCENE V
Cleopatra's palace.

Enter Cleopatra, Charmian, Iras, and Mardian

CLEOPATRA
Charmian!
CHARMIAN
Madam?
CLEOPATRA   *(yawning)*
Ha-ha.
Give me to drink mandragora.
CHARMIAN   Why, madam?
CLEOPATRA
That I might sleep out this great gap of time
My Antony is away.
CHARMIAN   You think of him too much.
CLEOPATRA
O, 'tis treason!
CHARMIAN   Madam, I trust, not so.
CLEOPATRA
You, eunuch Mardian!
MARDIAN   What's your highness' pleasure?
CLEOPATRA
Not now to hear you sing. I take no pleasure
In aught an eunuch has, 'Tis well for you
That, being emasculated, your freer thoughts
May not fly forth of Egypt. Have you affections?
MARDIAN
Yes, gracious madam.
CLEOPATRA
Indeed?
MARDIAN
Not in deed, madam; for I can do nothing
But what indeed is honest to be done.
Yet have I fierce affections, and think
What Venus did with Mars.

CLEOPATRA   O, Charmian,
  Where think you he is now? Stands he, or sits he?
  Or does he walk? Or is he on his horse?
  O happy horse, to bear the weight of Antony!
  Do bravely, horse, for know you whom you move?
  The demi-Atlas of this earth, the arm
  And head-piece of men. He's speaking now,
  Or murmuring 'Where's my serpent of old Nile?'
  For so he calls me. Now I feed myself
  With most delicious poison. Think of me,
  That am with Phoebus' amorous pinches black
  And wrinkled deep in time. Broad- fronted Caesar,
  When you were here above the ground, I was
  A morsel for a monarch; and great Pompey
  Would stand and make his eyes grow in my brow.
  There would he anchor his aspèct, and die
  With looking on his life.

    Enter Alexas

ALEXAS   Sovereign of Egypt, hail!
CLEOPATRA
  How much unlike are you Mark Antony!
  Yet, coming from him, that great medicine has
  With its tincture gilded you.
  How goes it with my brave Mark Antony?
ALEXAS
  Last thing he did, dear Queen,
  He kissed—the last of many doubled kisses—
  This orient pearl. His speech sticks in my heart.
CLEOPATRA
  My ear must pluck it thence.
ALEXAS   'Good friend,' said he,
  'Say the firm Roman to great Egypt sends
  This treasure of an oyster; at whose foot,
  To mend the petty present, I will piece
  Her opulent throne with kingdoms. All the East,

Say you, shall call her mistress.' So he nodded,
And soberly did mount an arrogant steed,
Which neighed so high that what I would have
    spoken
Was beastly dumbed by him.

CLEOPATRA   What, was he sad or merry?

ALEXAS
Like to the time of the year between the extremes
Of hot and cold, he was nor sad nor merry.

CLEOPATRA
O well-divided disposition! Note him,
Note him, good Charmian, 'tis the man; but note
    him!
He was not sad, for he would shine on those
That make their looks by his; he was not merry,
Which seemed to tell them his remembrance lay
In Egypt with his joy; but between both.
O heavenly mingle! Be you sad or merry,
The violence of either you becomes,
So does it no man else. Met you my posts?

ALEXAS
Ay, madam, twenty several messengers.
Why do you send so thick?

CLEOPATRA   Who's born that day
When I forget to send to Antony
Shall die a beggar. Ink and paper, Charmian.
Welcome, my good Alexas. Did I, Charmian,
Ever love Caesar so?

CHARMIAN   O, that brave Caesar!

CLEOPATRA
Be choked with such another emphasis!
Say 'the brave Antony'.

CHARMIAN   The valiant Caesar!

CLEOPATRA
By Isis, I will give you bloody teeth
If you with Caesar paragon again
My man of men.

CHARMIAN   By your most gracious pardon,
   I sing but after you.
CLEOPATRA   My salad days,
   When I was green in judgement, cold in blood,
   To say as I said then. But come, away,
   Get me ink and paper.
   He shall have every day a separate greeting,
   Or I'll unpeople Egypt.   *Exeunt*

Act II

SCENE I
Messina. Pompey's house.

Enter Pompey, Menecrates, and Menas, armed

POMPEY
If the great gods are just, they shall assist
The deeds of justest men.
MENECRATES   Know, worthy Pompey,
That what they do delay they not deny.
POMPEY
While we are suitors to their throne, decays
The thing we sue for.
MENECRATES   We, ignorant of ourselves,
Beg often our own harms, which the wise powers
Deny us for our good; so find we profit
By losing of our prayers.
POMPEY   I shall do well.
The people love me, and the sea is mine;
My powers are crescent, and my auguring hope
Says it will come to the full. Mark Antony
In Egypt sits at dinner, and will make
No wars without doors. Caesar gets money where
He loses hearts. Lepidus flatters both,
Of both is flattered; but he neither loves,
Nor either cares for him.
MENAS   Caesar and Lepidus
Are in the field. A mighty strength they carry.
POMPEY
Where have you this? 'Tis false.
MENAS   From Silvius, sir.

POMPEY

He dreams. I know they are in Rome together,
Looking for Antony. But all the charms of love,
Salt Cleopatra, soften your waned lip!
Let witchcraft join with beauty, lust with both!
Tie up the libertine in a field of feasts;
Keep his brain fuming. Epicurean cooks
Sharpen with cloyless sauce his appetite,
That sleep and feeding may prorogue his honour
Even till a Lethe'd dullness—

Enter Varrius

                                How now, Varrius?

VARRIUS

This is most certain that I shall deliver:
Mark Antony is every hour in Rome
Expected. Since he went from Egypt 'tis
A space for farther travel.

POMPEY   I could have given less matter
A better ear. Menas, I did not think
This amorous surfeiter would have donned his
    helmet
For such a petty war. His soldiership
Is twice the other twain. But let us rear
The higher our opinion, that our stirring
Can from the lap of Egypt's widow pluck
The never lust-wearied Antony.

MENAS   I cannot hope
Caesar and Antony shall well greet together.
His wife that's dead did trespasses to Caesar.
His brother warred upon him—although, I think,
Not moved by Antony.

POMPEY   I know not, Menas,
How lesser enmities may give way to greater.
Were it not that we stand up against them all,
'Twere pregnant they should square between
    themselves,

For they have entertained cause enough
To draw their swords. But how the fear of us
May cement their divisions and bind up
The petty difference, we yet not know.
Be it as our gods will have it! It only stands
That our lives depend upon our strongest hands.
Come Menas.   *Exeunt*

SCENE II
Rome. Lepidus' house.

Enter Enobarbus and Lepidus

LEPIDUS
    Good Enobarbus, it is a worthy deed,
    And shall become you well, to entreat your captain
    To soft and gentle speech.
ENOBARBUS   I shall entreat him
    To answer like himself. If Caesar moves him,
    Let Antony look over Caesar's head
    And speak as loud as Mars. By Jupiter,
    Were I the wearer of Antonius' beard,
    I would not shave it today.
LEPIDUS   'Tis not a time
    For private belly-aching.
ENOBARBUS   Every time
    Serves for the matter that is then born in it.
LEPIDUS
    But small to greater matters must give way.
ENOBARBUS
    Not if the small comes first.
LEPIDUS   Your speech is passion;
    But pray you stir no embers up. Here comes
    The noble Antony.

Enter Antony and Ventidius

ENOBARBUS   And yonder Caesar.

Enter Caesar, Maecenas, and Agrippa

ANTONY
   If we compose well here, to Parthia.
   Hark, Ventidius.
CAESAR   I do not know,
   Maecenas; ask Agrippa.
LEPIDUS   *(to Caesar and Antony)* Noble friends,
   That which combined us was most great, and let not
   A leaner action rend us. What's amiss,
   May it be gently heard. When we debate
   Our trivial difference loud, we do commit
   Murder in healing wounds. Then, noble partners,
   The rather for I earnestly beseech,
   Touch you the sourest points with sweetest terms,
   Nor curstness grow to the matter.
ANTONY   'Tis spoken well.
   Were we before our armies, and to fight,
   I should do thus.
            Flourish
CAESAR
   Welcome to Rome.
ANTONY
   Thank you.
CAESAR
   Sit.
ANTONY
   Sit, sir.
CAESAR
   Nay then.
ANTONY
   I learn you take things ill which are not so,
   Or, being, concern you not.
CAESAR   I must be laughed at
   If, or for nothing or a little, I
   Should say myself offended, and with you

Chiefly, in the world; more laughed at that I should
Once name you derogately, when to sound your
      name
It not concerned me.
ANTONY   My being in Egypt, Caesar,
What was it to you?
CAESAR
No more than my residing here at Rome
Might be to you in Egypt. Yet, if you were there
Did practise on my state, your being in Egypt
Might be my question.
ANTONY   How intend you—practised?
CAESAR
You may be pleased to catch at my intent
By what did here befall me. Your wife and brother
Made war upon me, and their contestation
Was theme for you: you were the word of war.
ANTONY
You do mistake your business. My brother never
Did urge me in his act. I did inquire it,
And have my learning from some true reports
That drew their swords with you. Did he not rather
Discredit my authority with yours,
And make the wars alike against my stomach,
Having alike your cause? Of this, my letters
Before did satisfy you. If you'll patch a quarrel,
As matter whole you'd have to make it with,
It must not be with this.
CAESAR   You praise yourself
By laying defects of judgement to me, but
You patched up your excuses.
ANTONY   Not so, not so;
I know you could not lack, I am certain of it,
Very necessity of this thought, that I,
Your partner in the cause against which he fought,
Could not with graceful eyes attend those wars
Which confronted my own peace. As for my wife,
I would you had her spirit in such another;

The third of the world is yours, which with a snaffle
You may pace easy, but not such a wife.
ENOBARBUS   Would we had all such wives, that the men
   might go to wars with the women.
ANTONY
   So much uncurbable, her tumults, Caesar,
   Made out of her impatience—which not wanted
   Shrewdness of policy too—I grieving grant
   Did you too much disquiet. For that you must
   But say I could not help it.
CAESAR   I wrote to you
   When, rioting in Alexandria, you
   Did pocket up my letters, and with taunts
   Did gibe my missive out of audience.
ANTONY   Sir,
   He fell upon me, ere admitted, then.
   Three kings I had newly feasted, and did want
   Of what I was in the morning; but next day
   I told him of myself, which was as much
   As to have asked him pardon. Let this fellow
   Be nothing of our strife; if we contend,
   Out of our question wipe him.
CAESAR   You have broken
   The article of your oath, which you shall never
   Have tongue to charge me with.
LEPIDUS   Soft, Caesar!
ANTONY
   No, Lepidus; let him speak.
   The honour is sacred which he talks of now,
   Supposing that I lacked it. But on, Caesar:
   The article of my oath—
CAESAR
   To lend me arms and aid when I required them,
   Which you both denied me.
ANTONY   Neglected rather;
   And then when poisoned hours had bound me up
   From my own knowledge. As nearly as I may,

I'll play the penitent to you; but my honesty
Shall not make poor my greatness, nor my power
Work without it. Truth is that Fulvia,
To have me out of Egypt, made war here,
For which myself, the ignorant motive, do
So far ask pardon as befits my honour
To stoop in such a case.

LEPIDUS   'Tis nobly spoken.

MAECENAS
If it might please you to enforce no further
The griefs between you to forget them quite
Speaks to unite you.

LEPIDUS   Worthily spoken, Maecenas.

ENOBARBUS   Or, if you borrow one another's love for the
instant, you may, when you hear no more words of
Pompey, return it again: you shall have time to
wrangle in when you have nothing else to do.

ANTONY
You are a soldier only. Speak no more.

ENOBARBUS   That truth should be silent I had almost
forgotten.

ANTONY
You wrong this presence; therefore speak no more.

ENOBARBUS   Go to, then; I am your considering stone.

CAESAR
I do not much dislike the matter, but
The manner of his speech; for it cannot be
We shall remain in friendship, our conditions
So differing in their acts. Yet if I knew
What hoop should hold us staunch, from edge to edge
Of the world I would pursue it.

AGRIPPA   Give me leave, Caesar.

CAESAR
Speak, Agrippa.

AGRIPPA
You have a sister by the mother's side,
Admired Octavia. Great Mark Antony
Is now a widower.

CAESAR   Say not so, Agrippa
   If Cleopatra heard you, your reproof
   Were well deserved of rashness.
ANTONY
   I am not married, Caesar. Let me hear
   Agrippa further speak.
AGRIPPA
   To hold you in perpetual amity,
   To make you brothers, and to knit your hearts
   With an unslipping knot, take Antony
   Octavia to his wife—whose beauty claims
   No worse a husband than the best of men;
   Whose virtue and whose general graces speak
   That which none else can utter. By this marriage
   All little jealousies, which now seem great,
   And all great fears, which now import their dangers,
   Would then be nothing. Truths would be tales,
   Where now half-tales be truths. Her love to both,
   Would each to other, and all loves to both,
   Draw after her. Pardon what I have spoken:
   It is a studied, not a present thought,
   By duty ruminated.
ANTONY   Will Caesar speak?
CAESAR
   Not till he hears how Antony is touched
   With what is spoken already.
ANTONY   What power is in Agrippa,
   If I would say 'Agrippa, be it so',
   To make this good?
CAESAR   The power of Caesar, and
   His power unto Octavia.
ANTONY   May I never
   To this good purpose, that so fairly shows,
   Dream of impediment! Let me have your hand.
   Further this act of grace, and from this hour
   The heart of brothers govern in our loves
   And sway our great designs.

CAESAR   There's my hand.
  A sister I bequeath you whom no brother
  Did ever love so dearly. Let her live
  To join our kingdoms and our hearts; and never
  Fly off our loves again.
LEPIDUS   Happily, amen.
ANTONY
  I did not think to draw my sword against Pompey,
  For he has laid strange courtesies and great
  Of late upon me. I must thank him only,
  Lest my remembrance suffers ill report;
  At heel of that, defy him.
LEPIDUS   Time calls upon us.
  Of us must Pompey presently be sought,
  Or else he seeks out us.
ANTONY   Where lies he?
CAESAR
  About the Mount Misena.
ANTONY   What is his strength?
CAESAR
  By land, great and increasing; but by sea
  He is an absolute master.
ANTONY   So is the fame.
  Would we had spoken together! Haste we for it.
  Yet, ere we put ourselves in arms, dispatch we
  The business we have talked of.
CAESAR   With most gladness;
  And do invite you to my sister's view,
  Whither straight I'll lead you.
ANTONY   Let us, Lepidus,
  Not lack your company.
LEPIDUS   Noble Antony,
  Not sickness should detain me.
                    Flourish. Exeunt all but Enobarbus,
                         Agrippa, and Maecenas
MAECENAS   Welcome from Egypt, sir.
ENOBARBUS   Half the heart of Caesar, worthy Maecenas.
  My honourable friend, Agrippa.

AGRIPPA   Good Enobarbus.

MAECENAS   We have cause to be glad that matters are so
    well digested. You stood up well to it in Egypt.

ENOBARBUS   Ay, sir, we did sleep day out of countenance
    and made the night light with drinking.

MAECENAS   Eight wild boars roasted whole at a break-
    fast, and but twelve persons there. Is this true?

ENOBARBUS   This was but as a fly by an eagle. We had
    much more monstrous matter of feast, which worthi-
    ly deserved noting.

MAECENAS   She's a most triumphant lady, if report is
    square to her.

ENOBARBUS   When she first met Mark Antony, she
    pursed up his heart, upon the river of Cydnus.

AGRIPPA   There she appeared indeed! Or my reporter
    devised well for her.

ENOBARBUS
    I will tell you.
    The barge she sat in, like a burnished throne,
    Burned on the water. The poop was beaten gold;
    Purple the sails, and so perfumèd that
    The winds were lovesick with them. The oars were
            silver,
    Which to the tune of flutes kept stroke and made
    The water which they beat to follow faster,
    As amorous of their strokes. For her own person,
    It beggared all description. She did lie
    In her pavilion, cloth-of-gold of tissue,
    O'erpicturing that Venus where we see
    The fancy outwork nature. On each side her
    Stood pretty dimpled boys, like smiling cupids,
    With divers-coloured fans, whose wind did seem
    To glow the delicate cheeks which they did cool,
    And what they undid did.

AGRIPPA   O, rare for Antony!

ENOBARBUS
    Her gentlewomen, like the Nereides,
    So many mermaids, tended her in the eyes,

And made their bends adornings. At the helm
A seeming mermaid steers. The silken tackle
Swell with the touches of those flower-soft hands,
That nimbly frame the office. From the barge
A strange invisible perfume hits the sense
Of the adjacent wharves. The city cast
Her people out upon her; and Antony,
Enthroned in the market-place, did sit alone,
Whistling to the air; which, but for vacancy,
Had gone to gaze on Cleopatra too,
And made a gap in nature.

AGRIPPA   Rare Egyptian!

ENOBARBUS
Upon her landing, Antony sent to her,
Invited her to supper. She replied
It should be better he became her guest—
Which she entreated. Our courteous Antony,
Whom never the word 'No' woman heard speak,
Being barbered ten times over, goes to the feast,
And, for his refreshment, pays his heart
For what his eyes eat only.

AGRIPPA   Royal wench!
She made great Caesar lay his sword to bed.
He ploughed her, and she conceived.

ENOBARBUS   I saw her once
Hop forty paces through the public street;
And, having lost her breath, she spoke, and panted,
That she did make defect perfectiòn,
And, breathless, power breathe forth.

MAECENAS
Now Antony must leave her utterly.

ENOBARBUS
Never; he will not.
Age cannot wither her, nor custom stale
Her infinite variety. Other women cloy
The appetites they feed, but she makes hungry
Where most she satisfies; for vilest things

Become themselves in her, that the holy priests
Bless her when she is randy.
MAECENAS
If beauty, wisdom, modesty, can settle
The heart of Antony, Octavia is
A blessed lottery to him.
AGRIPPA   Let us, go.
Good Enobarbus, make yourself my guest
While you abide here.
ENOBARBUS   Humbly sir, I thank you.

Exeunt

SCENE III
Caesar's house.

*Enter Antony and Caesar, with Octavia between
them*

ANTONY
The world and my great office will sometimes
Divide me from your bosom.
OCTAVIA   All which time,
Before the gods my knee shall bow my prayers
To them for you. Good night, sir.
ANTONY   My Octavia,
Read not my blemishes in the world's report.
I have not kept my square, but that to come
Shall all be done by the rule. Good night, dear lady.
Good night, sir.
CAESAR   Good night.   *Exeunt Caesar and Octavia*

Enter the Soothsayer

ANTONY   Now, man: you do wish yourself in Egypt?
SOOTHSAYER   Would I had never come from thence, nor
you thither.

ANTONY   If you can, your reason?

SOOTHSAYER   I see it in my spirit, have it not in my
  tongue; but yet hie you to Egypt again.

ANTONY
  Say to me, whose fortunes shall rise higher,
  Caesar's, or mine?

SOOTHSAYER
  Caesar's.
  Therefore, O Antony, stay not by his side.
  Your daemon—that your spirit which keeps
          you—is
  Noble, courageous, high, unmatchable,
  Where Caesar's is not. But near him your angel
  Becomes afraid, as if o'erpowered. Therefore
  Make space enough between you.

ANTONY   Speak this no more.

SOOTHSAYER
  To none but you; no more but when to you.
  If you do play with him at any game,
  You are sure to lose; and of that natural luck
  He beats you against the odds. Your lustre thickens
  When he shines by. I say again, your spirit
  Is all afraid to govern you near him;
  But, he away, 'tis noble.

ANTONY   Get you gone.
  Say to Ventidius I would speak with him.
  He shall to Parthia.

                                    Exit Soothsayer
                        Be it art or luck,
  He has spoken true. The very dice obey him,
  And in our sports my better cunning faints
  Under his chance. If we draw lots, he speeds;
  His cocks do win the battle always of mine
  When even at all to nought, his quails ever
  Beat mine, inhooped, at odds. I will to Egypt;
  And though I make this marriage for my peace,
  In the East my pleasure lies.

Enter Ventidius

                       O, come, Ventidius.
You must to Parthia. Your commission's ready;
Follow me, and receive it.   *Exeunt*

SCENE IV
Rome. A street.

Enter Lepidus, Maecenas, and Agrippa

LEPIDUS
Trouble yourselves no further. Pray you, hasten
Your generals after.
AGRIPPA   Sir, Mark Antony
Will even but kiss Octavia, and we'll follow.
LEPIDUS
Till I shall see you in your soldier's dress,
Which will become you both, farewell.
MAECENAS   We shall,
As I conceive the journey, be at the Mount
Before you, Lepidus.
LEPIDUS   Your way is shorter.
My purposes do draw me much about.
You'll win two days upon me.
MAECENAS *and* AGRIPPA   Sir, good success.
LEPIDUS
Farewell.   *Exeunt*

SCENE V
Cleopatra's palace.

Enter Cleopatra, Charmian, Iras, and Alexas

CLEOPATRA
  Give me some good music—music, moody food
  Of us that trade in love.
ALL   The music, ho!

  Enter Mardian

CLEOPATRA
  Let it alone! Let's to billiards. Come, Charmian.
CHARMIAN
  My arm is sore; best play with Mardian.
CLEOPATRA
  As well a woman with an eunuch played
  As with a woman. Come, you'll play with me, sir?
MARDIAN
  As well as I can, madam.
CLEOPATRA
  And when good will is shown, though it comes too
            short,
  The actor may plead pardon. I'll none now.
  Give me my tackle. We'll to the river; there,
  My music playing far off, I will betray
  Tawny-finned fishes. My bended hood shall pierce
  Their slimy jaws; and as I draw them up,
  I'll think them every one an Antony,
  And say 'Ah, ha! You are caught!'
CHARMIAN   'Twas merry when
  You wagered on your angling; when your diver
  Did hang a salt fish on his hook, which he
  With fervency drew up.
CLEOPATRA   That time—O times!
  I laughed him out of patience; and that night
  I laughed him into patience. And next morn,
  Ere the ninth hour, I drank him to his bed;
  Then put my dress and mantles on him, while
  I wore his sword Philippan.

  Enter a Messenger

                                              O, from Italy!
    Ram you your fruitful tidings in my ears,
    That long time have been barren.

MESSENGER   Madam, madam—

CLEOPATRA
    Antony's dead! If you say so, villain,
    You kill your mistress; but well and free,
    If you so yield him, there is gold and here
    My bluest veins to kiss; a hand that kings
    Have lipped, and trembled kissing.

MESSENGER
    First, madam, he is well.

CLEOPATRA   Why, there's more gold.
    But, fellow, mark, we use
    To say the dead are well. Bring it to that,
    The gold I give you will I melt and pour
    Down your ill-uttering throat.

MESSENGER
    Good madam, hear me.

CLEOPATRA   Well, go to, I will.
    But there's no goodness in your face if Antony
    Is free and healthful; so tart a favour
    To trumpet such good tidings. If not well,
    You should come like a Fury crowned with snakes,
    Not like a common man.

MESSENGER   Will it please you hear me?

CLEOPATRA
    I have a mind to strike you ere you speak.
    Yet, if you say Antony lives, is well,
    Or friends with Caesar, or not captive to him,
    I'll set you in a shower of gold, and hail
    Rich pearls upon you.

MESSENGER   Madam, he's well.

CLEOPATRA   Well said.

MESSENGER
    And friends with Caesar.

CLEOPATRA   You are an honest man.

MESSENGER
  Caesar and he are greater friends than ever.
CLEOPATRA
  Make you a fortune from me.
MESSENGER   But yet, madam—
CLEOPATRA
  I do not like 'But yet'; it does allay
  The good precèdence. Fie upon 'But yet'!
  'But yet' is a gaoler to bring forth
  Some monstrous malefactor. Pray you, friend,
  Pour out the pack of matter to my ear,
  The good and bad together. He's friends with Caesar,
  In state of health, you say, and you say, free.
MESSENGER
  Free, madam! No; I made no such report.
  He's bound unto Octavia.
CLEOPATRA   For what good turn?
MESSENGER
  For the best turn in the bed.
CLEOPATRA   I am pale, Charmian.
MESSENGER
  Madam, he's married to Octavia.
CLEOPATRA
  The most infectious pestilence upon you!
    She strikes him down
MESSENGER
  Good madam, patience.
CLEOPATRA   What say you?
    She strikes him
                                          Hence,
  Horrible villain, or I'll spurn your eyes
  Like balls before me! I'll unhair your head!
    She hales him up and down
  You shall be whipped with wire and stewed in brine,
  Smarting in lingering pickle!
MESSENGER   Gracious madam,
  I that do bring the news made not the match.

CLEOPATRA
>   Say 'tis not so, a province I will give you,
>   And make your fortunes proud. The blow you had
>   Shall make your peace for moving me to rage,
>   And I will enrich you with what gift beside
>   Your modesty can beg.

MESSENGER   He's married, madam.

CLEOPATRA
>   Rogue, you have lived too long.
>   *She draws a knife*

MESSENGER   Nay, then I'll run.
>   What mean you, madam? I have made no fault.
>>   *Exit*

CHARMIAN
>   Good madam, keep yourself within yourself.
>   The man is innocent.

CLEOPATRA
>   Some innocents escape not the thunderbolt.
>   Melt Egypt into Nile, and kindly creatures
>   Turn all to serpents! Call the slave again.
>   Though I am mad, I will not bite him. Call!

CHARMIAN
>   He is afraid to come.

CLEOPATRA   I will not hurt him.
>>   *Exit Charmian*
>   These hands do lack nobility, that they strike
>   A meaner than myself; since I myself
>   Have given myself the cause.
>   *Enter Charmian and the Messenger*
>   Come hither, sir.
>   Though it is honest, it is never good
>   To bring bad news. Give to a gracious message
>   A host of tongues, but let ill tidings tell
>   Themselves when they are felt.

MESSENGER   I have done my duty.

CLEOPATRA
>   Is he married?
>   I cannot hate you worse than I do

If you again say 'Yes'.
MESSENGER   He's married, madam.
CLEOPATRA
The gods confound you! Do you hold there still?
MESSENGER
Should I lie, madam?
CLEOPATRA   O, I would you did,
So half my Egypt were submerged and made
A cistern for scaled snakes! Go get you hence.
Had you Narcissus in your face, to me
You would appear most ugly. He is married?
MESSENGER
I crave your highness' pardon.
CLEOPATRA   He is married?
MESSENGER
Take no offence that I would not offend you;
To punish me for you make me do
Seems much unequal. He's married to Octavia.
CLEOPATRA
O, that his fault should make a knave of you,
That are not what you are sure of! Get you hence.
The merchandise which you have brought from Rome
Are all too dear for me. Lie they upon your hand,
And be undone by them.   *Exit Messenger*
CHARMIAN   Good your highness, patience.
CLEOPATRA
In praising Antony I have dispraised Caesar.
CHARMIAN
Many times, madam.
CLEOPATRA   I am paid for it now.
Lead me from hence;
I faint. O, Iras, Charmian! 'Tis no matter.
Go to the fellow, good Alexas; bid him
Report the feature of Octavia, her years,
Her inclination. Let him not leave out
The colour of her hair. Bring me word quickly.
                                   Exit Alexas

Let him for ever go—let him not, Charmian.
Though he is painted one way like a Gorgon,
The other way's a Mars. (*To Mardian*) Bid you Alexas
Bring me word how tall she is.—Pity me, Charmian,
But do not speak to me. Lead me to my chamber.

Exeunt

SCENE VI
Near Misena.

Flourish. Enter Pompey and Menas at one door, at another, Caesar, Lepidus, Antony, Enobarbus, Maecenas, Agrippa, with soldiers marching

POMPEY
  Your hostages I have; so have you mine;
  And we shall talk before we fight.
CAESAR   Most meet
  That first we come to words; and therefore have we
  Our written purposes before us sent.
  Which if you have considered, let us know
  If it will tie up your discontented sword
  And carry back to Sicily much tall youth
  That else must perish here.
POMPEY   To you all three,
  The senators alone of this great world,
  Chief factors for the gods: I do not know
  Wherefore my father should revengers want,
  Having a son and friends, since Julius Caesar,
  Who at Philippi the good Brutus ghosted,
  There saw you labouring for him. What was it
  That moved pale Cassius to conspire? And what
  Made the all-honoured, honest, Roman Brutus,
  With the armed rest, courtiers of beauteous freedom,
  To drench the Capitol, but that they would
  Have one man but a man? And that is it

Has made me rig my navy, at whose burden
The angered ocean foams; with which I meant
To scourge the ingratitude that despiteful Rome
Cast on my noble father.

CAESAR   Take your time.

ANTONY
You can not affright us, Pompey, with your sails.
We'll speak with you at sea. On land you know
How much we do o'ercount you.

POMPEY   On land indeed
You do o'ercount me of my father's house;
But since the cuckoo builds not for himself,
Remain in it as you may.

LEPIDUS   Be pleased to tell us—
For this is from the present—how you take
The offers we have sent you.

CAESAR   There is the point.

ANTONY
Which do not be entreated to, but weigh
What it is worth embraced.

CAESAR
To try a larger fortune.

POMPEY   You have made me offer
Of Sicily, Sardinia; and I must
Rid all the sea of pirates; then, to send
Measures of wheat to Rome. This agreed upon,
To part with unhacked edges and bear back
Our shields undinted.

ALL THE TRIUMVIRS   That's our offer.

POMPEY   Know, then,
I came before you here a man prepared
To take this offer. But Mark Antony
Put me to some impatience. Though I lose
The praise of it by telling, you must know,
When Caesar and your brother were at blows,
Your mother came to Sicily and did find
Her welcome friendly.

ANTONY   I have heard it, Pompey,
  And am well studied for a liberal thanks,
  Which I do owe you.
POMPEY   Let me have your hand.
  I did not think, sir, to have met you here.
ANTONY
  The beds in the East are soft; and thanks to you,
  That called me timelier than my purpose hither;
  For I have gained by it.
CAESAR (*to Pompey*)   Since I saw you last
  There is a change upon you.
POMPEY   Well, I know not
  What counts harsh Fortune casts upon my face,
  But in my bosom shall she never come
  To make my heart her vassal.
LEPIDUS   Well met here.
POMPEY
  I hope so, Lepidus. Thus we are agreed.
  I crave our composition may be written,
  And sealed between us.
CAESAR   That is the next to do.
POMPEY
  We'll feast each other ere we part, and let us
  Draw lots who shall begin.
ANTONY   That will I, Pompey.
POMPEY
  No, Antony, take the lot.
  But, first or last, your fine Egyptian cookery
  Shall have the fame. I have heard that Julius Caesar
  Grew fat with feasting there.
ANTONY   You have heard much.
POMPEY
  I have fair meanings, sir.
ANTONY   And fair words to them.
POMPEY
  Then so much have I heard.
  And I have heard Apollodorus carried—

ENOBARBUS
    No more of that: he did so.
POMPEY   What, I pray you?
ENOBARBUS
    A certain queen to Caesar in a mattress.
POMPEY
    I know you now. How fare you, soldier?
ENOBARBUS   Well;
    And well am like to do, for I perceive
    Four feasts are toward.
POMPEY   Let me shake your hand.
    I never hated you; I have seen you fight
    When I have envied your behaviour.
ENOBARBUS   Sir,
    I never loved you much; but I have praised you
    When you have well deserved ten times as much
    As I have said you did.
POMPEY   Enjoy your plainness;
    It nothing ill becomes you.
    Aboard my galley I invite you all.
    Will you lead, lords?
ALL   Show us the way, sir.
POMPEY   Come.
        Exeunt all but Enobarbus and Menas
MENAS *(aside)* Your father, Pompey, would never have
    made this treaty.—You and I have known, sir.
ENOBARBUS   At sea, I think.
MENAS   We have, sir.
ENOBARBUS   You have done well by water.
MENAS   And you by land.
ENOBARBUS   I will praise any man that will praise me;
    though it cannot be denied what I have done by land.
MENAS   Nor what I have done by water.
ENOBARBUS   Yes, something you can deny for your own
    safety: you have been a great thief by sea.
MENAS   And you by land.
ENOBARBUS   There I deny my land service. But give me

your hand, Menas. If our eyes had authority, here they
might take two thieves kissing.

MENAS   All men's faces are true, whatsoever their hands
are.

ENOBARBUS   But there is never a fair woman has a true
face.

MENAS   No slander; they steal hearts.

ENOBARBUS   We came hither to fight with you.

MENAS   For my part, I am sorry it is turned to a drinking.
Pompey does this day laugh away his fortune.

ENOBARBUS   If he does, sure he cannot weep it back
again.

MENAS   You have said, sir. We looked not for Mark
Antony here. Pray you, is he married to Cleopatra?

ENOBARBUS   Caesar's sister is called Octavia.

MENAS   True, sir; she was the wife of Caius Marcellus.

ENOBARBUS   But she is now the wife of Marcus
Antonius.

MENAS   Pray you, sir?

ENOBARBUS   'Tis true.

MENAS   Then are Caesar and he for ever knit together.

ENOBARBUS   If I were bound to divine of this unity, I
would not prophesy so.

MENAS   I think the policy of that purpose made more in
the marriage than the love of the parties.

ENOBARBUS   I think so too. But you shall find the bond
that seems to tie their friendship together will be the
very strangler of their amity. Octavia is of a holy, cold,
and still conversation.

MENAS   Who would not have his wife so?

ENOBARBUS   Not he that himself is not so; which is
Mark Antony. He will to his Egyptian dish again.
Then shall the sighs of Octavia blow the fire up in
Caesar, and, as I said before, that which is the
strength of their amity shall prove the immediate
author of their variance. Antony will use his affection
where it is. He married but his occasion here.

MENAS   And thus it may be. Come, sir, will you aboard?
   I have a health for you.
ENOBARBUS   I shall take it, sir. We have used our throats
   in Egypt.
MENAS   Come, let's away.   *Exeunt*

SCENE VII
Pompey's galley.

Music plays. Enter Servants, with a banquet

FIRST SERVANT   Here they'll be, man. Some of their
   plants are ill-rooted already; the least wind in the
   world will blow them down.
SECOND SERVANT   Lepidus is high-coloured.
FIRST SERVANT   They have made him drink alms drink.
SECOND SERVANT   As they pinch one another by the disposition, he cries out 'No more'; reconciles them to
   his entreaty, and himself to the drink.
FIRST SERVANT   But it raises the greater war between
   him and his discretion.
SECOND SERVANT   Why, this it is to have a name in great
   men's fellowship. I had as soon have a reed that will do
   me no service as a halberd I could not heave.
FIRST SERVANT   To be called into a huge sphere, and not
   to be seen to move in it, are the holes where eyes
   should be, which pitifully disaster the cheeks.
   A sennet sounded. Enter Caesar, Antony, Pompey,
   Lepidus, Agrippa, Maecenas, Enobarbus, Menas,
   with other captains
ANTONY   (*to Lepidus*)
   Thus do they, sir: they take the flow of the Nile
   By certain scales in the pyramid. They know
   By the height, the lowness, or the mean if dearth
   Or plenty follow. The higher the Nile does swell,

The more it promises; as it ebbs, the seedsman
Upon the slime and ooze scatters his grain,
And shortly comes to harvest.

LEPIDUS   You have strange serpents there.

ANTONY   Ay, Lepidus.

LEPIDUS   Your serpent of Egypt is bred now of your mud
by the operation of your sun; so is your crocodile.

ANTONY   They are so.

POMPEY   Sit—and some wine! A health to Lepidus!

LEPIDUS   I am not so well as I should be, but I'll never
out.

ENOBARBUS   Not till you have slept; I fear you'll be in till
then.

LEPIDUS   Nay, certainly, I have heard the Ptolemies'
pyramids are very goodly things; without contradic-
tion I have heard that.

MENAS   (*aside to Pompey*)
Pompey, a word.

POMPEY   (*aside to Menas*) Say in my ear; what is it?

MENAS   (*aside to Pompey*)
Forsake your seat, I do beseech you, captain,
And hear me speak a word.

POMPEY   (*aside to Menas*) Forbear me till anon.
(*aloud*) This wine for Lepidus!

LEPIDUS   What manner of thing is your crocodile?

ANTONY   It is shaped, sir, like itself, and it is as broad as
it has breadth. It is just so high as it is, and moves
with its own organs. It lives by that which nourishes
it, and the elements once out of it, it transmigrates.

LEPIDUS   What colour is it of?

ANTONY   Of its own colour too.

LEPIDUS   'Tis a strange serpent.

ANTONY   It is so; and the tears of it are wet.

CAESAR   Will this description satisfy him?

ANTONY   With the health that Pompey gives him; else
he is a very epicure.
Menas whispers to Pompey

POMPEY   *(aside to Menas)*
    Go hang, sir, hang! Tell me of that? Away!
    Do as I bid you.—Where's this cup I called for?
MENAS   *(aside to Pompey)*
    If for the sake of merit you will hear me,
    Rise from your stool.
POMPEY   *(aside to Menas)* I think you are mad. The
    matter?
        He rises and they walk aside
MENAS
    I have ever held my cap off to your fortunes.
POMPEY
    You have served me with much faith. What's else to
        say?—
    Be jolly, lords.
ANTONY   These quicksands, Lepidus,
    Keep off them, for you sink.
MENAS
    Will you be lord of all the world?
POMPEY   What say you?
MENAS
    Will you be lord of the whole world? That's twice.
POMPEY
    How should that be?
MENAS   But entertain it,
    And though you think me poor, I am the man
    Will give you all the world.
POMPEY   Have you drunk well?
MENAS
    No, Pompey, I have kept me from the cup.
    You are, if you dare be, the earthly Jove;
    Whatever the ocean pales, or sky inclips,
    Is yours, if you will have it.
POMPEY   Show me which way.
MENAS
    These three world-sharers, these competitors,
    Are in your vessel. Let me cut the cable;

And when we are put off, fall to their throats.
All there is yours.

POMPEY   Ah, this you should have done,
And not have spoken of it. In me 'tis villainy;
In you it had been good service. You must know
'Tis not my profit that does lead my honour;
My honour, it. Repent that ever your tongue
Has so betrayed your act. Being done unknown,
I should have found it afterwards well done,
But must condemn it now. Desist, and drink.

MENAS   *(aside)*
I'll never follow your fallen fortunes more.
Who seeks, and will not take when once 'tis offered,
Shall never find it more.

POMPEY   This health to Lepidus!

ANTONY
Bear him ashore.—I'll pledge it for him, Pompey.

ENOBARBUS
Here's to you, Menas!

MENAS   Enobarbus, welcome.

POMPEY
Fill till the cup be hidden.

ENOBARBUS   *(pointing to the servant who is carrying off
Lepidus)*
There's a strong fellow, Menas.

MENAS
Why?

ENOBARBUS
He bears the third part of the world, man; see not?

MENAS
The third part then is drunk. Would it were all,
That it might go on wheels!

ENOBARBUS
Drink you; increase the reels.

MENAS
Come.

POMPEY
This is not yet an Alexandrian feast.

ANTONY

    It ripens towards it. Strike the vessels, ho!

    Here's to Caesar!

CAESAR   I could well forbear it.

    It's monstrous labour when I wash my brain

    And it grows fouler.

ANTONY   Be a child of the time.

CAESAR

    Possess it, I'll make answer.

    But I had rather fast from all, four days,

    Than drink so much in one.

ENOBARBUS   *[to Antony]* Ha, my brave emperor!

    Shall we dance now the Egyptian bacchanals

    And celebrate our drink?

POMPEY   Let's have it, good soldier.

ANTONY

    Come, let's all take hands

    Till the conquering wine has steeped our sense

    In soft and delicate Lethe.

ENOBARBUS   All take hands.

    Make battery to our ears with the loud music;

    The while I'll place you; then the boy shall sing.

    The holding every man shall beat as loud

    As his strong sides can volley.

      Music plays. Enobarbus places them hand in hand

BOY   *(sings)*

    Come, you monarch of the vine,

    Plump Bacchus with pink eyne! [eyes]

    In your vats our cares be drowned;

    With your grapes our hairs be crowned.

      Cup us till the world go round,

      Cup us till the world go round!

CAESAR

    What would you more? Pompey, good night.

    (To Antony) Good brother,

    Let me request you off. Our graver business

    Frowns at this levity. Gentle lords, let's part.

You see we have burnt our cheeks. Strong Enobarb
Is weaker than the wine, and my own tongue
Splits what it speaks. The wild disguise has almost
Buffooned us all. What needs more words? Good night.
Good Antony, your hand.

POMPEY   I'll try you on the shore.

ANTONY

And shall, sir. Give us your hand.

POMPEY   O, Antony,
You have my father's house. But what, we are
friends!
Come down into the boat.

Exeunt all but Enobarbus and Menas

ENOBARBUS   Take heed you fall not.
Menas, I'll not on shore.

MENAS   No, to my cabin.
These drums! These trumpets, flutes! What!
Let Neptune hear we bid a loud farewell
To these great fellows. Sound and be hanged, sound
out!

Sound a flourish, with drums

ENOBARBUS   Hoo, says he. There's my cap.

He throws his cap in the air

MENAS   Hoa! Noble captain, come.   *Exeunt*

Act III

SCENE I
A plain in Syria.

Enter Ventidius, with Silius and other officers and soldiers. Before Ventidius is borne the dead body of Pacorus

VENTIDIUS
Now, darting Parthia, are you struck; and now
Pleased Fortune does of Marcus Crassus' death
Make me revenger. Bear the King's son's body
Before our army. Your Pacorus, Orodes,
Pays this for Marcus Crassus.

SILIUS   Noble Ventidius,
While yet with Parthian blood your sword is warm,
The fugitive Parthians follow. Spur through Media,
Mesopotamia, and the shelters whither
The routed fly. So your grand captain, Antony,
Shall set you on triumphant chariots, and
Put garlands on your head.

VENTIDIUS   O Silius, Silius,
I have done enough. A lower place, note well,
May make too great an act. For learn this, Silius:
Better to leave undone than by our deed
Acquire too high a fame when him we serve is away.
Caesar and Antony have ever won
More in their officer than person. Sossius,
One of my place in Syria, his lieutenant,
For quick accumulation of renown,
Which he achieved by the minute, lost his favour.
Who does in the wars more than his captain can
Becomes his captain's captain; and ambition,

73

The soldier's virtue, rather makes choice of loss
Than gain which darkens him.
I could do more to do Antonius good,
But it would offend him, and in his offence
Should my performance perish.
SILIUS   You have, Ventidius, that
Without which a soldier and his sword
Grants scarce distinction. You will write to Antony?
VENTIDIUS
I'll humbly signify what in his name,
That magical word of war, we have effected.
How, with his banners and his well-paid ranks,
The never-yet-beaten horse of Parthia
We have jaded out of the field.
SILIUS   Where is he now?
VENTIDIUS
He purposes to Athens; whither, with what haste
The weight we must convey with us will permit,
We shall appear before him.—On, there. Pass along.
                                                    Exeunt

SCENE II
Caesar's house.

Enter Agrippa at one door, Enobarbus at another

AGRIPPA
What, are the brothers parted?
ENOBARBUS
They have dispatched with Pompey; he is gone.
The other three are sealing. Octavia weeps
To part from Rome; Caesar is sad, and Lepidus
Since Pompey's feast, as Menas says, is troubled
With the green-sickness.
AGRIPPA   'Tis a noble Lepidus.
ENOBARBUS
A very fine one. O, how he loves Caesar!

AGRIPPA

Nay, but how dearly he adores Mark Antony!

ENOBARBUS

Caesar? Why, he is the Jupiter of men.

AGRIPPA

What's Antony? The god of Jupiter.

ENOBARBUS

Spoke you of Caesar? How! The nonpareil!

AGRIPPA

O Antony! O you Arabian bird!

ENOBARBUS

Would you praise Caesar, say 'Caesar'—go no further.

AGRIPPA

Indeed, he plied them both with excellent praises.

ENOBARBUS

But he loves Caesar best, yet he loves Antony—

Hoo! Hearts, tongues, figures, scribes, bards, poets,
    cannot

Think, speak, cast, write, sing, number—hoo!—

His love to Antony. But as for Caesar,

Kneel down, kneel down, and wonder.

AGRIPPA   Both he loves.

ENOBARBUS

They are his wings, and he their beetle. So—

    (*Trumpet within*)

This is to horse. Adieu, noble Agrippa.

AGRIPPA

Good fortune, worthy soldier, and farewell!

    Enter Caesar, Antony, Lepidus, and Octavia

ANTONY

No further, sir.

CAESAR

You take from me a great part of myself;

Use me well in it. Sister, prove such a wife

As my thoughts make you, and as my farthest bond

Shall prove you to be. Most noble Antony,

Let not the piece of virtue which is set

Between us as the cement of our love,
To keep it builded, be the ram to batter
The fortress of it. For better might we
Have loved without this means, if on both parts
This is not cherished.

ANTONY   Make me not offended
In your distrust.

CAESAR   I have said.

ANTONY   You shall not find,
Though you are therein doubtful, the least cause
For what you seem to fear. So, the gods keep you,
And make the hearts of Romans serve your ends!
We will here part.

CAESAR
Farewell, my dearest sister, fare you well.
The elements be kind to you, and make
Your spirits all of comfort. Fare you well.

OCTAVIA (weeping)
My noble brother!

ANTONY
The April's in her eyes; it is love's spring,
And these the showers to bring it on. Be cheerful.

OCTAVIA
Sir, look well to my husband's house; and—

CAESAR   What,
Octavia?

OCTAVIA   I'll tell you in your ear.

ANTONY
Her tongue will not obey her heart, nor can
Her heart inform her tongue—the swan's-down
    feather
That stands upon the swell at the full of tide,
And neither way inclines.

ENOBARBUS   (aside to Agrippa) Will Caesar weep?

AGRIPPA   (aside to Enobarbus)
He has a cloud in his face.

ENOBARBUS   *(aside to Agrippa)*
   He were the worse for that, were he a horse;
   So is he, being a man.
AGRIPPA   *(aside to Enobarbus)* Why, Enobarbus,
   When Antony found Julius Caesar dead,
   He cried almost to roaring; and he wept
   When at Philippi he found Brutus slain.
ENOBARBUS   *(aside to Agrippa)*
   That year indeed he was troubled with a cold.
   What willingly he did destroy he wailed,
   Believe it, till I wept too.
CAESAR   No, sweet Octavia,
   You shall hear from me always—the time shall not
   Outgo my thinking of you.
ANTONY   Come, sir, come,
   I'll wrestle with you in my strength of love.
   Look, here I have you; thus I let you go,
   And give you to the gods.
CAESAR   Adieu; be happy!
LEPIDUS   *(to Octavia)*
   Let all the number of the stars give light
   To your fair way!
CAESAR   Farewell, farewell!
      He kisses Octavia
ANTONY   Farewell!
                        Trumpets sound. Exeunt

SCENE III
Cleopatra's palace.

Enter Cleopatra, Charmian, Iras, and Alexas

CLEOPATRA
   Where is the fellow?
ALEXAS   Half afraid to come.

CLEOPATRA
  Go to, go to.
      Enter the Messenger
          Come hither, sir.
ALEXAS   Good majesty,
  Herod of Jewry dares not look upon you
  But when you are well pleased.
CLEOPATRA   That Herod's head
  I'll have; but how, when Antony is gone,
  Through whom I might command it?—Come you
  near.
MESSENGER
  Most gracious majesty!
CLEOPATRA   Did you behold Octavia?
MESSENGER
  Ay, dread queen.
CLEOPATRA   Where?
MESSENGER   Madam, in Rome.
  I looked her in the face, and saw her led
  Between her brother and Mark Antony.
CLEOPATRA
  Is she as tall as me?
MESSENGER   She is not, madam.
CLEOPATRA
  Did hear her speak? Is she shrill-tongued or low?
MESSENGER
  Madam, I heard her speak; she is low-voiced.
CLEOPATRA
  That's not so good. He cannot like her long.
CHARMIAN
  Like her? O Isis! It is impossible.
CLEOPATRA
  I think so, Charmian. Dull of tongue, and dwarfish.
  What majesty is in her gait? Remember,
  If ever you look on majesty.
MESSENGER   She creeps;
  Her motion and her station are as one.

She shows a body rather than a life,
A statue than a breather.
CLEOPATRA   Is this certain?
MESSENGER
Or I have no observance.
CHARMIAN   Three in Egypt
Cannot make better note.
CLEOPATRA   He's very knowing,
I do perceive it. There's nothing in her yet.
The fellow has good judgement.
CHARMIAN   Excellent.
CLEOPATRA
Guess at her years, I pray you.
MESSENGER   Madam,
She was a widow—
CLEOPATRA   Widow? Charmian, hark.
MESSENGER
And I do think she's thirty.
CLEOPATRA
Bear you her face in mind? Is it long or round?
MESSENGER
Round, even to faultiness.
CLEOPATRA
For the most part, too, they are foolish that are so.
Her hair, what colour?
MESSENGER   Brown, madam; and her forehead
As low as she would wish it.
CLEOPATRA   There's gold for you.
You must not take my former sharpness ill.
I will employ you back again. I find you
Most fit for business. Go, make you ready.
Our letters are prepared.   *Exit Messenger*
CHARMIAN   A proper man.
CLEOPATRA
Indeed he is so: I repent me much
That so I harried him. Why, I think, by him,
This creature's no such thing.

CHARMIAN   Nothing, madam.
CLEOPATRA
    The man has seen some majesty, and should know.
CHARMIAN
    Has he seen majesty? Isis else defend,
    And serving you so long!
CLEOPATRA
    I have one thing more to ask him yet, good Charmian.
    But 'tis no matter; you shall bring him to me
    Where I will write. All may be well enough.
CHARMIAN
    I warrant you, madam.   *Exeunt*

SCENE IV
Athens. Antony's house.

Enter Antony and Octavia

ANTONY
    Nay, nay, Octavia, not only that;
    That were excusable, that and thousands more
    Of semblable import—but he has waged
    New wars against Pompey; made his will, and read it
    To public ear;
    Spoke scantly of me. When perforce he could not
    But pay me terms of honour, cold and sickly
    He vented them, most narrow measure lent me;
    When the best hint was given him, he not took it,
    Or did it from his teeth.
OCTAVIA   O, my good lord,
    Believe not all; or, if you must believe,
    Stomach not all. A more unhappy lady,
    If this division chances, never stood between,
    Praying for both parts.
    The good gods will mock me instantly
    When I shall pray 'O, bless my lord and husband!';

Undo that prayer by crying out as loud
'O, bless my brother!' Husband win, win brother,
Prays, and destroys the prayèr; no midway
Between these extremes at all.
ANTONY   Gentle Octavia,
Let your best love draw to that point which seeks
Best to preserve it. If I lose my honour,
I lose myself; better I were not yours
Than yours so armless. But, as you requested,
Yourself shall go between us. The meantime, lady,
I'll raise the preparation of a war
Shall harm your brother. Make your soonest haste;
So your desires are yours.
OCTAVIA   Thanks to my lord.
The Jove of power make me, most weak, most weak,
Your reconciler! Wars with you twain would be
As if the world should cleave, and that slain men
Should solder up the rift.
ANTONY
When it appears to you where this begins,
Turn your displeasure that way; for our faults
Can never be so equal that your love
Can equally move with them. Provide for your going;
Choose your own company, and command what cost
Your heart has mind to.   *Exeunt*

SCENE V
The same.

Enter Enobarbus and Eros

ENOBARBUS   How now, friend Eros?
EROS   There's strange news come, sir.
ENOBARBUS   What, man?
EROS   Caesar and Lepidus have made war upon Pompey.
ENOBARBUS   This is old. What is the outcome?

EROS   Caesar, having made use of him in the war against
    Pompey, presently denied him equality, would not let
    him partake in the glory of the action; and, not resting
    here, accuses him of letters he formerly wrote to
    Pompey; upon his accusation, seizes him; so the poor
    third is up, till death enlarges his confine.
ENOBARBUS
    Then, world, you have a pair of chaps, no more;
    And throw between them all the food you have,
    They'll grind the one the other. Where's Antony?
EROS
    He's walking in the garden—thus, and spurns
    The rush that lies before him; cries 'Fool Lepidus!'
    And threatens the throat of that officer of his
    That murdered Pompey.   Our great navy's rigged.
ENOBARBUS
EROS
    For Italy and Caesar. More, Domitius:
    My lord desires you now at once. My news
    I might have told hereafter.
ENOBARBUS   It will be naught;
    But let it be. Bring me to Antony.
EROS   Come, sir.   *Exeunt*

SCENE VI
Caesar's house.

Enter Agrippa, Maecenas, and Caesar

CAESAR
    Contemning Rome, he has done all this and more
    In Alexandria. Here's the manner of it:
    In the market-place on a tribunal silvered,
    Cleopatra and himself in chairs of gold
    Were publicly enthroned; at the feet sat
    Caesarion, whom they call my father's son,

And all the unlawful issue that their lust
Since then has made between them. Unto her
He gave the establishment of Egypt; made her
Of lower Syria, Cyprus, Lydia,
Absolute queen.

MAECENAS   This in the public eye?

CAESAR

In the common showplace, where they exercise.
His sons he there proclaimed the kings of kings;
Great Media, Parthia, and Armenia
He gave to Alexander; to Ptolemy he assigned
Syria, Cilicia, and Phoenicia. She
In the habiliments of the goddess Isis
That day appeared, and oft before gave audience,
As it is reported, so.

MAECENAS   Let Rome be thus informed.

AGRIPPA

Who, queasy with his insolence already,
Will their good thoughts call from him.

CAESAR

The people knows it, and have now received
His accusations.

AGRIPPA   Whom does he accuse?

CAESAR

Caesar; and that, having in Sicily
Sextus Pompeius spoiled, we had not rated him
His part of the isle. Then does he say he lent me
Some shipping, unrestored. Lastly, he frets
That Lepidus of the triumvirate
Should be deposed; so being, that we detain
All his revenue.

AGRIPPA   Sir, this should be answered.

CAESAR

It is done already, and the messenger gone.
I have told him Lepidus was grown too cruel,
That he his high authority abused,
And did deserve his change. For what I have conquered,

I grant him part; but then in his Armenia,
And other of his conquered kingdoms, I
Demand the like.

MAECENAS   He will never yield to that.

CAESAR

Nor must he then be yielded to in this.

Enter Octavia with attendants

OCTAVIA

Hail, Caesar and my lord! Hail, most dear Caesar!

CAESAR

That ever I should call you castaway!

OCTAVIA

You have not called me so, nor have you cause.

CAESAR

Why have you stolen upon us thus? You come not
Like Caesar's sister. The wife of Antony
Should have an army for an usher, and
The neighs of horse to tell of her approach
Long ere she did appear. The trees by the way
Should have borne men, and expectation fainted,
Longing for what it had not. Nay, the dust
Should have ascended to the roof of heaven,
Raised by your populous troops. But you are come
A market maid to Rome, and have forestalled
The ostentation of our love; which, left unshown,
Is often left unloved. We should have met you
By sea and land, supplying every stage
With an augmented greeting.

OCTAVIA   Good my lord,
To come thus was I not constrained, but did it
On my free will. My lord, Mark Antony,
Hearing that you prepared for war, acquainted
My grievèd ear with it; whereon I begged
His pardon for return.

CAESAR   Which soon he granted,
Being an obstruct between his lust and him.

OCTAVIA

Do not say so, my lord.

CAESAR   I have eyes upon him,
  And his affairs come to me on the wind.
  Where is he now?
OCTAVIA   My lord, in Athens.
CAESAR
  No, my most wrongèd sister; Cleopatra
  Has nodded him to her. He has given his empire
  Up to a whore; who now are levying
  The kings of the earth for war. He has assembled
  Bocchus, the King of Libya; Archelaus,
  Of Cappadocia; Philadelphos, King
  Of Paphlagonia; the Thracian king, Adallas;
  King Mauchus of Arabia; King of Pont;
  Herod of Jewry; Mithridates, King
  Of Comagene; Polemon and Amyntas,
  The Kings of Mede and Lycaonia;
  With a larger list of sceptres.
OCTAVIA   Ay me most wretched,
  That have my heart parted between two friends
  That do afflict each other!
CAESAR   Welcome hither.
  Your letters did withhold our breaking forth,
  Till we perceived both how you were wrong led
  And we in negligent danger. Cheer your heart;
  Be you not troubled with the time, which drives
  O'er your content these strong necessities;
  But let determined things to destiny
  Hold unbewailed their way. Welcome to Rome;
  Nothing more dear to me. You are abused
  Beyond the mark of thought, and the high gods,
  To do you justice, make his ministers
  Of us and those that love you. Best of comfort,
  And ever welcome to us.
AGRIPPA   Welcome, lady.
MAECENAS
  Welcome, dear madam.
  Each heart in Rome does love and pity you.

Only the adulterous Antony, most large
In his abominations, turns you off
And gives his potent régime to a trull
That noises it against us.

OCTAVIA   Is it so, sir?

CAESAR

Most certain. Sister, welcome. Pray you
Be ever known to patience. My dearest sister!

Exeunt

SCENE VII
Near Actium.

Enter Cleopatra and Enobarbus

CLEOPATRA

I will be even with you, doubt it not.

ENOBARBUS

But why, why, why?

CLEOPATRA

You have opposed my being in these wars,
And say it is not fit.

ENOBARBUS   Well, is it, is it?

CLEOPATRA

Is it not denounced against us? Why should not we
Be there in person?

ENOBARBUS   *(aside)* Well, I could reply:
If we should serve with horse and mares together,
The horse were merely lost; the mares would bear
A soldier and his horse.

CLEOPATRA   What is it you say?

ENOBARBUS

Your presence needs must puzzle Antony,
Take from his heart, take from his brain, from his
        time,
What should not then be spared. He is already

Traduced for levity; it is said in Rome
That Photinus, an eunuch, and your maids
Manage this war.
CLEOPATRA   Sink Rome, and their tongues rot
That speak against us! A charge we bear in the war,
And as the president of my kingdom will
Appear there for a man. Speak not against it;
I will not stay behind.

Enter Antony and Canidius

ENOBARBUS   Nay, I have done.
Here comes the Emperor.
ANTONY   Is it not strange, Canidius,
That from Tarentum and Brundisium
He could so quickly cut the Ionian sea
And take in Toryne?—You have heard of it, sweet?
CLEOPATRA
Celerity is never more admired
Than by the negligent.
ANTONY   A good rebuke,
Which might have well become the best of men
To taunt at slackness. Canidius, we
Will fight with him by sea.
CLEOPATRA   By sea; what else?
CANIDIUS
Why will my lord do so?
ANTONY   Because he dares us to it.
ENOBARBUS
So has my lord dared him to single fight.
CANIDIUS
Ay, and to wage this battle at Pharsalia,
Where Caesar fought with Pompey. But these offers,
Which serve not for his advantage, he shakes off;
And so should you.
ENOBARBUS   Your ships are not well manned.
Your mariners are mulemen, reapers, people

Gathered by swift impress. In Caesar's fleet
Are those that often have against Pompey fought;
Their ships are swift; yours, heavy. No disgrace
Shall fall on you for refusing him at sea,
Being prepared for land.

ANTONY   By sea, by sea.

ENOBARBUS

Most worthy sir, you therein throw away
The absolute soldiership you have by land,
Distract your army, which does most consist
Of war-marked footmen; leave unexecuted
Your own renownèd knowledge, quite forgo
The way which promises assurance, and
Give up yourself merely to chance and hazard
From firm security.

ANTONY   I will fight at sea.

CLEOPATRA

I have sixty sails, Caesar none better.

ANTONY

Our overplus of shipping will we burn,
And with the rest full-manned, from the head of
          Actium
Beat the approaching Caesar. But if we fail,
We then can do it on land.

          Enter a Messenger

                          Your business?

MESSENGER

The news is true, my lord; he is descried.
Caesar has taken Toryne.

ANTONY

Can he be there in person? 'Tis impossible;
Strange that his army should be. Canidius,
Our nineteen legions you shall hold by land
And our twelve thousand horse. We'll to our ship.
Away, my Thetis!

Enter a Soldier

                              How now, worthy soldier?
SOLDIER
   O noble emperor, do not fight by sea.
   Trust not to rotten planks. Do you misdoubt
   This sword and these my wounds? Let the Egyptians
   And the Phoenicians go a-ducking; we
   Have used to conquer standing on the earth
   And fighting foot to foot.
ANTONY   Well, well; away!
                 Exeunt Antony, Cleopatra, and Enobarbus
SOLDIER
   By Hercules, I think I am in the right.
CANIDIUS
   Soldier, you are; but his whole action grows
   Not in the power of it. So our leader's led,
   And we are women's men.
SOLDIER   You keep by land
   The legions and the horse whole, do you not?
CANIDIUS
   Marcus Octavius, Marcus Justeius,
   Publicola, and Caelius are for sea;
   But we keep whole by land. This speed of Caesar's
   Carries beyond belief.
SOLDIER   While he was yet in Rome,
   His army went out in such divisions as
   Beguiled all spies.
CANIDIUS   Who's his lieutenant, hear you?
SOLDIER
   They say one Taurus.
CANIDIUS   Well I know the man.

Enter a Messenger

MESSENGER
   The Emperor calls Canidius.

CANIDIUS
    With news the time's with labour and brings forth
    Each minute some.   *Exeunt*

SCENE VIII
The same.

Enter Caesar and Taurus, with their army, marching

CAESAR
    Taurus!
TAURUS
    My lord?
CAESAR
    Strike not by land; keep whole; provoke not battle
    Till we have done at sea. Do not exceed
    The prescript of this scroll. Our fortune lies
    Upon this throw.   *Exeunt*

SCENE IX
The same.

Enter Antony and Enobarbus

ANTONY
    Set we our squadrons on yon side of the hill
    In eye of Caesar's line; from which place
    We may the number of the ships behold,
    And so proceed accordingly.   *Exeunt*

SCENE X
The same.

Canidius marches with his troops one way over

the stage, and Taurus, with soldiers the other way.
After their going in is heard the noise of a sea fight.
Alarum. Enter Enobarbus

ENOBARBUS
   Naught, naught, all naught! I can behold no longer.
   The *Antoniad*, the Egyptian admiral,
   With all their sixty, fly and turn the rudder.
   To see it my eyes are blasted.

   Enter Scarus

SCARUS   Gods and goddesses,
   All the whole synod of them!
ENOBARBUS   What's your passion?
SCARUS
   The greater cantle of the world is lost
   With very ignorance. We have kissed away
   Kingdoms and provinces.
ENOBARBUS   How appears the fight?
SCARUS
   On our side like the tokened pestilence,
   Where death is sure. Yon rotten nag of Egypt—
   Whom leprosy o'ertake!—in the midst of the fight,
   When vantage like a pair of twins appeared,
   Both as the same, or rather ours the greater,
   The gadfly on her like a cow in June,
   Hoists sails and flies.
ENOBARBUS   That I beheld.
   My eyes did sicken at the sight, and could not
   Endure a further view.
SCARUS   She once being luffed
   The noble ruin of her magic, Antony,
   Claps on his sea wing and, like a doting mallard,
   Leaving the fight in height, flies after her.
   I never saw an action of such shame.
   Experience, manhood, honour, never before
   Did violate so itself.
ENOBARBUS   Alas, alas!

Enter Canidius

CANIDIUS

Our fortune on the sea is out of breath,
And sinks most lamentably. Had our general
Been what he knew himself, it had gone well.
O, he has given example for our flight
Most grossly by his own.

ENOBARBUS

Ay, are you there? Why then, good night indeed.

CANIDIUS

Toward Peloponnesus are they fled.

SCARUS

'Tis easy to it; and there I will attend
What further comes.

CANIDIUS   To Caesar will I render
My legions and my horse. Six kings already
Show me the way of yielding.

ENOBARBUS   I'll yet follow
The wounded chance of Antony, though my reason
Sits in the wind against me.   *Exeunt*

SCENE XI
Cleopatra's palace.

Enter Antony with attendants

ANTONY

Hark! The land bids me tread no more upon it;
It is ashamed to bear me. Friends, come hither.
I am so belated in the world that I
Have lost my way for ever. I have a ship
Laden with gold; take that; divide it. Fly,
And make your peace with Caesar.

ALL   Fly? Not we.

ANTONY

I have fled myself, and have instructed cowards
To run and show their shoulders. Friends, be gone.

I have myself resolved upon a course
Which has no need of you. Be gone.
My treasure's in the harbour. Take it. O,
I followed what I blush to look upon.
My very hairs do mutiny, for the white
Reprove the brown for rashness, and they them
For fear and doting. Friends, be gone; you shall
Have letters from me to some friends that will
Sweep your way for you. Pray you, look not sad,
Nor make replies of loathness; take the hint
Which my despair proclaims. Let that be left
Which leaves itself. To the seaside straightway!
I will possess you of that ship and treasure.
Leave me, I pray, a little. Pray you now,
Nay, do so; for indeed I have lost command.
Therefore I pray you. I'll see you by and by.

> *Exeunt attendants. Antony*
> *sits down*

Enter Cleopatra, led by Charmian, Iras, and Eros

EROS
   Nay, gentle madam, to him, comfort him.
IRAS   Do, most dear queen.
CHARMIAN   Do; why, what else?
CLEOPATRA   Let me sit down. O, Juno!
ANTONY   No, no, no, no, no.
EROS   See you here, sir?
ANTONY   O, fie, fie, fie!
CHARMIAN   Madam!
IRAS   Madam, O, good empress!
EROS   Sir, sir!
ANTONY
   Yes, my lord, yes. He at Philippi kept
   His sword even like a dancer, while I struck
   The lean and wrinkled Cassius; it was I
   That the mad Brutus ended. He alone

Leaned on lieutenantry, and no practice had
In the brave squares of war. Yet now—no matter.

CLEOPATRA   Ah, stand by.

EROS   The Queen, my lord, the Queen.

IRAS
Go to him, madam, speak to him;
He's unqualitied with very shame.

CLEOPATRA   Well then, sustain me. O!

EROS
Most noble sir, arise. The Queen approaches.
Her head's declined, and death will seize her but
Your comfort makes the rescue.

ANTONY
I have offended reputatiòn,
A most unnoble swerving.

EROS   Sir, the Queen.

ANTONY
O, whither have you led me, Egypt? See
How I convey my shame out of your eyes
By looking back what I have left behind
Destroyed in dishonour.

CLEOPATRA   O my lord, my lord,
Forgive my fearful sails! I little thought
You would have followed.

ANTONY   Egypt, you knew too well
My heart was to your rudder tied by the strings,
And you should tow me after. Over my spirit
Your full supremacy you knew, and that
Your beck might from the bidding of the gods
Command me.

CLEOPATRA   O, my pardon!

ANTONY   Now I must
To the young man send humble entreaties, dodge
And palter in the shifts of lowness, who
With half the bulk of the world played as I pleased,
Making and marring fortunes. You did know
How much you were my conqueror, and that

My sword, made weak by my affection, would
Obey it on all cause.
CLEOPATRA   Pardon, pardon!
ANTONY
Let fall no tear, I say; one of them rates
All that is won and lost. Give me a kiss.
Even this repays me.—We sent our schoolmaster;
Is he come back?—Love, I am full of lead.
Some wine, within there, and our viands! Fortune
      knows
We scorn her most when most she offers blows.

Exeunt

SCENE XII
Egypt, Caesar's camp.

*Enter Caesar, Agrippa, Dolabella, and Thidias,
with others.*

CAESAR
Let him appear that's come from Antony.
Know you him?
DOLABELLA   Caesar, 'tis his schoolmaster:
An argument that he is plucked, when hither
He sends so poor a pinion of his wing,
Who had superfluous kings for messengers
Not many moons gone by.

Enter Schoolmaster

CAESAR   Approach and speak.
SCHOOLMASTER
Such as I am, I come from Antony.
I was of late as petty to his ends
As is the morn-dew on the myrtle leaf
To its grand sea.

CAESAR   Be it so. Declare your office.

SCHOOLMASTER

    Lord of his fortunes he salutes you, and

    Requests to live in Egypt; which not granted,

    He lessens his request, and to you sues

    To let him breathe between the heavens and earth,

    A private man in Athens. This for him.

    Next, Cleopatra does confess your greatness,

    Submits her to your might, and of you craves

    The circle of the Ptolemies for her heirs,

    Now hazarded to your grace.

CAESAR   For Antony,

    I have no ears to his request. The Queen

    Of audience nor desire shall fail, if she

    From Egypt drives her all-disgracèd friend

    Or takes his life there. This if she performs,

    She shall not sue unheard. So to them both.

SCHOOLMASTER

    Fortune pursue you!

CAESAR   Bring him through the lines.

                                        Exit Schoolmaster

    (*To Thidias*) To try your eloquence now 'tis time.

        Dispatch.

    From Antony win Cleopatra. Promise,

    And in our name, what she requests; add more,

    From your invention, offers. Women are not

    In their best fortunes strong, but want will perjure

    The never-touched vestal. Try your cunning, Thidias.

    Make your own edict for your pains, which we

    Will answer as a law.

THIDIAS   Caesar, I go.

CAESAR

    Observe how Antony becomes his fall,

    And what you think his very action speaks

    In every power that moves.

THIDIAS   Caesar, I shall.

                                              Exeunt

SCENE XIII
Cleopatra's palace.

Enter Cleopatra, Enobarbus, Charmian, and Iras

CLEOPATRA
  What shall we do, Enobarbus?
ENOBARBUS   Think, and die.
CLEOPATRA
  Is Antony or we in fault for this?
ENOBARBUS
  Antony only, that would make his will
  Lord of his reason. What though you fled
  From that great face of war, whose several ranges
  Frightened each other? Why should he follow?
  The itch of his affection should not then
  Have nicked his captainship, at such a point—
  When half to half the world opposed, he being
  The very question. 'Twas a shame no less
  Than was his loss, to follow your flying flags
  And leave his navy gazing.
CLEOPATRA   Pray you, peace.

Enter the Ambassador, with Antony

ANTONY
  Is that his answer?
AMBASSADOR
  Ay, my lord.
ANTONY
  The Queen shall then have courtesy, if she
  Will yield us up.
AMBASSADOR   He says so.
ANTONY   Let her know it.—
  To the boy Caesar send this grizzled head,
  And he will fill your wishes to the brim
  With principalities.

CLEOPATRA   That head, my lord?
ANTONY   (to Ambassador)
  To him again! Tell him he wears the rose
  Of youth upon him; from which the world should
      note
  Something particular. His coin, ships, legions,
  May be a coward's, whose ministers would prevail
  Under the service of a child as soon
  As in the command of Caesar. I dare him therefore
  To lay his gay comparisons apart,
  And answer me declined, sword against sword,
  Ourselves alone. I'll write it. Follow me.
                          Exeunt Antony and Ambassador
ENOBARBUS   (aside)
  Yes, like enough, high-battled Caesar will
  Unstate his happiness and be staged to the show
  Against a sworder! I see men's judgements are
  A parcel of their fortunes, and things outward
  Do draw the inward quality after them
  To suffer all alike. That he should dream,
  Knowing all measures, the full Caesar will
  Answer his emptiness! Caesar, you have subdued
  His judgement too.

      Enter a Servant

SERVANT   A messenger from Caesar.
CLEOPATRA
  What, no more ceremony? See, my women,
  Against the blown rose may they stop their nose
  That kneeled unto the buds. Admit him, sir.
                                          Exit Servant
ENOBARBUS   (aside)
  My honesty and I begin to quarrel.
  The loyalty well held to fools does make
  Our faith mere folly. Yet he that can endure
  To follow with allegiance a fallen lord

Does conquer him that did his master conquer
And earns a place in the story.

Enter Thidias

CLEOPATRA   Caesar's will?
THIDIAS
  Hear it apart.
CLEOPATRA   None but friends; say boldly.
THIDIAS
  So, haply, are they friends to Antony.
ENOBARBUS
  He needs as many, sir, as Caesar has,
  Or needs as many, sir, as Caesar has,
  Or needs not us. If Caesar pleases, our master
  Whose he is we are, and that is Caesar's.
THIDIAS   So.
  Thus then you most renowned: Caesar entreats
  Not to consider in what case you stand
  Further than he is Caesar.
CLEOPATRA   Go on; right royal.
THIDIAS
  He knows that you embraced not Antony
  As you did love, but as you feared him.
CLEOPATRA   O!
THIDIAS
  The scars upon your honour therefore he
  Does pity, as constrainèd blemishes,
  Not as deserved.
CLEOPATRA   He is a god, and knows
  What is most right. My honour was not yielded,
  But conquered merely.
ENOBARBUS (aside) To be sure of that,
  I will ask Antony. Sir, sir, you are so leaky
  That we must leave you to your sinking, for
  Your dearest quit you.   *Exit*
THIDIAS   Shall I say to Caesar

What you request of him? For he partly begs
To be desired to give. It much would please him
That of his fortunes you should make a staff
To lean upon. But it would warm his spirits
To hear from me you had left Antony,
And put yourself under his shroud,
The universal landlord.

CLEOPATRA   What's your name?

THIDIAS

My name is Thidas.

CLEOPATRA   Most kind messenger,
Say to great Caesar this: in deputation
I kiss his conquering hand. Tell him I am prompt
To lay my crown at his feet, and there to kneel,
Till from his all-obeying breath I hear
The doom of Egypt.

THIDIAS   It is your noblest course.
Wisdom and fortune combating together,
If now the former dares but what it can,
No chance may shake it. Give me grace to lay
My duty on your hand.

CLEOPATRA   Your Caesar's father oft,
When he has mused of taking kingdoms in,
Bestowed his lips on that unworthy place,
As if it rained kisses.

Enter Antony and Enobarbus

ANTONY   Favours, by Jove that thunders!
What are you, fellow?

THIDIAS   One that but performs
The bidding of the fullest man, and worthiest
To have command obeyed.

ENOBARBUS *(aside)*   You will be whipped.

ANTONY

Approach there!—Ah, you kite! Now, gods and devils!
Authority melts from me. Of late, when I cried 'Ho!',

Like boys unto a top, kings would start forth
And cry 'Your will?' Have you no ears? I am
Antony yet.

     Enter servants

                  Take hence this Jack and whip him.
ENOBARBUS   *(aside)*
   'Tis better playing with a lion's whelp
   Than with an old one dying.
ANTONY   Moon and stars!
   Whip him! Were it twenty of the great tributaries
   That do acknowledge Caesar, should I find them
   So saucy with the hand of—what's her name
   Since she was Cleopatra? Whip him, fellows,
   Till like a boy you see him cringe his face
   And whine aloud for mercy. Take him hence.
THIDIAS
   Mark Antony—
ANTONY   Tug him away. Being whipped,
   Bring him again. The Jack of Caesar's shall
   Bear us an errand to him.
                Exeunt servants with Thidias
   You were half blasted ere I knew you. Ha!
   Have I my pillow left unpressed in Rome,
   Forborne the getting of a lawful race,
   And by a gem of women, to be abused
   By one that looks on slaves?
CLEOPATRA   Good my lord—
ANTONY
   You have been a waverer ever.
   But when we in our viciousness grow hard—
   O, misery of it!—the wise gods sew up our eyes,
   In our own filth drop our clear judgements, make us
   Adore our errors, laugh at us while we strut
   To our confusion.
CLEOPATRA   O, is it come to this?

ANTONY

    I found you as a morsel cold upon
    Dead Caesar's trencher. Nay, you were a fragment
    Of Gnaeus Pompey's, besides what hotter hours,
    Unregistered in vulgar fame, you have
    Lustfully picked out. For I am sure,
    Though you can guess what temperance should be,
    You know not what it is.

CLEOPATRA   Wherefore is this?

ANTONY

    To let a fellow that will take rewards
    And say 'God quit you!' be familiar with
    My playfellow, your hand, this kingly seal
    And plighter of high hearts! O that I were
    Upon the hill of Basan to outroar
    The hornèd herd! For I have savage cause,
    And to proclaim it civilly were like
    A haltered neck which does the hangman thank
    For being swift about him.

Enter a Servant with Thidias

                        Is he whipped?

SERVANT

    Soundly, my lord.

ANTONY   Cried he? And begged he pardon?

SERVANT

    He did ask favour.

ANTONY

    If your father lives, let him repent
    You were not made his daughter; and be you sorry
    To follow Caesar in his triumph, since
    You have been whipped for following him.
    Henceforth
    Let the white hand of a lady fever you;
    Shake you to look on it. Get you back to Caesar.
    Tell him your entertainment. Look you say

He makes me angry with him; for he seems
Proud and disdainful, harping on what I am,
Not what he knew I was. He makes me angry,
And this time most easy 'tis to do it,
When my good stars that were my former guides
Have empty left their orbs and shot their fires
Into the abysm of hell. If he mislikes
My speech and what is done, tell him he has
Hipparchus, my enfranchised bondman, whom
He may at pleasure whip, or hang, or torture,
As he shall like, to quit me. Urge it you.
Hence with your stripes, be gone!   *Exit Thidias*

CLEOPATRA
Have you done yet?

ANTONY   Alas, our terrene moon
Is now eclipsed, and it portends alone
The fall of Antony.

CLEOPATRA   I must stay his time.

ANTONY
To flatter Caesar, would you mingle eyes
With one that ties his points?

CLEOPATRA   Not know me yet?

ANTONY
Cold-hearted toward me?

CLEOPATRA   Ah, dear, if I am so,
From my cold heart let heaven engender hail,
And poison it in the source, and the first stone
Drop in my neck: as it determines, so
Dissolve my life! The next Caesarion smite,
Till by degrees the memory of my womb,
Together with my brave Egyptians all,
By the melting of this pelleted storm,
Lie graveless, till the flies and gnats of Nile
Have buried them for prey!

ANTONY   I am satisfied.
Caesar sits down in Alexandria, where
I will oppose his fate. Our force by land

Has nobly held; our severed navy too
Has knit again, and fleet, threatening most sea-like.
Where have you been, my heart? Do you hear, lady?
If from the field I shall return once more
To kiss these lips, I will appear in blood.
I and my sword will earn our chronicle.
There's hope in it yet.

CLEOPATRA   That's my brave lord!

ANTONY

I will be treble-sinewed, hearted, breathed,
And fight maliciously. For when my hours
Were fine and lucky, men did ransom lives
Of me for jests; but now I'll set my teeth
And send to darkness all that stop me. Come,
Let's have one other gaudy night. Call to me
All my sad captains. Fill our bowls once more.
Let's mock the midnight bell.

CLEOPATRA   It is my birthday.

I thought to have held it poor. But since my lord
Is Antony again, I will be Cleopatra.

ANTONY

We will yet do well.

CLEOPATRA

Call all his noble captains to my lord.

ANTONY

Do so, we'll speak to them; and tonight I'll force
The wine peep through their scars. Come on, my
          queen,
There's sap in it yet! The next time I do fight,
I'll make death love me, for I will contend
Even with his pestilent scythe.

Exeunt all but Enobarbus

ENOBARBUS

Now he'll outstare the lightning. To be furious
Is to be frighted out of fear, and in that mood
The dove will peck the hawk; and I see ever
A diminution in our captain's brain
Restores his heart. When valour preys on reason,

It eats the sword it fights with. I will seek
Some way to leave him.   *Exit*

Act IV

SCENE I
Before Alexandria. Caesar's camp.

Enter Caesar, Agrippa, and Maecenas, with troops, Caesar reading a letter

CAESAR
He calls me boy, and chides as he had power
To beat me out of Egypt. My messenger
Has whipped with rods; dares me to personal
   combat,
Caesar to Antony. Let the old ruffian know
I have many other ways to die; meantime
Laugh at his challenge.

MAECENAS   Caesar must think,
When one so great begins to rage, he's hunted
Even to falling. Give him no breath, but now
Make use of his distraction. Never anger
Made good guard for itself.

CAESAR   Let our best heads
Know that tomorrow the last of many battles
We mean to fight. Within our files there are,
Of those that served Mark Antony but late,
Enough to fetch him in. See it done,
And feast the army; we have store to do it,
And they have earned the waste. Poor Antony!

              Exeunt

SCENE II
Cleopatra's palace.

Enter Antony, Cleopatra, Enobarbus, Charmian,
Iras, Alexas, with others

ANTONY
He will not fight with me, Domitius?
ENOBARBUS   No.
ANTONY
Why should he not?
ENOBARBUS
He thinks, being twenty times of better fortune,
He is twenty men to one.
ANTONY   Tomorrow, soldier,
By sea and land I'll fight. Either I will live
Or bathe my dying honour in the blood
Shall make it live again. Will you fight well?
ENOBARBUS
I'll strike, and cry 'Take all.'
ANTONY   Well said; come on.
Call forth my household servants. Let's tonight
Be bounteous at our meal.

   Enter Servants
                          Give me your hand.
You have been rightly honest. So have you;
You, and you, and you. You have served me well,
And kings have been your fellows.
CLEOPATRA   *(aside to Enobarbus)* What means this?
ENOBARBUS   *(aside to Cleopatra)*
'Tis one of those odd tricks which sorrow shoots
Out of the mind.
ANTONY   And you are honest too.
I wish I could be made so many men,
And all of you clapped up together in
An Antony, that I might do you service
So good as you have done.

ALL THE SERVANTS   The gods forbid!
ANTONY
  Well, my good fellows, wait on me tonight.
  Scant not my cups, and make as much of me
  As when my empire was your fellow too
  And suffered my command.
CLEOPATRA   *(aside to Enobarbus)* What does he mean?
ENOBARBUS   *(aside to Cleopatra)*
  To make his followers weep.
ANTONY   Tend me tonight.
  May be it is the period of your duty.
  Haply you shall not see me more; or if,
  A mangled shadow. Perchance tomorrow
  You'll serve another master. I look on you
  As one that takes his leave. My honest friends,
  I turn you not away but, like a master
  Married to your good service, stay till death.
  Tend me tonight two hours, I ask no more,
  And the gods yield you for it!
ENOBARBUS   What mean you, sir,
  To give them this discomfort? Look, they weep,
  And I, an ass, am onion-eyed. For shame,
  Transform us not to women.
ANTONY   Ho, ho, ho!
  Now the witch take me if I meant it thus!
  Grace grow where those drops fall! My hearty
     friends,
  You take me in too dolorous a sense,
  For I spoke to you for your comfort, did desire you
  To burn this night with torches. Know, my hearts,
  I hope well of tomorrow, and will lead you
  Where rather I'll expect victorious life
  Than death and honour. Let's to supper, come,
  And drown consideration.   *Exeunt*

SCENE III
Before Cleopatra's palace.

Enter a party of Soldiers

FIRST SOLDIER
  Brother, good night. Tomorrow is the day.
SECOND SOLDIER
  It will determine one way. Fare you well.
  Heard you of nothing strange about the streets?
FIRST SOLDIER   Nothing. What news?
SECOND SOLDIER   Perhaps 'tis but a rumour. Good night
  to you.
FIRST SOLDIER   Well, sir, good night.
    They meet other Soldiers
SECOND SOLDIER   Soldiers, have careful watch.
THIRD SOLDIER   And you, Good night, good night.
    They place themselves in every corner of the stage
SECOND SOLDIER
  Here we. If tomorrow
  Our navy thrives, I have an absolute hope
  Our landsmen will stand up.
FIRST SOLDIER   'Tis a brave army,
  And full of purpose.
    Music of hautboys under the stage
SECOND SOLDIER   Peace! What noise?
FIRST SOLDIER   List, list!
SECOND SOLDIER
  Hark!
FIRST SOLDIER   Music in the air.
THIRD SOLDIER   Under the earth.
FOURTH SOLDIER
  It signs well, does it not?
THIRD SOLDIER   No.
FIRST SOLDIER   Peace, I say!
  What should this mean?

SECOND SOLDIER
It is the god Hercules, whom Antony loved,
Now leaves him.
FIRST SOLDIER   Walk; let's see if other watchmen
Do hear what we do.
SECOND SOLDIER   How now, masters?
ALL (*speaking together*) How now? How now? Do you
        hear this?
FIRST SOLDIER   Ay. Is it not strange?
THIRD SOLDIER   Do you hear, masters? Do you hear?
FIRST SOLDIER
Follow the noise so far as we have quarter.
Let's see how it will give off.
ALL   Content. 'Tis strange.   *Exeunt*

SCENE IV
Cleopatra's palace.

*Enter Antony and Cleopatra, with Charmian
and others*

ANTONY
Eros! My armour, Eros!
CLEOPATRA   Sleep a little.
ANTONY
No, my chuck. Eros! Come, my armour, Eros!

Enter Eros wtih armour

Come, good fellow, put your iron on.
If fortune is not ours today, it is
Because we brave her. Come.
CLEOPATRA   Nay, I'll help too.
What's this for?
ANTONY   Ah, let be, let be! You are
The armourer of my heart. False, false; this, this.

CLEOPATRA
Sooth, la, I'll help; thus it must be.
ANTONY   Well, well,
We shall thrive now. See you, my good fellow?
Go put on your defences.
EROS   Briefly, sir.
CLEOPATRA
Is not this buckled well?
ANTONY   Rarely, rarely.
He that unbuckles this, till we do please
To doff it for our repose, shall hear a storm.
You fumble, Eros, and my queen's a squire
More tight at this than you. Dispatch. O, love,
That you could see my wars today, and knew
The royal occupation; you should see
A workman in it.

    Enter an armed Soldier

                  Good morrow to you. Welcome.
You look like him that knows a warlike charge.
To business that we love we rise betimes
And go to it with delight.
SOLDIER   A thousand, sir,
Early though it is, have on their riveted trim,
And at the port expect you.
    Shout. Trumpets flourish. Enter Captains and
    soldiers
CAPTAIN
The morn is fair. Good morrow, General.
ALL THE SOLDIERS
Good morrow, General.
ANTONY   'Tis well blown, lads.
This morning, like the spirit of a youth
That means to be of note, begins betimes.
So, so. Come, give me that; this way; well said.
Fare you well, dame. Whatever becomes of me,

This is a soldier's kiss. Rebukeable
And worthy shameful check it were to stand
On more mechanic compliment. I'll leave you
Now like a man of steel. You that will fight,
Follow me close; I'll bring you to it. Adieu.
              Exeunt all but Cleopatra and Charmian

CHARMIAN
Please you retire to your chamber?

CLEOPATRA   Lead me.
He goes forth gallantly. That he and Caesar might
Determine this great war in single fight!
Then Antony—but now. Well, on.   *Exeunt*

SCENE V
Before Alexandria.

*Trumpets sound. Enter Antony and Eros, a Soldier
meeting them*

SOLDIER
The gods make this a happy day to Antony!

ANTONY
Would you and those your scars had once prevailed
To make me fight on land!

SOLDIER   Had you done so,
The kings that have revolted, and the soldier
That has this morning left you, would have still
Followed your heels.

ANTONY   Who's gone this morning?

SOLDIER   Who?
One ever near you; call for Enobarbus,
He shall not hear you, or from Caesar's camp
Say 'I am none of yours.'

ANTONY   What say you?

SOLDIER   Sir,
He is with Caesar.

EROS   Sir, his chests and treasure
    He has not with him.
ANTONY   Is he gone?
SOLDIER   Most certain.
ANTONY
    Go, Eros, send his treasure after; do it.
    Detain no jot, I charge you. Write to him—
    I will subscribe—gentle adieus and greetings.
    Say that I wish he never finds more cause
    To change a master. O, my fortunes have
    Corrupted honest men! Dispatch. Enobarbus!
                                                    Exeunt

SCENE VI
The same.

*Flourish. Enter Agrippa and Caesar, with
Enobarbus, and Dolabella*

CAESAR
    Go forth, Agrippa, and begin the fight.
    Our will is Antony be taken alive;
    Make it so known.
AGRIPPA   Caesar, I shall.   *Exit*
CAESAR
    The time of universal peace is near.
    Prove this a prosperous day, the three-nooked world
    Shall bear the olive freely.

        Enter a Messenger

MESSENGER   Antony
    Has come into the field.
CAESAR   Go charge Agrippa
    Plant those that have revolted in the van,
    That Antony may seem to spend his fury
    Upon himself.   *Exeunt all but Enobarbus*

ENOBARBUS

    Alexas did revolt and went to Jewry on
    Affairs of Antony; there did dissuade
    Great Herod to incline himself to Caesar
    And leave his master Antony. For these pains
    Caesar has hanged him. Canidius and the rest
    That fell away have entertainment, but
    No honourable trust. I have done ill,
    Of which I do accuse myself so sorely
    That I will joy no more.

      Enter a Soldier of Caesar's

SOLDIER   Enobarbus, Antony
    Has after you sent all your treasure, with
    His bounty overplus. The messenger
    Came on my guard, and at your tent is now
    Unloading of his mules.
ENOBARBUS   I give it you.
SOLDIER
    Mock not, Enobarbus.
    I tell you true. Best you safed the bringer
    Out of the host. I must attend my office
    Or would have done it myself. Your emperor
    Continues still a Jove.   *Exit*
ENOBARBUS
    I am alone the villain of the earth,
    And feel I am so most. O Antony,
    You mine of bounty, how would you have paid
    My better service, when my turpitude
    You do so crown with gold! This blows my heart.
    If swift thought breaks it not, a swifter means
    Shall outstrike thought; but thought will do it, I feel.
    I fight against you? No, I will go seek
    Some ditch wherein to die; the foulest best fits
    My latter part of life.   *Exit*

SCENE VII
The same.

Alarum. Drums and trumpets. Enter Agrippa and others

AGRIPPA
Retire! We have engaged ourselves too far.
Caesar himself has work, and our oppression
Exceeds what we expected.   *Exeunt*
Alarums. Enter Antony, and Scarus wounded

SCARUS
O my brave emperor, this is fought indeed!
Had we done so at first, we had driven them home
With clouts about their heads.

ANTONY   You bleed apace.

SCARUS
I had a wound here that was like a T,
But now 'tis made an H.
Retreat sounded far off

ANTONY   They do retire.

SCARUS
We'll beat them into bench-holes. I have yet
Room for six scotches more.

Enter Eros

EROS
They are beaten, sir, and our advantage serves
For a fair victory.

SCARUS   Let us score their backs
And snatch them up, as we take hares, behind.
'Tis sport to maul a runner.

ANTONY   I will reward you
Once for your sprightly comfort, and tenfold
For your good valour. Come you on.

SCARUS   I'll halt after
Exeunt

SCENE VIII
The same.

Alarum. Enter Antony, with Scarus and others, marching

ANTONY

We have beaten him to his camp. Run one before
And let the Queen know of our deeds. Tomorrow,
Before the sun shall see us, we'll spill the blood
That has today escaped. I thank you all,
For doughty-handed are you, and have fought
Not as you served the cause, but as it had been
Each man's like mine; you have shown all Hectors.
Enter the city, embrace your wives, your friends,
Tell them your feats, while they with joyful tears
Wash the congealment from your wounds, and kiss
The honoured gashes whole.

Enter Cleopatra

(*to Scarus*) Give me your hand.
To this great fairy I'll commend your acts,
Make her thanks bless you.—O you day of the
              world,
Chain my armed neck; leap you, attire and all,
Through proof of harness to my heart, and there
Ride on the pants triumphing.
CLEOPATRA   Lord of lords!
O infinite virtue, come you smiling from
The world's great snare uncaught?
ANTONY   My nightingale,
We have beaten them to their beds. What, girl!
              Though grey
Does something mingle with our younger brown, yet
              have we
A brain that nourishes our nerves, and can

Get goal for goal of youth. Behold this man.
Commend unto his lips your favouring hand.—
Kiss it, my warrior.—He has fought today
As if a god in hate of mankind had
Destroyed in such a shape.

CLEOPATRA   I'll give you, friend,
An armour all of gold; it was a king's.

ANTONY
He has deserved it, were it enjewellèd
Like holy Phoebus' car. Give me your hand.
Through Alexandria make a jolly march.
Bear our hacked shields like the men that own them.
Had our great palace the capacity
To camp this host, we all would sup together
And drink carouses to the next day's fate,
Which promises royal peril. Trumpeters,
With brazen din blast you the city's ear;
Make mingle with our rattling tambourines,
That heaven and earth may strike their sounds
          together,
Applauding our approach.

                              Trumpets sound. Exeunt

SCENE IX
The same.

Enter Sentinel and the watch. Enobarbus follows

SENTINEL
If we are not relieved within this hour,
We must return to the court of guard. The night
Is shiny, and they say we shall embattle
By the second hour in the morn.

FIRST WATCH   This last day was
A shrewd one to us.

ENOBARBUS   O, bear me witness, night—

SECOND WATCH
  What man is this?
FIRST WATCH   Stand close, and list him.
ENOBARBUS
  Be witness to me, O you blessèd moon,
  When men revolted shall upon recòrd
  Bear hateful memory, poor Enobarbus did
  Before your face repent!
SENTINEL   Enobarbus?
SECOND WATCH   Peace;
  Hark further.
ENOBARBUS
  O sovereign mistress of true melancholy,
  The poisonous damp of night disponge upon me,
  That life, a very rebel to my will,
  May hang no longer on me. Throw my heart
  Against the flint and hardness of my fault,
  Which, being dried with grief, will break to powder,
  And finish all foul thoughts. O Antony,
  Nobler than my revolt is infamous,
  Forgive me in your own particular,
  But let the world rank me in register
  A master-leaver and a fugitive.
  O Antony! O Antony!   *He dies*
FIRST WATCH   Let's speak to him.
SENTINEL
  Let's hear him, for the things he speaks
  May concern Caesar.
SECOND WATCH   Let's do so. But he sleeps.
SENTINEL
  Swoons rather, for so bad a prayer as his
  Was never yet for sleep.
FIRST WATCH   Go we to him.
SECOND WATCH
  Awake, sir, awake; speak to us.
FIRST WATCH   Hear you, sir?
SENTINEL
  The hand of death has reached him.

Drums afar off

Hark! The drums
Demurely wake the sleepers. Let us bear him
To the court of guard; he is of note. Our hour
Is fully out.

SECOND WATCH

Come on then; he may recover yet.

Exeunt with the body

SCENE X
The same.

Enter Antony and Scarus, with their army

ANTONY

Their preparation is today by sea;
We please them not by land.

SCARUS   For both, my lord.

ANTONY

I would they'd fight in the fire or in the air;
We'd fight there too. But this it is: our foot
Upon the hills adjoining to the city
Shall stay with us. Order for sea is given;
They have put forth from the haven—
Where their appointment we may best discover
And look on their endeavour.   *Exeunt*

SCENE XI
The same.

Enter Caesar and his army

CAESAR

But being charged, we will be still by land—
Which, as I take it, we shall, for his best force

Is forth to man his galleys. To the vales,
And hold our best advantage.   *Exeunt*

SCENE XII
The same.

Alarum afar off, as at a sea fight
Enter Antony and Scarus

ANTONY
    Yet they are not joined. Where yon pine does stand
    I shall discover all. I'll bring you word
    Straight how 'tis like to go.   *Exit*
SCARUS   Swallows have built
    In Cleopatra's sails their nests. The augurers
    Say they know not, they cannot tell, look grimly,
    And dare not speak their knowledge. Antony
    Is valiant, and dejected, and by starts
    His fretted fortunes give him hope and fear
    Of what he has and has not.

    Enter Antony

ANTONY   All is lost!
    This foul Egyptian has betrayèd me.
    My fleet has yielded to the foe, and yonder
    They cast their caps up and carouse together
    Like friends long lost. Triple-turned whore! 'Tis you
    Have sold me to this novice, and my heart
    Makes only wars on you. Bid them all fly;
    For when I am revenged upon my charm,
    I have done all. Bid them all fly, begone!
                                    Exit Scarus
    O, sun, your uprise shall I see no more.
    Fortune and Antony part here; even here
    Do we shake hands. All come to this? The hearts

That spanieled me at heels, to whom I gave
Their wishes, do discandy, melt their sweets
On blossoming Caesar; and this pine is barked
That overtopped them all. Betrayed I am.
O this false soul of Egypt! This grave charm,
Whose eye becked forth my wars, and called them
       home,
Whose bosom was my coronet, my chief end,
Like a right gipsy has at fast-and-loose
Beguiled me to the very heart of loss.
What, Eros, Eros!

    Enter Cleopatra

                Ah, you spell! Be gone!
CLEOPATRA
Why is my lord enraged against his love?
ANTONY
Vanish, or I shall give you your deserving
And blemish Caesar's triumph. Let him take you
And hoist you up to the shouting plebeians;
Follow his chariot, like the greatest spot
Of all your sex; most monster-like be shown
For poorest diminutives, for dolts, and let
Patient Octavia plough your visage up
With her preparèd nails.   *Exit Cleopatra*
              'Tis well you are gone,
If it is well to live; but better it were
You fell into my fury, for one death
Might have prevented many. Eros, ho!
The shirt of Nessus is upon me. Teach me,
Alcides, you my ancestor, your rage.
Let me lodge Lichas on the horns of the moon,
And with those hands that grasped the heaviest club
Subdue my worthiest self. The witch shall die.
To the young Roman boy she has sold me, and I fall
Under this plot; she dies for it. Eros, ho!   *Exit*

SCENE XIII
Cleopatra's palace.

Enter Cleopatra, Charmian, Iras, and Mardian

CLEOPATRA
Help me, my women! O, he's more mad
Than Telamon for his shield; the boar of Thessaly
Never so slavered.
CHARMIAN   To the monument!
There lock yourself, and send him word you are dead.
The soul and body rend not more in parting
Than greatness going off.
CLEOPATRA   To the monument!
Mardian, go tell him I have slain myself;
Say that the last I spoke was 'Antony',
And word it piteously. Hence, Mardian,
And bring me how he takes my death to the
          monument.

Exeunt

SCENE XIV
The same.

Enter Antony and Eros

ANTONY
Eros, you yet behold me?
EROS   Ay, noble lord.
ANTONY
Sometimes we see a cloud that's dragonish,
A vapour sometimes like a bear or lion,
A towered citadel, a pendent rock,
A forkèd mountain, or blue promontory
With trees upon it that nod unto the world
And mock our eyes with air. You have seen these
          signs;

They are black vesper's pageants.

EROS   Ay, my lord.

ANTONY

That which is now a horse, even with a thought
The cloud dissolves, and makes it indistinct
As water is in water.

EROS   It does, my lord.

ANTONY

My good knave Eros, now your captain is
Even such a body. Here I am Antony,
Yet cannot hold this visible shape, my boy.
I made these wars for Egypt; and the Queen—
Whose heart I thought I had, for she had mine,
Which, while it was mine, had annexed unto it
A million more, now lost—she, Eros, has
Packed cards with Caesar, and false-played my glory
Unto an enemy's triumph.
Nay, weep not, gentle Eros, there is left us
Ourselves to end ourselves.

Enter Mardian

                                          O, your vile lady!
She has robbed me of my sword.

MARDIAN   No, Antony;
My mistress loved you, and her fortunes mingled
With yours entirely.

ANTONY   Hence, saucy eunuch, peace!
She has betrayed me and shall die the death.

MARDIAN

Death of one person can be paid but once,
And that she has discharged. What you would do
Is done unto your hand. The last she spoke
Was 'Antony! Most noble Antony!'
Then in the midst a tearing groan did break
The name of Antony; it was divided
Between her heart and lips. She rendered life,
Your name so buried in her.

ANTONY   Dead, then?
MARDIAN   Dead.
ANTONY
    Unarm, Eros. The long day's task is done,
    And we must sleep. (*To Mardian*) That you depart
        hence safe
    Does pay your labour richly. Go.
                              Exit Mardian
                              Off, pluck off!
    The sevenfold shield of Ajax cannot keep
    The battery from my heart. O, cleave, my sides!
    Heart, once be stronger than your continent,
    Crack your frail case! Apace, Eros, apace!
    No more a soldier. Bruisèd pieces, go;
    You have been nobly borne.—From me awhile.
                              Exit Eros
    I will o'ertake you, Cleopatra, and
    Weep for my pardon. So it must be, for now
    All length is torture; since the torch is out,
    Lie down, and stray no farther. Now all labour
    Mars what it does; yea, very force entangles
    Itself with strength. Seal then, and all is done.
    Eros!—I come, my queen—Eros! Stay for me.
    Where souls do couch on flowers, we'll hand in hand,
    And with our sprightly look make the ghosts gaze:
    Dido and her Aeneas shall want troops,
    And all the haunt be ours.—Come, Eros, Eros!

    Enter Eros

EROS
    What would my lord?
ANTONY   Since Cleopatra died,
    I have lived in such dishonour that the gods
    Detest my baseness. I, that with my sword
    Quartered the world, and o'er green Neptune's back
    With ships made cities, condemn myself to lack

The courage of a woman; less noble mind
Than she who by her death our Caesar tells
'I am conqueror of myself.' You are sworn, Eros,
That, when the exigency comes, which now
Is come indeed, when I should see behind me
The inevitable prosecution of
Disgrace and horror, that on my command
You then would kill me. Do it; the time is come.
You strike not me; 'tis Caesar you defeat.
Put colour in your cheek.

EROS   The gods withold me!
Shall I do that which all the Parthian darts,
Though enemy, lost aim and could not?

ANTONY   Eros,
Would you be windowed in great Rome and see
Your master thus: with pleached arms, bending
          down
His corrigible neck, his face subdued
To penetrative shame, while the wheeled seat
Of fortunate Caesar, drawn before him, branded
His baseness that ensued?

EROS   I would not see it.

ANTONY
Come then; for with a wound I must be cured.
Draw that your honest sword, which you have worn
Most useful for your country.

EROS   O, sir, pardon me.

ANTONY
When I did make you free, swore you not then
To do this when I bade you? Do it at once,
Or your precèdent services are all
But accidents unpurposed. Draw, and come.

EROS
Turn from me then that noble countenance
Wherein the worship of the whole world lies.

ANTONY
Lo you!

          He turns from him

EROS
    My sword is drawn.
ANTONY   Then let it do at once
    The thing why you have drawn it.
EROS   My dear master,
    My captain, and my emperor, let me say,
    Before I strike this bloody stroke, farewell.
ANTONY
    'Tis said, man, and farewell.
EROS
    Farewell, great chief. Shall I strike now?
ANTONY   Now, Eros.
EROS
    Why, there then! Thus I do escape the sorrow
    Of Antony's death.   *He kills himself*
ANTONY   Thrice nobler than myself,
    You teach me, O valiant Eros, what
    I should, and you could not. My queen and Eros
    Have by their brave instruction got upon me
    A nobleness in record. But I will be
    A bridegroom in my death, and run into it
    As to a lover's bed. Come then; and, Eros,
    Your master dies your scholar. To do thus
    I learned of you.
            He falls on his sword
                        How? Not dead? Not dead?
    The guard, ho! O, dispatch me!

        Enter Decretas and Guard

FIRST GUARD   What's the noise?
ANTONY
    I have done my work ill, friends. O, make an end
    Of what I have begun.
SECOND GUARD   The star is fallen.
FIRST GUARD
    And time is at its period.

ALL THE GUARDS   Alas, and woe!
ANTONY
    Let him that loves me strike me dead.
FIRST GUARD   Not I.
SECOND GUARD
    Nor I.
THIRD GUARD
    Nor anyone.   *Exeunt Guard*
DECRETAS
    Your death and fortunes bid your followers fly.
    This sword but shown to Caesar, with these tidings,
    Shall enter me with him. *Takes up Antony's sword*

        Enter Diomedes

DIOMEDES
    Where's Antony?
DECRETAS   There, Diomed, there.
DIOMEDES   Lives he?
    Will you not answer, man?   *Exit Decretas*
ANTONY
    Are you there, Diomed? Draw your sword, and give me
    Sufficing strokes for death.
DIOMEDES   Most absolute lord,
    My mistress Cleopatra sent me to you.
ANTONY
    When did she send you?
DIOMEDES   Now, my lord.
ANTONY   Where is she?
DIOMEDES
    Locked in her monument. She had a prophesying fear
    Of what has come to pass; for when she saw—
    Which never shall be found—you did suspect
    She had agreed with Caesar, and that your rage
    Would not be purged, she sent you word she was
                    dead.
    But, fearing since how it might work, has sent

Me to proclaim the truth, and I am come,
I dread, too late.
ANTONY
Too late, good Diomed. Call my guard, I pray.
DIOMEDES
What ho! The Emperor's guard! The guard, what ho!
Come, your lord calls!

Enter Guard

ANTONY
Bear me, good friends, where Cleopatra bides.
'Tis the last service that I shall command you.
FIRST GUARD
Woe, woe are we, sir, you may not live to wear
All your true followers out.
ALL THE GUARDS   Most heavy day!
ANTONY
Nay, good my fellows, do not please sharp fate
To grace it with your sorrows. Bid that welcome
Which comes to punish us, and we punish it,
Seeming to bear it lightly. Take me up.
I have led you oft; carry me now, good friends,
And have my thanks for all.
                            Exeunt, bearing Antony

SCENE XV
Alexandria. The monument.

*Enter Cleopatra and her maids, above with
Charmian and Iras*

CLEOPATRA
O, Charmian, I will never go from hence.
CHARMIAN
Be comforted, dear madam.

CLEOPATRA   No, I will not.
All strange and terrible events are welcome,
But comforts we despise. Our size of sorrow,
Proportioned to our cause, must be as great
As that which makes it.

    Enter Diomedes below

                  How now? Is he dead?

DIOMEDES
His death is upon him, but not dead.
Look out of the other side of your monument;
His guard have brought him thither.

    Enter, below, the Guard, bearing Antony

CLEOPATRA   O sun,
Burn the great sphere you move in; darkling stand
The varying shore of the world! O Antony,
Antony, Antony! Help, Charmian, help, Iras, help!
Help, friends below! Let's draw him hither.
ANTONY   Peace!
Not Caesar's valour has o'erthrown Antony,
But Antony's has triumphed on itself.
CLEOPATRA
So it should be, that none but Antony
Should conquer Antony, but woe 'tis so!
ANTONY
I am dying, Egypt, dying; only
I here importune death awhile, until
Of many thousand kisses the poor last
I lay upon your lips.
CLEOPATRA   I dare not, dear;
Dear my lord, pardon. I dare not,
Lest I am taken. Not the imperious show
Of the full-fortuned Caesar ever shall
Be brooched with me. If knife, drugs, serpents, have
Edge, sting, or operation, I am safe.

Your wife Octavia, with her modest eyes
And still conclusion, shall acquire no honour
Frowning upon me. But come, come, Antony—
Help me, my women—we must draw you up.
Assist, good friends.

ANTONY   O, quick, or I am gone.

CLEOPATRA

Here's sport indeed! How heavy weighs my lord!
Our strength is all gone into heaviness,
That makes the weight. Had I great Juno's power,
The strong-winged Mercury should fetch you up
And set you by Jove's side. Yet come a little;
Wishers were ever fools. O, come, come, come.

They heave Antony aloft to Cleopatra

And welcome, welcome! Die where you have lived;
Quicken with kissing. Had my lips that power,
Thus would I wear them out.

ALL THE GUARDS   A heavy sight!

ANTONY

I am dying, Egypt, dying.
Give me some wine, and let me speak a little.

CLEOPATRA

No, let me speak, and let me rail so high
That the false housewife Fortune breaks her wheel,
Provoked by my offence.

ANTONY   One word, sweet queen.
Of Caesar seek your honour, with your safety. O!

CLEOPATRA

They do not go together.

ANTONY   Gentle, hear me:
None about Caesar trust but Proculeius.

CLEOPATRA

My resolution and my hands I'll trust,
None about Caesar.

ANTONY

The miserable change now at my end
Lament nor sorrow at, but please your thoughts

In feeding them with those my former fortunes,
Wherein I lived: the greatest prince of the world,
The noblest; and do now not basely die,
Not cowardly put off my helmet to
My countryman; a Roman, by a Roman
Valiantly vanquished. Now my spirit is going;
I can no more.

CLEOPATRA   Noblest of men, will you die?
Have you no care of me? Shall I abide
In this dull world, which in your absence is
No better than a sty? O, see, my women,

                                        Antony dies

The crown of the earth does melt. My lord!
O, withered is the garland of the war,
The soldier's pole is fallen; young boys and girls
Are level now with men. The odds are gone,
And there is nothing left remarkable
Beneath the visiting moon.

          She faints

CHARMIAN   O, quietness, lady!
IRAS
She's dead too, our sovereign.
CHARMIAN   Lady!
IRAS   Madam!
CHARMIAN
O madam, madam, madam!
IRAS
Royal Egypt! Empress!
CHARMIAN   Peace, peace, Iras!
CLEOPATRA
No more but even a woman, and commanded
By such poor passion as the maid that milks
And does the meanest chores. It were for me
To throw my sceptre at the injurious gods,
To tell them that this world did equal theirs
Till they had stolen our jewel. All is but naught.
Patience is sottish, and impatience does
Become a dog that's mad; then is it sin

To rush into the secret house of death
Ere death dares come to us? How do you, women?
What, what, good cheer! Why, how now, Charmian?
My noble girls! Ah, women, women, look,
Our lamp is spent, it's out. Good sirs, take heart.
We'll bury him; and then, what's brave, what's
        noble,
Let's do it after the high Roman fashion,
And make death proud to take us. Come, away.
This case of that huge spirit now is cold.
Ah, women, women! Come; we have no friend
But resolution, and the briefest end.
                    Exeunt, bearing off Antony's body

Act V

SCENE I
Caesar's camp.

Enter Caesar, Agrippa, Dolabella, Maecenas,
Gallus, Proculeius, with his council of war

CAESAR

    Go to him, Dolabella, bid him yield.
    Being so frustrated, tell him, he mocks
    The pauses that he makes.

DOLABELLA   Caesar, I shall.   *Exit*

Enter Decretas, with the sword of Antony

CAESAR

    Wherefore is that? And what are you that dare
    Appear thus to us?

DECRETAS   I am called Decretas.
    Mark Antony I served, who best was worthy
    Best to be served. While he stood up and spoke,
    He was my master, and I wore my life
    To spend upon his haters. If you please
    To take me to you, as I was to him
    I'll be to Caesar; if that pleases not,
    I yield you up my life.

CAESAR   What is it you say?

DECRETAS

    I say, O Caesar, Antony is dead.

CAESAR

    The breaking of so great a thing should make
    A greater crack. The round world
    Should have shaken lions into civil streets

And citizens to their dens. The death of Antony
Is not a single doom; in the name lay
A moiety of the world.

DECRETAS   He is dead, Caesar,
Not by a public minister of justice
Nor by a hirèd knife; but that self hand
Which wrote his honour in the acts it did
Has with the courage which the heart did lend it,
Splitted the heart. This is his sword;
I robbed his wound of it. Behold it stained
With his most noble blood.

CAESAR   Look you, sad friends.
The gods rebuke me, but it is tidings
To wash the eyes of kings.

AGRIPPA   And strange it is
That nature must compel us to lament
Our most persisted deeds.

MAECENAS   His taints and honours
Waged equal with him.

AGRIPPA   A rarer spirit never
Did steer humanity. But you gods will give us
Some faults to make us men. Caesar is touched.

MAECENAS
When such a spacious mirror's set before him,
He needs must see himself.

CAESAR   O Antony,
I have followed you to this. But we do launch
Diseases in our bodies. I must perforce
Have shown to you such a declining day
Or look on yours. We could not stall together
In the whole world. But yet let me lament
With tears as sovereign as the blood of hearts
That you, my brother, my competitor
In top of all design, my mate in empire,
Friend and companion in the front of war,
The arm of my own body, and the heart
Where mine his thoughts did kindle—that our
          stars,

Unreconciliable, should divide
Our equalness to this. Hear me, good friends—

(*Enter an Egyptian*)

But I will tell you at some meeter season.
The business of this man looks out of him;
We'll hear him what he says. Whence are you?
EGYPTIAN
A poor Egyptian yet, the Queen my mistress,
Confined in all she has, her monument,
Of your intents desires instruction,
That she preparèdly may frame herself
To the way she's forced to.
CAESAR   Bid her have good heart.
She soon shall know of us, by some of ours,
How honourable and how kindly we
Determine for her. For Caesar cannot live
To be ungentle.
EGYPTIAN   So the gods preserve you!   *Exit*
CAESAR
Come hither, Proculeius. Go and say
We purpose her no shame. Give her what comforts
The quality of her passion shall require,
Lest in her greatness, by some mortal stroke,
She does defeat us. For her life in Rome
Would be eternal in our triumph. Go,
And with your speediest bring us what she says
And how you find her.
PROCULEIUS   Caesar, I shall.   *Exit*
CAESAR
Gallus, go you along.   *Exit Gallus*
                        Where's Dolabella,
To second Proculeius?
ALL CAESAR'S ATTENDANTS   Dolabella!
CAESAR
Let him alone, for I remember now

How he's employed. He shall in time be ready.
Go with me to my tent, where you shall see
How hardly I was drawn into this war,
How calm and gentle I proceeded ever
In all my writings. Go with me, and see
What I can show in this.   *Exeunt*

SCENE II
The monument.

Enter Cleopatra, Charmian, Iras, and Mardian

CLEOPATRA
My desolation does begin to make
A better life. 'Tis paltry to be Caesar:
Not being Fortune, he's but Fortune's knave,
A minister of her will. And it is great
To do that thing that ends all other deeds,
Which shackles accidents and bolts up change;
Which sleeps, and never palates more the dung,
The beggar's nurse and Caesar's.

Enter, to the gates of the monument,
Proculeius, Gallus, and soldiers

PROCULEIUS
Caesar sends greeting to the Queen of Egypt,
And bids you study on what fair demands
You mean to have him grant you.
CLEOPATRA   What's your name?
PROCULEIUS
My name is Proculeius.
CLEOPATRA   Antony
Did tell me of you, bade me trust you, but
I do not greatly care to be deceived,
That have no use for trusting. If your master

Would have a queen his beggar, you must tell him
That majesty, to keep decorum, must
No less beg than a kingdom. If he pleases
To give me conquered Egypt for my son,
He gives me so much of my own as I
Will kneel to him with thanks.

PROCULEIUS   Be of good cheer;
You are fallen into a princely hand; fear nothing.
Make your full reference freely to my lord,
Who is so full of grace that it flows over
On all that need. Let me report to him
Your sweet dependency, and you shall find
A conqueror that will pray in aid for kindness,
Where he for grace is kneeled to.

CLEOPATRA   Pray you, tell him
I am his fortune's vassal, and I send him
The greatness he has got. I hourly learn
A doctrine of obedience, and would gladly
Look him in the face.

PROCULEIUS   This I'll report, dear lady.
Have comfort, for I know your plight is pitied
Of him that caused it.

The soldiers approach Cleopatra from behind

GALLUS
You see how easily she may be surprised.

They seize Cleopatra

Guard her till Caesar comes.   *Exit Gallus*

IRAS
Royal Queen!

CHARMIAN
O Cleopatra! You are taken, queen.

CLEOPATRA
Quick, quick, good hands!

She draws a dagger

PROCULEIUS   Hold, worthy lady, hold!

He disarms her

Do not yourself such wrong, who are in this
Relieved, but not betrayed.

CLEOPATRA   What, of death too,
That rids our dogs of languish?
PROCULEIUS   Cleopatra,
Do not abuse my master's bounty by
The undoing of yourself. Let the world see
His nobleness well acted, which your death
Will never let come forth.
CLEOPATRA   Where are you, death?
Come hither, come! Come, come, and take a queen
Worth many babes and beggars!
PROCULEIUS   O, temperance, lady!
CLEOPATRA
Sir, I will eat no meat, I'll not drink, sir—
If idle talk will once be necessary—
I'll not sleep either. This mortal house I'll ruin,
Do Caesar what he can. Know, sir, that I
Will not wait pinioned at your master's Court,
Nor once be chastised with the sober eye
Of dull Octavia. Shall they hoist me up
And show me to the shouting varletry
Of censuring Rome? Rather a ditch in Egypt
Be gentle grave unto me! Rather on Nile's mud
Lay me stark naked and let the waterflies
Blow me into abhorring! Rather make
My country's high pyramids my gibbet
And hang me up in chains!
PROCULEIUS   You do extend
These thoughts of horror further than you shall
Find cause in Caesar.

          Enter Dolabella

DOLABELLA   Proculeius,
What you have done your master Caesar knows,
And he has sent for you. For the Queen,
I'll take her to my guard.
PROCULEIUS   So, Dolabella,

It shall content me best. Be gentle to her.
(*To Cleopatra*) To Caesar I will speak what you shall
          please,
If you'll employ me to him.
CLEOPATRA   Say I would die.
                              Exeunt Proculeius and soldiers
DOLABELLA
Most noble empress, you have heard of me?
CLEOPATRA
I cannot tell.
DOLABELLA   Assuredly you know me.
CLEOPATRA
No matter, sir, what I have heard or known.
You laugh when boys or women tell their dreams;
Is it not your trick?
DOLABELLA   I understand not, madam.
CLEOPATRA
I dreamt there was an emperor Antony.
O, such another sleep, that I might see
But such another man!
DOLABELLA   If it might please you—
CLEOPATRA
His face was as the heavens, and therein stuck
A sun and moon, which kept their course and lighted
The little O of the earth.
DOLABELLA   Most sovereign creature—
CLEOPATRA
His legs bestrode the ocean; his reared arm
Crested the world; his voice was propertied
As all the tunèd spheres, and that to friends;
But when he meant to quail and shake the orb,
He was as rattling thunder. For his bounty,
There was no winter in it; an Antony it was
That grew the more by reaping. His delights
Were dolphin-like; they showed his back above
The element they lived in. In his livery
Walked crowns and crownets; realms and islands
          were

As plates dropped from his pocket.
DOLABELLA   Cleopatra—
CLEOPATRA
Think you there was or might be such a man
As this I dreamt of?
DOLABELLA   Gentle madam, no.
CLEOPATRA
You lie, up to the hearing of the gods.
But if there is or ever was one such,
It's past the size of dreaming. Nature wants stuff
To vie strange forms with fancy, yet to imagine
An Antony were nature's piece against fancy,
Condemning shadows quite.
DOLABELLA   Hear me, good madam.
Your loss is as yourself, great; and you bear it
As answering to the weight. Would I might never
O'ertake pursued ill-fortune but I feel,
By the rebound of yours, a grief that smites
My very heart at root.
CLEOPATRA   I thank you, sir.
Know you what Caesar means to do with me?
DOLABELLA
I am loth to tell you what I would you knew.
CLEOPATRA
Nay, pray you, sir.
DOLABELLA   Though he is honourable—
CLEOPATRA
He'll lead me, then, in triumph?
DOLABELLA
Madam, he will. I know it.

*Flourish. Enter Proculeius, Caesar, Gallus,
Maecenas, and others*

ALL
Make way there! Caesar!
CAESAR
Which is the Queen of Egypt?

DOLABELLA
  It is the Emperor, madam.
        Cleopatra kneels
CAESAR
  Arise! You shall not kneel.
  I pray you rise; rise, Egypt.
CLEOPATRA   Sir, the gods
  Will have it thus. My master and my lord
  I must obey.
CAESAR   Take to you no hard thoughts.
  The record of what injuries you did us,
  Though written in our flesh, we shall remember
  As things but done by chance.
CLEOPATRA   Sole sir of the world,
  I cannot project my own cause so well
  To make it clear, but do confess I have
  Been laden with like frailties which before
  Have often shamed our sex.
CAESAR   Cleopatra, know,
  We will extenuate rather than enforce.
  If you apply yourself to our intents,
  Which towards you are most gentle, you shall find
  A benefit in this change. But if you seek
  To lay on me a cruelty by taking
  Antony's course, you shall bereave yourself
  Of my good purposes, and put your children
  To that destruction which I'll guard them from
  If thereon you rely. I'll take my leave.
CLEOPATRA
  And may, through all the world; 'tis yours, and we,
  Your scutcheons and your signs of conquest, shall
  Hang in what place you please. Here, my good lord.
CAESAR
  You shall advise me in all for Cleopatra.
CLEOPATRA
  This is the brief of money, plate, and jewels
  I am possessed of. 'Tis exactly valued,
  Not petty things admitted. Where's Seleucus?

Enter Seleucus

SELEUCUS
Here, madam.

CLEOPATRA
This is my treasurer. Let him speak, my lord,
Upon his peril, that I have reserved
To myself nothing. Speak the truth, Seleucus.

SELEUCUS
Madam,
I had rather seal my lips than to my peril
Speak that which is not.

CLEOPATRA   What have I kept back?

SELEUCUS
Enough to purchase what you have made known.

CAESAR
Nay, blush not, Cleopatra. I approve
Your wisdom in the deed.

CLEOPATRA   See, Caesar; O behold,
How pomp is followed! Mine will now be yours,
And should we shift estates, yours will be mine.
The ingratitude of this Seleucus does
Even make me wild. O slave, of no more trust
Than love that's hired! What, go you back? You shall
Go back, I warrant you; but I'll catch your eyes,
Though they had wings. Slave, soulless villain, dog!
O rarely base!

CAESAR   Good queen, let us entreat you.

CLEOPATRA
O Caesar, what a wounding shame is this,
That you now deigning here to visit me,
Doing the honour of your lordliness
To one so meek, that my own servant should
Parcel the sum of my disgraces by
Addition of his envy. Say, good Caesar,
That I some lady trifles have reserved,
Trivial toys, things of such dignity
As we greet everyday friends with; and say

Some nobler token I have kept apart
For Livia and Octavia, to induce
Their mediation—must I be unfolded
By one that I have bred? The gods! It smites me
Beneath the fall I have. (*To Seleucus*) Pray you go
      hence,
Or I shall show the cinders of my spirits
Through the ashes of my chance. Were you a man,
You would have mercy on me.
CAESAR   Forbear, Seleucus.
                               Exit Seleucus

CLEOPATRA
Be it known that we, the greatest, are misthought
For things that others do; and when we fall,
We answer others' merits in our name,
Are therefore to be pitied.
CAESAR   Cleopatra,
Not what you have reserved nor what acknowledged
Put we in the roll of conquest. Still be it yours;
Bestow it at your pleasure, and believe
Caesar's no merchant, to make prize with you
Of things that merchants sold. Therefore be cheered.
Make not your thoughts your prisons. No, dear
      queen,
For we intend so to dispose you as
Yourself shall give us counsel. Feed and sleep.
Our care and pity is so much upon you
That we remain your friend; and so adieu.
CLEOPATRA
My master, and my lord!
CAESAR   Not so. Adieu.

   Flourish. Exeunt Caesar with attendants

CLEOPATRA
He words me, girls, he words me, that I should not
Be noble to myself. But hark you, Charmian.
   She whispers to Charmian

IRAS
  Finish, good lady; the bright day is done,
  And we are for the dark.
CLEOPATRA   Hie you again.
  I have spoken already, and it is provided;
  Go put it to the haste.
CHARMIAN   Madam, I will.

  Enter Dolabella

DOLABELLA
  Where's the Queen?
CHARMIAN   Behold, sir.   *Exit*
CLEOPATRA   Dolabella!
DOLABELLA
  Madam, as thereto sworn, by your command,
  Which my love makes religion to obey,
  I tell you this: Caesar through Syria
  Intends his journey, and within three days
  You with your children will he send before.
  Make your best use of this. I have performed
  Your pleasure and my promise.
CLEOPATRA   Dolabella,
  I shall remain your debtor.
DOLABELLA   I, your servant.
  Adieu, good queen; I must attend on Caesar.
CLEOPATRA
  Farewell, and thanks.   *Exit Dolabella*
                        Now, Iras, what think you?
  You, an Egyptian puppet, shall be shown
  In Rome as well as I. Mechanic slaves
  With greasy aprons, rules, and hammers shall
  Uplift us to the view. In their thick breaths,
  Rank of gross diet, shall we be enclouded,
  And forced to drink their vapour.
IRAS   The gods forbid!
CLEOPATRA
  Nay, 'tis most certain, Iras. Saucy lictors

Will catch at us like strumpets, and rhymers scurvy
Ballad us out of tune. The quick comedians
Extemporally will stage us, and present
Our Alexandrian revels. Antony
Shall be brought drunken forth, and I shall see
Some squeaking Cleopatra boy my greatness
In the posture of a whore.
IRAS   O, the good gods!
CLEOPATRA
Nay that's certain.
IRAS
I'll never see it! For I am sure my nails
Are stronger than my eyes.
CLEOPATRA   Why, that's the way
To fool their preparation, and to conquer
Their most absurd intents.

          Enter Charmian

                              Now, Charmian!
Show me, my women, like a queen. Go fetch
My best attires. I am again for Cydnus,
To meet Mark Antony. Fellow Iras, go.
Now, noble Charmian, we'll dispatch indeed,
And when you have done this chore, I'll give you
          leave
To play till doomsday.—Bring our crown and all.
                                        Exit Iras
          A noise within
Wherefore is this noise?

          Enter a Guardsman
GUARDSMAN   Here is a rural fellow
That will not be denied your highness' presence.
He brings you figs.
CLEOPATRA
Let him come in.   *Exit Guardsman*

                                    What poor an instrument
May do a noble deed! He brings me liberty.
My resolution's placed, and I have nothing
Of woman in me. Now from head to foot
I am marble-constant; now the fleeting moon
No planet is of mine.

Enter Guardsman and Clown with a basket

GUARDSMAN   This is the man.
CLEOPATRA
    Avoid, and leave him.   *Exit Guardsman*
    Have you the pretty snake of the Nile there now,
    That kills and pains not?
CLOWN   Truly I have him; but I would not be the party
    that should desire you to touch him, for his biting is
    immortal. Those that do die of it do seldom or never
    recover.
CLEOPATRA   Remember you any that have died of it?
CLOWN   Very many, men and women too. I heard of one
    of them no longer than yesterday; a very honest
    woman, but something given to lie, as a woman
    should not do but in the way of honesty; how she died
    of the biting of it, what pain she felt; truly, she makes
    a very good report of the snake. But he that will
    believe all that they say shall never be saved by half
    that they do. But this is most fallible, the snake's an
    odd snake.
CLEOPATRA   Get you hence, farewell.
CLOWN   I wish you all joy of the snake.
    He sets down the basket
CLEOPATRA   Farewell.
CLOWN   You must think this, look you, that the snake
    will do its work.
CLEOPATRA   Ay, ay, farewell.
CLOWN   Look you, the snake is not to be trusted but in
    the keeping of wise people; for indeed there is no good-
    ness in the serpent.

CLEOPATRA   Take you no care; it shall be heeded.

CLOWN   Very good. Give it nothing, I pray you, for it is
not worth the feeding.

CLEOPATRA   Will it eat me?

CLOWN   You must not think I am so simple but I know
the devil himself will not eat a woman. I know that a
woman is a dish for the gods, if the devil dresses her
not. But truly, these same devils do the gods great
harm in their women; for in every ten that they make,
the devils mar five.

CLEOPATRA   Well, get you gone, farewell.

CLOWN   Yes, sure. I wish you joy of the serpent.   *Exit*

Enter Iras with a robe, crown and sceptre

CLEOPATRA

Give me my robe; put on my crown; I have
Immortal longings in me. Now no more
The juice of Egypt's grape shall moist this lip.
Quickly, good Iras; quick—I think I hear
Antony call. I see him rouse himself
To praise my noble act. I hear him mock
The luck of Caesar, which the gods give men
To excuse their after-wrath. Husband, I come.
Now to that name my courage prove my title!
I am fire and air; my other elements
I give to baser life. So, have you done?
Come then, and take the last warmth of my lips.
Farewell, kind Charmian, Iras, long farewell.
          She kisses them. Iras falls and dies
Have I the asp now in my lips? You fall?
If you and nature can so gently part,
The stroke of death is as a lover's pinch,
Which hurts, and is desired. Do you lie still?
If thus you vanish, you may tell the world
It is not worth leave-taking.

CHARMIAN
    Dissolve, thick cloud, and rain, that I may say
    The gods themselves do weep.
CLEOPATRA   This proves me base;
    If she first meets the curlèd Antony,
    He'll make demand of her, and spend that kiss
    Which is my heaven to have. (*To an asp*) Come, you
           mortal wretch,
    With your sharp teeth this knot intrinsicate
    Of life at once untie. Poor venomous fool,
    Be angry, and dispatch. O, could you speak,
    That I might hear you call great Caesar ass
    Unpolicied!
CHARMIAN   O eastern star!
CLEOPATRA   Peace, peace!
    Do you not see my baby at my breast,
    That sucks the nurse asleep?
CHARMIAN   O, break! O, break!
CLEOPATRA
    As sweet as balm, as soft as air, as gentle—
    O, Antony! Nay, I will take you too.
      She applies another asp to her arm
    What should I stay—   *She dies*
CHARMIAN
    In this vile world? So, fare you well.
    Now boast you, death, in your possession lies
    A lass unparalleled. Downy windows, close;
    And golden Phoebus never be beheld
    Of eyes again so royal! Your crown's awry;
    I'll mend it, and then play—

      Enter the Guard, rustling in

FIRST GUARD
    Where's the Queen?
CHARMIAN   Speak softly, wake her not.
FIRST GUARD
    Caesar has sent—

CHARMIAN   Too slow a messenger.
  She applies an asp to herself
O, come apace, dispatch. I partly feel you.
FIRST GUARD
Approach, ho! All's no well; Caesar's beguiled.
SECOND GUARD
There's Dolabella sent from Caesar; call him.
FIRST GUARD
What work is here, Charmian? Is this well done?
CHARMIAN
It is well done, and fitting for a princess
Descended of so many royal kings.
Ah, soldier!   *Charmian dies*

  Enter Dolabella

DOLABELLA
How goes it here?
SECOND GUARD   All dead.
DOLABELLA   Caesar, your thoughts
Touch their effects in this. Yourself are coming
To see performed the dreaded act which you
So sought to hinder.

  Enter Caesar and his train, marching

ALL   A way there, a way for Caesar!
DOLABELLA
O, sir, you are too sure an augurer;
That you did fear is done.
CAESAR   Bravest at the last,
She levelled at our purposes and, being royal,
Took her own way. The manner of their deaths?
I do not see them bleed.
DOLABELLA   Who was last with them?
FIRST GUARD
A simple countryman, that brought her figs.
This was his basket.

CAESAR   Poisoned, then.
FIRST GUARD   O, Caesar,
   This Charmian lived but now; she stood and spoke.
   I found her trimming up the diadem
   On her dead mistress. Tremblingly she stood,
   And on the sudden dropped.
CAESAR   O, noble weakness!
   If they had swallowed poison, it would appear
   By external swelling; but she looks like sleep,
   As if she would catch another Antony
   In her strong toil of grace.
DOLABELLA   Here, on her breast,
   There is a vent of blood, and something blown;
   The like is on her arm.
FIRST GUARD
   This is an asp's trail, sure, and these fig leaves
   Have slime upon them, such as the asp does leave
   Upon the caves of Nile.
CAESAR   Most probable
   That so she died; for her physician tells me
   She has pursued conclusions infinite
   Of easy ways to die. Take up her bed,
   And bear her women from the monument.
   She shall be buried by her Antony.
   No grave upon the earth shall hold in it
   A pair so famous. High events as these
   Strike those that make them; and their story is
   No less in pity than his glory which
   Brought them to be lamented. Our army shall
   In solemn show attend this funeral,
   And then to Rome. Come, Dolabella, see
   High order in this great solemnity.   *Exeunt*

Measure for Measure

INTRODUCTION

Measure for Measure is one of the most philo-
sophic of Shakespeare's plays, replete with his
reflections—on life and death, on government
and authority. Indeed government is a leading theme
that sets the stage, as it were, for the development of the
drama, which then is concerned equally with that of the
moral responsibility of the individual—particularly in
regard to sex, in which Shakespeare had a special, an
absorbing, interest. Thus the tone of this play is deeply
ethical, indeed religious, with one statement of Christian belief bound to move one's heart:

> Why, all the souls that were were forfeit once,
> And He that might the vantage best have taken
> Found out the remedy. How would you be
> If He, which is the top of judgment, should
> But judge you as you are? O think on that. . .

There need be no doubt that William Shakespeare was a
believing Christian, an Anglican with a flavouring of the
old medieval faith; the one thing he was not was a
Puritan, though there is a good deal of the Bible in all his
works, most of all in this one.

The theme of government is announced in the first
speech of the Duke:

> Of government the properties to unfold. . .
>   the nature of our people,
> Our city's institutions, and the terms
> For common justice. . .

The Duke is retiring into the background for a while to observe how things will work under his severe Deputy, Angelo; himself has been more lax and permissive, and sex has run riot in the city. The play is remarkable as well for the realism of its depiction of low life, and for its suggestive bawdiness in keeping, in which Shakespeare was a virtuoso—to the apprehension of Victorians like Robert Bridges, who could not bear it.

However, we know that Elizabethan life was like that, and moderns will not flinch from it. (With Shakespeare, by the way, the word 'modern' meant normal.) A recent editor of the play says that 'its plot and much of its religious, moral, and political thinking belong to a Jacobean context into which we may find it difficult to project ourselves and with which we are not always wholly in sympathy.' Though this puts the point rather too strongly, we must see it in its Jacobean context. And this reservation relates to the central crux where modern sympathies may be withheld. The heroine's, (Isabella's), brother has been condemned to death by the rigorous Deputy for a sexual fault. To a modern taste this appears excessive—yet, in the next generation, the intolerable Puritans passed a law punishing adultery with death. The common sense of the country left it inoperative.

The crux is that Isabella refuses to consent to sacrifice her virginity, at the Deputy's demand, to purchase her brother's life. Here, a modern inflexion would indicate her yielding—so that, paradoxically, it is all the more necessary for us moderns to see the issue in Elizabethan terms. In all the older versions of the tale—Shakespeare got it from an earlier play by George Whetstone, who got it from an Italian novel by Cinthio—Isabella yielded. Why did Shakespeare deliberately reverse the decision she made in his source? There have been reams of ethical discussion on this matter; but the answer is quite simple—simply to make a more effective play. As in the case of Cordelia, who in the old play of *King Leir* does not die, Shakespeare's dramatic sense always opts for the extreme, his language in keeping, more urgent and moving, extravagant and increasingly more eccentric. All the more important to remove superfluous obscurities.

The result is a profoundly serious play, without ending tragically, as it might so well have done: a powerful and well-nigh perfect play, with much of Shakespeare's personal reflection on life in it.

No difficulty about the date: it was presented at Court on Innocents' Day, 26 December 1604. As usual, it gives recognisable indications of the time, even of the moment. The new king, James I—unlike the great actress, his predecessor—did not like the populace crowding round him. The upper-class dramatist puts the point sympathetically, with his usual tact:

> I love the people,
> But do not like to stage me to their eyes;
> Though it does well, I do not relish well
> Their loud applause and Aves vehement.

And again:

> The general [i.e. populace], subject to a well-
>   wished king
> Quit their own part, and in obsequious fondness
> Crowd to his presence, where their untaught love
> Must needs appear offence.

It is Shakespeare's familiarly superior tone, and in fact James had reacted against the crowds curious to see their new monarch. There follows a reflection, with the late Essex in mind:

> Nor do I think the man of safe discretion
> That does affect it.

As for the period, Mistress Overdone the bawd, sums up on her first appearance: 'what with the war, what with the sweat, what with the gallows, and what with poverty, I am custom-shrunk.' It was indeed a queasy

time: the long war was only just ending, the previous
year one of severe plague; the gallows had claimed some
notable exhibits, Lord Cobham's brother and Father Wat-
son, while Cobham, Sir Walter Ralegh and Sir Griffin
Markham only narrowly escaped, their sentences suspended. When Mistress Overdone's brothel was put
down by the 'precise' Deputy, she set up a 'hot-house',
i.e., a bath-house; while the hypocrite of a Deputy
appoints his assignation with Isabella in a retired
garden-house to which there is a key. It is all as we read of
it in Simon Forman's papers at the time, and so too the
characters,[1] Elbow the stupid constable and Pompey,
Mrs. Overdone's pimp—for all that they are caricatures,
with their malapropisms and misuse of words. It is all
very well to label them stock-figures which Shakespeare
had readily at hand, but they are true to the life of the age
and provide contrast. Even the prison scenes, with their
macabre comedy, are convincing and authentic—that is
how things were.

One of the truest things ever said about Shakespeare
was that of the great historian, Froude: 'his stories are
not put together and his characters are not conceived to
illustrate any particular law or principle.' Hence the
attempt to reduce his plays to ethical systematising are
beside the mark. 'He builds his fabrics as nature does,
on right and wrong, but he does not struggle to make
nature more systematic than she is.' He depicts with
fidelity the contradictoriness of life and the extreme
difficulty we find—if indeed we try—in achieving moral
consistency. The Deputy Angelo provides a striking example of this: overstraining his nature to achieve moral
consistency and impose an unnatural strictness on
himself and others, he is seduced by Isabella's purity
when ordinary sex-appeal would not prevail with him.

---

[1] cf my *Simon Forman: Sex and Society in Shakespeare's Age.*

Angelo is betrayed into villainy by the strain he puts
upon his own nature. This is a theme true to William
Shakespeare: we may be sure that the type, 'precise'—it
was the contemporary word for a Puritan—did not
appeal to him, and the Deputy is treated harshly in the
play. A decade earlier Shakespeare had said something of
the sort, in describing those

> Who, moving others, are themselves as stone,
> Unmovèd, cold and to temptation slow. . .

They are the lords and owners of their faces.
Angelo, however, is found out by a skilful concatenation
of circumstances. We watch the dramatist exploiting
the element of suspense, postponing the *dénoue-
ment*, stretching it out to a splendid final scene in which
all the complications are resolved, the threads brought
together, everybody receiving his measure.

So serious a play on such a theme gives rise not only to
fine speeches, but many reflections on life in which we
hear William Shakespeare speaking to us. On life, a view
without illusions (from which he never suffered, his vision too clear):

> If I do lose you, I do lose a thing
> That none but fools would keep; a breath you are
> Servile to all the skyey influences
> That do this habitation where you keep
> Hourly afflict.

Thus an older man; but the young man, Claudio:

> Ay, but to die, and go we know not where,
> To lie in cold obstruction and to rot;
> This sensible warm motion to become
> A kneaded clod. . .

The point is that, with William Shakespeare, both views
are true.

On society and the people we have Shakespeare's
regular line:

> O place, O form,
> How often do you with your case, your habit,

> Wrench awe from fools, and tie the wiser souls
> To your false seeming.

The theme of seeming, the contrast between what a man seems and what he is, is at the heart of this play. It is one of which an actor would naturally be conscious, but it had particular import for Shakespeare, for it recurs in several plays. For all that Ben Jonson tells us that Shakespeare's nature was candid and open, he had a way of protecting himself from the public gaze, unlike Jonson—perhaps finding the mask of an actor a defence, where Jonson, not much of an actor, became a public figure.

He was very conscious too of the scandal and calumny that attacked public figures, as we know from the Sonnets. And here we find,

> No might nor greatness in mortality
> Can censure escape; back-wounding calumny
> The whitest virtue strikes. What king so strong
> Can tie the gall up in the slanderous tongue?

Elizabeth I had had that to put up with all her life, and James I was not to be exempt—with more reason. 'There is scarce truth enough alive to make societies secure.'

> O place and greatness, millions of false eyes
> Are stuck upon you. Volumes of report
> Run with these false and most contrarious guests
> Upon your doings. . .

The reflection is no less apposite today: Presidents are no more exempt than kings and queens from the persecution of the press, the misrepresentations of the public.

Of more intimate personal touches we have a revealing one in a woman's wisdom:

> They say best men are moulded out of faults,
> And, for the most part, become much more the
>   better
> For being a little bad.

No doubt that spoke for himself—and he was always particularly sensitive to the woman's point of view. We cannot for a moment doubt the personal import of this, coming from the most musically minded of writers:

> Music oft has such a charm
> To make bad good, and good provoke to harm.

Had he not found that from personal experience?

As for poetry, one is electrified suddenly to come upon this, in the middle of a passage all prose:

Look, the unfolding star calls up the shepherd—nor can one fail to notice that it is a countryman's observation, as once again with the expert knowledge of falconry. We learn too that the odd word 'tun-dish', meaning funnel, in Lucio's bawdy description of Claudio's offence, 'filling a bottle with a tun-dish', has continued a Warwickshire dialect expression into modern times. Just as the Player's phrase in *Hamlet*, 'the mobled' queen—which has given rise to so much unnecessary discussion—has the simple explanation that it is West Midlands dialect for 'muffled'—where Shakespeare came from.

Dr. Johnson quotes the lines,

> You have nor youth, nor age:
> But as it were an after dinner's sleep,
> Dreaming on both. . .

and thought them 'exquisitely imagined'. He was much touched, as I have been myself, coming upon them suddenly, unexpectedly quoted, and—recognising the voice—found myself in tears. A modern critic has asked, 'What were Mariana's feelings after she had been deserted by Angelo? The question was posed not by A.C. Bradley, but by Tennyson.' The answer was his beautiful poem, 'Mariana in the Moated Grange', which 'shows how one great poet can respond to another in a way that beggars the best endeavours of all critics.' Of course.

The text of this splendid play, as it has come down to us, presents difficulties—transcribers and compositors alike seem to have had difficulty with Shakespeare's rapid writing and his old-fashioned hand. We need not go into these: all the more reason to remove obscurities where possible to make the meaning clear. Once more the malapropisms of lower-class speech may bother the reader; I have reduced the barbarisms and explained the less obvious in brackets. A few footnotes have been needed. As usual I have supplied accents where necessary to help reader and actor with the scansion.

CHARACTERS

VINCENTIO, Duke of Vienna
ANGELO, Deputy of the Duke
ESCALUS, an old Lord
CLAUDIO, a young Gentleman
LUCIO, a light Gentleman
Two other Gentlemen
PROVOST
FRIAR THOMAS
FRIAR PETER
ELBOW, a Constable
FROTH, a foolish Gentleman
POMPEY, servant to Mistress Overdone
ABHORSON, an Executioner
BARNARDINE, a dissolute Prisoner
A JUSTICE
VARRIUS
ISABELLA, sister to Claudio
MARIANA, betrothed to Angelo
JULIET, beloved of Claudio
FRANCISCA, a Nun
MISTRESS OVERDONE, a Bawd

Lords and Attendants
Officers
Citizens
A Prisoner
A Boy
A Messenger

Act I

SCENE I
The Duke's palace.

Enter Duke, Escalus, Lords, and Attendants

DUKE
Escalus.

ESCALUS
My lord.

DUKE
Of government the properties to unfold
Would seem in me to affect speech and discourse,
Since I am put to know that your own science
Exceeds, in that, the lists of all advice
My strength can give you. Then no more remains
But that. To your sufficiency, as your worth is able,
And let them work. The nature of our people,
Our city's institutions, and the terms
For common justice, you are as pregnant in
As art and practice have enrichèd any
That we remember. There is our commission,
From which we would not have you warp. Call hither,
I say, bid come before us Angelo. *Exit an Attendant*
What figure of us think you he will bear?
For you must know, we have with special soul
Elected him our absence to supply,
Lent him our terror, dressed him with our love,
And given his deputation all the organs
Of our own power. What think you of it?

ESCALUS
If any in Vienna is of worth

To undergo such ample grace and honour,
It is Lord Angelo.

Enter Angelo

DUKE   Look where he comes.
ANGELO
Always obedient to your grace's will,
I come to know your pleasure.
DUKE   Angelo,
There is a kind of character in your life
That to the observer does your history
Fully unfold. Yourself and your belongings
Are not your own so proper as to waste
Yourself upon your virtues, they on you.
Heaven does with us as we with torches do,
Not light them for themselves: for if our virtues
Did not go forth of us it were all alike
As if we had them not. Spirits are not finely touched
But to fine issues, and Nature never lends
The smallest scruple of her excellence
But, like a thrifty goddess, she determines
Herself the glory of a creditor,
Both thanks and use. But I do bend my speech
To one that can my part in him advèrtise.
Hold therefore, Angelo:
In our remove be you at full ourself.
Mortality and mercy in Vienna
Live in your tongue and heart. Old Escalus,
Though first in question, is your secondary.
Take your commission.
ANGELO   Now, good my lord,
Let there be some more test made of my metal
Before so noble and so great a figure
Be stamped upon it.
DUKE   No more evasiòn
We have with leavened and preparèd choice

Proceeded to you; therefore take your honours.
Our haste from hence is of so quick condition
That it prefers itself, and leaves unquestioned
Matters of needful value. We shall write to you,
As time and our concernings shall impòrtune,
How it goes with us, and do look to know
What does befall you here. So fare you well.
To the hopeful execution do I leave you
Of your commissions.

ANGELO   Yet give leave, my lord,
That we may bring you something on the way.

DUKE
My haste may not admit it;
Nor need you, on my honour, have to do
With any scruple. Your scope is as my own,
So to enforce or qualify the laws
As to your soul seems good. Give me your hand.
I'll privily away: I love the people,
But do not like to stage me to their eyes;
Though it does well, I do not relish well
Their loud applause and *Aves* vehement;
Nor do I think the man of safe discretion
That does affect it. Once more, fare you well.

ANGELO
The heavens give safety to your purposes!

ESCALUS
Lead forth and bring you back in happiness!

DUKE
I thank you. Fare you well.   *Exit*

ESCALUS
I shall desire you, sir, to give me leave
To have free speech with you, and it concerns me
To look into the bottom of my place.
A power I have, but of what strength and nature
I am not yet instructed.

ANGELO
It is so with me. Let us withdraw together,

And we may soon our satisfaction have
Touching that point.
ESCALUS   I will wait upon your honour.   *Exeunt*

SCENE II
A street.

Enter Lucio and two other Gentlemen

LUCIO   If the Duke, with the other dukes, comes not to
composition with the King of Hungary, why then all
the dukes fall upon the King.

FIRST GENTLEMAN   Heaven grant us its peace, but not
the King of Hungary's!

SECOND GENTLEMAN   Amen.

LUCIO   You conclude like the sanctimonious pirate, that
went to sea with the Ten Commandments, but
scraped one out of the table.

SECOND GENTLEMAN   'Thou shalt not steal'?

LUCIO   Ay, that he razed.

FIRST GENTLEMAN   Why, it was a commandment to
command the captain and all the rest from their functions. They put forth to steal. There's not a soldier of
us all that, in the thanksgiving before meat, does relish the petition well that prays for peace.

SECOND GENTLEMAN   I never heard any soldier dislike it.

LUCIO   I believe you, for I think you never were where
grace was said.

SECOND GENTLEMAN   No? A dozen times at least.

FIRST GENTLEMAN   What? In metre?

LUCIO   In any proportion, or in any language.

FIRST GENTLEMAN   I think, or in any religion.

LUCIO   Ay, why not? Grace is grace, despite of all contro-
versy; as, for example, you yourself are a wicked
villain, despite of all grace.

FIRST GENTLEMAN   Well, there went but a pair of shears
between us.

LUCIO   I grant: as there may between the list[1] and the velvet. You are the list.

FIRST GENTLEMAN   And you the velvet. You are good velvet. You are a three-piled piece, I warrant you. I had as soon be a list of an English kersey[2] as be piled, as you are piled, for a French velvet. Do I speak feelingly now?

LUCIO   I think you do, and indeed with most painful feeling of your speech. I will, out of your own confession, learn to begin your health, but, while I live, forget to drink after you.

FIRST GENTLEMAN   I think I have done myself wrong, have I not?

SECOND GENTLEMAN   Yes, that you have, whether you are tainted or free.

Enter Mistress Overdone

LUCIO   Behold, behold, where Madam Mitigation comes.

FIRST GENTLEMAN   I have purchased as many diseases under her roof as come to—

SECOND GENTLEMAN   To what, I pray?

LUCIO   Judge.

SECOND GENTLEMAN   To three thousand dolours a year.

FIRST GENTLEMAN   Ay, and more.

LUCIO   A French crown more.[3]

FIRST GENTLEMAN   You are always figuring diseases in me, but you are full of error. I am sound.

LUCIO   Nay, not, as one would say, healthy, but so sound as things that are hollow. Your bones are hollow. Impiety has made a feast of you.

FIRST GENTLEMAN   How now, which of your hips has the most profound sciatica?

---

[1] Edging of cloth.
[2] Coarse woollen.
[3] Baldness from venereal disease.

MISTRESS OVERDONE Well, well; there's one yonder arrested and carried to prison was worth five thousand of you all.

SECOND GENTLEMAN Who is that, I pray you?

MISTRESS OVERDONE Indeed, sir, that's Claudio, Signor Claudio.

FIRST GENTLEMAN Claudio to prison? 'Tis not so.

MISTRESS OVERDONE Nay, but I know it is so. I saw him arrested, saw him carried away and, which is more, within these three days his head to be chopped off.

LUCIO But, after all this fooling, I would not have it so. Are you sure of this?

MISTRESS OVERDONE I am too sure of it; and it is for getting Madam Julietta with child.

LUCIO Believe me, this may be. He promised to meet me two hours since, and he was ever precise in promise-keeping.

SECOND GENTLEMAN Besides, you know, it draws something near to the speech we had to such a purpose.

FIRST GENTLEMAN But most of all agreeing with the proclamation.

LUCIO Away. Let's go learn the truth of it.

Exeunt Lucio and Gentlemen

MISTRESS OVERDONE Thus, what with the war, what with the sweat, what with the gallows, and what with poverty, I am custom-shrunk.

Enter Pompey

How now? What's the news with you?

POMPEY Yonder man is carried to prison.

MISTRESS OVERDONE Well, what has he done?

POMPEY A woman.

MISTRESS OVERDONE But what is his offence?

POMPEY Groping for trouts in a peculiar river.

MISTRESS OVERDONE What? Is there a maid with child by him?

POMPEY No, but there's a woman with maid by him. You have not heard of the proclamation, have you?

MISTRESS OVERDONE What proclamation, man?

POMPEY All houses (brothels) in the suburbs of Vienna must be plucked down.

MISTRESS OVERDONE And what shall become of those in the city?

POMPEY They shall stand for seed. They had gone down too, but that a wise burgher put in for them.

MISTRESS OVERDONE But shall all our houses of resort in the suburbs be pulled down?

POMPEY To the ground, mistress.

MISTRESS OVERDONE Why, here is a change indeed in the commonwealth. What shall become of me?

POMPEY Come, fear not you; good counsellors lack no clients. Though you change your place, you need not change your trade. I'll be your tapster still. Courage, there will be pity taken on you. You that have worn your eyes almost out in the service, you will be considered.

MISTRESS OVERDONE What is to do here, Thomas Tapster? Let's withdraw.

POMPEY Here comes Signor Claudio, led by the provost to prison; and there's Madam Juliet. *Exeunt*

Enter Provost, Claudio, Juliet and Officers

CLAUDIO
Fellow, why do you show me thus to the world?
Bear me to prison, where I am committed.

PROVOST
I do it not in evil disposition,
But from Lord Angelo by special charge.

CLAUDIO
Thus can the demigod Authority
Make us pay down for our offence by weight
The words of heaven. On whom it will, it will;
On whom it will not, so: yet still it is just.

LUCIO

Why, how now, Claudio? Whence comes this
restraint?

CLAUDIO

From too much liberty, my Lucio, liberty.
As surfeit is the father of much fast,
So every scope by the immoderate use
Turns to restraint. Our natures do pursue,
Like rats that gulp down their own poison
A thirsty evil, and when we drink we die.

LUCIO   If I could speak so wisely under an arrest, I
would send for certain of my creditors. And yet, to say
the truth, I had as soon have the foppery of freedom as
the mortality of imprisonment. What's your offence,
Claudio?

CLAUDIO   What but to speak of would offend again.

LUCIO   What, is it murder?

CLAUDIO   No.

LUCIO   Lechery?

CLAUDIO   Call it so.

PROVOST   Away, sir, you must go.

CLAUDIO   One word, good friend. Lucio, a word with
you.

LUCIO

A hundred, if they'll do you any good.
Is lechery so looked after?

CLAUDIO

Thus stands it with me: upon a true contràct
I got possession of Julietta's bed.
You know the lady. She is fast my wife,
Save that we do denunciation lack
Of outward order. This we came not to,
Only for propagation of a dower
Remaining in the coffer of her friends;
From whom we thought it meet to hide our love
Till time had made them for us. But it chances
The stealth of our most mutual entertainment
With character too gross is written on Juliet.

LUCIO
  With child, perhaps?
CLAUDIO   Unhappily, even so.
  And the new deputy now for the Duke—
  Whether it is the fault and glimpse of newness,
  Or whether now the body public is
  A horse whereon the governor does ride,
  Who, newly in the seat, that it may know
  He can command, lets it straight feel the spur;
  Whether the tyranny is in his place,
  Or in his eminence that fills it up,
  I stagger in. But this new governor
  Awakes now all the enrollèd penalties
  Which have, like unscoured armour, hung by the wall
  So long that nineteen zodiacs have gone round
  And none of them been worn; and for a name
  Now puts the drowsy and neglected act
  Freshly on me. It is surely for a name.
LUCIO   I warrant it is, if your head stands so ticklish on
  your shoulders that a milkmaid, if she is in love, may
  sigh it off. Send after the Duke and appeal to him.
CLAUDIO
  I have done so, but he is not to be found.
  I pray you, Lucio, do me this kind service:
  This day my sister should the cloister enter,
  And there receive her approbatìon.
  Acquaint her with the danger of my state;
  Implore her, in my voice, that she makes friends
  To the strict deputy, bid herself assay him.
  I have great hope in that, for in her youth
  There is a pure and speechless dialect,
  Such as move men; beside, she has prosperous art
  When she will play with reason and discourse,
  And well she can persuade.
LUCIO   I pray she may, as well for the encouragement of
  the like, which else would stand under grievous im-
  position, as for the enjoying of your life; which I

would be sorry should be thus foolishly lost at a game
of tick-tack. I will to her.

CLAUDIO
I thank you, good friend Lucio.

LUCIO
Within two hours.

CLAUDIO   Come, officer, away.   *Exeunt*

SCENE III
A friary.

Enter Duke and Friar Thomas

DUKE
No, holy father, throw away that thought;
Believe not that the dribbling dart of love
Can pierce a complete bosom. Why I desire you
To give me secret harbour has a purpose
More grave and wrinkled than the aims and ends
Of burning youth.

FRIAR THOMAS   May your grace speak of it?

DUKE
My holy sir, none better knows than you
How I have ever loved the life removed,
And held in idle price to haunt assemblies
Where youth and cost a witless bravery keep.
I have delivered to Lord Angelo,
A man of stricture and firm abstinence,
My absolute power and place here in Vienna,
And he supposes me travelled to Poland,
For so I have strewed it in the common ear,
And so it is received. Now, pious sir,
You will demand of me why I do this.

FRIAR THOMAS
Gladly, my lord.

DUKE
We have strict statutes and most biting laws,

The needful bits and curbs to headstrong weeds,
Which for this fourteen years we have let slip;
Even like an overgrown lion in a cave,
That goes not out to prey. Now, as fond fathers,
Having bound up the threatening twigs of birch,
Only to stick it in their children's sight
For terror, not to use, in time the rod
Becomes more mocked than feared. So our decrees,
Dead to infliction, to themselves are dead,
And liberty plucks justice by the nose;
The baby beats the nurse, and quite athwart
Goes all decorum.

FRIAR THOMAS   It rested in your grace
To unloose this tied-up justice when you pleased,
And it in you more dreadful would have seemed
Than in Lord Angelo.

DUKE   I do fear, too dreadful.
Since 'twas my fault to give the people scope,
It would be my tyranny to strike and gall them
For what I bid them do: For we bid this be done
When evil deeds have their permissive pass
And not the punishment. Therefore, indeed, my father,
I have on Angelo imposed the office,
Who may, in the ambush of my name, strike home,
And yet my nature never in the sight
To do it slander. And to behold his sway
I will, as it were a brother of your order,
Visit both prince and people. Therefore, I pray,
Supply me with the habit, and instruct
How I may formally in person bear me
Like a true friar. More reasons for this action
At our more leisure shall I render you.
Only this one—Lord Angelo is precise,
Stands at a guard with malice, scarce confesses
That his blood flows, or that his appetite
Is more to bread than stone. Hence shall we see,
If power change purpose, what our seemers be.

Exeunt

SCENE IV
A nunnery.

Enter Isabella and Francisca, a nun

ISABELLA
And have you nuns no further privileges?
FRANCISCA
Are not these large enough?
ISABELLA
Yes, truly. I speak not as desiring more,
But rather wishing a more strict restraint
Upon the sisterhood, the votarists of Saint Clare.

Lucio within

LUCIO
Ho! Peace be in this place.
ISABELLA   Who's that who calls?
FRANCISCA
It is a man's voice. Gentle Isabella,
Turn you the key, and know his business of him.
You may, I may not; you are yet unsworn.
When you have vowed, you must not speak with men
But in the presence of the prioress;
Then, if you speak, you must not show your face,
Or, if you show your face, you must not speak.
He calls again. I pray you, answer him.
ISABELLA
Peace and prosperity! Who is it that calls?

Enter Lucio

LUCIO
Hail, virgin, if you are, as those cheek-roses
Proclaim you are no less. Can you so help me

As bring me to the sight of Isabella,
A novice of this place, and the fair sister
To her unhappy brother, Claudio?

ISABELLA

Why 'her unhappy brother'? Let me ask,
The rather for I now must make you know
I am that Isabella, and his sister.

LUCIO

Gentle and fair, your brother kindly greets you.
Not to be weary with you, he is in prison.

ISABELLA

Woe is me, for what?

LUCIO

For that which, if myself might be his judge,
He should receive his punishment in thanks.
He has got his friend with child.

ISABELLA

Sir, make me not your story.

LUCIO   It is true.
I would not, though 'tis my familiar sin
With maids to seem the lapwing and to jest,
Tongue far from heart, play with all virgins so.
I hold you as a thing enskied and sainted,
By your renouncement an immortal spirit
And to be talked with in sincerity,
As with a saint.

ISABELLA

You do blaspheme the good in mocking me.

LUCIO

Do not believe it. Fewness and truth, 'tis thus:
Your brother and his lover have embraced.
As those that feed grow full, as blossoming time
That from the seedness the bare fallow brings
To teeming harvest, even so her plenteous womb
Expresses his full tilth and husbandry.

ISABELLA

Someone with child by him? My cousin Juliet?

LUCIO
　Is she your cousin?
ISABELLA
　Adoptedly, as school-maids change their names
　By vain though apt affection.
LUCIO   She it is.
ISABELLA   O, let him marry her.
LUCIO   This is the point.
　The Duke is very strangely gone from hence,
　Gave many gentlemen, myself being one,
　To think and hope of action. But we do learn
　By those that know the very nerves of state,
　His givings-out were of an infinite distance
　From his true-meant design. Upon his place,
　And with full line of his authority,
　Governs Lord Angelo. A man whose blood
　Is very snow-broth, one who never feels
　The wanton stings and motions of the sense,
　But does devote and blunt his natural edge
　With profits of the mind, study and fast.
　He, to give fear to use and liberty,
　Which have for long run by the hideous law,
　As mice by lions, has picked out an act,
　Under whose heavy sense your brother's life
　Falls into forfeit. He arrests him on it,
　And follows close the rigour of the statute
　To make him an example. All hope is gone,
　Unless you have the grace by your fair prayer
　To soften Angelo. And that's my pith of business
　Between you and your poor brother.
ISABELLA
　Does he so seek his life?
LUCIO   Has censured him
　Already and, as I hear, the provost has
　A warrant for his execution.
ISABELLA
　Alas, what poor ability is in me
　To do him good?

LUCIO   Assay the power you have.

ISABELLA

  My power? Alas, I doubt.

LUCIO   Our doubts are traitors

  And make us lose the good we oft might win,

  By fearing to attempt. Go to Lord Angelo,

  And let him learn to know, when maidens sue,

  Men give like gods; but when they weep and kneel,

  All their petitions are as freely theirs

  As they themselves would grant them.

ISABELLA

  I'll see what I can do.

LUCIO   But speedily.

ISABELLA

  I will about it straight,

  No longer staying but to give the Mother

  Notice of my affair. I humbly thank you.

  Commend me to my brother. Soon at night

  I'll send him certain word of the result.

LUCIO

  I take my leave of you.

ISABELLA   Good sir, adieu.   *Exeunt*

Act II

SCENE I
Angelo's house.

Enter Angelo, Escalus, Justice and Attendants

ANGELO
    We must not make a scarecrow of the law,
    Setting it up to frighten the birds of prey,
    And let it keep one shape, till custom makes it
    Their perch and not their terror.

ESCALUS   Ay, but yet
    Let us be keen and rather cut a little
    Than fall, and bruise to death. Alas, this gentleman,
    Whom I would save, had a most noble father.
    Let but your honour know,
    Whom I believe to be most strait in virtue,
    That, in the working of your own affections,
    Had time cohered with place or place with wishing,
    Or that the resolute acting of your blood
    Could have attained the effect of your own purpose—
    Whether you had not sometime in your life
    Erred in this point which now you censure him,
    And pulled the law upon you.

ANGELO
    It is one thing to be tempted, Escalus,
    Another thing to fall. I not deny,
    The jury, passing on the prisoner's life,
    May in the sworn twelve have a thief or two
    Guiltier than him they try. What's open made to justice,
    That justice seizes; what know the laws
    That thieves do pass on thieves? 'Tis very clear

The jewel that we find, we stoop and take it
Because we see it; but what we do not see
We tread upon, and never think of it.
You may not so extenuate his offence
For I have had such faults; but rather tell me,
When I, that censure him, do so offend,
Let my own judgement pattern out my death
And nothing come in partial. Sir, he must die.

Enter Provost

ESCALUS
Be it as your wisdom wills.
ANGELO   Where is the provost?
PROVOST
Here, if it likes your honour.
ANGELO   See that Claudio
Is executed by tomorrow morning:
Bring his confessor, let him be prepared;
For that's the utmost of his pilgrimage.
                                                 Exit Provost
ESCALUS
Well, heaven forgive him, and forgive us all.
Some rise by sin, and some by virtue fall:
Some run from breaks of ice, and answer none,
And some condemned for one fault alone.

Enter Elbow, Froth, Pompey, Officers

ELBOW   Come, bring them away. If these are good people
in a commonweal that do nothing but use their
abuses in common houses, I know no law. Bring them
away.
ANGELO   How now, sir, what is your name? And what's
the matter?
ELBOW   If it please your honour, I am the poor Duke's
constable, and my name is Elbow. I do lean upon

justice, sir, and do bring in here before your good
honour two notorious benefactors.

ANGELO   Benefactors? Well, what benefactors are they?
Are they not malefactors?

ELBOW   If it please your honour, I know not well what
they are; but precise villains they are, that I am sure
of, and void of all profanation [preservation] in the
world that good Christians ought to have.

ESCALUS   This comes off well. Here's a wise officer.

ANGELO   Go to. What quality are they of? Elbow is your
name? Why do you not speak, Elbow?

POMPEY   He cannot, sir. He's out at elbow.

ANGELO   What are you, sir?

ELBOW   He, sir? A tapster, sir, part-time-bawd; one that
serves a bad woman, whose house, sir, was, as they
say, plucked down in the suburbs. And now she
professes a bath-house, which I think is a very ill
house too.

ESCALUS   How know you that?

ELBOW   My wife, sir, whom I detest [protest] before
heaven and your honour—

ESCALUS   How? Your wife?

ELBOW   Ay, sir, whom I thank heaven is an honest
woman—

ESCALUS   Do you detest her therefore?

ELBOW   I say, sir, I will detest myself also, as well as she,
that this house, if it is not a bawd's house, it is pity of
her life, for it is a naughty house.

ESCALUS   How do you know that, constable?

ELBOW   Sure, sir, by my wife, who, if she had been a
woman cardinally [carnally] given, might have been
accused in fornication, adultery, and all uncleanli-
ness there.

ESCALUS   By the woman's means?

ELBOW   Ay, sir, by Mistress Overdone's means; but as
she spat in his face, so she defied him.

POMPEY   Sir, if it please your honour, this is not so.

ELBOW   Prove it before these varlets here, you honourable man, prove it.

ESCALUS   Do you hear how he misuses words?

POMPEY   Sir, she came in great with child, and longing
—saving your honour's reverence—for stewed prunes.
Sir, we had but two in the house, which at that very
distant time stood, as it were, in a fruit dish, a dish of
some threepence. Your honours have seen such
dishes; they are not china dishes, but very good
dishes.

ESCALUS   Go to, go to; no matter for the dish, sir.

POMPEY   No, indeed, sir, not of a pin; you are therein in
the right: but to the point. As I say, this Mistress
Elbow being, as I say, with child, and being great-
bellied and longing, as I said, for prunes, and having
but two in the dish, as I said, Master Froth here, this
very man, having eaten the rest, as I said, and, as I say,
paying for them very honestly; for, as you know,
Master Froth, I could not give you threepence again.

FROTH   No, indeed.

POMPEY   Very well: you being then, if you remember,
cracking the stones of the aforesaid prunes—

FROTH   Ay, so I did, indeed.

POMPEY   Why, very well: I telling you then, if you remember, that such a one and such a one were past
cure of the thing you know of, unless they kept very
good diet, as I told you—

FROTH   All this is true.

POMPEY   Why, very well then—

ESCALUS   Come, you are a tedious fool. To the purpose.
What was done to Elbow's wife, that he has cause to
complain of? Come to what was done to her.

POMPEY   Sir, your honour cannot come to that yet.

ESCALUS   No, sir, and I mean it not.

POMPEY   Sir, but you shall come to it, by your honour's
leave. And I beseech you look into Master Froth here,
sir; a man of fourscore pound a year, whose father died

at Hallowmas. Was it not at Hallowmas, Master
Froth?

FROTH   Allhallows' Eve.

POMPEY   Why, very well. I hope here are truths. He, sir,
sitting, as I say, in a lower chair, sir—'twas in the
Bunch of Grapes, where indeed you have a delight to
sit, have you not?

FROTH   I have so, because it is an open room and good for
winter (summer).

POMPEY   Why, very well then, I hope here are truths.

ANGELO
This will last out a night in Russia
When nights are longest there. I'll take my leave,
And leave you to the hearing of the cause,
Hoping you'll find good cause to whip them all.

ESCALUS   I think no less. Good morrow to your lordship.
                                                                Exit Angelo
Now, sir, come on. What was done to Elbow's wife,
once more?

POMPEY   Once, sir? There was nothing done to her once.

ELBOW   I beseech you, sir, ask him what this man did to
my wife.

POMPEY   I beseech your honour, ask me.

ESCALUS   Well, sir, what did this gentleman to her?

POMPEY   I beseech you, sir, look in this gentleman's face.
Good Master Froth, look upon his honour; 'tis for a
good purpose. Does your honour mark his face?

ESCALUS   Ay, sir, very well.

POMPEY   Nay, I beseech you, mark it well.

ESCALUS   Well, I do so.

POMPEY   Does your honour see any harm in his face?

ESCALUS   Why, no.

POMPEY   I'll be supposed (deposed) upon a book, his face
is the worst thing about him. Good then; if his face is
the worst thing about him, how could Master Froth
do the constable's wife any harm? I would know that
of your honour.

ESCALUS   He's in the right. Constable, what say you to it?

ELBOW   First, if it likes you, the house is a respected house; next, this is a respected fellow, and his mistress is a respected woman.

POMPEY   By this hand, sir, his wife is a more respected person than any of us all.

ELBOW   Varlet, you lie; you lie, wicked varlet. The time is yet to come that she was ever respected (suspected) with man, woman, or child.

POMPEY   Sir, she was respected with him before he married with her.

ESCALUS   Which is the wiser here, Justice or Iniquity? Is this true?

ELBOW   O you rascal, O you varlet, O you wicked Hannibal! I respected with her before I was married to her? If ever I was respected with her, or she with me, let not your worship think me the poor Duke's officer. Prove this, you wicked Hannibal, or I'll have my action of battery on you.

ESCALUS   If he took you a box on the ear, you might have your action of slander, too.

ELBOW   Sure, I thank your good worship for it. What is it your worship's pleasure I shall do with this wicked rascal?

ESCALUS   Truly, officer, because he has some offences in him that you would discover, if you could, let him continue in his courses till you know what they are.

ELBOW   Sure, I thank your worship for it. You see you wicked varlet now, what's come upon you. You are to continue now, you varlet, you are to continue.

ESCALUS   Where were you born, friend?

FROTH   Here in Vienna, sir.

ESCALUS   Are you of fourscore pounds a year?

FROTH   Yes, if it please you, sir.

ESCALUS   So. What trade are you of, sir?

POMPEY   A tapster, a poor widow's tapster.

ESCALUS   Your mistress' name?

POMPEY   Mistress Overdone.

ESCALUS   Has she had any more than one husband?

POMPEY   Nine, sir. Overdone by the last.

ESCALUS   Nine? Come hither to me, Master Froth.
Master Froth, I would not have you acquainted with
tapsters; they will draw you, Master Froth, and you
will hang then. Get you gone, and let me hear no more
of you.

FROTH   I thank your worship. For my own part, I never
come into any room in a taphouse but I am drawn in.

ESCALUS   Well, no more of it, Master Froth. Farewell.

Exit Froth

Come you hither to me, Master Tapster. What's your
name, Master Tapster?

POMPEY   Pompey.

ESCALUS   What else?

POMPEY   Bum, sir.

ESCALUS   Truth, and your bum is the greatest thing
about you; so that, in the beastliest sense, you are
Pompey the Great. Pompey, you are partly a bawd,
Pompey, howsoever you colour it in being a tapster,
are you not? Come, tell me true. It shall be the better
for you.

POMPEY   Truly, sir, I am a poor fellow that would live.

ESCALUS   How would you live, Pompey? By being a
bawd? What do you think of the trade, Pompey? Is it a
lawful trade?

POMPEY   If the law would allow it, sir.

ESCALUS   But the law will not allow it, Pompey; and it
shall not be allowed in Vienna.

POMPEY   Does your worship mean to geld and castrate
all the youth of the city?

ESCALUS   No, Pompey.

POMPEY   Truly, sir, in my poor opinion, they will to it
then. If your worship will take order for the drabs and
the knaves, you need not to fear the bawds.

ESCALUS   There are pretty orders beginning, I can tell
   you. It is but heading and hanging.

POMPEY   If you head and hang all that offend that way
   but for ten year together, you'll be glad to give out a
   commission for more heads. If this law holds in
   Vienna ten year, I'll rent the fairest house in it after
   threepence a bay. If you live to see this come to pass,
   say Pompey told you so.

ESCALUS   Thank you, good Pompey; and, in requital of
   your prophecy, hark you: I advise you, let me not find
   you before me again upon any complaint whatsoever;
   no, not for dwelling where you do. If I do, Pompey, I
   shall beat you to your tent, and prove a harsh Caesar
   to you. In plain dealing, Pompey, I shall have you
   whipped. So, for this time, Pompey, fare you well.

POMPEY   I thank your worship for your good counsel;
   but I shall follow it as the flesh and fortune shall
   better determine.
   Whip me? No, no, let carman whip his jade.
   The valiant heart's not whipped out of his trade.

Exit

ESCALUS   Come hither to me, Master Elbow. Come
   hither, master constable. How long have you been in
   this place of constable?

ELBOW   Seven year and a half, sir.

ESCALUS   I thought, by your readiness in the office, you
   had continued in it some time. You say, seven years
   together?

ELBOW   And a half, sir.

ESCALUS   Alas, it has been great pains to you; they do
   you wrong to put you so oft upon it. Are there not men
   in your ward sufficient to serve it?

ELBOW   Faith, sir, few of any wit in such matters. As
   they are chosen, they are glad to choose me for them. I
   do it for some piece of money, and go through with all.

ESCALUS   Look you bring me in the names of some six or
   seven, the most sufficient of your parish.

ELBOW   To your worship's house, sir?
ESCALUS   To my house. Fare you well.   *Exit Elbow*
    What's o'clock, think you?
JUSTICE   Eleven, sir.
ESCALUS   I pray you home to dinner with me.
JUSTICE   I humbly thank you.
ESCALUS
    It grieves me for the death of Claudio,
    But there is no remedy.
JUSTICE
    Lord Angelo is severe.
ESCALUS   It is but needful.
    Mercy is not itself, that oft looks so;
    Pardon is still the nurse of second woe.
    But yet poor Claudio; there is no remedy.
    Come, sir.   *Exeunt*

SCENE II
The same.

Enter Provost, and a Servant

SERVANT
    He's hearing of a cause; he will come straight;
    I'll tell him of you.
PROVOST   Pray you, do.   *Exit Servant*
                      I'll know
    His pleasure; maybe he will relent. Alas,
    He has but as offended in a dream.
    All sects, all ages smack of this vice, and he
    To die for it!

Enter Angelo

ANGELO   Now, what's the matter, provost?
PROVOST
    Is it your will Claudio shall die tomorrow?

ANGELO
   Did not I tell you, yea? Had you not order?
   Why do you ask again?
PROVOST   Lest I might be too rash.
   Under your good correction, I have seen
   When, after execution, judgement has
   Repented its sentence.
ANGELO   Go to; let that be mine.
   Do you your office, or give up your place,
   And you shall well be spared.
PROVOST   I crave your honour's pardon.
   What shall be done, sir, with the groaning Juliet?
   She's very near her hour.
ANGELO   Dispose of her
   To some fitter place, and that with speed.

     Enter Servant

SERVANT
   Here is the sister of the man condemned
   Desires access to you.
ANGELO   Has he a sister?
PROVOST
   Ay, my good lord, a very virtuous maid,
   And to be shortly of a sisterhood,
   If not already.
ANGELO   Well, let her be admitted.   *Exit Servant*
   See you the fornicatress be removed;
   Let her have needful, but not lavish, means.
   There shall be order for it.

     Enter Lucio and Isabella

PROVOST   God save your honour.
ANGELO
   Stay a little while. (*To Isabella*) You are welcome.
   What's your will?

ISABELLA
  I am a woeful suitor to your honour,
  Please but your honour hear me.
ANGELO   Well, what is your suit?
ISABELLA
  There is a vice that most I do abhor,
  And most desire should meet the blow of justice,
  For which I would not plead, but that I must;
  For which I must not plead, but that I am
  At war between will and will not.
ANGELO   Well: the matter?
ISABELLA
  I have a brother is condemned to die.
  I do beseech you, let it be his fault,
  And not my brother.
PROVOST (*aside*)   Heaven give you moving graces.
ANGELO
  Condemn the fault, and not the actor of it?
  Why, every fault's condemned ere it is done.
  Mine were the very cipher of a function,
  To fine the faults whose fine stands in record,
  And let go by the actor.
ISABELLA   O just, but severe law!
  I had a brother then; heaven keep your honour.
LUCIO (*aside to Isabella*)
  Give not over so. To him again, entreat him,
  Kneel down before him, hang upon his gown;
  You are too cold. If you should need a pin,
  You could not with more tame a tongue desire it.
  To him, I say.
ISABELLA
  Must he needs die?
ANGELO   Maiden, no remedy.
ISABELLA
  Yes, I do think that you might pardon him,
  And neither heaven nor man grieve at the mercy.
ANGELO
  I will not do it.

ISABELLA   But can you if you would?

ANGELO

    Look what I will not, that I cannot do.

ISABELLA

    But might you do it, and do the world no wrong,
    If so your heart were touched with that remorse
    As mine is to him?

ANGELO

    He is sentenced; it's too late.

LUCIO (*aside to Isabella*)   You are too cold.

ISABELLA

    Too late? Why, no. I that do speak a word
    May call it back again. Well, believe this,
    No ceremony that to great ones belongs,
    Not the king's crown, nor the deputed sword,
    The marshal's truncheon, nor the judge's robe,
    Become them with one half so good a grace
    As mercy does.
    If he had been as you, and you as he,
    You would have slipped like him; but he, like you,
    Would not have been so stern.

ANGELO   Pray you, be gone.

ISABELLA

    I would to heaven I had your potency,
    And you were Isabel; should it then be thus?
    No, I would tell what 'twere to be a judge,
    And what a prisoner.

LUCIO   (*aside to Isabella*)

               Ay, touch him; there's the vein.

ANGELO

    Your brother is a forfeit of the law,
    And you but waste your words.

ISABELLA   Alas, alas;

    Why, all the souls that were were forfeit once,
    And He that might the vantage best have taken
    Found out the remedy. How would you be,
    If He, which is the top of judgement, should

But judge you as you are? O think on that,
And mercy then will breathe within your lips,
Like man new-made.

ANGELO   Be you content, fair maid,
It is the law, not I, condemns your brother;
Were he my kinsman, brother, or my son,
It should be thus with him. He must die tomorrow.

ISABELLA
Tomorrow? O, that's sudden; spare him, spare him.
He's not prepared for death. Even for our kitchens
We kill the fowl of season. Shall we serve heaven
With less respect than we do minister
To our gross selves? Good, good my lord, bethink
          you:
Who is it that has died for this offence?
There's many have committed it.

LUCIO (aside to Isabella)   Ay, well said.

ANGELO
The law has not been dead, though it has slept.
Those many had not dared to do that evil
If the first that did the edict infringe
Had answered for his deed. Now it is awake,
Takes note of what is done, and like a prophet
Looks in a glass that shows what future evils,
Either new, or by remissness, new conceived,
And so in progress to be hatched and born,
Are now to have no successive degrees,
But, ere they live, to end.

ISABELLA   Yet show some pity.

ANGELO
I show it most of all when I show justice,
For then I pity those I do not know—
Which a dismissed offence would after gall,
And do him right that, answering one foul wrong,
Lives not to act another. Be satisfied
Your brother dies tomorrow. Be content.

ISABELLA
So you must be the first that gives this sentence,

And he, that suffers. O, 'tis excellent
To have a giant's strength, but it is tyrannous
To use it like a giant.
LUCIO (*aside to Isabella*) That's well said.
ISABELLA
Could great men thunder
As Jove himself does, Jove would never be quiet,
For every paltry, petty officer
Would use his heaven for thunder,
Nothing but thunder. Merciful heaven,
You rather with your sharp and sulphurous bolt
Split the unwedgeable and gnarlèd oak
Than the soft myrtle. But man, proud man,
Dressed in a little brief authority,
Most ignorant of what he is most assured,
His glassy essence, like an angry ape
Plays such fantastic tricks before high heaven
As makes the angels weep; who, with our nature,
Would all themselves laugh mortally.
LUCIO (*aside to Isabella*)
O, to him, to him, wench; he will relent.
He's coming, I perceive it.
PROVOST (*aside*)   Pray heaven she wins him.
ISABELLA
We cannot weigh our brother with ourself.
Great men may jest with saints: 'tis wit in them,
But in the less, foul profanatìon.
LUCIO (*aside to Isabella*)
You are in the right, girl, more of that.
ISABELLA
That in the captain's but a choleric word
Which in the soldier is flat blasphemy.
LUCIO (*aside to Isabella*)
You are advised of that? More of it.
ANGELO
Why do you put these sayings upon me?
ISABELLA
Because authority, though it errs like others,

Has yet a kind of medicine in itself
That skins the vice on the top. Go to your bosom,
Knock there, and ask your heart what it does know
That's like my brother's fault. If it confesses
A natural guiltiness such as is his,
Let it not sound a thought upon your tongue
Against my brother's life.
ANGELO (*aside*)   She speaks, and 'tis
Such sense that my sense breeds with it. Fare you
        well.
ISABELLA
Gentle my lord, turn back.
ANGELO
I will bethink me. Come again tomorrow.
ISABELLA
Hark how I'll bribe you. Good my lord, turn back.
ANGELO
How? Bribe me?
ISABELLA
Ay, with such gifts that heaven shall share with you.
LUCIO (*aside to Isabella*)
You had marred all else.
ISABELLA
Not with fond shekels of the tested gold,
Or stones whose rate are either rich or poor
As fancy values them. But with true prayers
That shall be up at heaven and enter there
Ere sunrise: prayers from preservèd souls,
From fasting maids whose minds are dedicated
To nothing temporal.
ANGELO   Well, come to me tomorrow.
LUCIO (*aside to Isabella*)
Go to, 'tis well; away.
ISABELLA
Heaven keep your honour safe.
ANGELO (*aside*)   Amen.
For I am that way going to temptation,
Where prayèrs cross.

ISABELLA   At what hour tomorrow
Shall I attend your lordship?
ANGELO   At any time before noon.
ISABELLA
God save your honour.
                    Exeunt Isabella, Lucio, and Provost
ANGELO   From you: even from your virtue.
What's this? What's this? Is this her fault or mine?
The tempter, or the tempted, who sins most, ha?
Not she, nor does she tempt; but it is I
That, lying by the violet in the sun,
Do as the carrion does, not as the flower,
Corrupt with virtuous season. Can it be
That modesty may more betray our sense
Than woman's lightness? Having waste ground
          enough,
Shall we desire to raze the sanctuary
And pitch our evils there? O fie, fie, fie!
What do you? Or what are you, Angelo?
Do you desire her foully for those things
That make her good? O, let her brother live:
Thieves for their robbery have authority
When judges steal themselves. What, do I love her,
That I desire to hear her speak again,
And feast upon her eyes? What is it I dream on?
O cunning enemy that, to catch a saint,
With saints do bait your hook. Most dangerous
Is that temptation that does goad us on
To sin in loving virtue. Never could the strumpet
With all her double vigour, art and nature,
Once stir my temper; but this virtuous maid
Subdues me quite. Ever till now,
When men were fools, I smiled and wondered how.
                                          Exit

SCENE III
A prison.

Enter Duke, disguised as a friar, and Provost

DUKE
Hail to you, provost—so I think you are.
PROVOST
I am the provost. What's your will, good friar?
DUKE
Bound by my charity and my blessed order,
I come to visit the afflicted spirits
Here in the prison. Do me the common right
To let me see them and to make me know
The nature of their crimes, that I may minister
To them accordingly.
PROVOST
I would do more than that, if more were needful.

Enter Juliet

Look, here comes one: a gentlewoman of mine,
Who, falling in the flaws of her own youth,
Has blistered her report. She is with child,
And he that got it, sentenced: a young man
More fit to do another such offence
Than die for this.
DUKE
When must he die?
PROVOST   As I do think, tomorrow.
    (*To Juliet*) I have provided for you; stay a while
And you shall be conducted.
DUKE
Repent you, fair one, of the sin you carry?
JULIET
I do, and bear the shame most patiently.

DUKE

    I'll teach you how you shall arraign your conscience
    And try your penitence, if it is sound,
    Or hollowly put on.

JULIET   I'll gladly learn.

DUKE

    Love you the man that wronged you?

JULIET

    Yes, as I love the woman that wronged him.

DUKE

    So then it seems your most offenceful act
    Was mutually committed?

JULIET   Mutually.

DUKE

    Then was your sin of heavier kind than his.

JULIET

    I do confess it, and repent it, father.

DUKE

    'Tis meet so, daughter, but lest you do repent
    As that the sin has brought you to this shame,
    Which sorrow is always toward ourselves, not
            heaven,
    Showing we would not spare heaven as we love it,
    But as we stand in fear—

JULIET

    I do repent me as it is an evil,
    And take the shame with joy.

DUKE   There rest.

    Your partner, as I hear, must die tomorrow,
    And I am going with instruction to him
    Grace go with you. *Benedicite.* [Bless you]   *Exit*

JULIET

    Must die tomorrow? O injurious love,
    That respites me a life whose very comfort
    Is still a dying horror.

PROVOST   'Tis pity of him.   *Exeunt*

SCENE IV
Angelo's house.

Enter Angelo

ANGELO

When I would pray and think, I think and pray
To several subjects: heaven has my empty words,
While my invention, hearing not my tongue,
Anchors on Isabel: God in my mouth,
As if I did but only chew his name,
And in my heart the strong and swelling evil
Of my conception. The state, whereon I studied,
Is like a good thing, being often read,
Grown seared and tedious; yea, my gravity,
Wherein, let no man hear me, I take pride,
Could I gladly change for an idle plume
Which the air beats in vain. O place, O form,
How often do you with your case, your habit,
Wrench awe from fools, and tie the wiser souls
To your false seeming! Blood, you are blood;
Let's write 'good Angel' on the devil's horn,
'Tis not the devil's crest—How now? Who's there?

Enter Servant

SERVANT

One Isabel, a sister, desires access to you.

ANGELO

Teach her the way.   *Exit Servant*
                    O heavens,
Why does my blood thus muster to my heart,
Making both it unable for itself,
And dispossessing all my other parts
Of necessary fitness?
So play the foolish throngs with one that swoons,

Come all to help him, and so stop the air
By which he should revive. And even so
The people, subject to a well-wished king,
Quit their own part, and in obsequious fondness
Crowd to his presence, where their untaught love
Must needs appear offence.

Enter Isabella

                                    How now, fair maid!
ISABELLA
I am come to know your pleasure.
ANGELO
That you might know it, would much better please me
Than to demand what it is. Your brother cannot live.
ISABELLA
Even so. Heaven keep your honour.
ANGELO
Yet may he live a while; and it may be
As long as you or I, yet he must die.
ISABELLA
Under your sentence?
ANGELO
Yea.
ISABELLA
When, I beseech you? That in his reprieve,
Longer or shorter, he may be so fitted
That his soul sicken not.
ANGELO
Ha! fie, these filthy vices! It were as good
To pardon him that has from nature stolen
A man already made as to remit
Their saucy sweetness that do coin God's image
In stamps that are forbidden. It is as easy
Falsely to take away a life true made
As to put metal in restrainèd means
To make a false one.

ISABELLA
'Tis set down so in heaven, but not on earth.
ANGELO
Say you so? Then I shall pose you quickly.
Which had you rather, that the most just law
Now took your brother's life, or to redeem him
Give up your body to such sweet uncleanness
As she that he has stained?
ISABELLA   Sir, believe this,
I had rather give my body than my soul.
ANGELO
I talk not of your soul. Our compelled sins
Stand more for number than account.
ISABELLA   How say you?
ANGELO
Nay, I'll not warrant that, for I can speak
Against the thing I say. Answer to this:
I, now the voice of the recorded law,
Pronounce a sentence on your brother's life;
Might there not be a charity in sin
To save this brother's life?
ISABELLA   Please you to do it,
I'll take it as a peril to my soul;
It is no sin at all, but charity.
ANGELO
Pleased you to do it, at peril of your soul,
Were equal poise of sin and charity.
ISABELLA
That I do beg his life, if it is sin,
Heaven let me bear it: you granting of my suit,
If that is sin, I'll make it my morning prayer
To have it added to the faults of mine
And nothing of your answer.
ANGELO   Nay, but hear me;
Your sense pursues not mine. Either you are ignorant,
Or seem so craftily; and that's not good.
ISABELLA
Let me be ignorant, and in nothing good

But graciously to know I am no better.

ANGELO

Thus wisdom wishes to appear most bright
When it does tax itself, as these black masks
Proclaim a shielded beauty ten times louder
Than beauty could, displayed. But mark me;
To be receivèd plain, I'll speak more gross:
Your brother is to die.

ISABELLA

So.

ANGELO

And his offence is so, as it appears,
Accountant to the law upon that pain.

ISABELLA

True.

ANGELO

Admit no other way to save his life—
As I subscribe not that, nor any other,
But in the loss of question—that you, his sister,
Finding yourself desired of such a person
Whose credit with the judge, or own great place,
Could fetch your brother from the manacles
Of the all-binding law; and that there were
No earthly means to save him, but that either
You must lay down the treasures of your body
To this supposed, or else to let him suffer—
What would you do?

ISABELLA

As much for my poor brother as myself:
That is, were I under the terms of death,
The impression of keen whips I'd wear as rubies,
And strip myself to death as to a bed
That long I have been sick for, ere I'd yield
My body up to shame.

ANGELO   Then must your brother die.

ISABELLA

And it were the cheaper way.

Better it were a brother died at once
Than that a sister, by redeeming him,
Should die for ever.

ANGELO

Were not you then as cruel as the sentence
That you have slandered so?

ISABELLA

Ignominy in ransom and free pardon
Are of two houses: lawful mercy is
Nothing kin to foul redemptiòn.

ANGELO

You seemed of late to make the law a tyrant,
And rather proved the sliding of your brother
A merriment than a vice.

ISABELLA

O pardon me, my lord; it oft falls out
To have what we would have, we speak not what we
       mean.
I something do excuse the thing I hate
For his advantage that I dearly love.

ANGELO

We are all frail.

ISABELLA   Else let my brother die,
If not a confederate, but only he,
Own and share your weakness.

ANGELO

Nay, women are frail too.

ISABELLA

Ay, as the glasses where they view themselves,
Which are as easy broken as they make forms.
Women, help heaven! Men their creation mar
In profiting by them. Nay, call us ten times frail,
For we are soft as our complexions are,
And credulous to false prints.

ANGELO   I think it well,
And from this testimony of your own sex—
Since I suppose we are made to be no stronger

Than faults may shake our frames—let me be bold.
I do arrest your words. Be that you are,
That is, a woman; if you are more, you're none.
If you are one, as you are well expressed
By all external warrants, show it now,
By putting on the destined livery.

ISABELLA
I have no tongue but one. Gentle my lord,
Let me entreat you speak the former language.

ANGELO
Plainly conceive, I love you.

ISABELLA
My brother did love Juliet,
And you tell me that he shall die for it.

ANGELO
He shall not, Isabel, if you give me love.

ISABELLA
I know your virtue has a licence in it,
Which seems a little fouler than it is,
To test on others.

ANGELO   Believe me, on my honour,
My words express my purpose.

ISABELLA
Ha! Little honour to be much believed,
And most pernicious purpose. Seeming, seeming!
I will proclaim you, Angelo, look for it!
Sign me a present pardon for my brother,
Or with an outstretched throat I'll tell the world
What man you are.

ANGELO   Who will believe you, Isabel?
My unsoiled name, the austereness of my life,
My word against you, and my place in the state,
Will so your accusation overweigh
That you shall stifle in your own report
And smell of calumny. I have begun,
And now I give my sensual race the rein.
Fit your consent to my sharp appetite,

Lay by all nicety and superfluous blushes,
That banish what they sue for. Redeem your brother
By yielding up your body to my will,
Or else he must not only die the death,
But your unkindness shall his death draw out
To lingering sufferance. Answer me tomorrow,
Or, by the affection that now guides me most,
I'll prove a tyrant to him. As for you,
Say what you can, my false o'erweighs your true.

Exit

ISABELLA

To whom should I complain? Did I tell this,
Who would believe me? O perilous mouths,
That bear in them one and the selfsame tongue,
Either of condemnation or approval,
Bidding the law make curtsy to their will,
Hooking both right and wrong to the appetite,
To follow as it draws. I'll to my brother.
Though he has fallen by prompting of the blood,
Yet has he in him such a mind of honour
That, had he twenty heads to tender down
On twenty bloody blocks, he'd yield them up,
Before his sister should her body stoop
To such abhorred pollutiòn.
Then, Isabel, live chaste and, brother, die.
More than our brother is our chastity.
I'll tell him yet of Angelo's request,
And fit his mind to death, for his soul's rest.   *Exit*

Act III

SCENE I
The prison.

Enter Duke, disguised as a friar, Claudio, and Provost

DUKE
So then you hope of pardon from Lord Angelo?

CLAUDIO
The miserable have no other medicine
But only hope:
I have hope to live, and am prepared to die.

DUKE
Be resolved for death: either death or life
Shall thereby be the sweeter. Reason thus with life:
If I do lose you, I do lose a thing
That none but fools would keep; a breath you are,
Servile to all the skyey influences
That do this habitation where you keep
Hourly afflict. Merely, you are death's fool,
For him you labour by your flight to shun,
And yet run toward him still. You are not noble,
For all the accommodations that you bear
Are nursed by baseness. You are by no means valiant,
For you do fear the soft and tender fork
Of a poor snake. Your best of rest is sleep,
And that you oft provoke, yet grossly fear
Your death, which is no more. You are not yourself,
For you exist on many a thousand grains
That issue out of dust. Happy you are not,
For what you have not, still you strive to get,
And what you have, forget. You are not certain,

For your complexion shifts to strange effects,
After the moon. If you are rich, you are poor,
For, like an ass, whose back with ingots bows,
You bear your heavy riches but a journey,
And death unloads you. Friend have you none,
For your own bowels, which do call you sire,
The mere effusion of your very loins,
Do curse the gout, skin disease, catarrh
For ending you no sooner. You have not youth or age,
But as it were an after-dinner's sleep,
Dreaming on both. For all your blessed youth
Becomes as agèd, and does beg the alms
Of palsied age: And when you are old and rich,
You have neither heat, affection, limb, nor beauty
To make your riches pleasant. What's yet in this
That bears the name of life? Yet in this life
Lie hidden more thousand deaths; yet death we fear,
That makes these odds all even.
CLAUDIO   I humbly thank you.
To sue to live, I find I seek to die,
And, seeking death, find life. Let it come on.

   Enter Isabella

ISABELLA What, ho! Peace here, grace and good
   company.
PROVOST Who's there? Come in. The wish deserves a
   welcome.
DUKE Dear sir, ere long I'll visit you again.
CLAUDIO Most holy sir, I thank you.
ISABELLA My business is a word or two with Claudio.
PROVOST And very welcome. Look, signor, here's your
   sister.
DUKE Provost, a word with you.
PROVOST As many as you please.
DUKE Bring me to hear them speak, where I may be
   concealed.
                              Exeunt Duke and Provost

CLAUDIO   Now, sister, what's the comfort?
ISABELLA
  Why,
  As all comforts are: most good, most good indeed.
  Lord Angelo, having affairs to heaven,
  Intends you for his swift ambassador,
  Where you shall be an everlasting subject.
  Therefore your best appointment make with speed;
  Tomorrow you set on.
CLAUDIO   Is there no remedy?
ISABELLA
  None, but such remedy as, to save a head,
  To cleave a heart in twain.
CLAUDIO   But is there any?
ISABELLA
  Yes, brother, you may live;
  There is a devilish mercy in the judge,
  If you'll implore it, that will free your life,
  But fetter you till death.
CLAUDIO   Perpetual durance?
ISABELLA
  Ay, just. Perpetual durance, a restraint,
  Through all the world's vastidity you had,
  To a determined scope.
CLAUDIO   But in what nature?
ISABELLA
  In such a one as, you consenting to it,
  Would bark your honour from that trunk you bear,
  And leave you naked.
CLAUDIO   Let me know the point.
ISABELLA
  O, I do fear you, Claudio, and I quake
  Lest you a feverous life should entertain,
  And six or seven winters more repect
  Than a perpetual honour. Dare you die?
  The sense of death is most in apprehension,
  And the poor beetle that we tread upon

In corporal sufferance finds a pang as great
As when a giant dies.

CLAUDIO   Why give you me this shame?
Think you I can a resolution fetch
From flowery tenderness? If I must die,
I will encounter darkness as a bride,
And hug it in my arms.

ISABELLA
There spoke my brother. There my father's grave
Did utter forth a voice. Yes, you must die.
You are too noble to conserve a life
In base appliances. This outward-sainted deputy,
Whose settled visage and deliberate word
Nip youth in the head, and follies does pursue
As falcon does the fowl, is yet a devil.
His filth within being cleared, he would appear
A pond as deep as hell.

CLAUDIO   The princely Angelo?

ISABELLA
O, 'tis the cunning livery of hell,
The damnedest body to invest and cover
In princely clothes. Do you think, Claudio,
If I would yield him my virginity,
You might be freed?

CLAUDIO   O heavens, it cannot be.

ISABELLA
Yes, he would give it you, from this rank offence,
So to offend him still. This night is the time
That I should do what I abhor to name,
Or else you die tomorrow.

CLAUDIO   You shall not do it.

ISABELLA
O, were it but my life,
I'd throw it down for your deliverance
As frankly as a pin.

CLAUDIO   Thanks, dear Isabel

ISABELLA
Be ready, Claudio, for your death tomorrow.

CLAUDIO
    Yes. Has he affections in him
    That thus can make him bite the law by the nose,
    When he would force it? Sure it is no sin,
    Or of the deadly seven it is the least.
ISABELLA
    Which is the least?
CLAUDIO
    If it were damnable, he being so wise,
    Why would he for the momentary trick
    Be perdurably fined? O Isabel!
ISABELLA
    What says my brother?
CLAUDIO   Death is a fearful thing.
ISABELLA
    And shamèd life a hateful.
CLAUDIO
    Ay, but to die, and go we know not where,
    To lie in cold obstruction and to rot;
    This sensible warm motion to become
    A kneaded clod; and the delighted spirit
    To bathe in fiery floods, or to reside
    In thrilling region of thick-ribbèd ice—
    To be imprisoned in the viewless winds
    And blown with restless violence round about
    The pendent world. Or to be worse than worst
    Of those that lawless and uncertain thoughts
    Imagine howling—it is too horrible.
    The weariest and most loathèd worldly life
    That age, ache, penury, and imprisonment
    Can lay on nature is a paradise
    To what we fear of death.
ISABELLA
    Alas, alas.
CLAUDIO   Sweet sister, let me live.
    What sin you do to save a brother's life,
    Nature dispenses with the deed so far

That it becomes a virtue.
ISABELLA   O you beast!
    O faithless coward! O dishonest wretch!
    Will you be made a man out of my vice?
    Is it not a kind of incest to take life
    From your own sister's shame? What should I think?
    Heaven shield my mother played my father fair,
    For such a warpèd slip of wildness never
    Issued from his blood. Take my defiance,
    Die, perish. Might but my bending down
    Reprieve you from your fate, it should proceed.
    I'll pray a thousand prayers for your death,
    No word to save you.
CLAUDIO
    Nay, hear me, Isabel.
ISABELLA   O, fie, fie, fie!
    Your sin's not accidental, but a trade.
    Mercy to you would prove itself a bawd,
    'Tis best that you die quickly.   *Going*
CLAUDIO   O hear me, Isabella.

    Enter Duke disguised

DUKE   Grant me a word, young sister, but one word.
ISABELLA   What is your will?
DUKE   Might you dispense with your leisure, I would by
    and by have some speech with you. The satisfaction I
    would require is likewise your own benefit.
ISABELLA   I have no superfluous leisure. My stay must
    be stolen out of other affairs, but I will attend you a
    while.
DUKE   *(aside)* Son, I have overheard what has passed
    between you and your sister. Angelo had never the
    purpose to corrupt her; only he has made an assay of
    her virtue to practise his judgement with the disposi-
    tion of natures. She, having the truth of honour in
    her, has made him that gracious denial which he is

most glad to receive. I am confessor to Angelo, and I know this to be true. Therefore prepare yourself to death. Do not satisfy your resolution with hopes that are fallible. Tomorrow you must die. Go to your knees and make ready.

CLAUDIO   Let me ask my sister pardon. I am so out of love with life that I will sue to be rid of it.

DUKE   Hold you there. Farewell.   *Exit Claudio*

Enter Provost

Provost, a word with you.

PROVOST   What is your will, father?

DUKE   That now you are come, you will be gone. Leave me a while with the maid. My mind promises with my habit no loss shall touch her by my company.

PROVOST   In good time.   *Exit*

DUKE   The hand that has made you fair has made you good. The goodness that is cheap in beauty makes beauty brief in goodness; but grace, being the soul of your complexion, shall keep the body of it ever fair. The assault that Angelo has made to you, fortune has conveyed to my understanding; and, but that frailty has examples for his falling, I should wonder at Angelo. How will you do to content this substitute, and to save your brother?

ISABELLA   I am now going to resolve him. I had rather my brother die by the law than my son should be unlawfully born. But O, how much is the good Duke deceived in Angelo! If ever he returns and I can speak to him, I will open my lips in vain, or discover his government.

DUKE   That shall not be much amiss. Yet, as the matter now stands, he will avoid your accusation; he made trial of you only. Therefore fasten your ear on my advisings. To the love I have in doing good a remedy presents itself. I do make myself believe that you may most uprighteously do a poor wronged lady a merited benefit, redeem your brother from the angry law, do no stain to your own gracious person, and much please the absent Duke—if peradventure he shall ever return to have hearing of this business.

ISABELLA   Let me hear you speak farther. I have spirit to do anything that appears not foul in the truth of my spirit.

DUKE   Virtue is bold, and goodness never fearful. Have you not heard speak of Mariana, the sister of Frederick, the great soldier who miscarried at sea?

ISABELLA   I have heard of the lady, and good words went with her name.

DUKE   She should this Angelo have married. He was affianced to her by oath, and the nuptials appointed; between which time of the contract and limit of the solemnity, her brother Frederick was wrecked at sea, having in that perished vessel the dowry of his sister. But mark how heavily this befell to the poor gentlewoman. There she lost a noble and renowned brother, in his love toward her ever most kind and natural; with him the portion and sinew of her fortune, her marriage dowry; with both, her betrothed husband, this well-seeming Angelo.

ISABELLA   Can this be so? Did Angelo so leave her?

DUKE   Left her in her tears, and dried not one of them with his comfort; swallowed his vows whole, pretending in her discoveries of dishonour. In short, bestowed her on her own lamentation, which she yet wears for his sake; and he, a marble to her tears, is washed with them, but relents not.

ISABELLA   What a merit were it in death to take this poor maid from the world! What corruption in this life, that it will let this man live! But how out of this can she avail?

DUKE   It is a rupture that you may easily heal, and the cure of it not only saves your brother, but keeps you from dishonour in doing it.

ISABELLA Show me how, good father.

DUKE This forenamed maid has yet in her the continuance of her first affection. His unjust unkindness, that in all reason should have quenched her
love, has like an impediment in the current, made it
more violent and unruly. Go you to Angelo, answer
his requiring with a plausible obedience, agree with
his demands to the point. Only refer yourself to this
advantage: first, that your stay with him may not be
long, that the time may have all shadow and silence
in it, and the place answer to convenience. This
being granted in course—and now follows all—we
shall advise this wronged maid to keep your appointment, go in your place. If the encounter acknowl-
edges itself hereafter, it may compel him to her
recompense. And here, by this is your brother saved,
your honour untainted, the poor Mariana advantaged,
and the corrupt deputy revealed. The maid will I
frame and make fit for his attempt. If you think well
to carry this, as you may, the doubleness of the benefit
defends the deceit from reproof. What think you of it?

ISABELLA The image of it gives me content already, and
I trust it will grow to a most prosperous perfection.

DUKE It lies much in your holding up. Haste you
speedily to Angelo. If for this night he entreats you to
his bed, give him promise of satisfaction. I will
presently to Saint Luke's. There, at the moated
grange, resides this dejected Mariana. At that place
call upon me, and dispatch with Angelo, that it may
be quickly.

ISABELLA I thank you for this comfort. Fare you well,
good father.   *Exit*

SCENE II
The same.

Enter Elbow, Pompey, and Officers

ELBOW Nay, if there is no remedy for it but that you
   will needs buy and sell men and women like beasts,
   we shall have all the world drink brown and white
   bastard.[1]

DUKE O heavens, what stuff is here?

POMPEY 'Twas never merry world since, of two
   usuries, the merrier was put down, and the worse
   allowed by order of law a furred gown to keep him
   warm; and furred with fox and lamb skins too, to
   signify that craft, being richer than innocency,
   stands for the trimming.

ELBOW Come your way, sir. Bless you, good father friar.

DUKE And you, good brother father. What offence has
   this man made you, sir?

ELBOW Sure, sir, he has offended the law. And, sir, we
   take him to be a thief too, sir, for we have found upon
   him, sir, a strange picklock, which we have sent to
   the deputy.

DUKE
   Fie, fellow, a bawd, a wicked bawd!
   The evil that you cause yet to be done,
   That is your means to live. Do you but think
   What it is to cram a maw or clothe a back
   From such a filthy vice. Say to yourself,
   From their abominable and beastly touches
   I drink, I eat, array myself, and live.
   Can you believe your living is a life,
   So stinkingly depending? Go mend, go mend.

---

[1]A cheap sweet wine.

POMPEY Indeed, it does stink in some sort, sir, but yet,
sir, I would prove—

DUKE
Nay, if the devil has given you proofs for sin,
You will prove his. Take him to prison, officer.
Correction and instruction must both work
Ere this rude beast will profit.

ELBOW He must before the deputy, sir. He has given
him warning. The deputy cannot abide a whore-
master. If he is a whoremonger, and comes before
him, he were as good go a mile on his errand.

DUKE
That we were all, as some would seem to be,
Free from our faults, as faults from seeming free.

Enter Lucio

ELBOW His neck will come to your waist—a cord, sir.

POMPEY I spy comfort, I cry bail. Here's a gentleman
and a friend of mine.

LUCIO How now, noble Pompey? What, at the wheels
of Caesar? Are you led in triumph? What, is there
none of Pygmalion's images, newly made woman, to
be had now, for putting the hand in the pocket and
extracting it clutched? What reply? Ha? What say
you to this tune, matter, and method? Is it not
drowned in the last rain, ha? What say you hack? Is
the world as it was, man? Which is the way? Is it sad,
and few words? Or how? The trick of it?

DUKE Still thus, and thus, still worse?

LUCIO How does my dear morsel, your mistress?
Procures she still, ha?

POMPEY Truth, sir, she has eaten up all her beef, and
she is herself in the tub.

LUCIO Why, 'tis good. It is the right of it. It must be so.
Ever your fresh whore and your pickled bawd. An un-
shunned consequence, it must be so. Going to
prison, Pompey?

POMPEY   Yes, faith, sir.

LUCIO   Why, 'tis not amiss, Pompey. Farewell. Go, say I
sent you thither. For debt, Pompey? Or how?

ELBOW   For being a bawd, for being a bawd.

LUCIO   Well, then, imprison him. If imprisonment is
the due of a bawd, why, it is his right. Bawd is he
doubtless, and of antiquity too; bawd-born. Farewell,
good Pompey. Commend me to the prison, Pompey.
You will turn good husband now, Pompey. You will
keep the house.

POMPEY   I hope, sir, your good worship will be my bail.

LUCIO   No, indeed will I not, Pompey; it is not the wear.
I will pray, Pompey, to increase your bondage. If you
take it not patiently, why, your mettle is the more.
Adieu, trusty Pompey. Bless you, friar.

DUKE   And you.

LUCIO   Does Bridget paint still, Pompey, ha?

ELBOW   Come your ways, sir, come.

POMPEY   You will not bail me then, sir?

LUCIO   Not then, Pompey, nor now. What news abroad,
friar, what news?

ELBOW   Come your ways, sir, come.

LUCIO   Go to kennel, Pompey, go.
                    Exeunt Elbow, Pompey, and Officers
What news, friar, of the Duke?

DUKE   I know none. Can you tell me of any?

LUCIO   Some say he is with the Emperor of Russia;
others, he is in Rome. But where is he, think you?

DUKE   I know not where, but wheresoever, I wish him
well.

LUCIO   It was a mad fantastical trick of him to steal
from the state, and usurp the beggary he was never
born to. Lord Angelo dukes it well in his absence. He
puts transgression to it.

DUKE   He does well in it.

LUCIO   A little more lenity to lechery would do no
harm in him. Something too crabbed that way, friar.

DUKE   It is too general a vice, and severity must cure it.

LUCIO   Yes, in good truth, the vice is of a great kindred. It is well allied, but it is impossible to extirp it quite, friar, till eating and drinking are put down. They say this Angelo was not made by man and woman after this downright way of creation. Is it true, think you?

DUKE   How should he be made, then?

LUCIO   Some report a sea-maid spawned him. Some that he was begot between two cod-fishes. But it is certain that when he makes water his urine is congealed ice. That I know to be true. And he is a eunuch. That's infallible.

DUKE   You are pleasant, sir, and speak apace.

LUCIO   Why, what a ruthless thing is this in him, for the rebellion of a cod-piece to take away the life of a man! Would the Duke that is absent have done this? Ere he would have hanged a man for the getting a hundred bastards, he would have paid for the nursing a thousand. He had some feeling of the sport. He knew the service, and that instructed him to mercy.

DUKE   I never heard the absent Duke much detected for women. He was not inclined that way.

LUCIO   O, sir, you are deceived.

DUKE   It is not possible.

LUCIO   Who? Not the Duke? Yes, your beggar of fifty, and his use was to put a ducat in her clack-dish. The Duke had crotchets in him. He would be drunk, too; that let me inform you.

DUKE   You do him wrong, surely.

LUCIO   Sir, I was an inward of his. A shy fellow was the Duke, and I believe I know the cause of his withdrawing.

DUKE   What, I pray, might be the cause?

LUCIO   No, pardon. 'Tis a secret must be locked within the teeth and the lips. But this I can let you understand, the greater file of the subject held the Duke to be wise.

DUKE   Wise? Why, no question but he was.

LUCIO   A very superficial, ignorant, unweighing fellow.

DUKE   Either this is malice in you, folly, or mistaking. The very stream of his life and the business he has helmed must, upon a warranted need, give him a better proclamation. Let him be but testimonied in his own bringings-forth, and he shall appear to the envious a scholar, a statesman, and a soldier. Therefore you speak unskillfully; or, if your knowledge is more, it is much darkened in your malice.

LUCIO   Sir, I know him, and I love him.

DUKE   Love talks with better knowledge, and knowledge with dearer love.

LUCIO   Come, sir, I know what I know.

DUKE   I can hardly believe that, since you know not what you speak. But if ever the Duke returns—as our prayers are he may—let me desire you to make your answer before him. If it is honest what you have spoken, you have courage to maintain it. I am bound to call upon you and, I pray you, your name?

LUCIO   Sir, my name is Lucio, well known to the Duke.

DUKE   He shall know you better, sir, if I may live to report you.

LUCIO   I fear you not.

DUKE   O, you hope the Duke will return no more, or you imagine me too unhurtful an opposite. But indeed I can do you little harm; you will forswear this again.

LUCIO   I'll be hanged first. You are deceived in me, friar. But no more of this. Can you tell if Claudio dies tomorrow or no?

DUKE   Why should he die, sir?

LUCIO   Why? For filling a bottle with a funnel. I would the Duke we talk of were returned again. This ungenitured agent will unpeople the province with continency. Sparrows must not build in his house-eaves because they are lecherous. The Duke yet would have dark deeds darkly answered. He would never bring them to light. Would he were returned. In fact, this Claudio is condemned for untrussing. Farewell, good friar. I pray, pray for me. The Duke, I say to you again, would eat mutton on Fridays. He's not past it yet, and I say to you, he would mouth with a beggar, though she smelt brown bread and garlic. Say that I said so. Farewell.   *Exit*

DUKE

No might nor greatness in mortality
Can censure escape; back-wounding calumny
The whitest virtue strikes. What king so strong
Can tie the gall up in the slanderous tongue?
But who comes here?

Enter Escalus, Provost, and Officers with Mistress Overdone

ESCALUS   Go! Away with her to prison.

MISTRESS OVERDONE   Good my lord, be good to me. Your honour is accounted a merciful man, good my lord.

ESCALUS   Double and treble admonition, and still forfeit in the same kind? This would make mercy swear, and play the tyrant.

PROVOST   A bawd of eleven years' continuance, may it please your honour.

MISTRESS OVERDONE   My lord, this is one Lucio's information against me. Mistress Kate Keepdown was with child by him in the Duke's time. He promised her marriage. His child is a year and a quarter old, come Philip and Jacob. I have kept it myself, and see how he goes about to abuse me.

ESCALUS   That fellow is a fellow of much licence. Let him be called before us. Away with her to prison. Go to, no more words.

Exeunt Officers with Mistress Overdone

Provost, my brother Angelo will not be altered.

Claudio must die tomorrow. Let him be furnished with divines, and have all charitable preparation. If my brother wrought by my pity, it should not be so with him.

PROVOST   So please you, this friar has been with him, and advised him for the entertainment of death.

ESCALUS   Good even, good father.

DUKE   Bliss and goodness on you!

ESCALUS   Of whence are you?

DUKE

Not of this country, though my chance is now
To use it for my time. I am a brother
Of gracious order, late come from the See,
In special business from his Holiness.

ESCALUS   What news abroad in the world?

DUKE   None, but that there is so great a fever on goodness that the dissolution of it must cure it. Novelty is only in request, and it is as dangerous to be aged in any kind of course as it is virtuous to be constant in any undertaking. There is scarce truth enough alive to make societies secure, but security enough to make fellowships accursed. Much upon this riddle runs the wisdom of the world. This news is old enough, yet it is every day's news. I pray you, sir, of what disposition was the Duke?

ESCALUS   One that, above all other strifes, contended especially to know himself.

DUKE   What pleasure was he given to?

ESCALUS   Rather rejoicing to see another merry than merry at anything which professed to make him rejoice: a gentleman of all temperance. But leave we him to his events, with a prayer they may prove prosperous, and let me desire to know how you find Claudio prepared. I am made to understand that you have lent him visitation.

DUKE   He professes to have received no sinister measure from his judge, but most willingly humbles himself to the determination of justice. Yet had he framed to himself, by the instruction of his frailty, many deceiving promises of life, which I, by my good leisure, have discredited to him, and now is he resolved to die.

ESCALUS You have paid the heavens your function, and the prisoner the very debt of your calling. I have laboured for the poor gentleman to the extremest shore of my modesty, but my brother-justice have I found so severe that he has forced me to tell him he is indeed Justice.

DUKE If his own life answers the straitness of his proceeding, it shall become him well; wherein if he chances to fail, he has sentenced himself.

ESCALUS I am going to visit the prisoner. Fare you well.

DUKE Peace be with you!

Exeunt Escalus and Provost

He who the sword of heaven will bear
Should be as holy as severe;
Pattern in himself to know,
Grace to stand, and virtue go;
No more nor less to others paying
Than by self-offences weighing.
Shame to him whose cruel striking
Kills for faults of his own liking.
Twice treble shame on Angelo,
To weed my vice and let his grow.
O, what may man within him hide,
Though angel on the outward side?
How may likeness made in crimes,
Experimenting on the times,
To draw with idle spiders' strings
Most ponderous and substantial things!
Craft against vice I must apply.
With Angelo tonight shall lie
His old betrothèd, but despised:
So disguise shall by the disguised
Pay with falsehood, false exacting,
And perform an old contracting.   *Exit*

Act IV

SCENE I
The moated grange.

Enter Mariana, and Boy singing

BOY (*sings*)
    Take, O take those lips away
      That so sweetly were forsworn;
    And those eyes, the break of day,
      Lights that do mislead the morn:
    But my kisses bring again, bring again;
    Seals of love, but sealed in vain, sealed in vain.

Enter Duke as a friar

MARIANA
    Break off your song, and haste you quick away.
    Here comes a man of comfort, whose advice
    Has often stilled my brawling discontent. *Exit Boy*
    I cry you mercy, sir, and well could wish
    You had not found me here so musical.
    Let me excuse me, and believe me so,
    My mirth it much displeased, but pleased my woe.
DUKE
    'Tis good, though music oft has such a charm
    To make bad good, and good provoke to harm.
    I pray you tell me, has anybody inquired for me here
    today? Much upon this time have I promised here to
    meet.
MARIANA   You have not been inquired after. I have sat
  here all day.

Enter Isabella

DUKE   I do constantly believe you. The time is come
even now. I shall crave your forbearance a little. May
be I will call upon you anon for some advantage to
yourself.

MARIANA   I am always bound to you.   *Exit*

DUKE
Very well met, and welcome.
What is the news from this good deputy?

ISABELLA
He has a garden circummured with brick,
Whose western side is with a vineyard backed;
And to that vineyard is a plankèd gate,
That makes its opening with this bigger key.
This other does command a little door
Which from the vineyard to the garden leads.
There have I made my promise,
Upon the heavy middle of the night,
To call upon him.

DUKE
But shall you on your knowledge find this way?

ISABELLA
I have taken a due and wary note upon it.
With whispering and most guilty diligence,
In action all of precept, he did show me
The way twice over.

DUKE   Are there no other tokens
Between you agreed concerning her observance?

ISABELLA
No, none, but only a repair in the dark,
And that I have possessed him my most stay
Can be but brief. For I have made him know
I have a servant comes with me along,
That stays upon me, whose persuasion is
I come about my brother.

DUKE   'Tis well borne up.

I have not yet made known to Mariana
A word of this. What ho, within. Come forth.

Enter Mariana

I pray you, be acquainted with this maid;
She comes to do you good.
ISABELLA   I do desire the like.
DUKE
Do you persuade yourself that I respect you?
MARIANA
Good friar, I know you do, and so have found it.
DUKE
Take then this your companion by the hand,
Who has a story ready for your ear.
I shall attend your leisure, but make haste.
The vaporous night approaches.
MARIANA
Will it please you walk aside?
                              Exeunt Mariana and Isabella
DUKE
O place and greatness, millions of false eyes
Are stuck upon you. Volumes of report
Run with these false and most contrarious quests
Upon your doings; thousand escapes of wit
Make you the father of their idle dream,
And rack you in their fancies.

Enter Mariana and Isabella

                              Welcome, how agreed?
ISABELLA
She'll take the enterprise upon her, father,
If you advise it.
DUKE   It is not my consent,
But my entreaty too.
ISABELLA   Little have you to say

When you depart from him but, soft and low,
'Remember now my brother.'
MARIANA   Fear me not.
DUKE
Nor, gentle daughter, fear you not at all.
He is your husband on a pre-contràct.
To bring you thus together, 'tis no sin,
Since the justice of your title to him
Does flourish the deceit. Come, let us go;
Our corn's to reap, for yet our tilth's to sow.

Exeunt

SCENE II
The prison.

Enter Provost and Pompey

PROVOST   Come hither, fellow. Can you cut off a man's
head?

POMPEY   If the man is a bachelor, sir, I can; but if he is a
married man, he's his wife's head, and I can never cut
off a woman's head.

PROVOST   Come, sir, leave me your snatches, and yield
me a direct answer. Tomorrow morning are to die
Claudio and Barnardine. Here is in our prison a
common executioner, who in his office lacks a
helper. If you will take it on you to assist him, it shall
redeem you from your fetters. If not, you shall have
your full time of imprisonment, and your
deliverance with an unpitied whipping, for you have
been a notorious bawd.

POMPEY   Sir, I have been an unlawful bawd time out of
mind, but yet I will be content to be a lawful
hangman. I would be glad to receive some instruction from my fellow partner.

PROVOST   What ho, Abhorson! Where's Abhorson,
there?

Enter Abhorson

ABHORSON   Do you call, sir?

PROVOST   Here's a fellow will help you tomorrow in your execution. If you think it meet, compound with him by the year, and let him abide here with you; if not, use him for the present and dismiss him. He cannot plead his estimation with you. He has been a bawd.

ABHORSON   A bawd, sir? Fie upon him, he will discredit our mystery [craft].

PROVOST   Go to, sir, you weigh equally. A feather will turn the scale.

POMPEY   Pray, sir, by your good favour—for surely, sir, a good favour [feature] you have, but that you have a hanging look—do you call, sir, your occupation a mystery?

ABHORSON   Ay, sir, a mystery.

POMPEY   Painting, sir, I have heard say, is a mystery, and your whores, sir, being members of my occupation, using painting, do prove my occupation a mystery. But what mystery there should be in hanging, if I should be hanged, I cannot imagine.

ABHORSON   Sir, it is a mystery.

POMPEY   Proof?

ABHORSON   Every true man's apparel fits your thief. If it is too little for your thief, your true man thinks it big enough. If it is too big for your thief, your thief thinks it little enough. So every true man's apparel fits your thief.

Enter Provost

PROVOST   Are you agreed?

POMPEY   Sir, I will serve him, for I do find your hangman is a more penitent trade than your bawd. He does oftener ask forgiveness.

PROVOST   You, man, provide your block and your axe tomorrow four o'clock.

ABHORSON   Come, on, bawd. I will instruct you in my
  trade. Follow!
POMPEY   I do desire to learn, sir, and I hope, if you have
  occasion to use me for your own turn, you shall find
  me brisk. For truly, sir, for your kindness I owe you a
  good turn.
PROVOST
  Call hither Barnardine and Claudio.
                        Exeunt Pompey and Abhorson
  The one has my pity; not a jot the other,
  Being a murderer, though he were my brother.

  Enter Claudio

  Look, here's the warrant, Claudio, for your death.
  'Tis now dead midnight, and by eight tomorrow
  You must be made immortal. Where's Barnardine?
CLAUDIO
  As fast locked up in sleep as guiltless labour
  When it lies starkly in the traveller's bones.
  He will not wake.
PROVOST   Who can do good on him?
  Well, go, prepare yourself.

  Knocking

                    But hark, what noise?
  Heaven give your spirits comfort.
                                      Exit Claudio
                    By and by.
  I hope it is some pardon or reprieve
  For the most gentle Claudio.

  Enter Duke disguised

                              Welcome, father.

DUKE
    The best and wholesomest spirits of the night
    Envelop you, good provost. Who called here of late?
PROVOST
    None since the curfew rang.
DUKE
    Not Isabel?
PROVOST   No.
DUKE   They will then, ere it be long.
PROVOST
    What comfort is for Claudio?
DUKE
    There's some in hope.
PROVOST   It is a bitter deputy.
DUKE
    Not so, not so; his life is paralleled
    Even with the stroke and line of his great justice.
    He does with holy abstinence subdue
    That in himself which he spurs on his power
    To qualify in others. Were he stained with that
    Which he corrects, then were he tyrannous,
    But this being so, he is just.

        Knocking

                            Now are they come.
                                Exit Provost
    This is a gentle provost; seldom when
    The steelèd gaoler is the friend of men.

        Knocking

    How now? What noise? That spirit's possessed
        with haste
    That wounds the unresisting postern with these
        strokes.

        Enter Provost

PROVOST
  There he must stay until the officer
  Arises to let him in. He is called up.
DUKE
  Have you no countermand for Claudio yet,
  But he must die tomorrow?
PROVOST   None, sir, none.
DUKE
  As near the dawning, provost, as it is,
  You shall hear more ere morning.
PROVOST   Happily
  You something know, yet I believe there comes
  No countermand; no such example have we.
  Besides, upon the very seat of justice,
  Lord Angelo has to the public ear
  Professed the contrary.

        Enter a Messenger

DUKE   This is his lordship's man.
PROVOST   And here comes Claudio's pardon.
MESSENGER   My lord has sent you this note, and by me
     this further charge: that you swerve not from the
     smallest article of it, neither in time, matter, or other
     circumstance. Good morrow; for, as I take it, it is
     almost day.
PROVOST   I shall obey him.   *Exit Messenger*
DUKE (*aside*)
  This is his pardon, purchased by such sin
  For which the pardoner himself is in:
  Hence has offence its quick celerity,
  When it is borne in high authority.
  When vice makes mercy, mercy's so extended
  That for the fault's love is the offender friended.
  Now, sir, what news?
PROVOST   I told you. Lord Angelo, perhaps thinking me
     remiss in my office, awakens me with this unwonted

urging—it seems strangely, for he has not used it
before.

DUKE   Pray you, let's hear.

PROVOST   (*reads the letter*) *Whatsoever you may hear to
the contrary, let Claudio be executed by four of the
clock and, in the afternoon, Barnardine. For my better satisfaction, let me have Claudio's head sent me
by five. Let this be duly performed, with a thought
that more depends on it than we must yet deliver.
Thus fail not to do your office, as you will answer it at
your peril.*

What say you to this, sir?

DUKE   What is that Barnardine who is to be executed in
the afternoon?

PROVOST   A Bohemian born, but here nursed up and
bred. One that is a prisoner nine years old.

DUKE   How came it that the absent Duke had not either
delivered him to his liberty or executed him? I have
heard it was ever his manner to do so.

PROVOST   His friends still wrought reprieves for him;
and, indeed, his fact, till now in the government of
Lord Angelo, came not to an undoubtful proof.

DUKE   It is now apparent?

PROVOST   Most manifest, and not denied by himself.

DUKE   Has he borne himself penitently in prison? How
seems he to be touched?

PROVOST   A man that apprehends death no more dread-
fully but as a drunken sleep; careless, reckless, and
fearless of what's past, present, or to come; insensible
of mortality, and desperately mortal.

DUKE   He wants advice.

PROVOST   He will hear none. He has evermore had the
liberty of the prison. Give him leave to escape hence,
he would not. Drunk many times a day, if not many
days entirely drunk. We have very oft awakened him,
as if to carry him to execution, and showed him a
seeming warrant for it. It has not moved him at all.

DUKE   More of him anon. There are written in your
brow, provost, honesty and constancy. If I read it not
truly, my ancient skill beguiles me; but in the bold-
ness of my cunning I will lay myself in hazard.
Claudio, whom here you have warrant to execute, is
no greater forfeit to the law than Angelo who has
sentenced him. To make you understand this in a
manifested effect, I crave but four days' respite, for
which you are to do me both a present and a
dangerous courtesy.

PROVOST   Pray, sir, in what?

DUKE   In the delaying death.

PROVOST   Alas, how may I do it, having the hour limited,
and an express command, under penalty, to deliver
his head in the view of Angelo? I may make my case as
Claudio's to cross this in the smallest.

DUKE   By the vow of my order I warrant you, if my in-
structions may be your guide. Let this Barnardine be
this morning executed, and his head borne to Angelo.

PROVOST   Angelo has seen them both, and will discover
the features.

DUKE   O, death's a great disguiser, and you may add to it.
Shave the head, and tie the beard, and say it was the
desire of the penitent to be so bared before his death.
You know the course is common. If anything falls to
you upon this, more than thanks and good fortune, by
the saint whom I profess, I will plead against it with
my life.

PROVOST   Pardon me, good father, it is against my oath.

DUKE   Were you sworn to the Duke or to the deputy?

PROVOST   To him, and to his substitutes.

DUKE   You will think you have made no offence if the
Duke confirms the justice of your dealing?

PROVOST   But what likelihood is in that?

DUKE   Not a resemblance, but a certainty. Yet since I
see you fearful, that neither my coat, integrity, nor

persuasion can with ease attempt you, I will go
further than I meant, to pluck all fears out of you.
Look you, sir, here is the hand and seal of the Duke.
You know the character, I doubt not, and the signet is
not strange to you.

PROVOST I know them both.

DUKE The contents of this is the return of the Duke.
You shall anon over-read it at your pleasure, where
you shall find within these two days he will be here.
This is a thing that Angelo knows not, for he this very
day receives letters of strange tenor, perchance of the
Duke's death, perchance entering into some
monastery, but by chance nothing of what is written.
Look, the unfolding star calls up the shepherd. Put
not yourself into amazement how these things
should be. All difficulties are but easy when they are
known. Call your executioner, and off with Barnardine's head. I will give him a present shrift and advise
him for a better place. Yet you are amazed, but this
shall absolutely resolve you. Come away, it is almost
clear dawn.

Exit with Provost

SCENE III
The prison, another room.

Enter Pompey

POMPEY I am as well acquainted here as I was in our
house of profession. One would think it was Mistress
Overdone's own house, for here are many of her old
customers. First, here's young Master Rash. He's in for
a commodity of brown paper and old ginger, nine-
score and seventeen pounds, of which he made five
marks ready money. Sure, then ginger was not much
in request, or the old women were all dead. Then is

there here one Master Caper, at the suit of Master
Threepile the mercer, for some four suits of peach-
coloured satin, which now peaches [impeaches] him
a beggar. Then have we here young Dizzy, and young
Master Deepvow, and Master Copperspur; and Master Starve-lackey, the rapier and dagger man, and
young Dropheir that killed lusty Pudding; and Master Forthright the tilter, and brave Master Shoetie the
great traveller, and wild Half-can that stabbed Pots.
And I think forty more, all great doers in our trade,
and are now 'for the Lord's sake'.

    Enter Abhorson

ABHORSON   Fellow, bring Barnardine hither.
POMPEY   Master Barnardine, you must rise and be
hanged, Master Barnardine.
ABHORSON   What ho, Barnardine!
BARNARDINE *(within)* A pox on your throats! Who
makes that noise there? What are you?
POMPEY   Your friends, sir, the hangman. You must be so
good, sir, to rise and be put to death.
BARNARDINE *(within)* Away, you rogue, away! I am
sleepy.
ABHORSON   Tell him he must awake, and that quickly
too.
POMPEY   Pray, Master Barnardine, awake till you are
executed, and sleep afterwards.
ABHORSON   Go in to him, and fetch him out.
POMPEY   He is coming, sir, he is coming. I hear his straw
rustle.

    Enter Barnardine

ABHORSON   Is the axe upon the block, man?
POMPEY   Very ready, sir.
BARNARDINE   How now, Abhorson, what's the news
with you?

ABHORSON   Truly, sir, I would desire you to clap into
your prayers, for look you, the warrant's come.

BARNARDINE   You rogue, I have been drinking all night. I
am not fitted for it.

POMPEY   O, the better, sir, for he that drinks all night,
and is hanged betimes in the morning, may sleep the
sounder all the next day.

Enter Duke disguised

ABHORSON   Look you, sir, here comes your ghostly
father. Do we jest now, think you?

DUKE   Sir, induced by my charity, and hearing how
hastily you are to depart, I am come to advise you,
comfort you, and pray with you.

BARNARDINE   Friar, not I. I have been drinking hard all
night and I will have more time to prepare me, or they
shall beat out my brains with billets. I will not
consent to die this day, that's certain.

DUKE   O, sir, you must, and therefore I beseech you look
forward on the journey you shall go.

BARNARDINE   I swear I will not die today for any man's
persuasion.

DUKE   But hear you.

BARNARDINE   Not a word. If you have anything to say to
me, come to my ward, for thence will not I today.

Exit

Enter Provost

DUKE

Unfit to live or die. O gravel heart!
After him, fellows: bring him to the block.

Exeunt Abhorson and Pompey

PROVOST

Now, sir, how do you find the prisoner?

DUKE

A creature unprepared, unmeet for death,

And to transport him in the mind he is
Were damnable.

PROVOST   Here in the prison, father,
There died this morning of a cruel fever
One Ragozine, a most notorious pirate,
A man of Claudio's years, his beard and head
Just of his colour. What if we do omit
This reprobate till he were well inclined,
And satisfy the deputy with the visage
Of Ragozine, more like to Claudio?

DUKE
O, 'tis an accident that heaven provides.
Dispatch it instantly; the hour draws on
Prefixed by Angelo. See this is done,
And sent according to command, while I
Persuade this rude wretch willingly to die.

PROVOST
This shall be done, good father, immediately,
But Barnardine must die this afternoon;
And how shall we continue Claudio,
To save me from the danger that might come
If he were known alive?

DUKE   Let this be done.
Put them in secret holds, both Barnardine
And Claudio. Ere twice the sun has made
His journal greeting to yonder generation,
You shall find your safety manifested.

PROVOST
I am your free dependant.

DUKE
Quick, dispatch, and send the head to Angelo.
                                        Exit Provost
Now will I write letters to Varrius—
The provost, he shall bear them—whose contents
Shall witness to him I am near at home,
And that by great injunctions I am bound
To enter publicly. Him I'll desire
To meet me at the consecrated fount

A league below the city, and from thence,
By cold gradation and well-balanced form,
We shall proceed with Angelo.

Enter Provost

PROVOST
Here is the head. I'll carry it myself.
DUKE
Convenient is it. Make a swift return,
For I would commune with you of such things
That want no ear but yours.
PROVOST   I'll make all speed.   *Exit*
ISABELLA *(within)*
Peace, ho, be here.
DUKE
The tongue of Isabel. She's come to know
If yet her brother's pardon is come hither,
But I will keep her ignorant of her good,
To make her heavenly comforts of despair
When it is least expected.

Enter Isabella

ISABELLA   Ho, by your leave!
DUKE
Good morning to you, fair and gracious daughter.
ISABELLA
The better, given me by so holy a man.
Has yet the deputy sent my brother's pardon?
DUKE
He has released him, Isabel, from the world.
His head is off and sent to Angelo.
ISABELLA
Nay, but it is not so.
DUKE
It is no other. Show your wisdom, daughter,
In your close patience.

ISABELLA
  O, I will to him and pluck out his eyes!
DUKE
  You shall not be admitted to his sight.
ISABELLA
  Unhappy Claudio! Wretched Isabel!
  Injurious world! Most damnèd Angelo!
DUKE
  This neither hurts him nor profits you a jot;
  Forbear it therefore, give your cause to heaven.
  Mark what I say, which you shall find
  By every syllable a faithful verity.
  The Duke comes home tomorrow—nay, dry your
            eyes—
  One of our convent, and his cònfessòr,
  Gives me this instance. Already he has carried
  Notice to Escalus and Angelo,
  Who do prepare to meet him at the gates,
  There to give up their power. If you can, pace your
            wisdom
  In that good path that I would wish it go,
  And you shall have your bosom on this wretch,
  Grace of the Duke, revenges to your heart,
  And general honour.
ISABELLA   I am directed by you.
DUKE
  This letter then to Friar Peter give.
  'Tis that he sent me of the Duke's return.
  Say, by this token, I desire his company
  At Mariana's house tonight. Her cause and yours
  I'll pèrfect him with then, and he shall bring you
  Before the Duke; and to the head of Angelo
  Accuse him home and home. For my poor self,
  I am combinèd by a sacred vow
  And shall be absent. Wend you with this letter.
  Command these fretting waters from your eyes
  With a light heart. Trust not my holy order
  If I pervert your course. Who's here?

Enter Lucio

LUCIO   Good even. Friar, where's the provost?

DUKE   Not within, sir

LUCIO   O pretty Isabella, I am pale at my heart to see your eyes so red. You must be patient. I am bound to dine and sup with water and bran. I dare not for my head fill my belly; one fruitful meal would set me to it. But they say the Duke will be here tomorrow. By my word, Isabel, I loved your brother. If the old fantastical Duke of dark corners had been at home, he had lived.

Exit Isabella

DUKE   Sir, the Duke is marvellous little beholding to your reports; but the best is, he lives not in them.

LUCIO   Friar, you know not the Duke so well as I do. He's a better womaniser than you take him for.

DUKE   Well, you'll answer this one day. Fare ye well.

LUCIO   Nay, tarry, I'll go along with you. I can tell you pretty tales of the Duke.

DUKE   You have told me too many of him already, sir, if they are true; if not true, none is enough.

LUCIO   I was once before him for getting a wench with child.

DUKE   Did you such a thing?

LUCIO   Yes, marry, did I, but I was fain to forswear it. They would else have married me to the rotten medlar.

DUKE   Sir, your company is fairer than honest. Rest you well.

LUCIO   By my word, I'll go with you to the lane's end. If bawdy talk offends you, we'll have very little of it. Nay, friar, I am a kind of burr, I shall stick. *Exeunt*

SCENE IV
Angelo's house.

Enter Angelo and Escalus

ESCALUS Every letter he has written has contradicted
the other.

ANGELO In most uneven and distracted manner. His
actions show much like to madness. Pray heaven his
wisdom is not tainted. And why meet him at the
gates, and redeliver our authorities there?

ESCALUS I guess not.

ANGELO And why should we proclaim it in an hour
before his entering, that if any crave redress of injustice, they should exhibit their petitions in the
street?

ESCALUS He shows his reason for that—to have a dispatch of complaints, and to deliver us from devices
hereafter, which shall then have no power to stand
against us.

ANGELO
Well, I beseech you let it be proclaimed.
Betimes in the morn I'll call you at your house.
Give notice to such men of sort and suit
As are to meet him.

ESCALUS   I shall, sir. Fare you well.

ANGELO
Good night.   *Exit Escalus*
This deed unshapes me quite, makes me unready
And dull to all proceedings. A deflowered maid,
And by an eminent body that enforced
The law against it! But that her tender shame
Will not proclaim against her maiden loss,
How might she tongue me? Yet reason dares her no,
For my authority bears a credent bulk
That no particular scandal once can touch

But it confounds the breather. He should have lived,
Save that his riotous youth with dangerous sense
Might in the times to come have taken revenge,
By so receiving a dishonoured life
With ransom of such shame. Would yet he had lived.
Alas, when once our grace we have forgot,
Nothing goes right. We would, and we would not.

Exit

SCENE V
Before the city.

Enter Duke, in his own habit, and Friar Peter

DUKE
These letters at fit time deliver me.
The provost knows our purpose and our plot.
The matter being afoot, keep your instruction,
And hold you ever to our special drift,
Though sometimes you do blench from this to that,
As cause does minister. Go call at Flavius' house,
And tell him where I stay. Give the like notice
To Valentius, Rowland, and to Crassus,
And bid them bring the trumpets to the gate;
But send me Flavius first.
FRIAR PETER   It shall be speeded well.

Exit

    Enter Varrius

DUKE
I thank you, Varrius, you have made good haste.
Come, we will walk. There are others of our friends
Will greet us here anon, my gentle Varrius. *Exeunt*

SCENE VI
A street.

Enter Isabella and Mariana

ISABELLA

To speak so indirectly I am loth.
I would say the truth, but to accuse him so,
That is your part. Yet I am advised to do it,
He says, to veil full purpose.

MARIANA   Be ruled by him.

ISABELLA

Besides, he tells me that if peradventure
He speaks against me on the adverse side,
I should not think it strange, for 'tis a physic
That's bitter to sweet end.

MARIANA

I would Friar Peter—

Enter Friar Peter

ISABELLA   O, peace, the friar is come.

FRIAR PETER

Come, I have found you out a stand most fit,
Where you may have such vantage on the Duke
He shall not pass you. Twice have the trumpets
          sounded.
The generous and gravest citizens
Hold the gates, and very near upon
The Duke is entering. Therefore hence, away.

                                              Exeunt

Act V

SCENE I
A public place.

Enter Duke, Varrius, Lords, Angelo, Escalus,
Lucio, Provost, Officers, and Citizens at separate
doors

DUKE
  My very worthy cousin, fairly met.
  Our old and faithful friend, we are glad to see you.
ANGELO *and* ESCALUS
  Happy return be to your royal grace.
DUKE
  Many and hearty thankings to you both.
  We have made inquiry of you, and we hear
  Such goodness of your justice that our soul
  Cannot but yield you forth to public thanks,
  Forerunning more requital.
ANGELO   You make my bonds still greater.
DUKE
  O, your desert speaks loud, and I should wrong it
  To lock it in the wards of covert bosom,
  When it deserves with characters of brass
  A forted residence against the tooth of time
  And razure of oblivion. Give me your hand,
  And let the subject see, to make them know
  That outward courtesies would fain proclaim
  Favours that keep within. Come, Escalus,
  You must walk by us on our other hand,
  And good supporters are you.

Enter Friar Peter and Isabella

FRIAR PETER
 Now is your time. Speak loud and kneel before him.
ISABELLA
 Justice, O royal Duke! Send your regard
 Upon a wronged—I would fain have said, a maid.
 O worthy prince, dishonour not your eye
 By throwing it on any other object
 Till you have heard me in my true complaint,
 And given me justice, justice, justice, justice!
DUKE
 Relate your wrongs. In what? By whom? Be brief.
 Here is Lord Angelo shall give you justice.
 Reveal yourself to him.
ISABELLA   O worthy Duke,
 You bid me seek redemption of the devil.
 Hear me yourself, for that which I must speak
 Must either punish me, not being believed,
 Or wring redress from you. Hear me, O hear me, hear.
ANGELO
 My lord, her wits, I fear me, are not firm.
 She has been a suitor to me for her brother,
 Cut off by course of justice—
ISABELLA   By course of justice!
ANGELO
 And she will speak most bitterly and strange.
ISABELLA
 Most strange, but yet most truly, will I speak.
 That Angelo's forsworn, is it not strange?
 That Angelo's a murderer, is it not strange?
 That Angelo is an adulterous thief,
 An hypocrite, a virgin-violator,
 Is it not strange, and strange?
DUKE   Nay, it is ten times strange.
ISABELLA
 It is not truer he is Angelo
 Than this is all as true as it is strange.
 Nay, it is ten times true, for truth is truth
 To the end of reckoning.

DUKE   Away with her. Poor soul,
    She speaks this in the infirmity of sense.
ISABELLA
    O prince, I conjure you, as you believe
    There is another comfort than this world,
    That you neglect me not with that opinion
    That I am touched with madness. Make not
                impossible
    That which but seems unlike. 'Tis not impossible
    But one, the wickedest villain on the ground,
    May seem as shy, as grave, as just, as absolute
    As Angelo. Even so may Angelo,
    In all his dressings, emblems, titles, forms,
    Be an arch-villain. Believe it, royal prince.
    If he is less, he's nothing: but he's more,
    Had I more name for badness.
DUKE   By my honesty,
    If she is mad, as I believe no other,
    Her madness has the oddest frame of sense,
    Such a dependency of thing on thing,
    As ever I heard in madness.
ISABELLA   O gracious Duke,
    Harp not on that, and do not banish reason
    For inequality, but let your reason serve
    To make the truth appear where it seems hidden,
    And hide the false seems true.
DUKE   Many that are not mad
    Have sure more lack of reason. What would you say?
ISABELLA
    I am the sister of one Claudio,
    Condemned upon the act of fornication
    To lose his head, condemned by Angelo.
    I, in probation of a sisterhood,
    Was sent to by my brother. One Lucio
    As, then the messenger—
LUCIO   That's I, so, please your grace.
    I came to her from Claudio, and desired her

To try her gracious fortune with Lord Angelo
For her poor brother's pardon.
ISABELLA   That's he indeed.
DUKE
You were not bidden to speak.
LUCIO   No, my good lord,
Nor wished to hold my peace.
DUKE   I wish you now, then.
Pray you, take note of it, and when you have
A business for yourself, pray heaven you then
Be perfect.
LUCIO   I warrant your honour.
DUKE
The warrant's for yourself: take heed to it.
ISABELLA
This gentleman told somewhat of my tale.
LUCIO
Right.
DUKE
It may be right, but your are in the wrong
To speak before your time. Proceed.
ISABELLA   I went
To this pernicious villain deputy—
DUKE
That's somewhat madly spoken.
ISABELLA   Pardon it,
The phrase is to the matter.
DUKE
Mended again. The matter. Proceed.
ISABELLA
In brief, to set the needless process by,
How I persuaded, how I prayed, and kneeled,
How he repelled me, and how I replied—
For this was of much length—the vile conclusion
I now begin with grief and shame to utter.
He would not, but by gift of my chaste body
To his concupiscible intemperate lust,

Release my brother. And after much debatement
My sisterly remorse confutes my honour,
And I did yield to him. But the next morn betimes.
His purpose surfeiting, he sends a warrant
For my poor brother's head.

DUKE   This is most likely!

ISABELLA

O, that it were as like as it is true.

DUKE

By heaven, poor wretch, you know not what you
        speak,
Or else you are suborned against his honour
In hateful intrigue. First, his integrity
Stands without blemish. Next, it imports no reason
That with such vehemency he should pursue
Faults proper to himself. If he had so offended,
He would have weighed your brother by himself,
And not have cut him off. Someone has set you on.
Confess the truth, and say by whose advice
You came here to complain.

ISABELLA   And is this all?

Then, O you blessèd ministers above,
Keep me in patience, and with ripened time
Unfold the evil which is here wrapped up
In countenance. Heaven shield your grace from woe,
As I thus wronged hence unbelievèd go.

DUKE

I know you'd fain be gone. An officer!
To prison with her. Shall we thus permit
A blasting and a scandalous breath to fall
On him so near us? This needs must be a trick.
Who knew of your intent and coming hither?

ISABELLA

One that I would were here, Friar Lodowick.

DUKE

A ghostly father, perhaps. Who knows that
        Lodowick?

LUCIO

My lord, I know him, 'tis a meddling friar;
I do not like the man. Had he been lay, my lord,
For certain words he spoke against your grace
In your retirement I had whipped him soundly.

DUKE

Words against me? This a good friar, indeed,
And to set on this wretched woman here
Against our substitute! Let this friar be found.

LUCIO

But yesternight, my lord, she and that friar,
I saw them at the prison. A saucy friar,
A very scurvy fellow.

FRIAR PETER

Blessed be your royal grace,
I have stood by, my lord, and I have heard
Your royal ear abused. First has this woman
Most wrongfully accused your substitute,
Who is as free from touch or soil with her
As she from one ungot.

DUKE   We did believe no less.

Know you that Friar Lodowick that she speaks of?

FRIAR PETER

I know him for a man divine and holy,
Not scurvy, nor a temporary meddler,
As he's reported by this gentleman;
And, on my trust, a man that never yet
Did—as he says—misreport your grace.

LUCIO

My lord, most villainously, believe it.

FRIAR PETER

Well, he in time may come to clear himself,
But at this instant he is sick, my lord,
Of a strange fever. Upon his mere request,
Being come to knowledge that there was complaint
Intended against Lord Angelo, came I hither:
To speak, as from his mouth, what he does know

Is true and false, and what he with his oath
And all probation will make up full clear,
When ever he is summoned. First, for this woman,
To justify this worthy nobleman,
So vulgarly and personally accused,
Her shall you hear disprovèd to her eyes,
Till she herself confesses it.

DUKE   Good friar, let's hear it.

Isabella is led off, guarded

Enter Mariana

Do you not smile at this, Lord Angelo?
O heaven, the vanity of wretched fools!
Give us some seats. Come, cousin Angelo,
In this I'll be impartial. Be you judge
Of your own cause. Is this the witness, friar?
First, let her show her face, and after speak.

MARIANA
Pardon, my lord, I will not show my face
Until my husband bids me.

DUKE   What, are you married?

MARIANA   No, my lord.

DUKE   Are you a maid?

MARIANA   No, my lord.

DUKE   A widow, then?

MARIANA   Neither, my lord.

DUKE   Why, you are nothing then. Neither maid,
widow, nor wife?

LUCIO   My lord, she may be a whore. For many of them
are neither maid, widow nor wife.

DUKE
Silence that fellow. I would he had some cause
To prattle for himself.

LUCIO   Well, my lord.

MARIANA
My lord, I do confess I never was married,

And I confess besides I am no maid;
I have known my husband, yet my husband
Knows not that ever he knew me.

LUCIO   He was drunk, then, my lord. It can be no better.

DUKE   For the benefit of silence, would you were so too.

LUCIO   Well, my lord.

DUKE
This is no witness for Lord Angelo.

MARIANA
Now I come to it, my lord:
She that accuses him of fornication
In selfsame manner does accuse my husband;
And charges him, my lord, with such a time
When, I'll depose, I had him in my arms,
With all the effect of love.

ANGELO
Charges she more than me?

MARIANA   Not that I know.

DUKE
No? You say your husband?

MARIANA
Why, just, my lord, and that is Angelo,
Who thinks he knows he never knew my body,
But knows, he thinks, that he knows Isabel's.

ANGELO
This is a strange abuse. Let's see your face.

MARIANA
My husband bids me. Now I will unmask.

   She unveils

This is that face, you cruel Angelo,
Which once you swore was worth the looking on.
This is the hand which, with a vowed contràct,
Was fast belocked in yours. This is the body
That took away the match from Isabel,
And did supply you at your garden-house

In her imagined person.

DUKE   Know you this woman?

LUCIO

Carnally, she says.

DUKE   Fellow, no more!

LUCIO

Enough, my lord.

ANGELO

My lord, I must confess I know this woamn,
And five years since there was some speech of
            marriage
Between myself and her, which was broken off—
Partly because her promisèd proportions
Came short of composition, but in chief
Because her reputation was disvalued
In levity. Since which time five years
I never spoke with her, saw her, nor heard from her,
Upon my faith and honour.

MARIANA   Noble prince,
As there comes light from heaven and words from
            breath,
As there is sense in truth and truth in virtue,
I am affianced this man's wife as strongly
As words could make up vows. And, my good lord,
But Tuesday night last gone in this garden-house
He knew me as a wife. As this is true,
Let me in safety raise me from my knees
Or else forever be confixèd here
A marble monument.

ANGELO   I did but smile till now.
Now, good my lord, give me the scope of justice.
My patience here is touched. I do perceive
These poor disordered women are no more
But instruments of some more mighty member
That sets them on. Let me have way, my lord,
To find this intrigue out.

DUKE   Ay, with my heart,

And punish them to your height of pleasure.
You foolish friar, and you pernicious woman,
In league with her that's gone, think you your oaths,
Though they would swear down each particular
    saint,
Were testimonies against his worth and credit
That's sealed in approbation? You, Lord Escalus,
Sit with my cousin, lend him your kind pains
To find out this abuse, whence it is derived.
There is another friar that set them on;
Let him be sent for.

FRIAR PETER
Would he were here, my lord, for he indeed
Has set the women on to this complaint.
Your provost knows the place where he abides
And he may fetch him.

DUKE   Go do it instantly;
                              Exit Provost
And you, my noble and well-warranted cousin,
Whom it concerns to hear this matter forth,
Do with your injuries as seems you best,
In any chastisement. I for a while
Will leave, but stir not you till you have well
Determinèd upon these slanderers.

ESCALUS
My lord, we'll do it thoroughly.   .*Exit Duke*
Signor Lucio, did not you say you knew that Friar
Lodowick to be a dishonest person?

LUCIO   *Cucullus non facit monachum.*[1] Honest in nothing but in his clothes, and one that has spoken most
villainous speeches of the Duke.

ESCALUS   We shall entreat you to abide here till he
comes and enforce them against him. We shall find
this friar a notable fellow.

LUCIO   As any in Vienna, on my word.

ESCALUS   Call that same Isabel here once again. I would
speak with her.
                            Exit an Attendant

_____
[1] The cowl does not make the monk.

Pray you, my lord, give me leave to question. You shall
see how I'll handle her.

LUCIO Not better than he, by her own report.

ESCALUS Say you?

LUCIO Sure, sir, I think, if you handled her privately, she
would sooner confess. Perchance publicly she'll be
ashamed.

Enter Duke, disguised, Provost, Isabella, and
Officers

ESCALUS I will go darkly to work with her.

LUCIO That's the way, for women are light at midnight.

ESCALUS Come on, mistress, here's a gentlewoman
denies all that you have said.

LUCIO My lord, here comes the rascal I spoke of—here
with the provost.

ESCALUS In very good time. Speak not you to him, till
we call upon you.

LUCIO Mum.

ESCALUS Come, sir, did you set these women on to
slander Lord Angelo? They have confessed you did.

DUKE It is false.

ESCALUS How? Know you where you are?

DUKE

Respect to your great place, and let the devil
Be sometimes honoured for his burning throne.
Where is the Duke? 'Tis he should hear me speak.

ESCALUS

The Duke's in us, and we will hear you speak.
Look you speak justly.

DUKE

Boldly at least. But O, poor souls,
Come you to seek the lamb here of the fox?
Good night to your redress. Is the Duke gone?
Then is your cause gone too. The Duke's unjust,
Thus to retort your manifest appeal

And put your trial in the villain's mouth
Which here you come to accuse.

LUCIO

This is the rascal. This is he I spoke of.

ESCALUS

Why, you unreverend and unhallowed friar,
Is it not enough you have suborned these women
To accuse this worthy man but, in foul mouth,
And in the witness of his very ear,
To call him villain? And then to glance from him
To the Duke himself, to tax him with injustice?
Take him hence. To the rack with him. We'll tear you
Joint by joint, but we will know his purpose.
What? Unjust?

DUKE   Be not so hot. The Duke
Dares no more stretch this finger of mine than he
Dares rack his own. His subject am I not,
Nor here provincial. My business in this state
Made me a looker-on here in Vienna,
Where I have seen corruption boil and bubble
Till it overruns the stew. Laws for all faults,
But faults so countenanced that the strong statutes
Stand like the forfeits in a barber's shop,
As much in mock as mark.

ESCALUS

Slander to the state. Away with him to prison.

ANGLEO

What can you charge against him, Signor Lucio?
Is this the man that you did tell us of?

LUCIO 'Tis he, my lord. Come hither, goodman
baldpate. Do you know me?

DUKE I remember you, sir, by the sound of your voice. I
met you at the prison in the absence of the Duke.

LUCIO O, did you so? And do you remember what you
said of the Duke?

DUKE Most notedly, sir.

LUCIO Do you so, sir? And was the Duke a fleshmonger,

a fool, and a coward, as you then reported him to be?
DUKE   You must, sir, change persons with me, ere you
    make that my report. You, indeed, spoke so of him,
    and much more, much worse.
LUCIO   O you damnable fellow, did not I pluck you by
    the nose for your speeches?
DUKE   I protest I love the Duke as I love myself.
ANGLEO   Hark how the villain would close now, after
    his treasonable abuses.
ESCALUS   Such a fellow is not to be talked with. Away
    with him to prison. Where is the provost? Away with
    him to prison. Lay bolts enough upon him. Let him
    speak no more. Away with those harlots too, and with
    the other confederate companion.
DUKE   Stay, sir, stay a while.
ANGLEO   What, resists he? Help him Lucio.
LUCIO   Come, sir, come, sir, come, sir! Foh, sir! Why, you
    bald-pated, lying rascal, you must be hooded, must
    you? Show your knave's visage, with a pox to you.
    Show your sheep-biting face, and be hanged an hour.
    Will it not off?

       *He pulls off the Friar's hood, and discovers the
       Duke*

DUKE
    You are the first knave that ever made a duke.
    First, provost, let me bail these gentle three—
    (to Lucio) Sneak not away, sir, for the friar and you
    Must have a word anon. Lay hold on him.
LUCIO
    This may prove worse than hanging.
DUKE *(to Escalus)*
    What you have spoken I pardon. Sit you down.
    We'll borrow place of him. *(To Angelo)* Sir, by your
            leave.
    Have you word, or wit, or impudence

That yet can do you office? If you have,
Rely upon it till my tale is heard,
And hold no longer out.

ANGELO   O my dread lord,
I should be guiltier than my guiltiness
To think I can be undiscernible,
When I perceive your grace, like power divine,
Has looked upon my passes. Then, good prince,
No longer session hold upon my shame,
But let my trial be my own confession.
Immediate sentence, then, and sequent death
Is all the grace I beg.

DUKE   Come hither, Mariana.
Say, were you ever contracted to this woman?

ANGELO
I was, my lord.

DUKE
Go take her hence, and marry her instantly.
Do you the office, friar, which consummate,
Return him here again. Go with him, provost.

Exit Angelo, with Mariana, Friar Peter, and Provost

ESCALUS
My lord, I am more amazed at his dishonour
Than at then strangeness of it.

DUKE   Come hither, Isabel.
Your friar is now your prince. As I was then
Advertising and holy to your business,
Not changing heart with habit, I am still
Attorneyed at your service.

ISABELLA   O, give me pardon,
That I, your vassal, have employed and pained
Your unknown sovereignty.

DUKE   You are pardoned, Isabel.
And now, dear maid, be you as free to us.
Your brother's death, I know, sits at your heart,
And you may marvel why I obscured myself,
Labouring to save his life, and would not rather

Make rash remonstrance of my hidden power
Than let him so be lost. O most kind maid,
It was the swift celerity of his death,
Which I did think with slower foot came on,
That brained my purpose; but peace be with him.
That life is better life past fearing death
Than that which lives to fear. Make it your comfort,
So happy is your brother.

Enter Angelo, Mariana, Friar Peter, Provost

ISABELLA   I do, my lord.
DUKE
For this new-married man approaching here,
Whose keen imagination yet has wronged
Your well-defended honour, you must pardon
For Mariana's sake. But as he judged your brother,
Being criminal, in double violation
Of sacred chastity, and of promise-breach—
Thereon dependent, for your brother's life—
The very mercy of the law cries out
Most audible, even from his very tongue,
'An Angelo for Claudio, death for death!'
Haste still pays haste, and leisure answers leisure,
Like does quit like, and Measure still for Measure.
Then, Angelo, your faults thus manifested,
Which, though you would deny, denies you profit
We do condemn you to the very block
Where Claudio stooped to death, and with like haste.
Away with him.
MARIANA   O, my most gracious lord,
I hope you will not mock me with a husband.
DUKE
It is your husband mocked you with a husband.
Consenting to the safeguard of your honour
I thought your marriage fit; else imputation,
Because he knew you, might reproach your life

And choke your good to come. For his possessions,
Although by confiscation they are ours,
We do instate and widow you with all,
To buy you a better husband.

MARIANA   O my dear lord,
I crave no other, nor any better man.

DUKE
Never crave him. We are definitive.

MARIANA
Gentle my liege!—

DUKE   You do but lose your labour.
Away with him to death. (*To Lucio*) Now, sir, to you.

MARIANA
O my good lord! Sweet Isabel, take my part,
Lend me your knees, and all my life to come
I'll lend you all my life to do you service.

DUKE
Against all sense you do importune her.
Should she kneel down in mercy of this fact,
Her brother's ghost his pavèd bed would break,
And take her hence in horror.

MARIANA   Isabel,
Sweet Isabel, do yet but kneel by me.
Hold up your hands, say nothing, I'll speak all.
They say best men are moulded out of faults,
And, for the most, become much more the better
For being a little bad. So may my husband.
O Isabel, will you not lend a knee?

DUKE
He dies for Claudio's death.

ISABELLA (*kneeling*)   Most bounteous sir,
Look, if it please you, on this man condemned
As if my brother lived. I partly think
A due sincerity governèd his deeds
Till he did look on me. Since it is so,
Let him not die. My brother had but justice,
In that he did the thing for which he died.
For Angelo,

His act did not o'vertake his bad intent,
And must be buried but as an intent
That perished by the way. Thoughts are no subjects,
Intents but merely thoughts.

MARIANA   Merely, my lord.

DUKE

Your suit's unprofitable. Stand up, I say.
I have bethought me of another fault.
Provost, how came it Claudio was beheaded
At an unusual hour?

PROVOST   It was commanded so.

DUKE

Had you a special warrant for the deed?

PROVOST

No, my good lord, it was by private message.

DUKE

For which I do discharge you of your office;
Give up your keys.

PROVOST   Pardon me, noble lord,
I thought it was a fault, but knew it not,
Yet did repent me after more advice;
For testimony whereof, one in the prison
That should by private order else have died
I have reserved alive.

DUKE   What's he?

PROVOST   His name is Barnardine.

DUKE

I would you had done so by Claudio.
Go, fetch him hither. Let me look upon him.

                                   Exit Provost

ESCALUS

I am sorry one so learned and so wise
As you, Lord Angelo, have still appeared,
Should slip so grossly, both in the heat of blood
And lack of tempered judgement afterward.

ANGELO

I am sorry that such sorrow I procure,

And so deep sticks it in my penitent heart
That I crave death more willingly than mercy.
'Tis my deserving, and I do entreat it.

Enter Barnardine and Provost, Claudio
muffled, Juliet

DUKE   Which is that Barnardine?
PROVOST   This, my lord.
DUKE
There was a friar told me of this man.
Fellow, you are said to have a stubborn soul,
That apprehends no further than this world,
And square your life according. You are condemned,
But, for those earthly faults, I quit them all;
And pray you take this mercy to provide
For better times to come. Friar, advise him:
I leave him to your hand. What muffled fellow's that?
PROVOST
This is another prisoner that I saved,
Who should have died when Claudio lost his head,
As like almost to Claudio as himself.

He unmuffles Claudio

DUKE (*To Isabella*)
If he is like your brother, for his sake
Is he pardoned, and for your lovely sake,
Give me your hand and say you will be mine.
He is my brother too. But fitter time for that.
By this Lord Angelo perceives he's safe;
I think I see a quickening in his eye.
Well, Angelo, your evil quits you well.
Look that you love your wife, her worth, worth yours.
I find an apt remission in myself,
And yet here's one in place I cannot pardon.
(*To Lucio*) You, fellow, that knew me for a fool, a
        coward,

One all of lechery, an ass, a madman,
Wherein have I so deserved of you,
That you extol me thus?

LUCIO 'Faith, my lord, I spoke it but according to the
times. If you will hang me for it, you may. But I had
rather it would please you I might be whipped.

DUKE
Whipped first, sir, and hanged after.
Proclaim it, provost, round about the city,
If any woman wronged by this lewd fellow—
As I have heard him swear himself there's one
Whom he begot with child—let her appear,
And he shall marry her. The nuptials finished,
Let him be whipped and hanged.

LUCIO I beseech your highness, do not marry me to a
whore. Your highness said even now, I made you a
duke. Good my lord, do not recompense me in making
me a cuckold.

DUKE
Upon my honour, you shall marry her.
Your slanders I forgive, and therewith too
Remit your other forfeits. Take him to prison,
And see our pleasure herein executed.

LUCIO Marrying a whore, my lord, is pressing to death,
whipping, and hanging.

DUKE
Slandering a prince deserves it.
                         Exeunt Officers with Lucio
She, Claudio, that you wronged, look you restore.
Joy to you, Mariana. Love her, Angelo.
I have confessed her and I know her virtue.
Thanks, good friend Escalus, for your much goodness.
There's more behind that is more grateful too.
Thanks, provost, for your care and secrecy.
We shall employ you in a worthier place.
Forgive him, Angelo, that brought you home
The head of Ragozine for Claudio's.

The offence pardons itself. Dear Isabel,
I have a motion much imports your good,
Whereto if you'll a willing ear incline,
What's mine is yours, and what is yours is mine.
So, bring us to our palace, where we'll show
What's yet behind, that's meet you all should know.

Exeunt

The Merry Wives of Windsor

INTRODUCTION

The Merry Wives of Windsor is the most sheerly amusing play that Shakespeare ever wrote—riotous fun from beginning to end, and incredibly ingenious in construction, characters, language—everything. It is a brilliant farce, always successful on the stage and has inspired operas, Nicolai's, Verdi's *Falstaff*, Vaughan Williams's *Sir John in Love*, as well as Elgar's nostalgic symphonic re-creation. Our leading textual critic, Fredson Bowers, makes the salutary observation: 'that it has proved less delightful to Shakespearean critics only goes to show that, with this kind of play at least, spectators in the theatre are better judges of values than readers in the study.'

Everything corroborates the early tradition that the Queen expressed a desire to see Falstaff in love—she may have been disappointed, like others, from his having been dropped from *Henry V*, after Shakespeare's promise that there would be more of him. The tradition is that the play was rapidly composed for a feast of the Order of the Garter at Windsor—obviously true. It is nearly all in prose, with a number of loose ends; it concludes with a salute to the Order and a personal tribute to the Queen. Familiarity with the Windsor scene is no less obvious, from performances there when the Court was in residence.

Nor need there be any difficulty as to dating, about which there has been so much discussion. The play obviously came after both *Henry IV* and *Henry V*; its most likely occasion being the Garter Feast at Windsor on St George's day 1600, when no new knights were created but the French were in strength for Henri IV's installation by proxy. Shakespeare had been reading Ralegh's *Guiana*, which came out in 1596: it is amusing to note that Falstaff, like most Elizabethans, thought of potatoes (sweet) as aphrodisiacs. Much play is made of Dr Caius's broken English—he is a French physician. Where did Shakespeare acquire that convincing acquaintance with it? It was about this time that he was lodging in Silver Street in the household of the French Montjoies, tire-makers or headdress-makers. The intimate knowledge displayed of 'the ship-tire, the tire-valiant, or any tire of Venetian admittance [fashion]' is rather corroborative. And where did he get the rare word 'oeuillades' from?

In 1598 he played in Ben Jonson's *Everyman in his Humour*. Great play is made of Corporal Nym's addiction to the word 'humour', it comes into every other sentence he utters—until the page settles his hash with 'The humour of it', says he! 'Here's a fellow frights English out of its wits.' Was this a score against Ben?—a good-humoured and friendly exchange. Actually Shakespeare probably took up the suggestion of Ford's jealousy over his wife—which is equally exposed along with Falstaff from the jealous husband in Ben Jonson's play.

What has not been sufficiently appreciated is the importance of Falstaff's knighthood, the class significance which is apparent in the play. For it is the fact that Falstaff is a knight—so much more honorific then—that enables him to get away with so much, even apart from his companionship with the heir to the throne. Here, Mrs Ford confides to Mrs Page, 'if it were not for one trifling respect, I could come to such honour. . . If I would but go to hell for an eternal moment or so, I could be knighted.' Mrs Page advises her not to think of moving out of her class.

In his attempt to seduce Mrs Ford Falstaff wishes her husband dead: 'I'll speak it before the best lord, I would make you my lady.' Respectable middle-class Mrs Ford: 'Alas, I should be a pitiful lady.' Sir John thinks he could make her presentable at Court in a fine semi-circled farthingale. As a knight Sir John has the *entrée* at Court. When he has been tricked by the good *bourgeoises*, Mrs Ford and Mrs Page, and had to be smuggled out of the house as the 'fat woman of Brentford', his fear is that 'if it should come to the ear of the Court. . .they would whip me with their fine wits till I were as crestfallen as a dried pear. I never prospered since I forswore myself at primero'—the card game most in fashion at Court. If it had not been for his 'admirable dexterity' in counterfeiting the old woman, 'the knave constable had set me in the stocks, in the common stocks!' This would be the greatest indignity for a knight: the punishment was reserved for the lower orders. In a lifetime of Elizabethan research l have not come across any knight set in the parish stocks.

And we should notice too that Falstaff's natural speech is upper-class—he is capable of rather grandiloquent Court speech, in fact relapses into it at intervals. All this adds point to his exposure, his public shaming at the hands of the *bons bourgeois* of Windsor—and must have been all the more funny to the courtiers who saw it. As always in the plays we see the theatre in the author's mind, ever present even in incidental references. Falstaff sees his penetration of Ford's house and his first encounter with his wife alone as speaking but 'the prologue of our comedy.' In a letter Anne Page wrote to her lover, young Fenton (a Stratford name at the time), she describes the goings-on at Windsor in

which 'fat Falstaff has a great scene.' He had indeed—marvellously comic.

Fredson Bowers reminds us of the sheer 'delight that
Shakespeare always found in pure eccentricity. . .and
oddity'—and we remember Aubrey's information about
both Shakespeare and Jonson, keeping an eye open for
people's humours and whimsies wherever they went.
This play has indeed 'as striking an array of comic
creations as he ever contrived'—and again there is the
linguistic virtuosity in rendering their speech. Besides
Dr Caius's comic English we have Parson Evans's Welsh
lingo: Shakespeare would have opportunities of picking
up that at Stratford with its close association with
Wales and the cattle trade. Evans murders Marlowe's
famous lines, mixing them up with one from the
Psalms. (Marlowe is never far away from Shakespeare's
mind—and Falstaff can quote a line from Sidney's
Sonnets.) Mistress Quickly is her questionably good
self, as given to malapropisms as ever and still playing
pander to men's desires. Shallow and Slender are
recognisable from their country background in the
Cotswolds; Pistol still speaks his inflated rhodomontade, and we learn that Nym speaks in a drawling,
affected way. Young Master Fenton speaks, as a
gentleman should, in blank verse, which was ex-
traordinarily close to upper class conversational speech.

We cannot but note the jollity of these townspeople's
lives, the fun and frolics; for all the element of carica-
ture, the picture is realistic, the middle-class life of
Stratford was just like that. But the actor knew his
Windsor: we have the Castle ditch or moat, the Petty
Ward and the Park Ward, the way to Frogmore, and
Datchet Mead where Falstaff was tumbled with all the
dirty linen into the Thames. Below in the meadows is
endearing Eton—where sweet Anne Page was married
at length—frowned down upon by the forbidding
ramparts of the Castle, where even then the Queen had

made a gallery and a terrace with pavilion at end.[1]

Hence the tribute to Elizabeth I:

> Search Windsor Castle, elves, within and out,
> Strew good luck, ouphs [fays], on every sacred
> room,
> That it may stand till the perpetual doom,
> In state as wholesome as in state 'tis fit,
> Worthy the owner and the owner it.

He knew the Garter Inn, and the story of the earlier visit of Count Mompelgart—'cozen Garmombles'—and his German entourage who went off without paying their debts. This was later altered to 'cozen—Germans', for Mompelgart, having become Duke of Würtemberg, got his Garter in 1597. A more significant alteration was that of the name Brook, under which Ford disguised himself to ferret out Falstaff's intentions towards his wife. Brook was the family name of Lord Cobham, and Shakespeare had to change the name to Broom as before he had had to change to Falstaff from Sir John Oldcastle, a precursor in the Cobham family. (In this text the original Brook is retained.) He knew the fairy lore of Windsor Park, the haunted Herne's Oak, where Falstaff was finally and publicly shown up.

Indications of contemporary and personal life are fairly full and telling. The popular songs 'Greensleeves' and 'Fortune my foe' are cited. We have bear-baiting frequently enough, but here we find the famous bear Sackerson, that performed at Paris Garden near the Globe theatre. Slender has seen him loose twenty times, yet has 'taken him by the chain'! To deer-hunting, as always, we now add birding and ferreting among the sports the countryman had been so addicted to. Slender, though not a spirited man, had at least fought with a 'warrener', a gamekeeper. And how revealing is the comparison of a great round beard to 'a

---

[1] cf my *Windsor Castle in the History of England.*

glover's paring knife'!—the glover's son would know. The rare word 'fap', meaning drunk, is a West Midlands dialect word again. We hear of Banbury cheese, not far away, and the joke about luces (pikes) in Shallow's coat of arms probably picks up that of the Lucys of Charlecote, brought to mind by the death of Sir Thomas in this year 1600. Schoolmaster-curate Evans, taking William through his Latin accidence, once more attests Shakespeare's familiarity with schoolmastering.

It is evident that a work in which so much play is made with words—where 'fritters of English' are made by both French Dr Caius and Welsh Evans, as well as the frequent malapropisms of Slender and Mrs Quickly, the lingos of Pistol and Nym, in addition to the usual verbal virtuosity—makes the task of presenting it in modern English more difficult than usual. But, by the same token, more necessary than ever. Hence a number of explanatory footnotes have been necessitated; sometimes it has been possible to give an equivalent word simply in brackets; occasionally it has been necessary to reduce the rebarbativeness of the garbled English a little to make it recognisable. Dr Caius's frequent swear word, 'By gar', was disapproved of by the religious Dr Johnson with the severe words, 'there are laws of higher authority than those of criticism.' The form 'By gore' is still not unknown in lower class provincial usage: it stands for 'By God', and so I have left it.

CHARACTERS

SIR JOHN FALSTAFF
FENTON, a young gentleman
SHALLOW, a country justice
SLENDER, cousin to Shallow
FORD ⎱
PAGE ⎰ two townsmen of Windsor
WILLIAM PAGE, a boy, son to Page
SIR HUGH EVANS, a Welsh curate
DOCTOR CAIUS, a French physician
HOST OF THE GARTER INN
BARDOLPH ⎫
PISTOL ⎬ followers of Falstaff
NYM ⎭
ROBIN, page to Falstaff
SIMPLE, servant to Slender
RUGBY, servant to Doctor Caius
MISTRESS FORD
MISTRESS PAGE
ANNE PAGE, her daughter, in love with Fenton
MISTRESS QUICKLY, servant to Doctor Caius
SERVANTS   to Page, Ford, etc.

Act I

SCENE I
Before Page's house.

Enter Justice Shallow, Slender, and Sir Hugh Evans.

SHALLOW   Sir Hugh, persuade me not—I will make a Star-chamber matter of it. If he were twenty Sir John Falstaffs he shall not abuse Robert Shallow, Esquire.

SLENDER   In the county of Gloucester, Justice of Peace, and Coram.[1]

SHALLOW   Ay, cousin Slender, and Custalorum.

SLENDER   Ay, and Ratolorum too; and a gentleman born, Master Parson, who writes himself Armigero, in any bill, warrant, quittance, or obligation—Armigero!

SHALLOW   Ay, that I do, and have done any time these three hundred years.

SLENDER   All his successors [predecessors] gone before him have done it; and all his ancestors [successors] that come after him may. They may give the dozen white luces in their coat.

SHALLOW   It is an old coat.

EVANS   The dozen white louses do become an old coat well. It agrees well, passant; it is a familiar peast to man, and signifies love.

SHALLOW   The luce is the fresh fish, the salt fish—is an old coat.

SLENDER   I may quarter, cousin?

---

[1]Malapropisms: Coram for quorum, i.e., a select number of J.P.s. Custalorum, i.e., Custos Rotulorum, Clerk of the Peace. Armigero, i.e., Esquire.

SHALLOW   You may, by marrying.

EVANS   It is marrying indeed, if he quarters it.

SHALLOW   Not a whit.

EVANS   Yes by our Lady. If he has a quarter of your coat, there are but three skirts for yourself, in my simple conjectures. But that is all one. If Sir John Falstaff has committed disparagements unto you, I am of the Church, and will be glad to do my benevolence to make atonements and compromises between you.

SHALLOW   The Council shall hear it. It is a riot.

EVANS   It is not meet the Council hear a riot. There is no fear of Got in a riot. The Council, look you, shall desire to hear the fear of Got, and not to hear a riot. Take your vizaments [advisements] in that.

SHALLOW   Ha! On my life, if I were young again, the sword should end it.

EVANS   It is better that friends is the sword, and end it. And there is also another device in my brain, which peradventure brings goot discretions with it. There is Anne Page, which is daughter to Master George Page, which is pretty virginity.

SLENDER   Mistress Anne Page? She has brown hair, and speaks small like a woman?

EVANS   It is that very person for all the world, as just as you will desire. And seven hundred pounds of money, and gold and silver, is her grandsire, upon his death's-bed—Got deliver to a joyful resurrection—give, when she is able to overtake seventeen years old. It were a goot motion if we leave our pribbles and prabbles [quibbles and babbles] and desire a marriage between Master Abraham and Mistress Anne Page.

SHALLOW   Did her grandsire leave her seven hundred pound?

EVANS   Ay, and her father is to make her a better penny.

SHALLOW   I know the young gentlewoman. She has good gifts.

EVANS   Seven hundred pounds and possibilities is goot
gifts.

SHALLOW   Well, let us see honest Master Page. Is
Falstaff there?

EVANS   Shall I tell you a lie? I do despise a liar as I do
despise one that is false, or as I despise one that is not
true. The knight Sir John is there; and, I beseech you,
be ruled by your well-willers. I will beat the door for
Master Page. [Knocks.] What, ho! Got bless your
house here.

PAGE   [within] Who's there?

EVANS   Here is Got's blessing, and your friend, and
Justice Shallow; and here young Master Slender, that
peradventure shall tell you another tale, if matters
grow to your liking.

Enter Master Page.

PAGE   I am glad to see your worships well. I thank you
for my venison, Master Shallow.

SHALLOW   Master Page, I am glad to see you. Much good
do it your heart! I wished your venison better—it was
ill killed. How does good Mistress Page? And I thank
you always with my heart, la; with my heart.

PAGE   Sir, I thank you.

SHALLOW   Sir, I thank you; by yea and no, I do.

PAGE   I am glad to see you, good Master Slender.

SLENDER   How does your fallow greyhound, sir? I heard
say he was outrun on Cotsall [Cotswolds].

PAGE   It could not be judged, sir.

SLENDER   You will not confess, you will not confess.

SHALLOW   That he will not—it is your fault, it is your
fault.—It is a good dog.

PAGE   A cur, sir.

SHALLOW   Sir, he is a good dog, and a fair dog. Can there
be more said? He is good and fair. Is Sir John Falstaff
here?

PAGE   Sir, he is within. And I would I could do a good office between you.

EVANS   It is spoken as a Christian ought to speak.

SHALLOW   He has wronged me, Master Page.

PAGE   Sir, he does in some sort confess it.

SHALLOW   If it is confessed, it is not redressed. Is not that so, Master Page? He has wronged me; indeed, he has. At a word, he has, believe me. Robert Shallow, Esquire, says he is wronged.

PAGE   Here comes Sir John.

Enter Falstaff, Bardolph, Nym, and Pistol.

FALSTAFF   Now, Master Shallow, you will complain of me to the King?

SHALLOW   Knight, you have beaten my men, killed my deer, and broken open my lodge.

FALSTAFF   But not kissed your keeper's daughter?

SHALLOW   Tut, a pin! This shall be answered.

FALSTAFF   I will answer it straight—I have done all this. That is now answered.

SHALLOW   The Council shall know this.

FALSTAFF   It were better for you if it were known in counsel—you'll be laughed at.

EVANS   Pauca verba, Sir John; goot worts. [Few words]

FALSTAFF   Good worts? good cabbage! Slender, I broke your head. What matter have you against me?

SLENDER   Indeed, sir, I have matter in my head against you, and against your cony-catching [cheating] rascals, Bardolph, Nym, and Pistol.

BARDOLPH   You Banbury cheese!

SLENDER   Ay, it is no matter.

PISTOL   How now, Mephistophilus!

SLENDER   Ay, it is no matter.

NYM   Slice, l say! Pauca, pauca. [Shut up] Slice! that's my humor.

SLENDER   Where's Simple, my man? Can you tell, cousin?

EVANS   Peace, I pray you. Now let us understand. There
are three umpires in this matter, as I understand;
that is—Master Page, videlicet [namely] Master Page;
and there is myself, videlicet, myself; and the three
party is, lastly and finally, my Host of the Garter.

PAGE   We three to hear it and end it between them.

EVANS   Very goot. I will make a brief of it in my
notebook, and we will afterwards work upon the
cause with as great discreetly as we can.

FALSTAFF   Pistol.

PISTOL   He hears with ears.

EVANS   The devil and his dam! What phrase is this, 'He
hears with ear'? Why, it is affectations.

FALSTAFF   Pistol, did you pick Master Slender's purse?

SLENDER   Ay, by these gloves, did he—or I would I
might never come in my own great chamber again
else—of seven groats in mill-sixpences, and two
Edward shovel-boards, [shillings] that cost me two
shilling and two pence apiece of Ned Miller, by these
gloves.

FALSTAFF   Is this true, Pistol?

EVANS   No, it is false, if it is a pick-purse.

PISTOL   Ha, you mountain-foreigner! Sir John and
master mine,
I combat challenge of this latten bilbo. [brass sword]
Word of denial in your labras [lips] here!
Word of denial! Froth and scum, you lie.

SLENDER   By these gloves, then it was he.

NYM   Be advised, sir, and pass good humors. I will say
'marry trap'[2] with you, if you run the constable's
humor on me. That is the very note of it.

SLENDER   By this hat, then he in the red face had it; for
though I cannot remember what I did when you
made me drunk, yet I am not altogether an ass.

FALSTAFF   What say you, Scarlet and John?[3]

---

[2] A children's game.
[3] Robin Hood's fellows.

BARDOLPH   Why, sir, for my part, I say the gentleman
  had drunk himself out of his five sentences.
EVANS   It is his 'five senses.' Fie, what the ignorance is.
BARDOLPH   And being fap,[4] sir, was, as they say, cash-
  iered; and so conclusions passed the careers.
SLENDER   Ay, you spoke in Latin then too. But 'tis no
  matter. I'll never be drunk while I live again, but in
  honest, civil, godly company, for this trick. If I am
  drunk, I'll be drunk with those that have the fear of
  God, and not with drunken knaves.
EVANS   So Got judge me, that is a virtuous mind.
FALSTAFF   You hear all these matters denied, gentlemen. You hear it.

  *Enter Anne Page with wine, Mistress Ford and
  Mistress Page.*

PAGE   Nay, daughter, carry the wine in—we'll drink
  within.   *Exit Anne Page.*
SLENDER   O heaven, this is Mistress Anne Page.
PAGE   How now, Mistress Ford.
FALSTAFF   Mistress Ford, by my word, you are very well
  met. By your leave, good mistress.   [*Kisses her.*]
PAGE   Wife, bid these gentlemen welcome. Come, we
  have a hot venison pasty to dinner. Come,
  gentlemen, I hope we shall drink down all unkind-
  ness.
       [*Exeunt all but Shallow, Slender, and Evans.*]
SLENDER   I had rather than forty shillings I had my
  Book of Songs and Sonnets here.[5]

  Enter Simple.

---

[4]Drunk—West Midlands dialect.
[5]Tottel's Miscellany, the most popular anthology.

How now, Simple; where have you been? I must wait on myself, must I? You have not the Book of Riddles about you, have you?

SIMPLE Book of Riddles? Why did you not lend it to Alice Shortcake upon Allhallowmas last, a fortnight before Michaelmas?[6]

SHALLOW Come coz [cousin], come, coz; we stay for you. A word with you, coz. Marry, this, coz—there is as it were a tender, a kind of tender, made afar off by Sir Hugh here. Do you understand me?

SLENDER Ay, sir, you shall find me reasonable. If it is so, I shall do that that is reason.

SHALLOW Nay, but understand me.

SLENDER So I do, sir.

EVANS Give ear to his motions. Master Slender, I will description [describe] the matter to you, if you are capacity [capable] of it.

SLENDER Nay, I will do as my cousin Shallow says—I pray you pardon me. He's a Justice of Peace in his county, simple though I stand here.

EVANS But that is not the question. The question is concerning your marriage.

SHALLOW Ay, there's the point, sir.

EVANS Indeed, is it, the very point of it—to Mistress Anne Page.

SLENDER Why, if it is so, I will marry her upon any reasonable demands.

EVANS But can you affection [affect] the woman? Let us command to know that of your mouth, or of your lips—for divers philosophers hold that the lips are parcel of the mouth. Therefore, precisely, can you carry your goot will to the maid?

SHALLOW Cousin Abraham Slender, can you love her?

SLENDER I hope, sir, I will do as it shall become one that would do reason.

EVANS Nay, Got's lords and his ladies! You must speak

---

[6]All Saints' day, 1 November; Michaelmas, 25 September.

positable, [positively], if you can carry your desires towards her.

SHALLOW That you must. Will you, upon good dowry, marry her?

SLENDER I will do a greater thing than that upon your request, cousin, in any reason.

SHALLOW Nay, conceive [understand] me, conceive me, sweet coz—what I do is to pleasure you, coz. Can you love the maid?

SLENDER I will marry her, sir, at your request. But if there is no great love in the beginning, yet heaven may decrease [increase], it upon better acquaintance when we are married and have more occasion to know one another. I hope upon familiarity will grow more contempt.[7] But if you say, 'Marry her,' I will marry her; that I am freely dissolved [resolved,] and dissolutely.

EVANS It is a very discretion [discreet] answer, save the fault is in the wort 'dissolutely': the wort is, according to our meaning, 'resolutely.' His meaning is goot.

SHALLOW Ay, I think my cousin meant well.

SLENDER Ay, or else I would I might be hanged, la.

Enter Anne Page.

SHALLOW Here comes fair Mistress Anne. Would I were young for your sake, Mistress Anne.

ANNE The dinner is on the table. My father desires your worships' company.

SHALLOW I will wait on him, fair Mistress Anne.

EVANS God's blessed will! I will not be absent at the grace.   *[Exeunt Shallow and Evans.]*

ANNE Will it please your worship to come in, sir?

SLENDER No, I thank you, indeed, heartily—I am very well.

ANNE The dinner attends you, sir.

---

[7]The popular saying, 'Familiarity breeds contempt.'

SLENDER   I am not a-hungry, I thank you all the same.
Go, fellow, for all you are my man, go wait upon my
cousin Shallow. [*Exit Simple.*] A Justice of Peace
sometimes may be beholding to his friend for a man.
I keep but three men and a boy yet, till my mother is
dead. But what though? Yet I live like a poor
gentleman born.

ANNE   I may not go in without your worship; they will
not sit till you come.

SLENDER   In faith, I'll eat nothing. I thank you as much
as though I did.

ANNE   I pray you, sir, walk in.

SLENDER   I had rather walk here, I thank you. I bruised
my shin the other day with playing at sword and
dagger with a master of fence—three bouts for a dish
of stewed prunes.[8] And, by my word, I cannot abide
the smell of hot meat since. Why do your dogs bark
so? Are there bears in the town?

ANNE   I think there are, sir; I heard them talked of.

SLENDER   I love the sport well, but I shall as soon
quarrel at it as any man in England. You are afraid if
you see the bear loose, are you not?

ANNE   Ay, indeed, sir.

SLENDER   That's meat and drink to me, now. I have
seen Sackerson loose twenty times, and have taken
him by the chain.[9] But, I warrant you, the women
have so cried and shrieked at it, that it passed. But
women, indeed, cannot abide them; they are very ill-
looking rough things.

Enter Page.

PAGE   Come, gentle Master Slender, come. We stay for
you.

---

[8]Bawdy suggestion: prostitutes were supposed to fancy prunes.
[9]A famous bear.

SLENDER   I'll eat nothing, I thank you, sir.

PAGE   By cock and pie,[10] you shall not choose, sir!
Come, come.

SLENDER   Nay, pray you lead the way.

PAGE   Come on, sir.

SLENDER   Mistress Anne, yourself shall go first.

ANNE   Not I, sir; pray you keep on.

SLENDER   Truly, I will not go first; truly, la. I will not do
you that wrong.

ANNE   I pray you, sir.

SLENDER   I'll rather be unmannerly than troublesome.
You do yourself wrong, indeed, la.   *Exeunt.*

SCENE II
The same.

Enter Evans and Simple.

EVANS   Go your ways, and ask of Doctor Caius'[11] house,
which is the way; and there dwells one Mistress
Quickly, who is in the manner of his nurse, or his dry
nurse, or his cook, or his laundry, his washer, and his
wringer.

SIMPLE   Well, sir.

EVANS   Nay, it is better yet. Give her this letter, for it is
a woman that altogether's acquainted with Mistress
Anne Page; and the letter is to desire and require her
to solicit your master's desires to Mistress Anne
Page. I pray you be gone. I will make an end of my
dinner—there's pipins and seese [cheese] to come.

---

[10]By God and religion.

[11]Pronounced Keys.

SCENE III
The Garter Inn.

Enter Falstaff, Host, Bardolph, Nym, Pistol, and Robin.

FALSTAFF   My Host of the Garter.

HOST   What says my bully boy? Speak scholarly and wisely.

FALSTAFF   Truly, my Host, I must turn away some of my followers.

HOST   Discard, bully Hercules, cashier. Let them be off; trot, trot.

FALSTAFF   I spend ten pounds a week.

HOST   You are an emperor—Caesar, Keisar, and Pheazar. I will entertain Bardolph: he shall draw, he shall tap. Said I well, bully Hector?

FALSTAFF   Do so, good my Host.

HOST   I have spoken; let him follow. *[to Bardolph]* Let me see you froth and lime.[12] I am at a work; follow.
[Exit]

FALSTAFF   Bardolph, follow him. A tapster is a good trade. An old cloak makes a new jerkin; a withered servingman, a fresh tapster. Go, adieu.

BARDOLPH   It is a life that I have desired. I will thrive.

PISTOL   O base Hungarian wight! Will you the spigot wield?   *[Exit Bardolph.]*

NYM   He was gotten in drink. Is not the humor good?

FALSTAFF   I am glad I am so quit of this tinderbox. His thefts were too open. His filching was like an unskilful singer: he kept not time.

NYM   The good humor is to steal at a minute's rest.

PISTOL   'Convey,' the wise it call. 'Steal?' foh, a fico [fig] for the phrase!

FALSTAFF   Well, sirs. I am almost out at heels.

PISTOL   Why then, let chilblains ensue.

---

[12]Give short measure and adulterate the drink.

FALSTAFF There is no remedy—I must cheat, I must
shift.

PISTOL Young ravens must have food.

FALSTAFF Which of you know Ford of this town?

PISTOL I ken the wight. He is of substance good.

FALSTAFF My honest lads, I will tell you what I am
about.

PISTOL Two yards, and more.

FALSTAFF No quips now, Pistol. Indeed, I am in the
waist two yards about—but I am now about no
waste; I am about thrift. Briefly, I do mean to make
love to Ford's wife. I spy entertainment in her: she
discourses, she carves, she gives the leer of invita-
tion. I can construe the action of her familiar style;
and the hardest voice of her behavior, to be Englished
rightly, is, 'I am Sir John Falstaff's.'

PISTOL He has studied her well, and translated her
well, out of honesty into English.

NYM The anchor is deep. Will that humor pass?

FALSTAFF Now, the report goes she has all the rule of
her husband's purse. He has a legion of angels. [gold
coins.]

PISTOL As many devils entertain—and 'To her, boy,'
say I.

NYM The humor rises—it is good. Humor me the
angels.

FALSTAFF I have written here a letter to her; and here
another to Page's wife, who even now gave me good
eyes too, examined my parts with most judicious
oeillades. [looks] Sometimes the beam of her view
gilded my foot, sometimes my portly belly.

PISTOL [aside] Then did the sun on dunghill shine.

NYM [aside] I thank you for that humor.

FALSTAFF O, she did so course over my exteriors with
such a greedy intention that the appetite of her eye
did seem to scorch me up like a burning-glass. Here's
another letter to her. She bears the purse too; she is a

region in Guiana, all gold and bounty. I will be escheator[13] to them both, and they shall be exchequers to me. They shall be my East and West Indies, and I will trade to them both. *[to Pistol]* Go, bear you this letter to Mistress Page; *[to Nym]* and you this to Mistress Ford. We will thrive, lads, we will thrive.

PISTOL Shall I Sir Pandarus of Troy become,
And by my side wear steel? Then Lucifer take all!

NYM I will run no base humor. Here, take the humor-letter. I will keep the bearing of reputation.

FALSTAFF *[to Robin]* Hold, boy, bear you these letters tightly:
Sail like my pinnace to these golden shores.
[Exit Robin.]
Rogues, hence, away! Vanish like hailstones, go;
Trudge, plod away on the hoof; seek shelter, be off!
Falstaff will learn the humor of the age:
French thrift,[14] you rogues—myself and skirted page.
[Exit.]

PISTOL Let vultures grip your guts! for gourd and fullam[15] holds,
And high and low beguile the rich and poor.
Sixpence I'll have in pouch when you shall lack,
Base Phrygian Turk!

NYM I have operations which are humors of revenge.

PISTOL Will you revenge?

NYM By heaven and its star!

PISTOL With wit or steel?

NYM With both the humors, I.
I will discuss the humor of this love to Page.

PISTOL And I to Ford shall eke [also] unfold
How Falstaff, varlet vile,
His dove will prove, his gold will hold,

---

[13]Tax official, with a pun on cheating.
[14]i.e., keep only one attendant.
[15]False dice.

And his soft couch defile.

NYM   My humor shall not cool. I will incense Page to
deal with poison. I will possess him with yellowness,
[jealousy], for the revolt of mine is dangerous. That is
my true humor.

PISTOL   You are the Mars of malcontents. I second you;
troop on.   *Exeunt.*

SCENE IV
Doctor Caius' house.

Enter Mistress Quickly, Simple, and John Rugby.

QUICKLY   What, John Rugby. I pray you, go to the
casement and see if you can see my master, Master
Doctor Caius, coming. If he does in faith, and find
anybody in the house, here will be an old abusing of
God's patience and the King's English.

RUGBY   I'll go watch.

QUICKLY   Go, and we'll have a night-cap for it soon at
night, in faith, at the latter end of a sea-coal fire. *[Exit
Rugby.]* An honest, willing, kind fellow, as ever
servant shall come in house; and, I warrant you, no
telltale, and no mischiefmaker. His worst fault is
that he is given to prayer; he is something peevish
that way, but nobody but has his fault. But let that
pass. Peter Simple you say your name is?

SIMPLE   Ay, for fault of a better.

QUICKLY   And Master Slender's your master?

SIMPLE   Ay, please.

QUICKLY   Does he not wear a great round beard like a
glover's paring knife?

SIMPLE   No, please. He has but a little whey face, with a
little yellow beard—a Cain-colored beard.

QUICKLY   A softly-spirited man, is he not?

SIMPLE   Ay, sure. But he is as tall a man of his hands as

any is between this and his head: he has fought with
a gamekeeper.

QUICKLY   How say you?—O! I should remember him.
Does he not hold up his head, as it were, and strut in
his gait?

SIMPLE   Yes, indeed does he.

QUICKLY   Well, heaven send Anne Page no worse
fortune. Tell Master Parson Evans I will do what I can
for your master. Anne is a good girl, and I wish—

Enter Rugby.

RUGBY   Out, alas, here comes my master!

QUICKLY   We shall all be scolded. Run in here, good
young man; go into this closet. He will not stay long.
[*Shuts Simple in the closet.*] What, John Rugby. John,
what, John, I say! Go, John, go inquire for my master.
I fear he is not well, that he comes not home. [*Exit
Rugby.*]

[*Sings.*] 'And down, down, adown-a,' etc.

Enter Doctor Caius.

CAIUS   Vat is you sing? I do not like dese games. Pray
you go and vetch me in my closet un boitier vert—a
box, a green-a box. Do hear vat I speak? A green-a
box.

QUICKLY   Ay, sure, I'll fetch it you. [*aside*] I am glad he
went in himself. If he had found the young man, he
would have been horn-mad.

CAIUS   Fe, fe, fe, fe! ma foi, il fait fort chaud. Je m'en vais
à la cour—la grande affaire.[16]

QUICKLY   Is it this, sir?

---

[16]Faith, it is very warm. I am going to Court on important
business.

CAIUS   Oui; mette-le au mon pocket; dépêche,[17] quickly.—Vere is dat knave Rugby?

QUICKLY   What, John Rugby? John!

Enter Rugby.

RUGBY   Here, sir.

CAIUS   You are John Rugby, and you are Jack Rugby.
Come, take-a your rapier and come after my heel to
de Court.

RUGBY   'Tis ready, sir, here in the porch.

CAIUS   By my word, I tarry too long. God's me! Qu'ai
j'oublié?[18] Dere is some simples in my closet dat I vill
not vor de vorld I shall leave behind.

QUICKLY   *[aside]* Ay me, he'll find the young man there,
and be mad.

CAIUS   O diable! diable![19] Vat is in my closet?—
Villainy! Larron![20] *[Pulls Simple out.]* Rugby, my
rapier!

QUICKLY   Good master, be content.

CAIUS   Verefore shall I be content-a?

QUICKLY   The young man is an honest man.

CAIUS   Vat shall de honest man do in my closet? Dere is
no honest man dat shall come in my closet.

QUICKLY   I beseech you, be not so phlegmatic.[21] Hear
the truth of it: he came of an errand to me from
Parson Hugh.

CAIUS   Vell?

SIMPLE   Ay, sure, to desire her to—

QUICKLY   Peace, I pray you.

CAIUS   Peace-a your tongue. Speak-a your tale.

SIMPLE   To desire this honest gentlewoman, your maid,

---

[17]Yes, put it in my pocket. Hurry.
[18]What have I forgotten?
[19]Devil
[20]Thief
[21]Full of phlegm, she means.

to speak a good word to Mistress Anne Page for my
master in the way of marriage.

QUICKLY   This is all, indeed, la; but I'll never put my
finger in the fire, and need not.

CAIUS   Sir Hugh send-a you? Rugby, baille [fetch] me
some paper. Tarry you a little-a while.   [Writes.]

QUICKLY   [aside to Simple] I am glad he is so quiet: if
he had been thoroughly moved, you should have heard
him so loud, and so melancholy [surly]. But notwithstanding, man, I'll do your master what good I can;
and the very yea and the no is, the French doctor, my
master—I may call him my master, look you, for I
keep his house; and I wash, wring, brew, bake, scour,
dress meat and drink, make the beds, and do all
myself—

SIMPLE   [aside to Quickly] 'Tis a great charge to come
under one body's hand.

QUICKLY   [aside to Simple] Are you aware of that? You
shall find it a great charge. And to be up early and
down late; but notwithstanding—to tell you in your
ear—I would have no words of it—my master himself
is in love with Mistress Anne Page. But notwithstanding that, I know Anne's mind. That's neither
here nor there.

CAIUS   You jackanape, give-a dis letter to Sir Hugh. By
God, it is a shallenge: I vill cut his throat in de Park;
and I vill teach a survy jackanape priest to meddle or
make. You may be gone; it is not good you tarry
here.—By God, I vill cut all his two stones; by God,
he shall not have a stone to throw at his dog.

                                            [Exit Simple.]

QUICKLY   Alas, he speaks but for his friend.

CAIUS   It is no matter-a vor dat.—Do not you tell-a me
dat I shall have Anne Page for myself? By God, I vill
kill de Jack priest; and I have appointed my Host of de
Jarteer to measure our weapon. By God, I vill myself
have Anne Page.

QUICKLY   Sir, the maid loves you, and all shall be well.
We must give folks leave to prate—what the hell!

CAIUS   Rugby, come to the Court vit me. By God, if I
have not Anne Page, I shall turn your head out of my
door. Follow my heels, Rugby.

[Exeunt Caius and Rugby.]

QUICKLY   You shall have—Anne-fool's-head of your own.
No, I know Anne's mind for that. Never a woman in
Windsor knows more of Anne's mind than I do, nor
can do more than I do with her, I thank heaven.

FENTON   *[within]* Who's within there, ho?

QUICKLY   Who's there, I trust? Come near the house, I
pray you.

FENTON   How now, good woman.—How do you?

QUICKLY   The better that it pleases your good worship
to ask.

FENTON   What news? How does pretty Mistress Anne?

QUICKLY   In truth, sir, and she is pretty, and honest,
and gentle; and one that is your friend, I can tell you
that by the way, I praise heaven for it.

FENTON   Shall I do any good, think you? Shall I not lose
my suit?

QUICKLY   Faith, sir, all is in his hands above. But
notwithstanding, Master Fenton, I'll be sworn on a
book she loves you. Has not your worship a wart
above your eye?

FENTON   Yes, indeed have I. What of that?

QUICKLY   Well, thereby hangs a tale. Good faith, it is
such another Nan; but, I detest, an honest maid as
ever broke bread. We had an hour's talk of that wart. I
shall never laugh but in that maid's company. But,
indeed, she is given too much to allicholy
[melancholy] and musing. But for you—well go to.

FENTON   Well, I shall see her to-day. Hold, there's
money for you; let me have your voice in my behalf.
If you see her before me, commend me.—

QUICKLY   Will I? In faith, that we will. And I will tell
your worship more of the wart the next time we have

confidence, [conference] and of other wooers.
FENTON   Well, farewell. I am in great haste now.
QUICKLY   Farewell to your worship. *[Exit Fenton.]*
Truly, an honest gentleman. But Anne loves him not,
for I know Anne's mind as well as another does. Out
upon it, what have I forgot?   *Exit.*

Act II

SCENE I
Before Page's house.

Enter Mistress Page with a letter.

MRS. PAGE What, have I escaped love letters in the holiday time of my beauty, and am I now a subject for them? Let me see.   *[Reads.]*
'Ask me no reason why I love you; for though Love uses Reason for his precisian, he admits him not for his counsellor. You are not young, no more am I. Go to then, there is sympathy. You are merry, so am I. Ha, ha! then there is more sympathy. You love sack, and so do I. Would you desire better sympathy? Let it suffice you, Mistress Page—at the least, if the love of soldier can suffice—that I love you. I will not say, pity me, it is not a soldier-like phrase, but I say, love me. By me,
> Your own true knight,
> By day or night,
> Or any kind of light,
> With all his might
> For you to fight,
>   JOHN FALSTAFF.'
What a Herod of Jewry is this! O wicked, wicked world. One that is well-nigh worn to pieces with age to show himself a young gallant. What an unweighed behavior has this Flemish drunkard picked—with the devil's name!—out of my conversation that he dares in this manner assay me? Why, he has not been thrice in my company. What should I say to him? I was then frugal of my mirth—heaven forgive me!

Why, I'll exhibit a bill in the parliament for the putting down of men. How shall I be revenged on him?
for revenged I will be, as sure as his guts are made of
puddings.

Enter Mistress Ford.

MRS. FORD Mistress Page—trust me, I was going to
your house.
MRS. PAGE And, trust me, I was coming to you. You
look very ill.
MRS. FORD Nay, I'll never believe that. I have some-
thing to show to the contrary.
MRS. PAGE Faith, but you do, in my mind.
MRS. FORD Well, I do then; yet I say I could show you to
the contrary. O Mistress Page, give me some counsel.
MRS. PAGE What is the matter, woman?
MRS. FORD O woman, if it were not for one trifling
respect, I could come to such honor.
MRS. PAGE Hang the trifle, woman; take the honor.
What is it?—dispense with trifles—what is it?
MRS. FORD If I would but go to hell for an eternal
moment or so, I could be knighted.
MRS. PAGE What you lie. Sir Alice Ford? These knights
will hack; and so you should not alter the article of
your class.
MRS. FORD We burn daylight. Here, read, read: perceive
how I might be knighted. I shall think the worse of
fat men as long as I have an eye to make difference of
men's liking. And yet he would not swear; praised
women's modesty; and gave such orderly and well-
behaved reproof to all uncomeliness that I would
have sworn his disposition would have gone to the
truth of his words. But they do no more adhere and
keep place together than the Hundredth Psalm to the
tune of 'Greensleeves.' What tempest, I wonder,
threw this whale, with so many tuns of oil in his

belly, ashore at Windsor? How shall I be revenged on
him? I think the best way were to entertain him with
hope till the wicked fire of lust has melted him in his
own grease. Did you ever hear the like?

MRS. PAGE   Letter for letter, but that the name of Page
and Ford differs. To your great comfort in this
mystery of ill opinions, here's the twin brother of
your letter. But let yours inherit first, for I protest
mine never shall. I warrant he has a thousand of
these letters, written with blank space for different
names—sure, more—and these are of the second edition. He will print them, out of doubt; for he cares
not what he puts into the press, when he would put
us two. I had rather be a giantess and lie under Mount
Pelion. Well, I will find you twenty lascivious turtles
ere one chaste man.

MRS. FORD   Why, this is the very same: the very hand,
the very words. What does he think of us?

MRS. PAGE   Nay, I know not. It makes me almost ready
to wrangle with my own honesty. I'll entertain
myself like one that I am not acquainted with; for
sure, unless he knows some strain in me that I know
not myself, he would never have boarded me in this
fury.

MRS. FORD   Boarding call you it? I'll be sure to keep him
above deck.

MRS. PAGE   So will I—if he comes under my hatches, I'll
never to sea again. Let's be revenged on him. Let's
appoint him a meeting, give him a show of comfort in
his suit, and lead him on with a fine-baited delay till
he has pawned his horses to my Host of the Garter.

MRS. FORD   Nay, I will consent to act any villainy
against him that may not sully the chariness of our
honesty. O that my husband saw this letter! It would
give eternal food to his jealousy.

MRS. PAGE   Why, look where he comes, and my
goodman too. He's as far from jealousy as I am from

giving him cause; and that, I hope, is an un-
measurable distance.

MRS. FORD   You are the happier woman.

MRS. PAGE   Let us consult together against this greasy
knight. Come hither.   *[They retire.]*

*Enter Master Page, with Nym, and Master Ford,
with Pistol.*

FORD   Well, I hope it is not so.

PISTOL   Hope is a curtal dog in some affairs.
Sir John affects your wife.

FORD   Why, sir, my wife is not young.

PISTOL   He woos both high and low, both rich and poor,
Both young and old, one with another, Ford.
He loves the gallimaufry.¹ Ford, perpend.

FORD   Love my wife?

PISTOL   With liver burning hot. Prevent, or go you, Like
Sir Actaeon he with Ringwood at your heels.²
O, odious is the name!

FORD   What name, sir?

PISTOL   The horn, I say. Farewell.
Take heed, have open eye, for thieves do foot by night.
Take heed, ere summer comes or cuckoo birds do
sing.
Away, Sir Corporal Nym!
Believe it, Page; he speaks sense.   *[Exit.]*

FORD   *[aside]* I will be patient; I will find out this.

NYM   *[to Page]* And this is true; I like not the humor of
lying. He has wronged me in some humors. I should
have borne the humored letter to her, but I have
sword and it shall bite upon my necessity. He loves
your wife—there's the short and the long. My name
is Corporal Nym; I speak, and I affirm it is true. My
name is Nym, and Falstaff loves your wife. Adieu. I

---

¹The whole mixed-up lot.
²Actaeon hunted to death by Diana's hounds.

love not the humor of bread and cheese—and there's
the humor of it. Adieu.   *[Exit.]*
PAGE   'The humor of it,' says he! Here's a fellow frights
English out of its wits.
FORD   *[aside]* I will seek out Falstaff.
PAGE   *[aside]* I never heard such a drawling, affected
rogue.
FORD   *[aside]* If I do find it—well.
PAGE   *[aside]* I will not believe such a Cathaian,[3]
though the priest of the town commended him for a
true man.
FORD   *[aside]* It was a good sensible fellow—well.

    Mrs. Page and Mrs. Ford come forward.

PAGE   How now, Meg.
MRS. PAGE   Whither go you, George? Hark you.
                                              [Whispers.]
MRS. FORD   How now, sweet Frank. Why are you melan-
choly?
FORD   I melancholy? I am not melancholy. Get you
home, go.
MRS. FORD   Faith, you have some crotchets in your head
now. Will you go, Mistress Page?
MRS. PAGE   Have with you. You'll come to dinner,
George?

    Enter Mistress Quickly.

[Aside to Mrs. Ford] Look who comes yonder. She
shall be our messenger to this paltry knight.
MRS. FORD   *[aside to Mrs. Page]* Trust me, I thought on
her: she will fit it.
MRS. PAGE   You are come to see my daughter Anne?
QUICKLY   Ay, indeed: and I pray, how does good
Mistress Anne?

---

[3]Sharper, from Cathay.

MRS. PAGE   Go in with us and see. We have an hour's
talk with you.

[Exeunt Mistress Page, Mistress Ford,
and Mistress Quickly.]

PAGE   How now, Master Ford.

FORD   You heard what this knave told me, did you not?

PAGE   Yes, and you heard what the other told me?

FORD   Do you think there is truth in them?

PAGE   Hang them, slaves! I do not think the knight
would offer it. But these that acuse him in his intent
towards our wives are a pair of his discarded
men—very rogues, now they are out of service.

FORD   Were they his men?

PAGE   Indeed were they.

FORD   I like it never the better for that. Does he lie at
the Garter?

PAGE   Ay, indeed does he. If he should intend this
voyage toward my wife, I would turn her loose to
him; and what he gets more of her than sharp words,
let it lie on my head.

FORD   I do not misdoubt my wife, but I would be loth
to turn them together. A man may be too confident. I
would have nothing lie on my head. I cannot be thus
satisfied.

Enter Host.

PAGE   Look, where my ranting Host of the Garter
comes. There is either liquor in his pate or money in
his purse when he looks so merrily. How now, my
Host.

HOST   How now, bully boy, you are a gentleman.
Cavaliero Justice, I say!

Enter Shallow.

SHALLOW   I follow, my Host, I follow. Good even and

twenty, good Master Page. Master Page, will you go
with us? We have sport in hand.

HOST   Tell him, Cavaliero Justice: tell him, bully boy.

SHALLOW   Sir, there is a fray to be fought between Sir
Hugh the Welsh priest and Caius the French doctor.

FORD   Good my Host of the Garter, a word with you.

HOST   What say you, my bully boy? *[They go aside.]*

SHALLOW   *[to Page]* Will you go with us to behold it?
My merry Host has had the measuring of their
weapons and, I think, has appointed them contrary
places: for, believe me, I hear the Parson is no jester.
Hark, I will tell you what our sport shall be.

                                        [They go aside.]

HOST   Have you no suit against my knight, my Guest
Cavaliero?

FORD   None, I protest. But I'll give you a pottle of hot
sack to give me recourse to him and tell him my
name is Brook—only for a jest.

HOST   My hand, bully. You shall have egress and
regress—said I well?—and your name shall be Brook.
It is a merry knight. Will you go, mynheers?

SHALLOW   Have with you, my Host.

PAGE   I have heard the Frenchman has good skill in his
rapier.

SHALLOW   Tut, sir, I could have told you more. In these
times you stand on distance, your passes, thrusts, and
I know not what. It is the heart, Master Page; 'tis
here, 'tis here. I have seen the time with my long
sword I would have made four tall fellows skip like
rats.

HOST   Here, boys, here, here! Shall we wag?

PAGE   Have with you. I had rather hear them scold than
fight.   *Exeunt Host, Shallow, and Page.*

FORD   Though Page is a secure fool and stands so firmly
on his wife's frailty, yet I cannot put off my opinion
so easily. She was in his company at Page's house,
and what they made there, I know not. Well, I will

look further into it; and I have a disguise to sound
Falstaff. If I find her honest, I lose not my labor. If she
is otherwise, it is labor well bestowed.   *[Exit.]*

SCENE II
The Garter Inn.

Enter Falstaff and Pistol.

FALSTAFF   I will not lend you a penny.

PISTOL   Why, then the world's my oyster,
Which I with sword will open.
I will retort the sum in equipage [equipment].

FALSTAFF   Not a penny.
I have been content, sir, you should lay my
countenance to pawn. I have grated upon my good
friends for three reprieves for you and your coach-
fellow Nym, or else you had looked through the
grate, like a pair of baboons. I am damned in hell for
swearing to gentlemen my friends you were good
soldiers and tall fellows. And when Mistress Bridget
lost the handle of her fan, I took it upon my honor
you had it not.

PISTOL   Did you not share? Had you not fifteen pence?

FALSTAFF   Reason, you rogue, reason: think you, I'll
endanger my soul gratis? At a word, hang no more
about me—I am no gibbet for you. Go! a short knife
and a throng!—to your manor of Pickt-hatch, go.
You'll not bear a letter for me, you rogue? You stand
upon your honor! Why, you unconfinable baseness,
it is as much as I can do to keep the terms of my
honor precise. I, I, I myself sometimes, leaving the
fear of God on the left hand and hiding my honor in
my necessity, am fain to shuffle, to hedge, and to
lurch. And yet you, rogue, will ensconce your rags,
your cat-a-mountain looks, your alehouse phrases,

and your bull-baiting oaths, under the shelter of your
honor! You will not do it, you!

PISTOL   I do relent. What would you more of man?

Enter Robin.

ROBIN   Sir, here's a woman would speak with you.

FALSTAFF   Let her approach.

Enter Mistress Quickly.

QUICKLY   Give your worship good morrow.

FALSTAFF   Good morrow, goodwife.

QUICKLY   Not so, if it please your worship.

FALSTAFF   Good maid then.

QUICKLY   I'll be sworn, as my mother was, the first hour
I was born.

FALSTAFF   I do believe the swearer. What with me?

QUICKLY   Shall I vouchsafe your worship a word or two?

FALSTAFF   Two thousand, fair woman, and I'll vouchsafe you the hearing.

QUICKLY   There is one Mistress Ford, sir—I pray, come
a little nearer this ways.—I myself dwell with Master
Doctor Caius.

FALSTAFF   Well, on: Mistress Ford, you say—

QUICKLY   Your worship says very true—I pray your
worship, come a little nearer this ways.

FALSTAFF   I warrant you nobody hears—my own people,
my own people.

QUICKLY   Are they so? God bless them and make them
his servants!   *[They go aside.]*

FALSTAFF   Well, Mistress Ford—what of her?

QUICKLY   Why, sir, she's a good creature. Lord, Lord, your
worship's a wanton! Well, heaven forgive you, and all
of us, I pray.

FALSTAFF   Mistress Ford—come, Mistress Ford—

QUICKLY   Sure, this is the short and long of it. You have

brought her into such a canaries [quandary] as it is wonderful. The best courtier of them all, when the Court lay at Windsor, could never have brought her to such a canary. Yet there have been knights, and lords, and gentlemen, with their coaches. I warrant you, coach after coach, letter after letter, gift after gift; smelling so sweetly—all musk—and so rushling [rustling], I warrant you, in silk and gold; and in such alligant [elegant] terms; and in such wine and sugar of the best and the fairest that would have won any woman's heart. And I warrant you they could never get an eye-wink of her. I had myself twenty angels given me this morning: but I defy all angels—in any such sort, as they say—but in the way of honesty; and I warrant you they could never get her so much as sip on a cup with the proudest of them all. And yet there have been earls—nay, which is more, Pensioners;[4] but, I warrant you, all is one with her.

FALSTAFF   But what says she to me? Be brief, my good she-Mercury.

QUICKLY   Sure, she has received your letter: for which she thanks you a thousand times: and she gives you to notify that her husband will be absent from his house between ten and eleven.

FALSTAFF   Ten and eleven.

QUICKLY   Ay, to be sure: and then you may come and see the picture, she says, that you know of. Master Ford her husband will be from home. Alas, the sweet woman leads an ill life with him; he's a very jealousy man; she leads a very frampold [uneasy] life with him, good heart.

FALSTAFF   Ten and eleven. Woman, commend me to her; I will not fail her.

QUICKLY   Why, you say well. But I have another messenger to your worship. Mistress Page has her hearty commendations to you too; and let me tell

---
[4] Queen's bodyguard.

you in your ear, she's as fartuous [virtuous] a civil
modest wife, and one, I tell you, that will not miss
you morning nor evening prayer, as any is in
Windsor, whoever is the other. And she bade me tell
your worship that her husband is seldom from home,
but she hopes there will come a time. I never knew a
woman so dote upon a man. Surely I think you have
charms, la; yes, in truth.

FALSTAFF   Not I, I assure you. Setting the attraction of
my good parts aside, I have no other charms.

QUICKLY   Blessing on your heart for it!

FALSTAFF   But, I pray you tell me this: have Ford's wife
and Page's wife acquainted each other how they love
me?

QUICKLY   That were a jest indeed! They have not so
little grace, I hope; that were a trick indeed! But
Mistress Page would desire you to send her your little
page, of all loves. Her husband has a marvellous in-
fection [affection] to the little page; and truly Master
Page is an honest man. Never a wife in Windsor leads
a better life than she does. Do what she will, say
what she will, take all, pay all, go to bed when she
likes, all is as she will. And truly she deserves it; for if
there is a kind woman in Windsor, she is one. You
must send her your page—no remedy.

FALSTAFF   Why, I will.

QUICKLY   Nay, but do so then: and look you, he may
come and go between you both. And in any case have
a watch-word, that you may know one another's
mind, and the boy never needs to understand anything; for 'tis not good that children should know any
wickedness. Old folks, you know, have discretion, as
they say, and know the world.

FALSTAFF   Fare you well, commend me to them both.
There's my purse; I am yet your debtor.—Boy, go
along with this woman. [Exeunt Mistress Quickly
and Robin.] This news distracts me.

PISTOL *[aside]* This strumpet is one of Cupid's carriers.
Clap on more sails; pursue; up with your fights;
Give fire! She is my prize, or ocean whelm them all!
                                                    [Exit.]
FALSTAFF Say you so, old Jack? Go your ways; I'll make
more of your old body than I have done. Will they yet
look after you? Will you, after the expense of so much
money, be now a gainer? Good body, I thank you. Let
them say it is grossly done; so it be fairly done, no
matter.

Enter Bardolph.

BARDOLPH Sir John, there's one Master Brook below
would fain speak with you, and be acquainted with
you; and has sent your worship a morning's draught
of sack.
FALSTAFF Brook is his name?
BARDOLPH Ay, sir.
FALSTAFF Call him in. *[Exit Bardolph.]* Such Brooks are
welcome to me, that overflow such liquor. Aha!
Mistress Ford and Mistress Page, have I encompassed
you? Go to; well!

Enter Bardolph, with Ford disguised.

FORD Bless you, sir.
FALSTAFF And you, sir; would you speak with me?
FORD I make bold to press with so little preparation
upon you.
FALSTAFF You're welcome. What's your will? Give us
leave, drawer.   *[Exit Bardolph.]*
FORD Sir, I am a gentleman that has spent much. My
name is Brook.
FALSTAFF Good Master Brook, I desire more acquain-
tance of you.
FORD Good Sir John, I sue for yours—not to charge

you—for I must let you understand I think myself in
better plight for a lender than you are, which has
something emboldened me to this unseasoned intru-
sion; for they say if money goes before, all ways do lie
open.

FALSTAFF   Money is a good soldier, sir, and will on.

FORD   Truth, and I have a bag of money here troubles
me. If you will help to bear it, Sir John, take all, or
half, for easing me of the carriage.

FALSTAFF   Sir, I know not how I may deserve to be your
porter.

FORD   I will tell you sir, if you will give me the hearing.

FALSTAFF   Speak, good Master Brook. I shall be glad to be
your servant.

FORD   Sir, I hear you are a scholar—I will be brief with
you—and you have been a man long known to me,
though I had never so good means as desire to make
myself acquainted with you. I shall discover a thing
to you wherein I must very much lay open my own
imperfection. But, good Sir John, as you have one eye
upon my follies, as you hear them unfolded, turn
another into the register of your own, that I may pass
with a reproof the easier, since you yourself know
how easy it is to be such an offender.

FALSTAFF   Very well, sir—proceed.

FORD   There is a gentlewoman in this town, her
husband's name is Ford.

FALSTAFF   Well, sir.

FORD   I have long loved her and, I protest to you, bestowed much on her, followed her with a doting
observance, engrossed opportunities to meet her,
fee'd every slight occasion that could but niggardly
give me sight of her; not only bought many presents
to give her but have given largely to many to know
what she would have given. Briefly, I have pursued
her as love has pursued me, which has been on the

wing of all occasions. But whatsoever I have merited
—either in my mind or in my means—reward, I am
sure, I have received none, unless experience is a
jewel. That I have purchased at an infinite rate, and
that has taught me to say this,
>'Love like a shadow flies when substance love
>   pursues;
>Pursuing that that flies, and flying what pursues.'

FALSTAFF Have you received no promise of satisfaction
at her hands?

FORD Never.

FALSTAFF Have you importuned her to such a purpose?

FORD Never.

FALSTAFF Of what quality was your love then?

FORD Like a fair house built on another man's ground,
so that I have lost my edifice by mistaking the place
where I erected it.

FALSTAFF To what purpose have you unfolded this to
me?

FORD When I have told you that, I have told you all.
Some say that though she appears honest to me, yet
in other places she enlarges her mirth so far that
there is poor construction made of her. Now, Sir
John, here is the heart of my purpose. You are a
gentleman of excellent breeding, admirable discourse, in great favour, authentic in your place and
person, generally allowed for your many warlike,
courtlike, and learned preparations.

FALSTAFF O sir!

FORD Believe it, for you know it. There is money.
Spend it, spend it; spend more; spend all I have. Only
give me so much of your time in exchange of it as to
lay an amiable siege to the honesty of this Ford's
wife. Use your art of wooing, win her to consent to
you; if any man may, you may as soon as any.

FALSTAFF Would it apply well to the vehemency of your
affection that I should win what you would enjoy? I
think you prescribe to yourself very preposterously.

FORD   O, understand my drift. She dwells so securely on the excellency of her honor that the folly of my soul dares not present itself. She is too bright to be looked against. Now, could I come to her with any detection in my hand, my desires had instance and argument to commend themselves. I could drive her then from the ward of her purity, her reputation, her marriage vow, and a thousand other defenses, which now are too too strongly embattled against me. What say you to it, Sir John?

FALSTAFF   Master Brook, I will first make bold with your money; next, give me your hand; and last, as I am a gentleman, you shall, if you will, enjoy Ford's wife.

FORD   O good sir!

FALSTAFF   I say you shall.

FORD   Want no money, Sir John; you shall want none.

FALSTAFF   Want no Mistress Ford, Master Brook; you shall want none. I shall be with her, I may tell you, by her own appointment—even as you come in to me, her assistant or go-between parted from me. I say I shall be with her between ten and eleven, for at that time the jealous rascally knave her husband will be forth. Come you to me at night; you shall know how I speed.

FORD   I am blest in your acquaintance. Do you know Ford, sir?

FALSTAFF   Hang him, poor cuckoldly knave! I know him not. Yet I wrong him to call him poor: they say the jealous cuckoldly knave has masses of money; for which his wife seems to me good-looking. I will use her as the key of the cuckoldly rogue's coffer, and there's my harvest-home.

FORD   I would you knew Ford, sir, that you might avoid him if you saw him.

FALSTAFF   Hang him, mechanical salt-butter rogue! I will stare him out of his wits. I will awe him with my cudgel; it shall hang like a meteor over the cuckold's horns. Master Brook, you shall know I will predominate over the peasant, and you shall lie with his wife. Come to me soon at night. Ford is a knave, and I will aggravate his style. You, Master Brook, shall know him for knave and cuckold. Come to me soon at night   [Exit.]

FORD What a damned Epicurean rascal is this! My heart is ready to crack with impatience. Who says this is improvident jealousy? My wife has sent to him, the hour is fixed, the match is made. Would any man have thought this? See the hell of having a false woman! My bed shall be abused, my coffers ransacked, my reputation gnawn at. And I shall not only receive this villainous wrong, but stand under the adoption of abominable terms, and by him that does me this wrong. Terms! names! Amaimon sounds well; Lucifer, well? Barbason, well; yet they are devils' additions, the names of fiends. But Cuckold! Witless!—Cuckold! the devil himself has not such a name. Page is an ass, a secure ass. He will trust his wife; he will not he jealous. I will rather trust a Fleming with my butter, Parson Hugh the Welshman with my cheese, an Irishman with my whisky bottle, or a thief to walk my ambling gelding, than my wife with herself. Then she plots, then she ruminates, then she devises. And what they think in their hearts they may effect, they will break their hearts but they will effect. God be praised for my jealousy. Eleven o'clock the hour. I will forestall this, detect my wife, be revenged on Falstaff, and laugh at Page. I will about it; better three hours too soon than a minute too late. Fie, fie, fie! cuckold! cuckold! cuckold!   [Exit.]

SCENE III
Near Windsor.

Enter Doctor Caius and Rugby.

CAIUS Jack Rugby.—

RUGBY Sir?

CAIUS Vat is de clock, Jack?

RUGBY 'Tis past the hour, sir, that Sir Hugh promised to meet.

CAIUS By God he has saved his soul dat he is not come. He has prayed his Bible vell dat he is not come. By God, Jack Rugby, he is dead already if he is come.

RUGBY He is wise, sir. He knew your worship would kill him if he came.

CAIUS By God, de herring is not dead so as I vill kill him. Take your rapier, Jack; I vill tell you how I vill kill him.

RUGBY Alas, sir, I cannot fence.

CAIUS Villain, take your rapier.

RUGBY Forbear; here's company.

Enter Page, Shallow, Slender, and Host.

HOST 'Bless you, bully Doctor.

SHALLOW 'Save you, Master Doctor Caius.

PAGE Now, good Master Doctor.

SLENDER 'Give you good morrow, sir.

CAIUS Vat be all you, one, two, tree, four, come for?

HOST To see you fight, to see you thrust, to see you traverse; to see you here, to see you there; to see you pass your point, your stock, your reverse, your distance, your upthrust. Is he dead, my Ethiopian? Is he dead, my Francisco? Ha, bully? What says my Aesculapius? my Galen? my heart of elder? Ha, is he dead, bully piss? is he dead?

CAIUS By God, he is de coward Jack-priest of de vorld. He is not show his face.

HOST You are a Castilian King-Urinal! Hector of Greece, my boy!

CAIUS I pray you bear vitness dat I have stayed six or seven, two, tree hours for him, and he is not come.

SHALLOW He is the wiser man, Master Doctor. He is a curer of souls, and you a curer of bodies. If you should fight, you go against the hair of your professions. Is it not true, Master Page?

PAGE Master Shallow, you have yourself been a great fighter, though now a man of peace.

SHALLOW Bodykins, Master Page, though l now am old and of the peace, if I see a sword out, my finger itches to make one. Though we are justices and doctors and churchmen, Master Page, we have some salt of our youth in us. We are the sons of women, Master Page.

PAGE 'Tis true, Master Shallow.

SHALLOW It will be found so, Master Page. Master Doctor Caius, I am come to fetch you home. I am sworn of the peace. You have shown yourself a wise physician, and Sir Hugh has shown himself a wise and patient churchman. You must go with me, Master Doctor.

HOST Pardon, Guest-Justice. A word, Monsieur Make-water.

CAIUS Make-vater? vat is dat?

HOST Make-water, in our English tongue, is valor, bully.

CAIUS By God, den, I have as much make-vater as de Englishman. Scurvy jack-dog priest! By God, I vill cut his ears.

HOST He will clapperclaw [thrash] you tightly, bully.

CAIUS Clapper-de-claw? vat is dat?

HOST That is, he will make you amends.

CAIUS By God, I do look he shall clapper-de-claw me; for, by God, I vill have it.

HOST   And I will provoke him to it, or let him trot.

CAIUS   I tank you vor dat.

HOST   And moreover, bully *[aside]* But first, Master Guest, and Master Page, and also Cavaliero Slender, go you through the town to Frogmore.

PAGE   Sir Hugh is there, is he?

HOST   He is there; see what humor he is in. And I will bring the doctor about by the fields. Will it do well?

SHALLOW   We will do it.

PAGE, SHALLOW, AND SLENDER   Adieu, good Master Doctor.

> *[Exeunt Page, Shallow, and Slender.]*

CAIUS   By God I vill kill de priest, for he speak for a jackanape to Anne Page.

HOST   Let him die. Sheathe your impatience; throw cold water on your choler. Go about the fields with me through Frogmore. I will bring you where Mistress Anne Page is, at a farmhouse a-feasting; and you shall woo her. Cried game;[5] said I well?

CAIUS   By God, I tank you vor dat. I love you; and I shall procure-a you de good guest—de earl, de knight, de lords, de gentlemen, my patients.

HOST   For which I will be your adversary [advocate] toward Anne Page. Said I well?

CAIUS   By God, 'tis good; vell said.

HOST   Let us trot, then.

CAIUS   Come at my heels, Jack Rugby.   *Exeunt.*

---

[5]The sport is on.

Act III

SCENE I
Near Frogmore.

Enter Evans and Simple.

EVANS I pray you now, good Master Slender's serving-man, and friend Simple by your name, which way have you looked for Master Caius, that calls himself Doctor of Physic?

SIMPLE Sure, sir, the Petty-ward the Park-ward, every way; old Windsor way, and every way but the town way.

EVANS I most vehemently desire you, you will also look that way.

SIMPLE I will, sir.   *[Exit.]*

EVANS Bless my soul, how full of cholers I am, and trembling of mind. I shall be glad if he has deceived me. How melancholies I am. I will knog his urinals about his knave's noddle when I have goot opportunities for the work. 'Bless my soul.

[Sings.]   'To shallow rivers, to whose falls
          Melodious birds sing madrigals;
          There will we make our beds of roses,
          And a thousand fragrant posies.
          To shallow—'[1]

Mercy on me, I have a great dispositions to cry.

---

[1] A garbled version of Marlowe's famous lines, with one from the Psalms.

[Sings.]   'Melodious birds sing madrigals,—
            Whenas I sat in Babylon,—
            And a thousand vagram [fragrant] posies.
            To shallow—'

Enter Simple.

SIMPLE   Yonder he is coming, this way, Sir Hugh.
EVANS   He is welcome.
    [Sings.]   'To shallow rivers, to whose falls—'
    Heaven prosper the right!—What weapons has he?
SIMPLE   No weapons, sir. There comes my master, Master Shallow, and another gentleman, from Frogmore, over the stile, this way.
EVANS   Pray you, give me my gown—or else keep it in your arms.   *[Reads in a book.]*

Enter Page, Shallow, Slender.

SHALLOW   How now, Master Parson. Good morrow, good Sir Hugh. Keep a gamester from the dice, and a good student from his book, and it is wonderful.
SLENDER   *[aside]* Ah sweet Anne Page!
PAGE   Save you, good Sir Hugh.
EVANS   Bless you from his mercy sake, all of you.
SHALLOW   What, the sword and the word? Do you study them both, Master Parson?
PAGE   And youthful still—in your doublet and hose this raw rheumatic day?
EVANS   There are reasons and causes for it.
PAGE   We are come to you to do a good office, Master Parson.
EVANS   Very well; what is it?
PAGE   Yonder is a most reverend gentleman who, perhaps having received wrong by some person, is at most odds with his own gravity and patience that ever you saw.
SHALLOW   I have lived fourscore years and upward; I

never heard a man of his place, gravity, and learning so wide of his own respect.

EVANS   What is he?

PAGE   I think you know him: Master Doctor Caius, the renowned French physician.

EVANS   Got's will, and his passion of my heart! I had as soon you would tell me of a mess of porridge.

PAGE   Why?

EVANS   He is no more knowledge in Hippocrates and Galen—and he is a knave besides, a cowardly knave as you would desire to be acquainted with.

PAGE   I warrant you, he is the man should fight with him.

SLENDER   *[aside]* O sweet Anne Page!

SHALLOW   It appears so by his weapons.

Enter Host, Caius, and Rugby.

Keep them asunder; here comes Doctor Caius.

PAGE   Nay, good Master Parson, keep in your weapon.

SHALLOW   So do you, good Master Doctor.

HOST   Disarm them, and let them question. Let them keep their limbs whole and hack our English.

CAIUS   I pray you let-a me speak a word vit your ear. Verefore vill you not meet-a me?

EVANS   *[aside to Caius]* Pray you use your patience. *[aloud]* In good time.

CAIUS   By God, you are de coward, de Jack dog, John ape.

EVANS   *[aside to Caius]* Pray you let us not be laughing-stogs to other men's humors. I desire you in friendship, and I will one way or other make you amends. *[aloud]* I will knog your urinal about your knave's cogscomb for missing your meetings and appointments.

CAIUS   Diable!—Jack Rugby—my Host de Jarteer—have I not stayed for him to kill him? Have I not, at de place I did appoint?

EVANS   As I am a Christians soul, now, look you, this is the place appointed. I'll be judgment [judged] by my Host of the Garter.

HOST   Peace, I say, Gallia and Gaul, French and Welsh, soul-curer and body-curer.

CAIUS   Ay, dat is very good, excellent.

HOST   Peace, I say. Hear my Host of the Garter. Am I politic? am I subtle? am I a Machiavel? Shall I lose my doctor? No; he gives me the potions and the motions. Shall I lose my parson, my priest, my Sir Hugh? No; he gives me the proverbs and the no-verbs. Give me your hand, terrestrial; so. Give me your hand, celestial; so. Boys of art, I have deceived you both; I have directed you to wrong places. Your hearts are mighty, your skins are whole, and let hot sack be the issue. Come, lay their swords to pawn. Follow me, lad of peace; follow, follow, follow.

SHALLOW   Trust me, a mad Host. Follow, gentlemen, follow.

SLENDER   *[aside]* O sweet Anne Page!

       Exeunt Shallow, Slender, Page, and Host.

CAIUS   Ha, do I perceive dat? Have you make-a de sot of us, ha, ha?

EVANS   This is well—he has make us his flouting-stog. I desire you that we may be friends, and let us knog our brains together to be revenged on this same scald, scurvy, cheating companion, the Host of the Garter.

CAIUS   By God, vit all my heart. He promised to bring me vere is Anne Page. By God, he deceived me too.

EVANS   Well, I will smite his noodle. Pray you follow.

                                              [Exeunt.]

SCENE II
A Windsor street.

Enter Mistress Page and Robin.

MRS. PAGE   Nay, keep your way, little gallant—you were wont to be a follower, but now you are a leader. Whether had you rather lead my eyes, or eye your master's heels?

ROBIN   I had rather, sure, go before you like a man than follow him like a dwarf.

MRS. PAGE   O, you are a flattering boy. Now I see you will be a courtier.

Enter Ford.

FORD   Well met, Mistress Page. Whither go you?

MRS. PAGE   Truly, sir, to see your wife. Is she at home?

FORD   Ay, and as idle as she may hang together, for want of company. I think if your husbands were dead, you two would marry.

MRS. PAGE   Be sure of that—two other husbands.

FORD   Where had you this pretty weathercock?

MRS. PAGE   I cannot tell what the dickens his name is my husband had him of. What do you call your knight's name, pray?

ROBIN   Sir John Falstaff.

FORD   Sir John Falstaff!

MRS. PAGE   He, he; I can never hit on his name. There is such a league between my goodman and him.—Is your wife at home indeed?

FORD   Indeed she is.

MRS. PAGE   By your leave, sir. I am sick till I see her.
                    [Exeunt Mistress Page and Robin.]

FORD   Has Page any brains? Has he any eyes? has he any thinking? Sure, they sleep; he has no use of them. Why, this boy will carry a letter twenty miles as easy as a cannon will shoot pointblank twelve score. He pieces out his wife's inclination; he gives her folly motion and advantage—and now she's going to my wife, and Falstaff's boy with her. A man may hear this shower sing in the wind. And Falstaff's boy with her. Good plots! They are laid, and our revolted wives share damnation together. Well, I will take him, then torture my wife, pluck the borrowed veil of modesty from the so-seeming Mistress Page, divulge Page himself for a secure and wilful Actaeon; and to these violent proceedings all my neighbors shall applaud *[Clock strikes.]* The clock gives me my cue, and my assurance bids me search. There I shall find Falstaff. I shall be rather praised for this than mocked, for it is positive as the earth is firm that Falstaff is there. I will go.

Enter Page, Shallow, Slender, Host, Sir Hugh Evans, Caius, and Rugby.

SHALLOW, PAGE, etc.   Well met, Master Ford.

FORD   Trust me, a good knot. I have good cheer at home, and I pray you all go with me.

SHALLOW   I must excuse myself, Master Ford.

SLENDER   And so must I, sir. We have appointed to dine with Mistress Anne, and I would not break with her for more money than I'll speak of.

SHALLOW   We have lingered about a match between Anne Page and my cousin Slender, and this day we shall have our answer.

SLENDER   I hope I have your good will, father Page.

PAGE   You have, Master Slender—I stand wholly for you. But my wife, Master Doctor, is for you altogether.

CAIUS   Ay, by God, and de maid is love-a me—my nursh-a Quickly tell me so mush.

HOST   What say you to young Master Fenton? He capers, he dances, he has eyes of youth, he writes verses, he speaks holiday, he smells April and May. He will carry it, he will carry it; 'tis in his fortune; he will carry it.

PAGE   Not by my consent, I promose you. The gentleman is of no having. He kept company with the wild
Prince and Poins; he is of too high a region; he knows
too much. No, he shall not knit a knot in his fortunes
with the finger of my substance. If he takes her, let
him take her simply. The wealth I have waits on my
consent, and my consent goes not that way.

FORD   I beseech you heartily, some of you go home with
me to dinner. Besides your cheer, you shall have
sport—I will show you a monster. Master Doctor, you
shall go. So shall you, Master Page, and you, Sir Hugh.

SHALLOW   Well, fare you well. We shall have the freer
wooing at Master Page's.

> *[Exeunt Shallow and Slender.]*

CAIUS   Go home, John Rugby. I come anon.

> *[Exit Rugby.]*

HOST   Farewell, my hearts. I will to my honest knight
Falstaff, and drink canary with him.   *[Exit.]*

FORD   *[aside]* I think I shall drink in pipe-wine first
with him: I'll make him dance.—Will you go, gentles?

ALL   Have with you to see this monster.   *Exeunt.*

SCENE III
Ford's house.

Enter Mistress Ford and Mistress Page.

MRS. FORD   What, John; what, Robert.—
MRS. PAGE   Quickly, quickly. Is the buck-basket—[2]
MRS. FORD   I warrant. What, Robert, I say.—

Enter Servants with a basket.

---

[2]Dirty-linen basket.

MRS. PAGE   Come, come, come.

MRS. FORD   Here, set it down.

MRS. PAGE   Give your men the charge. We must be brief.

MRS. FORD   Sure, as I told you before, John, and Robert, be ready here hard by in the brewhouse; and when I suddenly call you, come forth, and without any pause or staggering, take this basket on your shoulders. That done trudge with it in all haste, and carry it among the bleachers in Datchet Mead, and there empty it in the muddy ditch, close by the Thames side.

MRS. PAGE   You will do it?

MRS. FORD   I have told them over and over—they lack no direction. Be gone, and come when you are called.

[Exeunt Servants.]

Enter Robin.

MRS. PAGE   Here comes little Robin.

MRS. FORD   How now, my little sparrow hawk, what news with you?

ROBIN   My master, Sir John, is come in at your back door, Mistress Ford, and requests your company.

MRS. PAGE   You little Jack-a-Lent, have you been true to us?

ROBIN   Ay, I'll be sworn. My master knows not of your being here, and has threatened to put me into everlasting liberty if I tell you of it; for he swears he'll turn me away.

MRS. PAGE   You are a good boy. This secrecy of yours shall be a tailor to you and shall make you a new doublet and hose. I'll go hide.

MRS. FORD   Do so. Go tell your master I am alone.

[Exit Robin.]

Mistress Page, remember your cue.

MRS. PAGE   I warrant you. If I do not act it, hiss me.

[Exit.]

MRS. FORD   Go to, then We'll use this unwholesome
humidity, this gross water-pumpkin—we'll teach
him to know turtles from jays.

Enter Falstaff.

FALSTAFF   'Have I caught thee, my heavenly jewel?'
Why, now let me die, for I have lived long enough.
This is the period of my ambition. O this blessed
hour!

MRS. FORD   O sweet Sir John!

FALSTAFF   Mistress Ford, I cannot flatter, I cannot prate,
Mistress Ford. Now shall I sin in my wish: I would
your husband were dead. I'll speak it before the best
lord, I would make you my lady.

MRS. FORD   I your lady, Sir John? Alas, I should be a
pitiful lady.

FALSTAFF   Let the Court of France show me such another.
I see how your eye would emulate the diamond. You
have the right arched beauty of the brow that
becomes the ship-tire, the tire-valiant, or any tire of
Venetian fashion.[3]

MRS. FORD   A plain kerchief, Sir John—my brows
become nothing else, nor that well either.

FALSTAFF   By the Lord, you are a tyrant to say so. You
would make an absolute courtier, and the firm fixture
of your foot would give an excellent motion to your
gait in a semicircled farthingale. I see what you were
if Fortune your foe were not, Nature your friend.
Come, you cannot hide it.

MRS. FORD   Believe me, there is no such thing in me.

FALSTAFF   What made me love you? Let that persuade
you there's something extraordinary in you. Come, I
cannot flatter and say you are this and that, like many
of these lisping hawthorn buds that come like women

---

[3]Various types of head-dress.

in men's apparel and smell like Bucklersbury in simple-time. I cannot. But I love you, none but you; and you deserve it.

MRS. FORD   Do not betray me, sir. I fear you love Mistress Page.

FALSTAFF   You might as well say I love to walk by the Counter-gate, [debtors' prison] which is as hateful to me as the reek of a limekiln.

MRS. FORD   Well, heaven knows how I love you, and you shall one day find it.

FALSTAFF   Keep in that mind—I'll deserve it.

MRS. FORD   Nay, I must tell you, so you do, or else I could not be in that mind.

Enter Robin.

ROBIN   Mistress Ford, Mistress Ford! Here's Mistress Page at the door, sweating and blowing and looking wildly, and would needs speak with you at once.

FALSTAFF   She shall not see me; I will ensconce me behind the arras.

MRS. FORD   Pray you, do so—she's a very tattling woman.

Falstaff hides himself.

Enter Mistress Page.

What's the matter? how now.—

MRS. PAGE   O Mistress Ford, what have you done? You're shamed, you're overthrown, you're undone for ever!

MRS. FORD   What's the matter, good Mistress Page?

MRS. PAGE   O well-a-day, Mistress Ford—having an honest man to your husband, to give him such cause of suspicion!

MRS. FORD   What cause of suspicion?

MRS. PAGE   What cause of suspicion! Out upon you, how am I mistaken in you!

MRS. FORD   Why, alas, what's the matter?

MRS. PAGE   Your husband's coming hither, woman, with
all the officers in Windsor, to search for a gentleman
that he says is here now in the house by your consent,
to take an ill advantage of his absence. You are undone.

MRS. FORD   'Tis not so, I hope.

MRS. PAGE   Pray heaven it is not so, that you have such a
man here! But 'tis most certain your husband's coming, with half Windsor at his heels, to search for such
a one. I come before to tell you. If you know yourself
clear, why, I am glad of it; but if you have a friend here,
convey, convey him out. Be not amazed, call all your
senses to you, defend your reputation—or bid farewell
to your good life for ever.

MRS. FORD   What shall I do?—There is a gentleman, my
dear friend; and I fear not my own shame so much as
his peril. I had rather than a thousand pound he were
out of the house.

MRS. PAGE   For shame! Never stand 'you had rather' and
'you had rather.' Your husband's here at hand; think of
some conveyance. In the house you cannot hide him.
O, how have you deceived me! Look, here is a basket.
If he is of any reasonable stature, he may creep in here;
and throw foul linen upon him, as if it were going to
washing. Or—it is bleaching-time—send him by your
two men to Datchet Mead.

MRS. FORD   He's too big to go in there. What shall I do?

FALSTAFF   *[coming forward]* Let me see it, let me see it,
O let me see it! I'll in, I'll in. Follow your friend's
counsel.   I'll in.

MRS. PAGE   What, Sir John Falstaff! *[aside]* Are these
your letters, knight?

FALSTAFF   *[aside]* I love you. Help me away. Let me creep
in here. I'll never—
*[Gets into the basket; they cover him with foul
linen.]*

MRS. PAGE   Help to cover your master, boy. Call your
men, Mistress Ford. *[aside]* You dissembling knight!
MRS. FORD   What, John! Robert! John!   *[Exit Robin.]*

Enter Servants.

Go take up these clothes here quickly. Where's the
basket-pole? Look how you dawdle! Carry them to the
laundress in Datchet Mead—quickly, come!

Enter Ford, Page, Caius, and Evans.

FORD   Pray you come near. If I suspect without cause,
why then make sport at me; then let me be your jest; I
deserve it. How now, whither bear you this?
SERVANTS   To the laundress, to be sure.
MRS. FORD   Why, what have you to do whither they bear
it? You were best meddle with buck-washing!
FORD   Buck? I would I could wash myself of the buck!
Buck, buck, buck! Ay, buck; I warrant you, buck; and
of the season too, it shall appear. *[Exeunt Servants
with the basket.]* Gentlemen, I have dreamed to-
night; I'll tell you my dream. Here, here, here are my
keys. Ascend my chambers; search, seek, find out. I'll
warrant we'll unkennel the fox. Let me stop this way
first. *[Locks the door.]* So, now unloose.
PAGE   Good Master Ford, be contented. You wrong
yourself too much.
FORD   True, Master Page. Up, gentlemen; you shall see
sport anon. Follow me, gentlemen.   *[Exit.]*
EVANS   This is very fantastical humors and jealousies.
CAIUS   By God, 'tis not de fashion of France; it is not
jealous in France.
PAGE   Nay, follow him, gentlemen—see the issue of his
search.   *[Exeunt Page, Caius, and Evans.]*
MRS. PAGE   Is there not a double excellency in this?
MRS. FORD   I know not which pleases me better: that my
husband is deceived, or Sir John.

MRS. PAGE   What a taking was he in when your husband asked what was in the basket!

MRS. FORD   I am half afraid he will have need of washing; so throwing him into the water will do him a benefit.

MRS. PAGE   Hang him, dishonest rascal! I would all of the same strain were in the same distress.

MRS. FORD   I think my husband has some special suspicion of Falstaff's being here, for I never saw him so gross in his jealousy till now.

MRS. PAGE   I will lay a plot to try that, and we will yet have more tricks with Falstaff. His dissolute disease will scarce obey this medicine.

MRS. FORD   Shall we send that foolish carrion Mistress Quickly to him, and excuse his throwing into the water; and give him another hope, to betray him to another punishment?

MRS. PAGE   We will do it. Let him be sent for to-morrow eight o'clock, to have amends.

Enter Ford, Page, Caius, and Evans.

FORD   I cannot find him—may be the knave bragged of that he could not compass.

MRS. PAGE   *[aside to Mrs. Ford]* Heard you that?

MRS. FORD   You use me well, Master Ford, do you?

FORD   Ay, I do so.

MRS. FORD   Heaven make you better than your thoughts!

FORD   Amen.

MRS. PAGE   You do yourself mighty wrong, Master Ford.

FORD   Ay, ay, I must bear it.

EVANS   If there be any body in the house, and in the chambers, and in the coffers, and in the presses, heaven forgive my sins at the day of judgement.

CAIUS   By God, nor I too, dere is nobodies.

PAGE   Fie, fie, Master Ford, are you not ashamed? What spirit, what devil suggests this imagination? I would

not have your distemper in this kind for the wealth of
Windsor Castle.

FORD   'Tis my fault, Master Page—I suffer for it.

EVANS   You suffer for a bad conscience. Your wife is an
honest a woman as I will desire among five thousand,
and five hundred too.

CAIUS   By God, I see 'tis an honest woman.

FORD   Well, I promised you a dinner. Come, come,
walk in the Park. I pray you pardon me, I will hereafter
make known to you why I have done this. Come, wife;
come, Mistress Page. I pray you pardon me; pray heartily pardon me.

PAGE   Let's go in, gentlemen; but, trust me, we'll mock
him. I do invite you to-morrow morning to my house
to breakfast. After, we'll a-birding together: I have a
fine hawk for the bush. Shall it be so?

FORD   Anything.

EVANS   If there is one or two in the company.

CAIUS   If dere be one, or two, I shall make-a de turd.

FORD   Pray you go, Master Page.

EVANS   I pray you now, remember to-morrow on the
lousy knave, my Host.

CAIUS   Dat is good; by God, vit all my heart.

EVANS   A lousy knave to have his gibes and his
mockeries!

Exeunt.

SCENE IV
Before Page's house.

Enter Fenton and Anne Page.

FENTON   I see I cannot get your father's love;
    Therefore no more turn me to him, sweet Nan.

ANNE   Alas, how then?

FENTON   Why, you must be yourself.

He does object I am too great of birth,
And that my state being galled with my expense,
I seek to heal it only by his wealth.
Besides these, other bars he lays before me,
My riots past, my wild societies;
And tells me it is a thing impossible
I should love you but as a property.
ANNE   May be he tells you true.
FENTON   No, heaven so speed me in my time to come!
Albeit I will confess your father's wealth
Was the first motive that I wooed you, Anne.
Yet, wooing you, I found you of more value
Than stamps in gold or sums in sealèd bags;
It is the very riches of yourself
That now I aim at.
ANNE   Gentle Master Fenton,
Yet seek my father's love; still seek it, sir.
If opportunity and humblest suit
Cannot attain it, why, then—hark you hither.
                                    [They talk apart.]

Enter Shallow, Slender, and Mistress Quickly.

SHALLOW   Break their talk, Mistress Quickly. My
kinsman shall speak for himself.
SLENDER   I'll make a shot or a try on it. Well, it is but
venturing.
SHALLOW   Be not dismayed.
SLENDER   No, she shall not dismay me. I care not for
that, but that I am afraid.
QUICKLY   Hark you, Master Slender would speak a word
with you.
ANNE   I come to him. *[aside]* This is my father's choice.
O, what a world of vile ill-favored faults
Looks handsome in three hundred pounds a year.
QUICKLY   And how does good Master Fenton? Pray you
a word with you.

SHALLOW   She's coming; to her, my boy. O boy, you had
a father!

SLENDER   I had a father, Mistress Anne—my uncle can
tell you good jests of him. Pray you, uncle, tell
Mistress Anne the jest how my father stole two geese
out of a pen, good uncle.

SHALLOW   Mistress Anne, my cousin loves you.

SLENDER   Ay, that I do, as well as I love any woman in
Gloucestershire.

SHALLOW   He will maintain you like a gentlewoman.

SLENDER   Ay, that I will, come what may, under the
degree of a squire.

SHALLOW   He will make you a hundred and fifty pounds
jointure.

ANNE   Good Master Shallow, let him woo for himself.

SHALLOW   Sure, I thank you for it, I thank you for that
good comfort. She calls you, my boy. I'll leave you.

ANNE   Now, Master Slender—

SLENDER   Now, good Mistress Anne—

ANNE   What is your will?

SLENDER   My will? God's heartlings, that's a pretty jest
indeed! I never made my will yet, I thank God. I am
not such a sickly creature, I give heaven praise.

ANNE   I mean, Master Slender, what would you with
me?

SLENDER   Truly, for my own part, I would little or nothing with you. Your father and my uncle have made
motions. If it is my luck, so; if not, good luck to him.
They can tell you how things go better than I can.
You may ask your father; here he comes.

Enter Page and Mistress Page.

PAGE   Now, Master Slender. Love him, daughter Anne.
Why, how now, what does Master Fenton here?
You wrong me, sir, thus still to haunt my house.
I told you, sir, my daughter is disposed of.

FENTON   Nay, Master Page, be not impatient.

MRS. PAGE   Good Master Fenton, come not to my child.

PAGE   She is no match for you.

FENTON   Sir, will you hear me?

PAGE   No, good Master Fenton.
Come, Master Shallow; come, son Slender, in.
Knowing my mind, you wrong me, Master Fenton.
                    [Exeunt Page, Shallow, and Slender.]

QUICKLY   Speak to Mistress Page.

FENTON   Good Mistress Page, because I love your
         daughter
In such a righteous fashion as I do,
Perforce, against all checks, rebukes, and manners,
I must advance the colors of my love
And not retire. Let me have your good will.

ANNE   Good mother, do not marry me to yon fool.

MRS. PAGE   I mean it not—I seek you a better husband.

QUICKLY   *[aside]* That's my master, Master Doctor.

ANNE   Alas, I had rather be set quick in the earth,
And bowled to death with turnips.

MRS. PAGE   Come, trouble not yourself. Good Master
         Fenton,
I will not be your friend, nor enemy.
My daughter will I question how she loves you,
And as I find her, so am I affected.
Till then, farewell, sir. She must needs go in;
Her father will be angry.

FENTON   Farewell, gentle mistress. Farewell, Nan.
                    Exeunt Mistress Page and Anne.

QUICKLY   This is my doing now. 'Nay,' said I, 'will you
cast away your child on a fool, and a physician? Look
on Master Fenton.' This is my doing.

FENTON   I thank you, and I pray you once to-night
Give my sweet Nan this ring. There's for your pains.

QUICKLY   Now heaven send you good fortune! *[Exit
Fenton.]* A kind heart he has. A woman would run
through fire and water for such a kind heart. But yet I

would my master had Mistress Anne; or I would
Master Slender had her; or, in truth, I would Master
Fenton had her. I will do what I can for them all three,
for so I have promised, and I'll be as good as my word;
but specially for Master Fenton. Well, I must of
another errand to Sir John Falstaff from my two
mistresses. What a beast am I to slack it!   *[Exit.]*

SCENE V
The Garter Inn.

Enter Falstaff and Bardolph.

FALSTAFF   Bardolph, I say.
BARDOLPH   Here, sir.
FALSTAFF   Go fetch me a quart of sack—put a toast in it.
[Exit Bardolph.] Have I lived to be carried in a basket
like a barrow of butcher's offal? And to be thrown in
the Thames! Well, if I am served such another trick,
I'll have my brains taken out, and buttered, and give
them to a dog for a New-Year's gift. The rogues
slighted me into the river with as little remorse as
they would have drowned a blind bitch's puppies,
fifteen in the litter—and you may know by my size
that I have a kind of alacrity in sinking; if the bottom
were as deep as hell, I should down. I had been
drowned but that the shore was shelvy and
shallow—a death that I abhor, for the water swells a
man, and what a thing should I have been when I had
been swelled. I should have been a mountain of
mummy.[4]

Enter Bardolph with wine.

---

[4]A concoction from mummified corpses.

BARDOLPH   Here's Mistress Quickly, sir, to speak with
you.

FALSTAFF   Come, let me pour in some sack to the
Thames water, for my belly's as cold as if I had
swallowed snowballs for pills to cool the reins. Call
her in.

BARDOLPH   Come in, woman.

Enter Mistress Quickly.

QUICKLY   By your leave; I cry you mercy. Give your
worship good morrow.

FALSTAFF   Take away these chalices. Go, brew me a
pottle of sack finely.

BARDOLPH   With eggs, sir?

FALSTAFF   Simple of itself—I'll no pullet-sperm in my
brewage. *[Exit Bardolph.]* How now?

QUICKLY   Sure, sir, I come to your worship from
Mistress Ford.

FALSTAFF   Mistress Ford? I have had ford enough; I was
thrown into the ford; I have my belly full of ford.

QUICKLY   Alas the day, good heart, that was not her
fault. She does so take on with her men—they
mistook their erection.

FALSTAFF   So did I mine, to build upon a foolish
woman's promise.

QUICKLY   Well, she laments, sir, for it that it would
yearn your heart to see it. Her husband goes this
morning a-birding. She desires you once more to
come to her between eight and nine. I must carry her
word quickly. She'll make you amends, I warrant
you.

FALSTAFF   Well, I will visit her, tell her so. And bid her
think what a man is—let her consider his frailty, and
then judge of my merit.

QUICKLY   I will tell her.

FALSTAFF   Do so. Between nine and ten say you?

QUICKLY   Eight and nine, sir.

FALSTAFF   Well, begone. I will not miss her.

QUICKLY   Peace be with you, sir.   *Exit.*

FALSTAFF   I marvel I hear not of Master Brook—he sent
me word to stay within. I like his money well.

Enter Ford

O, here he comes.

FORD   'Bless you, sir.—

FALSTAFF   Now, Master Brook, you come to know what
has passed between me and Ford's wife?

FORD   That, indeed, Sir John, is my business.

FALSTAFF   Master Brook, I will not lie to you. I was at
her house the hour she appointed me.

FORD   And sped you, sir?

FALSTAFF   Very ill-favoredly, Master Brook.

FORD   How so, sir? Did she change her determination?

FALSTAFF   No, Master Brook, but the sneaking cuckold
her husband, Master Brook, dwelling in a continual
alarum of jealousy, comes in the instant of our
encounter, after we had embraced, kissed, protested,
and as it were, spoken the prologue of our comedy.
And at his heels a rabble of his companions, thither
provoked and instigated by his distemper and, to be
sure, to search his house for his wife's love.

FORD   What, while you were there?

FALSTAFF   While I was there.

FORD   And did he search for you, and could not find
you?

FALSTAFF   You shall hear. As good luck would have it,
comes in one Mistress Page, gives intelligence of
Ford's approach, and in her invention and Ford's
wife's distraction, they conveyed me into a buck-
basket.

FORD   A buck-basket?

FALSTAFF   By the Lord, a buck-basket! Rammed me in
   with foul shirts and smocks, socks, foul stockings,
   greasy napkins that, Master Brook, there was the
   rankest compound of villainous smell that ever
   offended nostril.

FORD   And how long lay you there?

FALSTAFF   Nay, you shall hear, Master Brook, what I
   have suffered to bring this woman to evil for your
   good. Being thus crammed in the basket, a couple of
   Ford's knaves, his hinds, were called forth by their
   mistress to carry me in the name of foul clothes to
   Datchet Lane. They took me on their shoulders, met
   the jealous knave their master in the door, who asked
   them once or twice what they had in their basket. I
   quaked for fear lest the lunatic knave would have
   searched it; but fate, ordaining he should be a
   cuckold, held his hand. Well, on went he for a search,
   and away went I for foul clothes. But mark the
   sequel, Master Brook. I suffered the pangs of three
   several deaths: first, an intolerable fright to be
   detected by a jealous rotten old ram; next, to be
   compassed like a good sword in the circumference of
   a peck, hilt to point, heel to head; and then, to be
   stopped in, like a strong distillation, with stinking
   clothes that fretted in their own grease. Think of
   that, a man of my kidney—think of that—that am as
   subject to heat as butter; a man of continual dissolution and thaw. It was a miracle to escape suffocation.
   And in the height of this bath, when I was more than
   half stewed in grease like a Dutch dish, to be thrown
   into the Thames, and cooled, glowing hot, in that
   surge like a horseshoe. Think of that—hissing
   hot—think of that, Master Brook!

FORD   In good sadness, sir, I am sorry that for my sake
   you have suffered all this. My suit then is desperate.
   You'll undertake her no more?

FALSTAFF   Master Brook, I will be thrown into Aetna, as
   I have been into Thames, ere I will leave her thus.

Her husband is this morning gone a-birding. I have
received from her another embassy of meeting,
between eight and nine is the hour, Master Brook.

FORD   It is past eight already, sir.

FALSTAFF   Is it? I will then address me to my appointment. Come to me at your convenient leisure, and
you shall know how I speed; and the conclusion shall
be crowned with your enjoying her. Adieu. You shall
have her, Master Brook; Master Brook, you shall
cuckold Ford.   [Exit.]

FORD   Hum, ha! is this a vision? is this a dream? do I
sleep? Master Ford, awake; awake, Master Ford!
There's a hole made in your best coat, Master Ford.
This it is to be married; this it is to have linen and
buck-baskets! Well, I will proclaim myself what I
am. I will now take the lecher; he is at my house; he
cannot escape me; it is impossible he should. He
cannot creep into a halfpenny purse, nor into a
pepperbox; but, lest the devil that guides him should
aid him, I will search impossible places. Though
what I am I cannot avoid, yet to be what I would not,
shall not make me tame. If I have horns to make one
mad, let the proverb go with me—I'll be horn-mad.
                                                     [Exit.]

Act IV

SCENE I
Before Page's house.

Enter Mistress Page, Mistress Quickly, and William.

MRS. PAGE   Is he at Master Ford's already, think you?

QUICKLY   Sure he is by this, or will be presently. But truly, he is very courageous mad about his throwing into the water. Mistress Ford desires you to come suddenly.

MRS. PAGE   I'll be with her by and by. I'll but bring my young man here to school. Look where his master comes; it is a playing-day, I see.

Enter Evans.

How now, Sir Hugh; no school to-day?

EVANS   No. Master Slender is let the boys leave to play.

QUICKLY   Blessing of his heart.

MRS. PAGE   Sir Hugh, my husband says my son profits nothing in the world at his book. I pray you, ask him some questions in his grammar.

EVANS   Come hither, William. Hold up your head; come.

MRS. PAGE   Come on, boy; hold up your head; answer your master, be not afraid.

EVANS   William, how many numbers is in nouns?

WILLIAM   Two.

QUICKLY   Truly, I thought there had been one number more, because they say, 'God's nouns.' [God's wounds']

EVANS Peace your tattlings. What is 'fair,' William?

WILLIAM 'Pulcher.'

QUICKLY Polecats! There are fairer things than polecats, sure.

EVANS You are a very simplicity woman. I pray you peace. What is 'lapis,' William?

WILLIAM A stone.

EVANS And what is 'a stone,' William?

WILLIAM A pebble.

EVANS No, it is 'lapis.' I pray you remember in your brain.

WILLIAM 'Lapis.'

EVANS That is a good William. What is he, William, that does lend articles?

WILLIAM Articles are borrowed of the pronoun, and are thus declined: 'Singulariter, nominativo, hic, haec, hoc.'

EVANS 'Nominativo, hig, hag, hog.' Pray you mark: 'genitivo, hujus.' Well, what is your accusative case?

WILLIAM 'Accusativo, hinc.'

EVANS I pray you, have your remembrance, child: 'accusativo, hung, hang, hog.'

QUICKLY 'Hang-hog' is Latin for bacon, I warrant you.

EVANS Leave your prabbles, woman. What is the focative case, William?

WILLIAM 'O, vocativo, O.'

EVANS Remember, William; focative is 'caret.' [lacking]

QUICKLY And that's a good root.

EVANS Woman, forbear.

MRS. PAGE Peace.

EVANS What is your genitive case plural, William?

WILLIAM Genitive case?

EVANS Ay.

WILLIAM 'Genitivo, horum, harum, horum.'

QUICKLY Vengeance of Jenny's case! fie on her! Never name her, child, if she is a whore.

EVANS   For shame, woman.

QUICKLY   You do ill to teach the child such words. He teaches him to hick and to hack, which they'll do fast enough of themselves, and to call 'horum.' Fie upon you!

EVANS   Woman, are you lunatic? Have you no understanding for your cases and the numbers of the genders? You are as foolish Christian creature as I would desire.

MRS. PAGE   Pray hold your peace.

EVANS   Show me now, William, some declensions of your pronouns.

WILLIAM   Well now, I have forgotten.

EVANS   It is 'qui, quae, quod.' If you forget your 'qui's,' your 'quae's,' and your 'quod's,' you must be whipped. Go your ways and play, go.

MRS. PAGE   He is a better scholar than I thought he was.

EVANS   He is a good quick memory. Farewell, Mistress Page.

MRS. PAGE   Adieu, good Sir Hugh. *[Exit Evans.]* Get you home, boy. Come, we stay too long.   *Exeunt.*

SCENE II
Ford's house.

Enter Falstaff and Mistress Ford.

FALSTAFF   Mistress Ford, your sorrow has eaten up my sufferance. I see you are constant in your love, and I profess requital to a hair's breadth; not only, Mistress Ford, in the simple office of love, but in all the accoutrement, complement, and ceremony of it. But are you sure of your husband now?

MRS. FORD   He's a-birding, sweet Sir John.

MRS. PAGE   *[within]* What ho, gossip Ford. What ho!

MRS. FORD   Step into the chamber, Sir John.
[Exit Falstaff.]

Enter Mistress Page.

MRS. PAGE   How now, sweetheart; who's at home besides yourself?

MRS. FORD   Why, none but my own people.

MRS. PAGE   Indeed?

MRS. FORD   No, certainly.—*[aside to her]* speak louder.

MRS. PAGE   Truly, I am so glad you have nobody here.

MRS. FORD   Why?

MRS. PAGE   Why, woman, your husband is in his old fits again. He so takes on yonder with my husband; so rails against all married mankind; so curses all Eve's daughters, of what complexion soever. He so buffets himself on the forehead, crying, 'Peer out, peer out!' that any madness I ever yet beheld seemed but tameness, civility, and patience to this his distemper he is in now. I am glad the fat knight is not here.

MRS. FORD   Why, does he talk of him?

MRS. PAGE   Of none but him; and swears he was carried out, the last time he searched for him, in a basket; protests to my husband he is now here, and has drawn him and the rest of their company from their sport to make another experiment of his suspicion. But I am glad the knight is not here. Now he shall see his own foolery.

MRS. FORD   How near is he, Mistress Page?

MRS. PAGE   Hard by, at street end; he will be here anon.

MRS. FORD   I am undone! The knight is here.

MRS. PAGE   Why then you are utterly shamed, and he's but a dead man. What a woman are you! Away with him, away with him. Better shame than murder.

MRS. FORD   Which way should he go? How should I bestow him? Shall I put him into the basket again?

Enter Falstaff.

FALSTAFF No, I'll come no more in the basket. May I not go out ere he comes?

MRS. PAGE Alas, three of Master Ford's brothers watch the door with pistols that none shall issue out; otherwise you might slip away ere he came. But what make you here?

FALSTAFF What shall I do? I'll creep up into the chimney.

MRS. FORD There they always use to discharge their birding pieces.

MRS. PAGE Creep into the oven.

FALSTAFF Where is it?

MRS. FORD He will seek there, on my word. Neither press, coffer, chest, trunk, well, vault, but he has an abstract for the remembrance of such places, and goes to them by his note. There is no hiding you in the house.

FALSTAFF I'll go out, then.

MRS. PAGE If you go out in your own semblance, you die, Sir John. Unless you go out disguised.

MRS. FORD How might we disguise him?

MRS. PAGE Alas the day, I know not. There is no woman's gown big enough for him, otherwise, he might put on a hat, a muffler, and a kerchief, and so escape.

FALSTAFF Good hearts, devise something. Any extremity rather than a mischief.

MRS. FORD My maid's aunt, the fat woman of Brentford, has a gown above.

MRS. PAGE On my word, it will serve him; she is as big as he is. And there's her woollen hat and her muffler too. Run up, Sir John.

MRS. FORD Go, go, sweet Sir John. Mistress Page and I will look some linen for your head.

MRS. PAGE Quick, quick! We'll come dress you straight; put on the gown the while.

[Exit Falstaff.]

MRS. FORD I would my husband would meet him in this
shape. He cannot abide the old woman of Brentford;
he swears she's a witch, forbade her my house, and
has threatened to beat her.

MRS. PAGE Heaven guide him to your husband's cudgel,
and the devil guide his cudgel afterwards!

MRS. FORD But is my husband coming?

MRS. PAGE Ay, in good sadness, is he; and talks of the
basket too, howsoever he has had intelligence.

MRS. FORD We'll try that; for I'll appoint my men to
carry the basket again, to meet him at the door with
it, as they did last time.

MRS. PAGE Nay, but he'll be here presently. Let's go
dress him like the witch of Brentford.

MRS. FORD I'll first direct my men what they shall do
with the basket. Go up; I'll bring linen for him
straight.

[Exit.]

MRS. PAGE Hang him, dishonest varlet, we cannot
misuse him enough.
We'll leave a proof, by that which we will do,
Wives may be merry, and yet honest too.
We do not act that often jest and laugh;
'Tis old but true, 'Still swine eat all the draff.'

[Exit.]

Enter Mistress Ford, with two Servants.

MRS. FORD Go, sirs, take the basket again on your
shoulders. Your master is hard at door; if he bids you
set it down, obey him. Quickly, dispatch. [Exit.]

FIRST SERVANT Come, come, take it up.

SECOND SERVANT Pray heaven, it is not full of knight
again.

FIRST SERVANT I hope not; I had as soon bear so much
lead.

Enter Ford, Page, Caius, Evans, and Shallow.

FORD   Ay, but if it proves true, Master Page, have you
any way then to unfool me again? Set down the
basket, villains. Somebody call my wife. Youth in a
basket! O you panderly rascals! There's a knot, a
gang, a pack, a conspiracy against me. Now shall the
devil be shamed. What, wife, I say! Come, come
forth! Behold what honest clothes you send forth to
bleaching!
PAGE   Why, this passes! Master Ford, you are not to go
loose any longer; you must be pinioned.
EVANS   Why, this is lunatic, this is mad as a mad dog.
SHALLOW   Indeed, Master Ford, this is not well, indeed.
FORD   So say I too, sir.

Enter Mistress Ford.

Come hither Mistress Ford; Mistress Ford, the
honest woman, the modest wife, the virtuous crea-
ture that has the jealous fool to her husband! I
suspect without cause, mistress, do I?
MRS. FORD   Heaven be my witness, you do if you
suspect me in any dishonesty.
FORD   Well said, brazen- face; hold it out.—Come forth,
sir!
[Pulls clothes out of the basket.]
PAGE   This passes everything.
MRS. FORD   Are you not ashamed? Let the clothes alone.
FORD   I shall find you anon.
EVANS   It is unreasonable. Will you take up your wife's
clothes? Come away.
FORD   Empty the basket, I say!
MRS. FORD   Why, man, why?
FORD   Master Page, as I am an honest man, there was
one conveyed out of my house yesterday in this
basket. Why may not he be there again? In my house I
am sure he is—my intelligence is true; my jealousy is
reasonable. Pluck out all the linen.

MRS. FORD   If you find a man there, he shall die a flea's death.

PAGE   Here's no man.

SHALLOW   By my fidelity, this is not well, Master Ford—this wrongs you.

EVANS   Master Ford, you must pray, and not follow the imagination of your own heart. This is jealousies.

FORD   Well, he's not here I seek for.

PAGE   No, and nowhere else but in your brain.

FORD   Help to search my house this one time. If I find not what I seek, show no color for my extremity; let me for ever be your table-sport. Let them say of me, 'As jealous as Ford, that searched a hollow walnut for his wife's cover.' Satisfy me once more; once more search with me.

MRS. FORD   What ho, Mistress Page, come you and the old woman down. My husband will come into the chamber.

FORD   Old woman! What old woman's that?

MRS. FORD   Why, it is my maid's aunt of Brentford.

FORD   A witch, a quean, an old cozening quean! Have I not forbidden her my house? She comes on errands, does she? We are simple men; we do not know what's brought to pass under the profession of fortune-telling. She works by charms, by spells, by the figure, and such daubery as this is, beyond our element—we know nothing. Come down, you witch, you hag, you; come down, I say!

MRS. FORD   Nay, good, sweet husband! Good gentlemen, let him not strike the old woman.

Enter Falstaff in woman's clothes, and Mistress Page.

MRS. PAGE   Come, Mother Prat, come, give me your hand.

FORD   I'll 'prat' her.—*[Beats him.]* Out of my door you

witch, you hag, you baggage, you polecat, you run-
agate! Out, out! I'll conjure you, I'll fortune-tell you.
                              [Falstaff runs out.]
MRS. PAGE   Are you not ashamed? I think you have
killed the poor woman.
MRS. FORD   Nay, he will do it. 'Tis a goodly credit for
you.
FORD   Hang her, witch!
EVANS   *[aside]* By Jeshu, I think the woman is a witch
indeed. I like not when a woman has a great beard; I
spy a great beard under his muffler.
FORD   Will you follow, gentlemen? I beseech you,
follow. See but the issue of my jealousy. If I cry out
thus upon no trail, never trust me when I open again.
PAGE   Let's obey his humor a little further. Come,
gentlemen.
          [Exeunt Ford, Page, Shallow, Caius, and Evans.]
MRS. PAGE   Trust me, he beat him most pitifully.
MRS. FORD   Nay, by the mass, that he did not: he beat
him most unpitifully, I thought.
MRS. PAGE   I'll have the cudgel hallowed and hung over
the altar: it has done meritorious service.
MRS. FORD   What think you? May we, with the warrant
of womanhood and the witness of a good conscience,
pursue him with any further revenge?
MRS. PAGE   The spirit of wantonness is, sure, scared out
of him. If the devil has him not in fee simple, with fine
and recovery, he will never, I think, in the way of
waste, attempt us again.
MRS. FORD   Shall we tell our husbands how we have
served him?
MRS. PAGE   Yes, by all means, if it is but to scrape the
figures out of your husband's brains. If they can find in
their hearts the poor unvirtuous fat knight shall be
any further afflicted, we two will still be the
ministers.
MRS. FORD   I'll warrant they'll have him publicly

shamed, and I think there would be no point to the jest, should he not be publicly shamed.

MRS. PAGE   Come, to the forge with it; then shape it. I would not have things cool.

Exeunt.

SCENE III
The Garter Inn.

Enter Host and Bardolph.

BARDOLPH   Sir, the Germans desire to have three of your horses. The Duke himself will be to-morrow at Court, and they are going to meet him.

HOST   What duke should that be comes so secretly? I hear not of him in the Court. Let me speak with the gentlemen. They speak English?

BARDOLPH   Ay, sir; I'll call them to you.

HOST   They shall have my horses, but I'll make them pay; I'll sauce them. They have had my house a week at command. I have turned away my other guests. They must come off; I'll sauce them. Come.

Exeunt.

SCENE IV
Ford's house.

Enter Page, Ford, Mistress Page, Mistress Ford, and Evans.

EVANS   It is one of the best discretions of woman as ever I did look upon.

PAGE   And did he send you both these letters at an instant?

MRS. PAGE   Within a quarter of an hour.

FORD   Pardon me, wife. Henceforth do what you will:
I rather will suspect the sun with cold
Than you with wantonness. Now does your honor
    stand,
In him that was of late an heretic,
As firm as faith.
PAGE   'Tis well, 'tis well; no more.
Be not as extreme in submission as in offense.
But let our plot go forward. Let our wives
Yet once again, to make us public sport,
Appoint a meeting with this old fat fellow,
Where we may take him and disgrace him for it.
FORD   There is no better way than that they spoke of.
PAGE   How! to send him word they'll meet him in the
Park at midnight? Fie, fie, he'll never come.
EVANS   You say he has been thrown in the river, and has
been grievously beaten as an old woman. I think there
should be terror in him that he should not come. I
think his flesh is punished; he shall have no desires.
PAGE   So think I too.
MRS. FORD   Devise but how you'll use him when he
comes,
And let us two devise to bring him thither.
MRS. PAGE   There is an old tale goes that Herne the
    hunter,
Sometime a keeper here in Windsor Forest,
Does all the wintertime, at still midnight,
Walk round about an oak, with ragged horns;
And there he blasts the tree, and takes the cattle,
And makes milch kine yield blood, and shakes a
    chain
In a most hideous and dreadful manner.
You have heard of such a spirit, and well you know
The superstitious idle-headed elders
Received and did deliver to our age
This tale of Herne the Hunter for a truth.
PAGE   Why, yet there want not many that do fear

In deep of night to walk by this Herne's Oak.
But what of this?

MRS. FORD   Sure, this is our device:
That Falstaff at that oak shall meet with us,
Disguised like Herne, with huge horns on his head.

PAGE   Well, let it not be doubted but he'll come,
And in this shape when you have brought him
      thither,
What shall be done with him? What is your plot?

MRS. PAGE   That likewise have we thought upon, and
      thus:
Nan Page my daughter, and my little son,
And three or four more of their growth, we'll dress
Like goblins, elves, and fairies, green and white,
With rounds of waxen tapers on their heads,
And rattles in their hands. Upon a sudden,
As Falstaff, she, and I are newly met,
Let them from forth a sawpit rush at once
With some diffusèd song. Upon their sight,
We two in great amazedness will fly.
Then let them all encircle him about,
And, fairy-like, to pinch the unclean knight,
And ask him why, that hour of fairy revel,
In their so sacred paths he dares to tread
In shape profane.

MRS. FORD   And till he tells the truth,
Let the supposèd fairies pinch him sound
And burn him with their tapers.

MRS PAGE   The truth being known,
We'll all present ourselves, dis-horn the spirit,
And mock him home to Windsor.

FORD   The children must
Be practised well to this, or they'll never do it.

EVANS   I will teach the children their behavior; and I
will be like a jackanape also, to burn the knight with
my taper.

FORD   That will be excellent. I'll go buy them masks

MRS. PAGE   My Nan shall be the Queen of all the Fairies,
Finely attirèd in a robe of white.

PAGE   That silk will I go buy. *[aside]* And in that attire
Shall master Slender steal my Nan away.
And marry her at Eton.[1] Go, send to Falstaff straight.

FORD   Nay, I'll to him again in name of Brook.
He'll tell me all his purpose. Sure, he'll come.

MRS. PAGE   Fear not you that. Go, get us properties
And tricking for our fairies.

EVANS   Let us about it. It is admirable pleasure and very
honest knavery.   *[Exeunt Page, Ford, and Evans.]*

MRS. PAGE   Go, Mistress Ford,
Send Quickly to Sir John, to know his mind.
                                    [Exit Mistress Ford.]
I'll to the Doctor: he has my good will,
And none but he, to marry with Nan Page.
That Slender, though well-landed, is an idiot;
And him my husband best of all affects.
The Doctor is well moneyed, and his friends
Potent at Court. He, none but he, shall have her,
Though twenty thousand worthier come to crave her.
                                                [Exit.]

SCENE V
The Garter Inn.

Enter Host and Simple.

HOST   What would you have, boor? What, thick-
skin—speak, breathe, discuss; brief, short, quick,
snap.

SIMPLE   Sure, sir, I come to speak with Sir John Falstaff
from Master Slender.

HOST   There's his chamber, his house, his castle, his
standing-bed and truckle-bed. 'Tis painted about
with the story of the Prodigal, fresh and new. Go,

---

[1]Across the Thames from Windsor, below the Castle.

knock and call. He'll speak like an Anthropopha-
ginian unto you. Knock, I say.

SIMPLE   There's an old woman, a fat woman, gone up
into his chamber. I'll be so bold as stay, sir, till she
comes down. I come to speak with her, indeed.

HOST   Ha, a fat woman? The knight may be robbed: I'll
call. Bully knight, bully Sir John—speak from your
lungs military: are you there? It is your Host, your
Ephesian, calls.

FALSTAFF   *[within]* How now, my Host?

HOST   Here's a Bohemian-Tartar tarries the coming
down of your fat woman. Let her descend, bully, let
her descend. My chambers are honorable. Fie, privacy,
fie!

        Enter Falstaff.

FALSTAFF   There was, my Host, an old fat woman even
now with me, but she's gone.

SIMPLE   Pray you, sir, was it not the wise woman of
Brentford?

FALSTAFF   Ay, certainly, was it, mussel-shell. What
would you with her?

SIMPLE   My master, sir, Master Slender, sent to her, seeing her go through the streets, to know, sir, whether
one Nym, sir, that beguiled him of a chain, had the
chain or no.

FALSTAFF   I spoke with the old woman about it.

SIMPLE   And what says she, I pray, sir?

FALSTAFF   Certain, she says that the very same man that
be-guiled Master Slender of his chain cozened [cheat-
ed] him of it.

SIMPLE   I would I could have spoken with the woman
herself. I had other things to have spoken with her
too, from him.

FALSTAFF   What are they? Let us know.

HOST   Ay, come; quick.

SIMPLE   I may not conceal them, sir.

HOST   Conceal them, or you die.

SIMPLE   Why, sir, they were nothing but about Mistress
Anne Page; to know if it were my master's fortune to
have her, or no.

FALSTAFF   It is, it is his fortune.

SIMPLE   What, sir?

FALSTAFF   To have her, or no. Go, say the woman told me
so.

SIMPLE   May I be bold to say so, sir?

FALSTAFF   Ay, sir, like who more bold?

SIMPLE   I thank your worship: I shall make my master
glad with these tidings.   [Exit.]

HOST   You are clerkly, you are clever, Sir John. Was there
a wise woman with you?

FALSTAFF   Ay, that there was, my Host: one that has
taught me more wit than ever I learned before in my
life; and I paid nothing for it either, but was paid for
my learning.

Enter Bardolph.

BARDOLPH   Out, alas, sir, cozenage, mere cozenage!

HOST   Where are my horses? Speak well of them,
varletto.

BARDOLPH   Run away, with the cozeners; for so soon as I
came beyond Eton, they threw me off, from behind
one of them, in a slough of mire; and set spurs and
away, like three German devils, three Doctor
Faustuses.

HOST   They are gone but to meet the Duke, villain. Do
not say they are fled: Germans are honest men.

Enter Evans

EVANS   Where is my Host?

HOST   What is the matter, sir?

EVANS Have a care of your entertainments. There is a friend of mine come to town, tells me there are three cozen-germans that have cozened all the hosts of Reading, of Maidenhead, of Colebrook, of horses and money. I tell you for good will, look you: you are wise and full of gibes and flouting-stogs, and 'tis not convenient you should be cozened. Fare you well.

[Exit.]

Enter Caius.

CAIUS Vere is mine Host de Jarteer?

HOST Here, Master Doctor, in perplexity and doubtful dilemma.

CAIUS I cannot tell vat is dat; but it is tell-a me dat you make grand preparation for a Duke de Jarmany. By my trot, dere is no duke dat de Court is know to come. I tell you for good vill; adieu.   *[Exit.]*

HOST Hue and cry, villain, go! Assist me, knight. I am undone. Fly, run, hue and cry, villain! I am undone!

[Exeunt Host and Bardolph.]

FALSTAFF I would all the world might be cozened, for I have been cozened and beaten too. If it should come to the ear of the Court how I have been transformed, and how my transformation has been washed and cudgelled, they would melt me out of my fat drop by drop, and liquor fishermen's boots with me. I warrant they would whip me with their fine wits till I were as crestfallen as a dried pear. I never prospered since I forswore myself at primero.[2] Well, if my wind were but long enough to say my prayers, I would repent.

Enter Mistress Quickly.

Now, whence come you?

QUICKLY From the two parties to be sure.

---

[2]The card game most in fashion at Court.

FALSTAFF The devil take one party and his dam the
other!—and so they shall be both bestowed. I have
suffered more for their sakes, more than the villainous inconstancy of man's disposition is able to bear.

QUICKLY And have not they suffered? Yes, I warrant;
speciously one of them. Mistress Ford, good heart, is
beaten black and blue, that you cannot see a white
spot about her.

FALSTAFF What tell you me of black and blue? I was
beaten myself into all the colors of the rainbow; and I
was likely to be apprehended for the witch of Brentford. But that my admirable dexterity of wit, my
counterfeiting the action of an old woman, delivered
me, the knave constable had set me in the stocks, in
the common stocks, for a witch.

QUICKLY Sir, let me speak with you in your chamber.
You shall hear how things go and, I warrant, to your
content. Here is a letter will say somewhat. Good
hearts, what ado here is to bring you together. Sure,
one of you does not serve heaven well, that you are so
crossed.

FALSTAFF Come up into my chamber. *Exeunt.*

SCENE VI
The same.

Enter Fenton and Host.

HOST Master Fenton, talk not to me. My mind is heavy;
I will give over all.

FENTON Yet hear me speak. Assist me in my purpose,
And, as I am a gentleman, I'll give you
A hundred pound in gold more than your loss.

HOST I will hear you, Master Fenton, and I will, at the
least, keep your counsel.

FENTON From time to time I have acquainted you
With the dear love I bear to fair Anne Page,

Who mutually has answered my affection,
So far forth as herself might be her chooser,
Even to my wish. I have a letter from her
Of such contents as you will wonder at,
The mirth whereof so larded with my matter
That neither singly can be manifested
Without the show of both, wherein fat Falstaff
Has a great scene. The image of the jest
I'll show you here at large.   *[Shows a letter.]*
                                        Hark, good my Host:
To-night at Herne's Oak, between twelve and one,
Must my sweet Nan present the Fairy Queen—
The purpose why, is here—in which disguise,
While other jests are something rank on foot,
Her father has commanded her to slip
Away with Slender, and with him at Eton
Immediately to marry. She has consented.
Now, sir,
Her mother (even strong against that match
And firm for Doctor Caius) has appointed
That he shall likewise shuffle her away,
While other sports are tasking of their minds,
And at the deanery, where a priest attends,
Straight marry her. To this her mother's plot
She, seemingly obedient, likewise has
Made promise to the Doctor. Now, thus it rests:
Her father means she shall be all in white,
And in that habit, when Slender sees his time
To take her by the hand and bid her go
She shall go with him. Her mother has intended,
The better to denote her to the Doctor
(For they must all be masked and well disguised),
That quaint in green she shall be loose enrobed,
With ribands pendent, flaring about her head.
And when the Doctor spies his vantage ripe,
To pinch her by the hand, and on that token
The maid has given consent to go with him.

HOST Which means she to deceive, father or mother?
FENTON Both, my good Host, to go along with me.
  And here it rests, that you'll procure the vicar
  To stay for me at church between twelve and one,
  And, in the lawful name of marrying,
  To give our hearts united ceremony.
HOST Well, husband your device; I'll to the vicar.
  Bring you the maid, you shall not lack a priest.
FENTON So shall I evermore be bound to you;
  Besides, I'll make a present recompense.   *Exeunt.*

Act V

SCENE I
The Garter Inn.

Enter Falstaff and Mistress Quickly.

FALSTAFF   Pray no more prattling. Go: I'll hold. This is
the third time; I hope good luck lies in odd numbers.
Away; go. They say there is divinity in odd numbers,
either in nativity, chance, or death. Away.

QUICKLY   I'll provide you a chain, and I'll do what I can to
get you a pair of horns.

FALSTAFF   Away, I say; time wears. Hold up your head,
and mince off.   *[Exit Mistress Quickly.]*

Enter Ford.

How now, Master Brook. Master Brook, the matter
will be known to-night, or never. Be you in the Park
about midnight, at Herne's Oak, and you shall see
wonders.

FORD   Went you not to her yesterday, sir, as you told me
you had appointed?

FALSTAFF   I went to her, Master Brook, as you see, like a
poor old man; but I came from her, Master Brook,
like a poor old woman. That same knave Ford, her
husband, has the finest mad devil of jealousy in him,
Master Brook, that ever governed frenzy. I will tell
you: he beat me grievously, in the shape of a woman;
for in the shape of a man, Master Brook, I fear not
Goliath with a weaver's beam, because I know also
life is a shuttle. I am in haste. Go along with me; I'll
tell you all, Master Brook. Since I plucked geese,

played truant, and whipped top, I knew not what it
was to be beaten till lately. Follow me. I'll tell you
strange things of this knave Ford, on whom to-night I
will be revenged, and I will deliver his wife into your
hand. Follow. Strange things in hand, Master Brook!
Follow.

Exeunt.

SCENE II
Windsor Park.

Enter Page, Shallow, and Slender.

PAGE   Come, come; we'll couch in the Castle ditch till
we see the light of our fairies. Remember, son
Slender, my daughter.

SLENDER   Ay, sure; I have spoken with her and we have
a watchword how to know one another. I come to her
in white, and cry, 'mum'; she cries, 'budget'; and by
that we know one another.

SHALLOW   That's good too. But what needs either your
'mum,' or her 'budget'? The white will decipher her
well enough. It has struck ten o'clock.

PAGE   The night is dark; light and spirits will become it
well. Heaven prosper our sport. No man means evil
but the devil, and we shall know him by his horns.
Let's away; follow me.   *Exeunt.*

SCENE III
The Park.

*Enter Mistress Page, Mistress Ford, and Doctor
Caius.*

MRS. PAGE   Master Doctor, my daughter is in green.

When you see your time, take her by the hand, away
with her to the deanery, and dispatch it quickly. Go
before into the Park. We two must go together.

CAIUS   I know vat I have to do. Adieu.

MRS. PAGE   Fare you well, sir. *[Exit Caius.]* My husband
will not rejoice so much at the abuse of Falstaff, as he
will chafe at the Doctor's marrying my daughter. But
it is no matter: better a little chiding than a great deal
of heartbreak.

MRS. FORD   Where are Nan now and her troop of fairies,
and the Welsh devil, Hugh?

MRS. PAGE   They are all couched in a pit hard by Herne's
Oak, with obscured lights, which at the very instant
of Falstaff's and our meeting they will at once display
to the night.

MRS. FORD   That cannot choose but amaze him.

MRS. PAGE   If he is not amazed, he will be mocked; if he
is amazed, he will every way be mocked.

MRS. FORD   We'll betray him finely.

MRS. PAGE   Against such lechers and their lechery,
Those that betray them do no treachery.

MRS. FORD   The hour draws on. To the Oak, to the Oak!

Exeunt.

SCENE IV
The Park.

Enter Evans as a Satyr and others as Fairies.

EVANS   Trip, trip, fairies. Come, and remember your
parts. Be bold, I pray you. Follow me into the pit, and
when I give the watch-words, do as I bid you. Come,
come; trip, trip.   *Exeunt.*

SCENE V
The Park.

*Enter Falstaff disguised as Herne the Hunter
with a buck's head.*

FALSTAFF   The Windsor bell has struck twelve; the
minute draws on. Now, the hot-blooded gods assist
me! Remember, Jove, you were a bull for your
Europa; love set on your horns. O powerful love, that
in some respects makes a beast a man; in some
others, a man a beast. You were also, Jupiter, a swan
for the love of Leda. O omnipotent love, how near the
god drew to the complexion of a goose! A fault done
first in the form of a beast—O Jove, a beastly
fault!—and then another fault in the semblance of a
fowl. Think of it, Jove; a foul fault! When gods have
hot backs, what shall poor men do? For me, I am here
a Windsor stag; and the fattest, I think, in the forest.
Send me a cool rut-time, Jove, or who can blame me
to piss my tallow? Who comes here? my doe?

Enter Mistress Page and Mistress Ford.

MRS. FORD   Sir John? Are you there, my deer, my male
deer?

FALSTAFF   My doe with the black scut! Let the sky rain
potatoes; let it thunder to the tune of 'Greensleeves,'
hail kissing-comfits, and snow candies. Let there
come a tempest of provocation, I will shelter me
here.
                                                    [Embraces her.]

MRS. FORD   Mistress Page is come with me, sweetheart.

FALSTAFF   Divide me like a bribed buck, each a haunch.
I will keep my sides to myself, my shoulders for the
keeper of this walk, and my horns I bequeath your
husbands. Am I a hunter, ha? Speak I like Herne the

Hunter? Why, now is Cupid a child of conscience; he
makes restitution. As I am a true spirit, welcome!
                                    [Noise within.]

MRS. PAGE   Alas, what noise?

MRS. FORD   Heaven forgive our sins!

FALSTAFF   What should this be?

MRS. FORD ⎫
MRS. PAGE ⎭   Away, away!   *[They run off.]*

FALSTAFF   I think the devil will not have me damned,
    lest the oil that's in me should set hell on fire. He
    would never else cross me thus.

Enter Evans as a Satyr and others as Fairies.

QUICKLY   Fairies, black, grey, green, and white,
    You moonshine revellers, and shades of night,
    You orphan heirs of fixèd destiny,
    Attend your office and your quality.
    Crier Hobgoblin, make the fairy oyes.[1]

PISTOL   Elves, list your names; silence, you airy toys!
    Cricket, to Windsor chimneys shall you leap.
    Where fires you find unraked and hearths unswept,
    There pinch the maids as blue as bilberry.
    Our radiant Queen hates sluts and sluttery.

FALSTAFF   They are fairies; he that speaks to them shall
    die.
    I'll wink and couch; no man their works must eye.
                                    [Lies down upon his face.]

EVANS   Where's Bead? Go you, and where you find a
    maid
    That ere she sleeps has thrice her prayèrs said,
    Raise up the organs of her fantasy,
    Sleeps she as sound as careless infancy.
    But those that sleep and think not on their sins,
    Pinch them, arms, legs, backs, shoulders, sides and
    shins.

---

[1]Town crier's call.

ANNE PAGE   About, about—
Search Windsor Castle, elves, within and out.
Strew good luck, fays, on every sacred room,
That it may stand till the perpetual doom,
In state as wholesome as in state 'tis fit,
Worthy the owner, and the owner it.
The several chairs of order look you scour
With juice of balm and every precious flower.
Each fair instalment, coat, and separate crest,
With loyal bearings, evermore be blest.
And nightly, meadow-fairies, look you sing,
Like to the Garter's compass, in a ring.
The expression that it bears, green let it be,
More fertile-fresh than all the field to see;
And 'Honi soit qui mal y pense'[2] write
In emerald tufts, flowers purple, blue, and white,
Like sapphire, pearl, and rich embroidery,
Buckled below fair knighthood's bending knee.
Fairies use flowers for their charactery [writing].
Away, disperse. But till 'tis one o'clock,
Our dance of custom round about the Oak
Of Herne the Hunter, let us not forget.
EVANS   Pray you, lock hand in hand; yourselves in order
  set;
And twenty glowworms shall our lanterns be,
To guide our measure round about the tree.
But, stay—I smell a man of middle earth.[3]
FALSTAFF   Heavens defend me from that Welsh fairy,
  lest he transform me to a piece of cheese!
PISTOL   Vile worm, you were bewitched even in your
  birth.
QUICKLY   With trial-fire touch me his finger end.
If he is chaste, the flame will back descend
And turn him to no pain; but if he start,

---

[2]'Evil to him who evil thinks': the motto of the Order of the Garter.
[3]The planet inhabited by humans.

It is the flesh of a corrupted heart.
PISTOL   A trial, come.
EVANS   Come, will this wood take fire?
                    [They burn him with their tapers.]
FALSTAFF   O, O, O!
QUICKLY   Corrupt, corrupt, and tainted in desire!
About him, fairies, sing a scornful rhyme;
And, as you trip, still pinch him to your time.

                    The Song.

Fie on sinful fantasy!
Fie on lust and luxury! [lustfulness]
Lust is but a bloody fire,
Kindled with unchaste desire,
Fed in heart, whose flames aspire,
As thoughts do blow them, higher and higher.
Pinch him, fairies, mutually;
Pinch him for his villainy;
Pinch him, and burn him, and turn him about,
Till candles and starlight and moonshine be out.
*[During this song they pinch Falstaff. Doctor Caius
steals away a Fairy in green; Slender takes off a Fairy
in white; and Fenton steals away Anne Page. A noise
of hunting is heard within. All the Fairies run away.
Falstaff rises.]*

        *Enter Page, Ford, Mistress Page, and Mistress
        Ford.*

PAGE   Nay, do not fly: I think we have watched you
    now.
Will none but Herne the Hunter serve your turn?
MRS. PAGE   I pray you, come, hold up the jest no higher.
Now, good Sir John, how like you Windsor wives?
See you these, husband? Do not these fair horns
Become the forest better than the town?

FORD   Now sir, who's a cuckold now? Master Brook, Falstaff's a knave, a cuckoldly knave; here are his horns, Master Brook. And, Master Brook, he has enjoyed nothing of Ford's but his buck-basket, his cudgel, and twenty pounds of money, which must be paid too, Master Brook; his horses are arrested for it, Master Brook.

MRS. FORD   Sir John, we have had ill luck; we could never meet. I will never take you for my love again, but I will always count you my deer.

FALSTAFF   I do begin to perceive that I am made an ass.

FORD   Ay, and an ox too: both the proofs are extant.

FALSTAFF   And these are not fairies? I was three or four times in the thought they were not fairies; and yet the guiltiness of my mind, the sudden surprise of my powers, drove the grossness of the foppery into a received belief, in despite of the teeth of all rhyme and reason, that they were fairies. See now how wit may be made a Jack-a-Lent, when it is upon ill employment.

EVANS   Sir John Falstaff, serve Got and leave your desires, and fairies will not pinse you.

FORD   Well said, fairy Hugh.

EVANS   And leave you your jealousies too, I pray you.

FORD   I will never mistrust my wife again, till you are able to woo her in good English.

FALSTAFF   Have I laid my brain in the sun and dried it, that it wants matter to prevent so gross overreaching as this? Am I ridden with a Welsh goat too? Shall I have a coxcomb of Welsh cloth? 'Tis time I were choked with a piece of toasted cheese.

EVANS   Seese is not goot to give putter—your belly is all putter.

FALSTAFF   'Seese' and 'putter'! Have I lived to stand at the taunt of one that makes fritters of English? This is enough to be the decay of lust and late-walking through the realm.

MRS. PAGE   Why, Sir John, do you think, though we would have thrust virtue out of our hearts by the head and shoulders, and have given ourselves without scruple to hell, that ever the devil could have made you our delight?

FORD   What, a hogs'-pudding? a bag of flax?

MRS. PAGE   A puffed man?

PAGE   Old, cold, withered, and of intolerable entrails?

FORD   And one that is as slanderous as Satan?

PAGE   And as poor as Job?

FORD   And as wicked as his wife?

EVANS   And given to fornications, and to taverns, and sack and wine and metheglins,[4] and to drinkings and swearings and starings, pribbles and prabbles?

FALSTAFF   Well, I am your theme. You have the start of me;

I am dejected; I am not able to answer the Welsh flannel. Ignorance itself is a plummet over me[5]—use me as you will.

FORD   Sure, sir, we'll bring you to Windsor, to one Master Brook, that you have cozened of money, to whom you should have been a pander. Over and above that you have suffered, I think to repay that money will be a biting affliction.

PAGE   Yet be cheerful, knight. You shalt eat a posset tonight at my house, where I will desire you to laugh at my wife that now laughs at you. Tell her, Master Slender has married her daughter.

MRS. PAGE   [aside] Doctors doubt that. If Anne Page is my daughter, she is, by this, Doctor Caius' wife.

   Enter Slender.

SLENDER   Whoa, ho, ho, father Page!

---

[4]Welsh mead.
[5]i.e., has sounded to the bottom.

PAGE   Son, how now; how now, son. Have you dispatched?

SLENDER   Dispatched? I'll make the best in Gloucestershire know of it; would I were hanged, la, else.

PAGE   Of what, son?

Slender   I came yonder at Eton to marry Mistress Anne Page, and she's a great lubberly boy. If it had not been in the church, I would have swinged him, or he should have swinged me. If I did not think it had been Anne Page, would I might never stir—and 'tis a postmaster's boy.

PAGE   Upon my life, then, you took the wrong.

SLENDER   What need you tell me that? I think so, when I took a boy for a girl. If I had been married to him, for all he was in woman's apparel, I would not have had him.

PAGE   Why, this is your own folly. Did not I tell you how you should know my daughter my her garments?

SLENDER   I went to her in white, and cried, 'mum,' and she cried 'budget,' as Anne and I had appointed; and yet it was not Anne, but a postmaster's boy.

MRS. PAGE   Good George, be not angry. I knew of your purpose; turned my daughter into green; and indeed she is now with the Doctor at the deanery, and there married.

Enter Doctor Caius.

CAIUS   Vere is Mistress Page? By God, I am cozened—I have married un garçon, a boy; un paysan, by God, a boy; it is not Anne Page. By God, I am cozened.

MRS. PAGE   Why, did you not take her in green?

CAIUS   Ay, by God, and 'tis a boy. By God, I'll raise all Windsor.   [*Exit.*]

FORD   This is strange. Who has got the right Anne?

PAGE   My heart misgives me. Here comes Master Fenton.

Enter Fenton and Anne Page.

How now, Master Fenton?

ANNE Pardon, good father; good my mother, pardon.

PAGE Now, mistress, how chance you went not with
Master Slender?

MRS. PAGE Why went you not with Master Doctor,
maid?

FENTON You do amaze her. Hear the truth of it.—
You would have married her most shamefully,
Where there was no proportion held in love.
The truth is, she and I, long since contracted,
Are now so sure that nothing can dissolve us.
The offense is holy that she has committed,
And this deceit loses the name of craft,
Of disobedience, or unduteous title;
Since therein she does avoid and shun
A thousand irreligious cursèd hours,
Which forcèd marriage would have brought upon
her.

FORD Stand not amazed. Here is no remedy.
In love the heavens themselves do guide the state;
Money buys lands, and wives are sold by fate.

FALSTAFF I am glad, though you have taken a special
stand to strike at me, that your arrow has glanced.

PAGE Well, what remedy? Fenton, heaven give you joy!
What cannot be eschewed must be embraced.

FALSTAFF When night dogs run, all sorts of deer are
chased.

MRS. PAGE Well, I will muse no further. Master Fenton,
Heaven give you many, many merry days!
Good husband, let us every one go home,
And laugh this sport over by a country fire;
Sir John and all.

FORD   Let it be so. Sir John,
To Master Brook you yet shall hold your word;
For he to-night shall lie with Mistress Ford.

Exeunt.

Troilus and Cressida

INTRODUCTION

Troilus and Cressida is a very remarkable play, of a special character in Shakespeare's work. Though not one of the most popular, it is of surpassing intellectual interest. It was not in the first place written for a popular audience but for a sophisticated, one, probably at one of the Inns of Court, where its free talk about sex, its bawdiness and generous allowance of cynical comment on war and love, would be relished.

As usual the dramatist was responding to the circumstances of both the time and the theatre. The time, 1602, was the year after the disheartening fall of Essex, the war with Spain dragging on endlessly, the ageing Queen on her way out, people uncertain and nervous about the future. The phrase 'the bitter disposition of the time' reflects it perfectly. The theatre was dominated by the so-called War of the Theatres stirred up by Ben Jonson's testy disposition, between him—his satires shrilly voiced by the Boys' Companies—and the Men's Companies of Shakespeare, Dekker and Marston. With this Ben broke away from the Chamberlain's Company, where Shakespeare had given him his opening.

A Cambridge play, *The Return from Parnassus*, comments, 'our fellow Shakespeare puts them all down, aye and Ben Jonson too. . .Shakespeare hath given him a purge that made him beray [dirty] his credit.' Certainly the Prologue in this play has a tilt at the Prologue to Ben's *Poetaster* of the year before; while Ben's theme of 'humours' is caricatured in several plays of this time.

369

When the play was ultimately published in 1609, it was provided with a peculiar, personal-sounding Preface, saying that it was 'never staled with the stage, never clapper-clawed with the palms of the vulgar, and yet passing full of the palm comical; for it is a birth of your brain that never undertook anything comical vainly. . . Especially this author's comedies, that are so framed to the life. . .showing such a dexterity and power of wit that the most displeased with plays are pleased with his comedies. . . Amongst all there is none more witty than this'—though 'not sullied with the smoky breath of the multitude.' It is the oddest Preface, written—one would say—by someone close to Shakespeare. A curious feature is the word 'clapper-clawed', which had appeared before only in a work by Nashe, and occurs once again only in the play.

The play is best regarded as a satire, reflecting the contemporary situation—it is not to be regarded romantically or tragically. The general tone is decidedly disillusioned, and it is the cynical Thersites to whom it is given to speak the truth, about war and and love and the cause that had brought it about—the carrying off of Helen to Troy. 'Fools on both sides' is his crisp conclusion; and the consequences of war, plague and venereal disease, 'the curse dependent on those that war for a placket', i.e. a bitch. Even Troilus is shown up for a fool for believing in Cressida's promised faithfulness: with singularly little fuss she goes over to the Greek Diomedes. *His* view of Helen was no less cynical:

> For every false drop in her bawdy veins
> A Grecian's life has sunk; for every scruple
> Of her contaminated carrion weight
> A Trojan has been slain. . .

To what point? It would lead only to the destruction of Troy—a theme which, like Julius Caesar, always haunted Shakespeare's imagination. His mind was formed by his classical education from school and subsequent reading—one is continually surprised by his range of reference. However, where the Greeks were concerned, he saw the matter through medieval spectacles, in terms of Chaucer, Caxton's Troy story, which—with Chapman's recent *Iliad* (1598)—provided material. The fighting between Greeks and Trojans is in a medieval idiom, distinctly personal, with the infantile brags of the fighting fools on either side. Not William Shakespeare's view of life, as we see fairly consistently from the plays; but it appealed to the Elizabethan audience, the noise, the clashes, the drums and trumpets—after all their repertory of effects was rather limited.

The theatre itself as always provides images: Achilles' minion Patroclus mimics the fighting fools—

—like a strutting player whose conceit [thought]
Lies in his hamstring, and does think it rich
To hear the wooden dialogue and sound
Betwixt his stretched footing and the scaffoldage.

The contemporary audience, especially a sophisticated one, would recognise the obvious portrayal of Essex:

Things small as nothing, for request's sake only,
He makes important. Possessed he is with greatness,
And speaks not to himself but with a pride
That quarrels at self-breath. . .
He is so plaguy proud that the death-tokens of it
Cry 'No recovery.'

This is exactly as Essex had behaved with the Queen, always pressing her for jobs for his followers, then absenting himself from Court when he did not get his way, sulking in his tent like Achilles. Actually, sycophantic publications at the time referred to him as another Achilles. Southampton kept him company in his dangerous sulks; Essex was notably heterosexual; Southampton, though now married, was still ambivalent; it was Achilles who was bi-sexual.

Essex had been executed in 1601, Southampton was in

the Tower under sentence: the prudent dramatist, up to
his eyes in the theatre, could not but be affected by the
tragedy—especially to his former patron and friend. He
could observe from close at hand the facts of political life
and faction fighting. What happened after Essex's fall is
precisely described:

> What the declined is
> He shall as soon read in the eyes of others
> As feel in his own fall. For men, like butterflies,
> Show not their mealy [dusty] wings but to the
>   summer.

That is as it had been quite recently with Francis Bacon,
who read the signs before Essex's fall and deserted him.
Here is what William Shakespeare thought:

> And not a man, for being simply man,
> Has any honour, but honour for those honours
> That are without him—as place, riches and favour,
> Prizes of accident as oft as merit.
> Who when they fall, as being slippery standers,
> The love that leaned on them as slippery too,
> Does one pluck down another, and together
> Die in the fall.

Several had died along with Essex: Southampton was
under suspended sentence.   One can *see* William
Shakespeare in the images that come to mind:

> like a fashionable host
> That slightly shakes his parting guest by the hand
> And, with his arms outstretched as he would fly,
> Grasps in the comer.

Or again, in another personal observation —

> Like vassalage at unawares encountering
> The eye of Majesty.

From frequent appearances at Court he had encountered
those searching eyes often enough.

   Marlowe remains constant in his memory: Helen,
'whose price has launched a thousand ships', reflects one
of those memorable lines for which Marlowe was famous. It is more surprising to find Aristotle cited, for

only the second time in the plays: but Shakespeare knew
what he stood for, the pre-eminence of reason, and young
men's unfitness for moral, in which he included political, philosophy. Young Troilus argues all for love against
reason. The argument is brilliantly conducted; but,
since Shakespeare thought in images as well as abstrac-
tions, it is by no means easy to follow. All the more reason to simplify where we come up against obstacles to
understanding what he is saying.

The play is most famous for the splendid speeches of
the wise Ulysses on the theme ever present to
Shakespeare's mind from beginning to end: the prime
necessity of social order, of due rank in society according
to function, the proper observation of degree and authority if society is not to break down and evil consequences
ensue.

> O, when degree is shaked—
> Which is the ladder of all high designs—
> The enterprise is sick. . .
> Take but degree away, untune that string,
> And hark what discord follows. Each thing meets
> In mere oppugnancy.

How piercingly true this is the whole social map of our
own world today shows. The conflicts between classes,
of groups, between producer and consumer, become
open and inveterate: no reconciliation within the
community as a whole.

> How could communities,
> Degrees in schools, and brotherhoods in cities,
> Peaceful commerce

between nations, stand without proper division of function? Shake the fabric of society, undermine order and
social discipline—and see what happens:

> Then everything includes itself in power,
> Power into will, will into appetite,
> And appetite, an universal wolf. . .
> Must make perforce an universal prey
> And last eat up itself.

Everywhere in the world today we have reason to see how profoundly true this is. We should not be surprised, for Shakespeare understood human nature more completely than any other writer. And there is much more in this play which we can learn from.

From the character of the play the language is not easy, perhaps most of all from Thersites, an extraordinary character. He is a licensed jester, playing the part of Clown, but also that of Chorus, commenting on the action and the actors. 'Now they are clapper-clawing [mauling] one another; I'll go look on.' He sums up Achilles and Patroclus: 'with too much blood and too little brain, these two may run mad.' The great Agamemnon is 'an honest fellow enough, and one that loves quails, but he has not so much brain as ear-wax.' As for the blockish Ajax, a whole cataract of insults falls upon him—and of such linguistic virtuosity as to give us difficulty. At one point it is a catalogue of contemporary diseases, for which we have to find modern equivalents. At another we have inventive variations of vituperation. And the swear-words! What are we to do with the frequent word 'whoreson'? I suppose a modern equivalent would be bastard, son-of-a-bitch.

When Thersites is challenged by a bastard son of King Priam, he is not such a fool as to fight. 'I am a bastard too; I love bastards. I am a bastard begot, bastard instructed, bastard in mind, bastard in valour, in everything illegitimate. One bear will not bite another, and wherefore should one bastard?' Thersites the cynic, and Pandarus, who is what he is, have the last words in this satirical play. It is as if Jonathan Swift had written it.

A NEVER WRITER,
TO AN EVER READER.
NEWS.

Eternal reader, you have here a new play, never staled with the stage, never clapper-clawed with the palms of the vulgar, and yet passing full of the palm comical; for it is a birth of your brain that never undertook anything comical vainly. And were but the vain names of comedies changed for the titles of commodities, or of plays for pleas, you should see all those grand censors, that now style them such vanities, flock to them for the main grace of their gravities, especially this author's comedies, that are so framed to the life that they serve for the most common commentaries of all the actions of our lives, showing such a dexterity and power of wit that the most displeased with plays are pleased with his comedies. And all such dull and heavy-witted worldlings as were never capable of the wit of a comedy, coming by report of them to his representations, have found that wit there that they never found in themselves and have parted better witted than they came, feeling an edge of wit set upon them more than ever they dreamed they had brain to grind it on. So much and such savored salt of wit is in his comedies that they seem, for their height of pleasure, to be born in that sea that brought forth Venus. Amongst all there is none more witty than this: and had I time I would comment upon it, though I know it needs not, for so much as will make you think your sixpence well bestowed, but for so much worth as even poor I know to be stuffed in it. It deserves such a labor as well as the best comedy in

Terence or Plautus. And believe this, that when he is gone and his comedies out of sale, you will scramble for them and set up a new English Inquisition. Take this for a warning, and at the peril of your pleasure's loss, and judgment's, refuse not, nor like this the less for not being sullied with the smoky breath of the multitude; but thank fortune for the 'scape it hath made amongst you, since by the grand possessors' wills I believe you should have prayed for them rather than been prayed. And so I leave all such to be prayed for, for the state of their wits' healths, that will not praise it. Vale.

CHARACTERS

PRIAM, King of Troy

HECTOR
TROILUS
PARIS } his sons
DEIPHOBUS
HELENUS

MARGARELON, a bastard son of Priam

AENEAS
ANTENOR } Trojan commanders

CALCHAS, a Trojan priest,

PANDARUS, uncle to Cressida

AGAMEMNON, the Greek general

MENELAUS, his brother

ACHILLES
AJAX
ULYSSES } Greek commanders
NESTOR
DIOMEDES
PATROCLUS

THERSITES, a Greek cynic

ALEXANDER, servant to Cressida

HELEN, wife to Menelaus

ANDROMACHE, wife to Hector

CASSANDRA, daughter to Priam; a prophetess

CRESSIDA, daughter to Calchas

TROJAN and GREEK SOLDIERS, Attendants and Servants

Prologue

In Troy there lies the scene. From isles of Greece
The princes arrogant, their high blood chafed,
Have to the port of Athens sent their ships,
Fraught with the ministers and instruments
Of cruel war. Sixty and nine, that wore
Their crownets regal, from the Athenian bay
Put forth toward Phrygia; and their vow is made
To ransack Troy, within whose strong ramparts
The ravished Helen, Menelaus' queen,
With wanton Paris sleeps; and that's the quarrel.
To Tenedos they come,
And the deep-drawing barks do there disgorge
Their warlike freightage. Now on Dardan plains
The fresh and yet unbruisèd Greeks do pitch
Their brave pavilions. Priam's six-gated city,
Dardan, and Timbria, Helias, Chetas, Troien,
And Antenorides, with massy staples
And corresponsive and fulfilling bolts,
Shut up the sons of Troy.
Now expectations, tickling skittish spirits,
On one and other side, Trojan and Greek,
Sets all on hazard. And hither am I come,
A prologue armed, but not in confidence
Of author's pen or actor's voice, but suited
In like conditions as our argument—
To tell you, fair beholders, that our play
Leaps over the first beginnings of those broils,
Beginning in the middle, starting thence away
To what may be digested in a play.
Like or find fault; do as your pleasures are:
Now good or bad, 'tis but the chance of war.

Act I

SCENE I
Troy. Before Priam's palace.

Enter Pandarus and Troilus.

TROILUS
> Call here my varlet, I'll unarm again.
> Why should I war without the walls of Troy
> That find such cruel battle here within?
> Each Trojan that is master of his heart,
> Let him to field; Troilus, alas, has none.

PANDARUS
> Will this business never be mended?

TROILUS
> The Greeks are strong, and skillful to their strength,
> Fierce to their skill, and to their fierceness valiant;
> But I am weaker than a woman's tear,
> Tamer than sleep, more foolish than ignorance,
> Less valiant than the virgin in the night,
> And skilless as unpractised infancy.

PANDARUS   Well, I have told you enough of this. For my
part, I'll not meddle nor make any farther. He that will
have a cake out of the wheat must tarry the grinding.

TROILUS   Have I not tarried?

PANDARUS   Ay, the grinding; but you must tarry the
sifting.

TROILUS   Have I not tarried?

PANDARUS   Ay, the sifting; but you must tarry the
leavening.

TROILUS   Still have I tarried.

PANDARUS   Ay, to the leavening; but here's yet in the
word 'hereafter' the kneading, the making of the cake,

381

the heating of the oven, and the baking. Nay, you must
stay the cooling too, or you may chance to burn your
lips.

TROILUS

Patience herself, what goddess ever she is,
Does lesser blench at sufferance than I do.
At Priam's royal table do I sit,
And when fair Cressid comes into my thoughts—
So, traitor, then she comes when she is thence.

PANDARUS   Well, she looked yesternight fairer than ever
I saw her look, or any woman else.

TROILUS

I was about to tell you, when my heart,
As wedgèd with a sigh, would rive in twain,
Lest Hector or my father should perceive me:
I have, as when the sun does light askance,
Buried this sigh in wrinkle of a smile.
But sorrow, that is couched in seeming gladness,
Is like that mirth fate turns to sudden sadness.

PANDARUS   If her hair were not somewhat darker than
Helen's—well, go to—there were no more comparison
between the women. But, for my part, she is my kins-
woman; I would somebody had heard her talk yesterday, as I did. I will not dispraise your sister Cassandra's
wit, but—

TROILUS

O Pandarus! I tell you, Pandarus—
When I do tell you, there my hopes lie drowned,
Reply not in how many fathoms deep
They lie indrenched. I tell you I am mad
In Cressid's love; you answer she is fair;
Pour in the open ulcer of my heart
Her eyes, her hair, her cheek, her gait, her voice;
Handle in your discourse, O, that her hand,
In whose comparison all whites are ink,
Writing their own reproach; to whose soft seizure
The cygnet's down is harsh, and spirit of sense
Hard as the palm of ploughman. This you tell me,

As true you tell me, when I say I love her;
But, saying thus, instead of oil and balm,
You lay in every gash that love has given me
The knife that made it.

PANDARUS   I speak no more than truth.

TROILUS   You do not speak so much.

PANDARUS   Faith, I'll not meddle in it. Let her be as she
is. If she is fair, 'tis the better for her; if she is not, she
has the mends in her own hands.

TROILUS   Good Pandarus, how now, Pandarus?

PANDARUS   I have had my labor for my travail; ill-
thought-on of her, and ill-thought-on of you; gone
between and between, but small thanks for my labor.

TROILUS   What, are you angry, Pandarus? What, with
me?

PANDARUS   Because she's kin to me, therefore she's not
so fair as Helen. If she were not kin to me, she would
be as fair on Friday as Helen is on Sunday. But what
care I? I care not if she were a blackamoor; 'tis all one
to me.

TROILUS   Say I she is not fair?

PANDARUS   I do not care whether you do or no. She's a
fool to stay behind her father. Let her to the Greeks,
and so I'll tell her the next time I see her. For my part,
I'll not meddle nor make any more in the matter.

TROILUS   Pandarus—

PANDARUS   Not I.

TROILUS   Sweet Pandarus—

PANDARUS   Pray you, speak no more to me. I will leave
all as I found it, and there an end.

Exit. Sound alarum.

TROILUS
Peace, you ungracious clamors! Peace, rude sounds!
Fools on both sides! Helen must needs be fair,
When with your blood you daily paint her thus.
I cannot fight upon this argument;
It is too starved a subject for my sword.
But Pandarus—O gods, how do you plague me!

I cannot come to Cressid but by Pandar;
And he's as tetchy to be wooed to woo
As she is stubborn, chaste, against all suit.
Tell me, Apollo, for your Daphne's love,
What Cressid is, what Pandar, and what we.
Her bed is India; there she lies, a pearl.
Between our Ilium and where she resides
Let it be called the wild and wandering flood,
Ourself the merchant, and this sailing Pandar
Our doubtful hope, our convoy and our bark.

> *Alarum. Enter Aeneas.*

AENEAS
How now, Prince Troilus, wherefore not afield?
TROILUS
Because not there. This woman's answer suits,
For womanish it is to be from thence.
What news, Aeneas, from the field to-day?
AENEAS
That Paris is returnèd home, and hurt.
TROILUS
By whom, Aeneas?
AENEAS   Troilus, by Menelaus.
TROILUS
Let Paris bleed; 'tis but a scar to scorn.
Paris is gored with Menelaus' horn.
            Alarum.
AENEAS
Hark what good sport is out of town to-day!
TROILUS
Better at home, if 'would I might' were 'may.'
But to the sport abroad. Are you bound thither?
AENEAS
In all swift haste.
TROILUS   Come, go we then together.
                                        Exeunt.

SCENE II
The same.

Enter Cressida and Alexander, her man.

CRESSIDA

Who were those went by?

ALEXANDER   Queen Hecuba and Helen.

CRESSIDA

And whither go they?

ALEXANDER   Up to the eastern tower,
Whose height commands as subject all the vale,
To see the battle. Hector, whose patiènce
Is as a virtue fixed, to-day was moved.
He chid Andròmache, and struck his armorer,
And, like as there were husbandry in war,
Before the sun rose he was harnessed light,
And to the field goes he; where every flower
Did, as a prophet, weep what it foresaw
In Hector's wrath.

CRESSIDA   What was his cause of anger?

ALEXANDER

The noise goes, this: there is among the Greeks
A lord of Trojan blood, nephew to Hector;
They call him Ajax.

CRESSIDA   Good; and what of him?

ALEXANDER

They say he is a very man per se [by himself]
And stands alone.

CRESSIDA   So do all men unless they are drunk, sick, or
have no legs.

ALEXANDER   This man, lady, has robbed many beasts of
their particular additions: he is as valiant as the lion,
churlish as the bear, slow as the elephant; a man into
whom nature has so crowded humors that his valor is
crushed into folly, his folly sauced with discretion.

There is no man has a virtue that he has not a glimpse of, nor any man an attaint but he carries some stain of it. He is melancholy without cause and merry against the grain. He has the joints of everything, but everything so out of joint that he is a gouty Briareus: many hands and no use, or purblind Argus, all eyes and no sight.

CRESSIDA   But how should this man that makes me smile make Hector angry?

ALEXANDER   They say he yesterday coped with Hector in the battle and struck him down; the disdain and shame whereof have ever since kept Hector fasting and waking.

Enter Pandarus

CRESSIDA   Who comes here?

ALEXANDER   Madam, your uncle Pandarus.

CRESSIDA   Hector is a gallant man.

ALEXANDER   As may be in the world, lady.

PANDARUS   What's that? What's that?

CRESSIDA   Good morrow, uncle Pandarus.

PANDARUS   Good morrow, niece Cressid. What do you talk of? Good morrow, Alexander. How do you, niece? When were you at Ilium?

CRESSIDA   This morning, uncle.

PANDARUS   What were you talking of when I came? Was Hector armed and gone ere you came to Ilium? Helen was not up, was she?

CRESSIDA   Hector was gone, but Helen was not up.

PANDARUS   Even so, Hector was stirring early.

CRESSIDA   That were we talking of, and of his anger.

PANDARUS   Was he angry?

CRESSIDA   So he says here.

PANDARUS   True, he was so. I know the cause too. He will lay about him to-day, I can tell them that; and there's Troilus will not come far behind him. Let them take heed of Troilus, I can tell them that too.

CRESSIDA   What, is he angry too?

PANDARUS   Who, Troilus? Troilus is the better man of
the two.

CRESSIDA   O Jupiter! there's no comparison.

PANDARUS   What, not between Troilus and Hector? Do
you know a man if you see him?

CRESSIDA   Ay, if I ever saw him before and knew him.

PANDARUS   Well, I say Troilus is Troilus.

CRESSIDA   Then you say as I say, for I am sure he is not
Hector.

PANDARUS   No, and Hector is not Troilus in some
degrees.

CRESSIDA   'Tis just to each of them; he is himself.

PANDARUS   Himself? Alas, poor Troilus, I would he
were.

CRESSIDA   So he is.

PANDARUS   Condition, I had gone barefoot to India.

CRESSIDA   He is not Hector.

PANDARUS   Himself? no, he is not himself. Would he
were himself! Well, the gods are above; time must
friend or end. Well, Troilus, well, I would my heart
were in her body. No, Hector is not a better man than
Troilus.

CRESSIDA   Excuse me.

PANDARUS   He is older.

CRESSIDA   Pardon me, pardon me.

PANDARUS   The other's not come to it; you shall tell me
another tale when the other is come to it. Hector shall
not have his wit this year.

CRESSIDA   He shall not need it if he has his own.

PANDARUS   Nor his qualities.

CRESSIDA   No matter.

PANDARUS   Nor his beauty.

CRESSIDA   It would not become him; his own is better.

PANDARUS   You have no judgment, niece. Helen herself
swore the other day that Troilus, for a brown complexion—for so it is, I must confess, not brown either—

CRESSIDA   No, but brown.

PANDARUS   Faith, to say truth, brown and not brown.

CRESSIDA   To say the truth, true and not true.

PANDARUS   She praised his complexion above Paris.

CRESSIDA   Why, Paris has color enough.

PANDARUS   So he has.

CRESSIDA   Then Troilus should have too much. If she praised him above, his complexion is higher than his. He having color enough, and the other higher, is too flaming a praise for a good complexion. I had as soon Helen's golden tongue had commended Troilus for a copper nose.

PANDARUS   I swear to you, I think Helen loves him better than Paris.

CRESSIDA   Then she is a gay Greek indeed.

PANDARUS   Nay, I am sure she does. She came to him the other day into the bay window, and, you know, he has not past three or four hairs on his chin—

CRESSIDA   Indeed, a tapster's arithmetic may soon bring his particulars therein to a total.

PANDARUS   Why, he is very young; and yet will he, within three pound, lift as much as his brother Hector.

CRESSIDA   Is he so young a man, and so old a lifter?

PANDARUS   But to prove to you that Helen loves him, she came and puts her white hand to his cloven chin—

CRESSIDA   Juno have mercy! how came it cloven?

PANDARUS   Why, you know it is dimpled. I think his smiling becomes him better than any man in Phrygia.

CRESSIDA   O, he smiles valiantly.

PANDARUS   Does he not?

CRESSIDA   O, yes, as if a cloud in autumn.

PANDARUS   Why, go to then. But to prove to you that Helen loves Troilus—

CRESSIDA   Troilus will stand to the proof, if you will prove it so.

PANDARUS   Troilus? Why, he esteems her no more than I esteem an addled egg.

CRESSIDA   If you love an addled egg as well as you love an idle head, you would eat chickens in the shell.

PANDARUS   I cannot choose but laugh to think how she tickled his chin. Indeed, she has a marvellous white hand, I must needs confess.

CRESSIDA   Without racking.

PANDARUS   And she takes upon her to spy a white hair on his chin.

CRESSIDA   Alas poor chin, many a wart is richer.

PANDARUS   But there was such laughing: Queen Hecuba laughed that her eyes ran over.

CRESSIDA   With millstones.

PANDARUS   And Cassandra laughed.

CRESSIDA   But there was a more temperate fire under the pot of her eyes. Did her eyes run over too?

PANDARUS   And Hector laughed.

CRESSIDA   At what was all this laughing?

PANDARUS   Sure, at the white hair that Helen spied on Troilus' chin.

CRESSIDA   If it had been a green hair, I should have laughed too.

PANDARUS   They laughed not so much at the hair as at his pretty answer.

CRESSIDA   What was his answer?

PANDARUS   Said she, 'Here's but two-and-fifty hairs on your chin, and one of them is white.'

CRESSIDA   This is her question.

PANDARUS   That's true; make no question of that. 'Two-and-fifty hairs,' said he, 'and one white. That white hair is my father, and all the rest are his sons.' 'Jupiter!' said she, 'which of these hairs is Paris, my husband?' 'The forked one,' said he; 'pluck it out, and give it him.' But there was such laughing, and Helen so blushed, and Paris so chafed, and all the rest so laughed, that it passed.

CRESSIDA   So let it now, for it has been a great while going by.

PANDARUS   Well, niece, I told you a thing yesterday; think on it.

CRESSIDA   So I do.

PANDARUS   I'll be sworn it is true; he will weep, as if it were a man born in April.

A retreat sounds.

CRESSIDA   And I'll spring up in his tears, as though a nettle against May.

PANDARUS   Hark, they are coming from the field. Shall we stand up here and see them as they pass toward Ilium? Good niece, do; sweet niece, Cressida.

CRESSIDA   At your pleasure.

PANDARUS   Here, here, here's an excellent place; here we may see most bravely. I'll tell you them all by their names as they pass by, but mark Troilus above the rest.

Enter Aeneas.

CRESSIDA   Speak not so loud.

PANDARUS   That's Aeneas. Is not that a brave man? He is one of the flowers of Troy, I can tell you. But mark Troilus; you shall see anon.

Enter Antenor.

CRESSIDA   Who's that?

PANDARUS   That's Antenor. He has a shrewd wit, I can tell you; and he's a man good enough. He is one of the soundest judgments in Troy whosoever, and a proper man of person. When comes Troilus? I'll show you Troilus anon. If he sees me, you shall see him nod at me.

CRESSIDA   Will he give you the nod?

PANDARUS   You shall see.

CRESSIDA   If he does, the rich shall have more.

Enter Hector.

PANDARUS   That's Hector, that, that, look you, that;
  there's a fellow! Go your way, Hector! There's a brave
  man, niece. O brave Hector! Look how he looks;
  there's a countenance! Is it not a brave man?
CRESSIDA   O, a brave man!
PANDARUS   Is he not? It does a man's heart good. Look
  you what hacks are on his helmet. Look you yonder,
  do you see? Look you there. There's no jesting; there's
  laying on, take it off who will, as they say. There are
  hacks!
CRESSIDA   Are those with swords?
PANDARUS   Swords, anything; he cares not; if the devil
  comes to him, it's all one. By God's lid, it does one's
  heart good.

Enter Paris.

Yonder comes Paris, yonder comes Paris. Look you
yonder, niece. Is it not a gallant man too, is it not? Why,
this is brave now. Who said he came hurt home to-day?
He is not hurt. Why, this will do Helen's heart good
now, ha! Would I could see Troilus now. You shall see
Troilus anon.
CRESSIDA   Who's that?

Enter Helenus.

PANDARUS   That's Helenus. I marvel where Troilus is.
  That's Helenus. I think he went not forth to-day.
  That's Helenus.
CRESSIDA   Can Helenus fight, uncle?
PANDARUS   Helenus? No. Yes, he will fight indifferently
  well. I marvel where Troilus is. Hark, do you not hear
  the people cry 'Troilus'? Helenus is a priest.
CRESSIDA   What sneaking fellow comes yonder?

Enter Troilus.

PANDARUS Where? Yonder? That's Deiphobus. 'Tis
Troilus! There's a man, niece! Hem! Brave Troilus, the
prince of chivalry!

CRESSIDA Peace, for shame, peace!

PANDARUS Mark him, note him. O brave Troilus! Look
well upon him, niece. Look you how his sword is
bloodied, and his helm more hacked than Hector's;
and how he looks, and how he walks. O admirable
youth! he never saw three-and-twenty. Go your way,
Troilus, go your way! Had I a sister a grace, or a
daughter a goddess, he should take his choice. O
admirable man! Paris? Paris is dirt to him; and I
warrant Helen, to change, would give an eye too.

Enter Common Soldiers.

CRESSIDA Here come more.

PANDARUS Asses, fools, dolts; chaff and bran, chaff and
bran; porridge after meat. I could live and die in the
eyes of Troilus. Never look, never look. The eagles are
gone; crows and daws, crows and daws. I had rather be
such a man as Troilus than Agamemnon and all
Greece.

CRESSIDA There is among the Greeks Achilles, a better
man than Troilus.

PANDARUS Achilles? A drayman, a porter, a very camel.

CRESSIDA Well, well.

PANDARUS 'Well, well'? Why, have you any discretion,
have you any eyes, do you know what a man is? Are
not birth, beauty, good shape, discourse, manhood,
learning, gentleness, virtue, youth, liberality, and
such like, the spice and salt that season a man?

CRESSIDA Ay, a mincing man; and then to be baked with
no date in the pie, for then the man's date is out.

PANDARUS You are such a woman a man knows not at
what fence you lie.

CRESSIDA   Upon my back, to defend my belly; upon my
wit, to defend my wiles; upon my secrecy, to defend
my honesty; my mask, to defend my beauty; and you,
to defend all these. And at all these defences I lie, at a
thousand watches.

PANDARUS   Say one of your watches.

CRESSIDA   Nay, I'll watch you for that; and that's one of
the chiefest of them too. If I cannot defend what I
would not have hit, I can watch you for telling how I
took the blow; unless it swells past hiding, and then
it's past watching.

PANDARUS   You are such another woman.

   Enter Troilus' Boy.

BOY   Sir, my lord would instantly speak with you.

PANDARUS   Where?

BOY   At your own house. There he unarms him.

PANDARUS   Good boy, tell him I come. *Exit Boy.* I fear he
is hurt. Fare you well, good niece.

CRESSIDA   Adieu, uncle.

PANDARUS   I will be with you, niece, by and by.

CRESSIDA   To bring, uncle?

PANDARUS   Ay, a token from Troilus.

CRESSIDA   By the same token, you are a bawd.
                                         Exit Pandarus.
Words, vows, gifts, tears, and love's full sacrifice
He offers in another's enterprise;
But more in Troilus thousandfold I see
Than in the glass of Pandar's praise may be.
Yet hold I off: women are angels, wooing;
Things won are done, joy's soul lies in the doing.
That she beloved knows nought that knows not this:
Men prize the thing ungained more than it is;
That she was never yet, that ever knew
Love got so sweet as when desire did sue.
Therefore this maxim out of love I teach:
Achievement is command; ungained, beseech.

Then, though my heart's content firm love does bear,
Nothing of that shall from my eyes appear.

                                                    Exit.

SCENE III
The Greek camp.
Before Agamemnon's tent.

*Sennet. Enter Agamemnon, Nestor, Ulysses,
Diomedes, Menelaus, with others.*

AGAMEMNON
    Princes,
    What grief has set the jaundice on your cheeks?
    The ample proposition that hope makes
    In all designs begun on earth below
    Fails in the promised largeness. Checks and disasters
    Grow in the veins of actions highest reared,
    As knots, by the conflux of meeting sap,
    Infect the sound pine and divert its grain
    Tortuous and errant from its course of growth.
    Nor, princes, is it matter new to us
    That we come short of our suppose so far
    That after seven years' siege yet Troy walls stand.
    Since every action that has gone before,
    Whereof we have record, trial did draw
    Bias and thwart, not answering the aim
    And that unbodied figure of the thought
    That gave it surmised shape. Why then, you princes,
    Do you with cheeks abashed behold our works
    And call them shames, which are indeed nought else
    But the protractive trials of great Jove
    To find persistive constancy in men?
    The fineness of which metal is not found
    In Fortune's love; for then, the bold and coward,
    The wise and fool, the artist and unread,
    The hard and soft, seem all allied and kin.

But, in the wind and tempest of her frown,
Distinction, with a broad and powerful fan,
Puffing at all, winnows the light away;
And what has mass or matter by itself
Lies rich in virtue and unmingled.

NESTOR
With due observance of your godlike seat,
Great Agamemnon, Nestor shall apply
Your latest words. In the reproof of chance
Lies the true proof of men. The sea being smooth,
How many shallow bauble boats dare sail
Upon her patient breast, making their way
With those of nobler bulk?
But let the ruffian Boreas once enrage
The gentle Thetis, and anon behold
The strong-ribbed bark through liquid mountains
        cut,
Bounding between the two moist elements
Like Perseus' horse: where's then the saucy boat,
Whose weak untimbered sides but even now
Co-rivalled greatness? Either to harbor fled,
Or made a toast for Neptune. Even so
Do valor's show and valor's worth divide
In storms of fortune. For in her ray and brightness
The herd has more annoyance by the gadfly
Than by the tiger. But when the splitting wind
Makes flexible the knees of knotted oaks,
And flies fled under shade, why then the thing of
        courage,
As roused with rage, with rage does sympathize,
And with an accent tuned in self-same key
Returns to chiding fortune.

ULYSSES   Agamemnon,
You great commander, nerve and bone of Greece,
Heart of our numbers, soul and only spirit,
In whom the tempers and the minds of all
Should be enclosed, hear what Ulysses speaks.
Besides the applause and approbatìon

Which, *[to Agamemnon]* most mighty for your place
     and sway,

     To Nestor
And you most reverend for your stretched-out life,
I give to both your speeches; which were such
As Agamemnon and the hand of Greece
Should hold up high in brass. And such again
As venerable Nestor, hatched in silver,
Should with a bond of air, strong as the axle-tree
On which heaven rides, knit all the Greekish ears
To his experienced tongue. Yet let it please both,
You great, and wise, to hear Ulysses speak.

AGAMEMNON
Speak, Prince of Ithaca; and let us less expect
That matter needless, of importless burden,
Divide your lips than we are confident,
When rank Thersites opens his bitter jaws,
We shall hear music, wit, and oracle.

ULYSSES
Troy, yet upon its basis, had been down,
And the great Hector's sword had lacked a master,
But for these instances.
The specialty of rule has been neglected;
And look, how many Grecian tents do stand
Hollow upon this plain, so many hollow factions.
When the general is not like the hive
To whom the foragers shall all repair,
What honey is expected? Degree being masked,
The unworthiest shows as fairly in the mask.
The heavens themselves, the planets, and this centre
Observe degree, priority, and place,
Persistence, course, proportion, season, form,
Office, and custom, in all line of order.
And therefore is the glorious planet Sol
In noble eminence enthroned and sphered
Amid the others; whose medicinal eye
Corrects the influence of evil planets,

And posts, like the commandment of a king,
Without check to good and bad. But when the planets
In evil mixture to disorder wander,
What plagues, and what portents, what mutiny,
What raging of the sea, shaking of earth,
Commotion in the winds, frights, changes, horrors,
Divert and crack, rend and deracinate
The unity and married calm of states
Quite from their fixture? O, when degree is shaked,
Which is the ladder of all high designs,
The enterprise is sick. How could communities,
Degrees in schools, and brotherhoods in cities,
Peaceful commerce from dividable shores,
The primogeniture and due of birth,
Prerogative of age, crowns, sceptres, laurels,
But by degree, stand in authentic place?
Take but degree away, untune that string,
And hark what discord follows. Each thing meets
In mere oppugnancy. The bounded waters
Should lift their bosoms higher than the shores
And make a sop of all this solid globe.
Strength should be lord of all simplicity,
And the rude son should strike his father dead;
Force should be right, or rather right and wrong,
Between whose endless jar justice resides,
Should lose their names, and so should justice too.
Then everything includes itself in power,
Power into will, will into appetite.
And appetite, an universal wolf,
So doubly seconded with will and power,
Must make perforce an universal prey
And last eat up itself. Great Agamemnon,
This chaos, when degree is suffocated,
Follows the choking.
And this neglection of degree it is
That by a pace goes backward with a purpose
It has to climb. The general is disdained
By him one step below, he by the next,

That next by him beneath. So every step,
Exampled by the first pace that is sick
Of its superior, grows to an envious fever
Of pale and bloodless emulatiòn.
It is this fever that keeps Troy on foot,
Not her own sinews. To end a tale of length,
Troy in our weakness stands, not in her strength.

NESTOR
Most wisely has Ulysses here discovered
The fever whereof all our power is sick.

AGAMEMNON
The nature of the sickness found, Ulysses,
What is the remedy?

ULYSSES
The great Achilles, whom opinion crowns
The sinew and the forehand of our host,
Having his ear full of his airy fame,
Grows dainty of his worth, and in his tent
Lies mocking our designs. With him Patroclus
Upon a lazy bed the livelong day
Breaks scurrilous jests,
And with ridiculous and silly action
(Which, slanderer, he imitation calls)
He pageants us. Sometimes, great Agamemnon,
Your supreme power he puts on
And—like a strutting player, whose conceit
Lies in his hamstring, and does think it rich
To hear the wooden dialogue and sound
Between his stretched footing and the scaffoldage—
Such to-be-pitied and o'er-wrested seeming
He acts your greatness in. And when he speaks,
'Tis like a chime a-mending, with terms unsquared,
Which, from the tongue of roaring Typhon dropped,
Would seem hyperboles. At this fusty stuff
The large Achilles, on his pressed bed lolling,
From his deep chest laughs out a loud applause,
Cries, 'Excellent! 'tis Agamemnon right.
Now play me Nestor; hem, and stroke your beard,

As he being drest to some oratiòn.'
That's done, as near as the extremest ends
Of parallels, as like as Vulcan and his wife,
Yet god Achilles still cries, 'Excellent!
'Tis Nestor right. Now play him me, Patroclus,
Arming to answer in a night alarm.'
And then, for sure, the faint defects of age
Must be the scene of mirth; to cough and spit,
And with a palsy fumbling on his gorget,
Shake in and out the rivet. And at this sport
Sir Valor dies; cries,'O! enough, Patroclus,
Or give me ribs of steel; I shall split all
In pleasure of my lungs.' And in this fashion
All our abilities, gifts, natures, shapes,
Special and general qualities exact,
Achievements, plots, orders, preventiòns,
Excitements to the field or speech for truce,
Success or loss, what is or is not, serves
As stuff for these two to make paradoxes.

NESTOR

And in the imitation of these twain,
Who, as Ulysses says, opinion crowns
With an imperial voice, many are infected.
Ajax is grown self-willed, and bears his head
In such a way, in full as proud a place
As broad Achilles; keeps his tent like him;
Makes factious feasts; rails on our state of war,
Bold as an oracle. And sets Thersites,
A slave whose gall coins slanders like a mint,
To match us in comparisons with dirt,
To weaken and discredit our exposure,
How rank soever rounded in with danger.

ULYSSES

They tax our policy and call it cowardice,
Count wisdom as no member of the war,
Forestall prescience, and esteem no act
But that of hand. The still and mental parts

That do contrive how many hands shall strike
When fitness calls them on, and know by measure
Of their observant toil the enemies' weight—
Why, this has not a finger's dignity.
They call this bed-work, mappery, closet-war;
So that the ram that batters down the wall,
For the great swing and rudeness of its poise,
They place before his hand that made the engine,
Or those that with the fineness of their souls
By reason guide its execution.

NESTOR
Let this be granted, and Achilles' horse
Makes many Thetis' sons.

Tucket.

AGAMEMNON
What trumpet? Look, Menelaus.
MENELAUS
From Troy.

Enter Aeneas.

AGAMEMNON
What would you before our tent?
AENEAS
Is this great Agamemnon's tent, I pray you?
AGAMEMNON
Even this.
AENEAS
May one that is a herald and a prince
Do a fair message to his kingly eyes?
AGAMEMNON
With surety stronger than Achilles' arm
Before all the Greekish heads, which with one voice
Call Agamemnon head and general.
AENEAS
Fair leave and large security. How may

A stranger to those most imperial looks
Know them from eyes of other mortals?

AGAMEMNON   How?

AENEAS

Ay.
I ask, that I might waken reverence,
And bid the cheek be ready with a blush
Modest as morning when she coldly eyes
The youthful Phoebus,
Which is that god in office, guiding men?
Which is the high and mighty Agamemnon?

AGAMEMNON

This Trojan scorns us, or the men of Troy
Are ceremonious courtiers.

AENEAS

Courtiers as free, as debonair, unarmed,
As bending angels; that's their fame in peace.
But when they would seem soldiers, they have galls,
Good arms, strong joints, true swords; and, Jove's
    accord,
Nothing so full of heart. But peace, Aeneas;
Peace, Trojan; lay your finger on your lips.
The worthiness of praise does stain his worth,
If the praised himself brings the praise forth.
But what the repining enemy commends,
That breath fame blows; that praise, sole pure, tran-
    scends.

AGAMEMNON

Sir, you of Troy, call you yourself Aeneas?

AENEAS

Ay, Greek, that is my name.

AGAMEMNON

What is your affair, I pray you?

AENEAS

Sir, pardon; it is for Agamemnon's ears.

AGAMEMNON

He hears nought privately that comes from Troy.

AENEAS
   And I from Troy come not to whisper him:
   I bring a trumpet to awake his ear,
   To set his seat on the attentive bent,
   And then to speak.
AGAMEMNON   Speak frankly as the wind;
   It is not Agamemnon's sleeping hour.
   That you shall know, Trojan, he is awake,
   He tells you so himself.
AENEAS   Trumpet, blow loud,
   Send your brass voice through all these lazy tents;
   And every Greek of mettle, let him know,
   What Troy means fairly shall be spoken aloud.

     Sound trumpet.

   We have, great Agamemnon, here in Troy
   A prince called Hector—Priam is his father—
   Who in this dull and long-continued truce
   Is rusty grown. He bade me take a trumpet,
   And to this purpose speak: Kings, princes, lords,
   If there is one among the fairest of Greece
   That holds his honor higher than his ease,
   That seeks his praise more than he fears his peril,
   That knows his valor and knows not his fear;
   That loves his mistress more than in confession
   With truant vows to her own lips he loves,
   And dares avow her beauty and her worth
   In other arms than hers—to him this challenge.
   Hector, in view of Trojans and of Greeks,
   Shall make it good, or do his best to do it,
   He has a lady wiser, fairer, truer,
   Than ever Greek did compass in his arms;
   And will to-morrow with his trumpet call,
   Midway between your tents and walls of Troy,
   To rouse a Grecian that is true in love.
   If any comes, Hector shall honor him;
   If none, he'll say in Troy when he retires,

The Grecian dames are sunburnt and not worth
The splinter of a lance. Even so much.

AGAMEMNON

This shall be told our lovers, Lord Aeneas;
If none of them have soul in such a kind,
We left them all at home. But we are soldiers;
And may that soldier a mere miscreant prove,
That means not, has not, or is not in love!
If then one is, or has, or means to be,
That one meets Hector; if none else, I am he.

NESTOR

Tell him of Nestor, one that was a man
When Hector's grandsire sucked. He is old now,
But if there is not in our Grecian host
A noble man that has one spark of fire
To answer for his love, tell him from me,
I'll hide my silver beard in a gold beaver [face-guard]
And in my armour put this withered brawn,
And, meeting him, will tell him that my lady
Was fairer than his grandam, and as chaste
As may be in the world. His youth in flood,
I'll prove this truth with my three drops of blood.

AENEAS

Now heavens forfend such scarcity of youth!

ULYSSES

Amen.

AGAMEMNON

For Lord Aeneas, let me touch your hand;
To our pavilion shall I lead you first.
Achilles shall have word of this intent;
So shall each lord of Greece, from tent to tent.
Yourself shall feast with us before you go,
And find the welcome of a noble foe.

Exeunt, except Ulysses and Nestor.

ULYSSES

Nestor.

NESTOR

What says Ulysses?

ULYSSES

    I have a young conception in my brain;

    Be you my time to bring it to some shape.

NESTOR

    What is it?

ULYSSES

    This it is:

    Blunt wedges split hard knots; the seeded pride

    That has to this maturity blown up

    In rank Achilles, must either now be cropped

    Or, shedding, breed a nursery of like evil

    To overbulk us all.

NESTOR   Well, and how?

ULYSSES

    This challenge that the gallant Hector sends,

    However it is spread in general name,

    Relates in purpose only to Achilles.

NESTOR

    True, the purpose is perspicuous as substance

    Whose grossness little characters sum up;

    And, in the publication, make no strain

    But that Achilles, were his brain as barren

    As banks of Libya—though, Apollo knows,

    It is dry enough—will with great speed of judgment,

    Ay with celerity, find Hector's purpose

    Pointing on him.

ULYSSES

    And wake him to the answer, think you?

NESTOR

    Why, it is most meet. Who may you else oppose

    That can from Hector bring his honor off,

    If not Achilles? Though it is a sportful combat,

    Yet in this trial much opinion dwells;

    For here the Trojans taste our dearest repute

    With their finest palate; trust to me, Ulysses,

    Our imputation shall be oddly poised

    In this sportive action. For the success,

    Although particular, shall give a sample

Of good or bad unto the whole army.
And in such indexes, although small pricks
To their subsequent volumes, there is seen
The baby figure of the giant mass
Of things to come at large. It is supposed
He that meets Hector issues from our choice;
And choice, being mutual act of all our souls
Makes merit her election, and does boil,
As if from forth us all, a man distilled
Out of our virtues: who miscarrying,
What heart receives from hence a conquering part,
To steel a strong opinion to themselves!
Which entertained, limbs are his instruments,
In no less working than are swords and bows
Directive by the limbs.

ULYSSES

Give pardon to my speech: therefore it is meet
Achilles meets not Hector. Let us, like merchants,
First show foul wares, and think perchance they'll
      sell;
If not, the lustre of the better shall exceed
By showing the worse first. Do not consent
That ever Hector and Achilles meet;
For both our honor and our shame in this
Are dogged with two strange followers.

NESTOR

I see them not with my old eyes. What are they?

ULYSSES

What glory our Achilles shares from Hector,
Were he not proud, we all should share with him.
But he already is too insolent,
And we were better parch in African sun
Than in the pride and salt scorn of his eyes,
Should he escape Hector fair. If he were foiled,
Why then we did our main opinion crush
In taint of our best man. No, make a lottery;
And by device let blockish Ajax draw

Act II

SCENE I
The Greek camp.

Enter Ajax and Thersites.

AJAX Thersites!

THERSITES Agamemnon, how if he had boils—full, all over, generally?

AJAX Thersites!

THERSITES And those boils did run?—say so. Did not the general run then? Were not that a botchy core?

AJAX Dog!

THERSITES Then would come some matter from him. I see none now.

AJAX You bitch-wolf's son, can you not hear? Feel then.

Strikes him.

THERSITES The plague of Greece upon you, you mongrel beef-witted lord!

AJAX Speak then, you mouldiest leaven, speak. I will beat you into handsomeness.

THERSITES I shall sooner rail you into wit and holiness; but I think your horse will sooner learn an oration than you learn a prayer without book. You can strike, can you? A red plague on your jade's tricks!

AJAX Toadstool, teach me the proclamation.

THERSITES Do you think I have no sense, you strike me thus?

AJAX The proclamation!

THERSITES You are proclaimed fool, I think.

AJAX Do not, porcupine, do not; my fingers itch.

THERSITES I would you did itch from head to foot; if I
   had the scratching of you, I would make you the loath-
   somest scab in Greece. When you are forth in the excursions, you strike as slow as another.

AJAX I say, the proclamation!

THERSITES You grumble and rail every hour on Achilles,
   and you are as full of envy at his greatness as Cerberus
   is at Proserpina's beauty, ay that you bark at him.

AJAX Mistress Thersites!

THERSITES You should strike him.

AJAX Crusty loaf!

THERSITES He would pound you into shivers with his
   fist, as a sailor breaks a biscuit.

AJAX You filthy cur!

   Beating him.

THERSITES Do, do.

AJAX You stool for a witch!

THERSITES Ay, do, do, you sodden-witted lord! You have
   no more brain than I have in my elbows; a donkey may
   tutor you. You scurvy-valiant ass, you are here but to
   thrash Trojans, and you are bought and sold among
   those of any wit like a barbarian slave. If you go on
   beating me, I will begin at your heel, and tell what you
   are by inches, you thing of no bowels, you!

AJAX You dog!

THERSITES You scurvy lord!

AJAX You cur!

   Beating him.

THERSITES Mars's idiot! Do, rudeness; do, camel; do, do.

   Enter Achilles and Patroclus.

ACHILLES Why, how now, Ajax, wherefore do you thus?
   How now, Thersites, what's the matter, man?

THERSITES   You see him there, do you?

ACHILLES   Ay, what's the matter?

THERSITES   Nay, look upon him.

ACHILLES   So I do. What's the matter?

THERSITES   Nay, but regard him well.

ACHILLES   'Well'—why so I do.

THERSITES   But yet you look not well upon him; for, whosoever you take him to be, he is Ajax.

ACHILLES   I know that, fool.

THERSITES   Ay, but that fool knows not himself.

AJAX   Therefore I beat you.

THERSITES   Lo, lo, lo, lo, what modicums of wit he utters! His evasions have ears thus long. I have banged his brain more than he has beaten my bones. I will buy nine sparrows for a penny, and his cerebellum is not worth the ninth part of a sparrow. This lord, Achilles, Ajax, who wears his wit in his belly and his guts in his head, I'll tell you what I say of him.

ACHILLES   What?

THERSITES   I say, this Ajax—

Ajax offers to strike him.

ACHILLES   Nay, good Ajax.

THERSITES   Has not so much wit—

ACHILLES   Nay, I must hold you.

THERSITES   As will stop the eye of Helen's needle, for whom he comes to fight.

ACHILLES   Peace, fool!

THERSITES   I would have peace and quietness, but the fool will not—he there, that he. Look you there.

AJAX   O you damned cur, I shall—

ACHILLES   Will you set your wit to a fool's?

THERSITES   No, I warrant you; the fool's will shame it.

PATROCLUS   Good words, Thersites.

ACHILLES   What's the quarrel?

AJAX   I bade the vile owl go teach me the tenor of the proclamation, and he rails upon me.

THERSITES   I serve you not.

AJAX   Well, go to, go to.

THERSITES   I serve here voluntary.

ACHILLES   Your last service was sufferance, it was not voluntary; no man is beaten voluntarily. Ajax was here the voluntary, and you as under an impress.

THERSITES   Even so. A great deal of your wit, too, lies in your sinews, or else there are liars. Hector shall have a great catch if he knocks out either of your brains. He were as good crack a fusty nut with no kernel.

ACHILLES   What, with me too, Thersites?

THERSITES   There are Ulysses and old Nestor, whose wit was mouldy ere your grandsires had nails on their toes, yoke you like draught-oxen and make you plough up the wars.

ACHILLES   What, what?

THERSITES   Yes, good truth. To, Achilles; to, Ajax; to—

AJAX   I shall cut out your tongue.

THERSITES   'Tis no matter; I shall speak as much as you afterwards.

PATROCLUS   No more words, Thersites; peace!

THERSITES   I will hold my peace when Achilles' bitch bids me, shall I?

ACHILLES   There's for you, Patroclus.

THERSITES   I will see you hanged, like blockheads, ere I come any more to your tents. I will keep where there is wit stirring and leave the faction of fools.   *Exit.*

PATROCLUS   A good riddance.

ACHILLES

Indeed, this, sir, is proclaimed through all our host:
That Hector, by the fifth hour of the sun,
Will, with a trumpet, between our tents and Troy
To-morrow morning call some knight to arms
That has a stomach, and such a one that dares
Maintain—I know not what; 'tis trash. Farewell.

AJAX

Farewell? Who shall answer him?

ACHILLES

I know not. 'Tis put to lottery. Otherwise,
He knew his man.

AJAX

O, meaning you? I will go learn more of it. *Exeunt.*

Scene II
Troy: Priam's palace.

Enter Priam, Hector, Troilus, Paris, and Helenus.

PRIAM

After so many hours, lives, speeches spent,
Thus once again says Nestor from the Greeks:
'Deliver Helen, and all damage else,
As honor, loss of time, travail, expense,
Wounds, friends, and what else dear that is consumed
In hot digestion of this cormorant war,
Shall be struck off.' Hector, what say you to it?

HECTOR

Though no man lesser fears the Greeks than I,
As far as touches my particular,
Yet, dread Priam,
There is no lady of any softer bowels,
More spongy to suck in the sense of fear,
More ready to cry out, 'Who knows what follows?'
Than Hector is. The wound of peace is surety,
Surety secure; but modest doubt is called
The beacon of the wise, the probe that searches
To the bottom of the worst. Let Helen go.
Since the first sword was drawn about this question,
Every tenth soul, among many thousand tens,
Has been as dear as Helen; I mean, of ours.
If we have lost so many tenths of ours
To guard a thing not ours nor worth to us,
Had it our name, the value of one ten,

What merit is in that reason which denies
The yielding of her up?
TROILUS   Fie, fie, my brother!
Weigh you the worth and honor of a king
So great as our dread father in a scale
Of common ounces? Will you with counters sum
The past proportion of his infinite,
And buckle in a waist most fathomless
With spans and inches so diminutive
As fears and reasons? Fie, for godly shame!
HELENUS
No marvel, though you bite so sharp at reasons,
You are so empty of them. Should not our father
Bear the great sway of his affairs with reason,
Because your speech has none that tells him so?
TROILUS
You are for dreams and slumbers, brother priest;
You fur your gloves with reason. Here are your
          reasons:
You know an enemy intends you harm;
You know a sword employed is perilous,
And reason flies the object of all harm.
Who marvels then, when Helenus beholds
A Grecian and his sword, if he does set
The very wings of reason to his heels
And fly like chidden Mercury from Jove,
Or like a star disorbed? Nay, if we talk of reason,
Let's shut our gates and sleep. Manhood and honor
Should have hare-hearts, would they but fat their
          thoughts
With this crammed reason. Reason and respect
Make livers pale and lustihood deject.
HECTOR
Brother, she is not worth what she does cost
The keeping.
TROILUS   What's aught but as it is valued?
HECTOR
But value dwells not in particular will;

It holds its estimate and dignity
As well wherein 'tis precious of itself
As in the prizer. It is mad idolatry
To make the service greater than the god;
And the will dotes that is attributive
To what infectiously itself affects,
Without some image of the affected merit.

TROILUS
I take to-day a wife, and my election
Is led on in the conduct of my will—
My will enkindled by my eyes and ears,
Two traded pilots between the dangerous shores
Of will and judgment. How may I avoid,
Although my will distastes what it elected,
The wife I chose? There can be no evasion
To blench from this and to stand firm by honor.
We turn not back the silks upon the merchant
When we have soiled them, nor the remainder viands
We do not throw in unrespective sieve
Because we now are full. It was thought meet
Paris should do some vengeance on the Greeks.
Your breath with full consent bellied his sails;
The seas and winds, old wranglers, took a truce
And did him service. He touched the ports desired,
And for an old aunt whom the Greeks held captive
He brought a Grecian queen, whose youth and
    freshness
Wrinkle Apollo's and makes stale the morning.
Why keep we her? The Grecians keep our aunt.
Is she worth keeping? Why, she is a pearl
Whose price has launched above a thousand ships
And turned crowned kings to merchants.
If you'll affirm it was wisdom Paris went—
As you must needs, for you all cried, 'Go, go'—
If you'll confess he brought home worthy prize—
As you must needs, for you all clapped your hands,
And cried, 'Inestimable!'—why do you now
The issue of your own wisdoms rate,

And do a deed that never Fortune did:
Beggar the estimation which you prized
Richer than sea and land? O theft most base,
That we have stolen what we do fear to keep!
But thieves unworthy of a thing so stolen,
That in their country did them that disgrace
We fear to warrant in our native place.

CASSANDRA *[within]*
    Cry, Trojans, cry!

PRIAM   What noise? what shriek is this?

TROILUS
    'Tis our mad sister. I do know her voice.

CASSANDRA *[within]* Cry, Trojans!

HECTOR   It is Cassandra.

        Enter Cassandra raving.

CASSANDRA
    Cry, Trojans, cry! Lend me ten thousand eyes,
    And I will fill them with prophetic tears.

HECTOR
    Peace, sister, peace!

CASSANDRA
    Virgins and boys, mid-age and wrinkled elders,
    Soft infancy, that nothing can but cry,
    Add to my clamors! Let us pay betimes
    A moiety of that mass of moan to come.
    Cry, Trojans, cry! Practise your eyes with tears!
    Troy must not be, nor goodly Ilion stand;
    Our firebrand brother, Paris, burns us all.
    Cry, Trojans, cry! A Helen and a woe!
    Cry, cry! Troy burns, or else let Helen go.   *Exit.*

HECTOR
    Now, youthful Troilus, do not these high strains
    Of divination in our sister work
    Some touches of remorse? Or is your blood
    So madly hot that no discourse of reason,

Nor fear of bad fortune ın a bad cause,
Can qualify the same?
TROILUS   Why, Brother Hector,
We may not think the justness of each act
Such and no other than event does form it,
Nor once deject the courage of our minds
Because Cassandra's mad. Her brainsick raptures
Cannot distaste the goodness of a quarrel
Which has our several honors all engaged
To make it gracious. For my private part,
I am no more touched than all Priam's sons;
And Jove forbid there should be done among us
Such things as might offend the weakest spirit
To fight for and maintain.
PARIS
Else might the world convince of levity
As well my undertakings as your counsels;
But I attest the gods, your full consent
Gave wings to my propulsion and cut off
All fears attending on so dire a project.
For what, alas, can these my single arms?
What propugnation is in one man's valor
To stand the push and enmity of those
This quarrel would excite? Yet, I protest,
Were I alone to pass the difficulties,
And had as ample power as I have will,
Paris should never retract what he has done
Nor faint in the pursuit.
PRIAM   Paris, you speak
Like one besotted on your sweet delights.
You have the honey still, but these the gall;
So to be valiant is no praise at all.
PARIS
Sir, I propose not merely to myself
The pleasures such a beauty brings with it;
But I would have the soil of her fair rape
Wiped off in honorable keeping her.
What treason were it to the captured queen,

Disgrace to your great worths, and shame to me,
Now to deliver her possession up
On terms of base compulsion! Can it be
That so degenerate a strain as this
Should once set footing in your generous bosoms?
There's not the meanest spirit on our part
Without a heart to dare or sword to draw
When Helen is defended, and none so noble
Whose life were ill bestowed or death unfamed
Where Helen is the subject. Then, I say,
Well may we fight for her, whom we know well
The world's large spaces cannot parallel.

HECTOR
Paris and Troilus, you have both said well;
And on the cause and question now in hand
Have glossed, but superficially; not much
Unlike young men, whom Aristotle thought
Unfit to hear moral philosophy.
The reasons you allege do more conduce
To the hot passion of distempered red blood
Than to make up a free determination
Between right and wrong; for pleasure and revenge
Have ears more deaf than adders to the voice
Of any true decision. Nature craves
All dues be rendered to their owners. Now,
What nearer debt in all humanity
Than wife is to the husband? If this law
Of nature is corrupted through desire,
And if great minds, of favouring indulgence
To their benumbèd wills, resist the same,
There is a law in each well-ordered nation
To curb those raging appetites that are
Most disobedient and refractory.
If Helen, then, is wife to Sparta's king,
As it is known she is, these moral laws
Of nature and of nations speak aloud
To have her back returned. Thus to persist
In doing wrong extenuates not wrong,

But makes it much more heavy. Hector's opinion
Is this in way of truth; yet nevertheless,
My spritely brethren, I incline to you
In resolution to keep Helen still;
For 'tis a cause that has no mean dependence
Upon our joint and several dignities.

TROILUS

Why, there you touched the life of our design.
Were it not glory that we more aimed at
Than the performance of our heaving hearts,
I would not wish a drop of Trojan blood
Spent more in her defense. But, worthy Hector,
She is a theme of honor and renown,
A spur to valiant and magnanimous deeds,
Whose present courage may beat down our foes
And fame in time to come canònize us.
For I presume brave Hector would not lose
So rich advantage of a promised glory
As smiles upon the forehead of this action
For the wide world's revènue.

HECTOR   I am yours,
You valiant offspring of great Priamus.
I have a roistering challenge sent among
The dull and factious nobles of the Greeks
Will strike amazement to their drowsy spirits.
I was advèrtised their great general slept
While emulation in the army crept.
This, I presume, will wake him.   *Exeunt.*

SCENE III
The Greek camp. Before Achilles' tent.

Enter Thersites.

THERSITES How now, Thersites? What, lost in the
labyrinth of your fury? Shall the elephant Ajax carry
it thus? He beats me, and I rail at him. O worthy

satisfaction! Would it were otherwise—that I could beat him, while he railed at me. God's foot, I'll learn to conjure and raise devils, but I'll see some issue of my spiteful execrations. Then there's Achilles, a rare engineer. If Troy is not taken till these two undermine it, the walls will stand till they fall of themselves. O you great thunder-darter of Olympus, forget that you are Jove, the king of gods; and, Mercury, lose all the serpentine craft of your caduceus, [staff] if you take not that little, little, less than little wit from them that they have. Which short-armed ignorance itself knows is so abundant scarce, it will not in circumvention deliver a fly from a spider, without drawing their massy irons and cutting the web. After this the vengeance on the whole camp! or, rather, the Neapolitan bone-ache, [syphilis] for that, I think, is the curse depending on those that war for a bitch. I have said my prayers, and devil Envy say 'Amen.' What ho, my Lord Achilles!

Enter Patroclus.

PATROCLUS   Who's there? Thersites? Good Thersites, come in and rail.

THERSITES   If I could have remembered a gilt counterfeit, you would not have slipped out of my contemplation. But it is no matter; yourself upon yourself! The common curse of mankind, folly and ignorance, be yours in great revenue. Heaven save you from a tutor, and discipline come not near you. Let your blood be your direction till your death. Then, if she that lays you out says you are a fair corpse, I'll be sworn and sworn upon it she never shrouded any but lepers. Amen. Where is Achilles?

PATROCLUS   What are you devout? Were you in prayer?

THERSITES   Ay; the heavens hear me!

PATROCLUS   Amen.

Enter Achilles.

ACHILLES   Who's there?

PATROCLUS   Thersites, my lord.

ACHILLES   Where, where, O, where? Are you come? Why, my cheese, my digestion, why have you not served yourself in to my table so many meals? Come, what is Agamemnon?

THERSITES   Your commander, Achilles. Then tell me, Patroclus, what is Achilles?

PATROCLUS   Your lord, Thersites. Then tell me, I pray you, what's yourself?

THERSITES   Your knower, Patroclus. Then tell me, Patroclus, what are you?

PATROCLUS   You must tell that know.

ACHILLES   O tell, tell.

THERSITES   I'll decline the whole question. Agamemnon commands Achilles, Achilles is my lord, I am Patroclus' knower, and Patroclus is a fool.

PATROCLUS   You rascal!

THERSITES   Peace, fool! I have not done.

ACHILLES   He is a privileged man. Proceed, Thersites.

THERSITES   Agamemnon is a fool, Achilles is a fool, Thersites is a fool and, as aforesaid, Patroclus is a fool.

ACHILLES   Derive this; come.

THERSITES   Agamemnon is a fool to offer to command Achilles, Achilles is a fool to be commanded by Agamemnon, Thersites is a fool to serve such a fool, and this Patroclus is a fool positive.

PATROCLUS   Why am I a fool?

THERSITES   Make that demand of the Creator. It suffices me you are. Look you, who comes here?

Enter Agamemnon, Ulysses, Nestor,
Diomedes, Ajax, and Calchas.

ACHILLES   Come, Patroclus, I'll speak with nobody. Come in with me, Thersites.   *Exit.*

THERSITES   Here is such foolery, such juggling, and such
    knavery. All the argument is a whore and a cuckold, a
    good quarrel to draw emulous factions and bleed to
    death upon. Now, the dry impetigo on the subject, and
    war and lechery confound all!   *Exit.*
AGAMEMNON   Where is Achilles?
PATROCLUS
    Within his tent, but ill-disposed, my lord.
AGAMEMNON
    Let it be known to him that we are here.
    He scorned our messengers, and we lay by
    Our rights of rank in visiting of him.
    Let him be told so, lest perchance he thinks
    We dare not move the question of our place
    Or know not what we are.
PATROCLUS   I shall so say to him. *Exit.*
ULYSSES   We saw him at the opening of his tent. He is
    not sick.
AJAX   Yes, lion-sick, sick of proud heart. You may call it
    melancholy if you will favor the man; but, by my
    head, it is pride. But why, why? Let him show us a
    cause. A word, my lord.

        Takes Agamemnon aside.

NESTOR   What moves Ajax thus to bay at him.
ULYSSES   Achilles has inveigled his fool from him.
NESTOR   Who, Thersites?
ULYSSES   He.
NESTOR   Then will Ajax lack matter, if he has lost his
    argument.
ULYSSES   No, you see, he is his argument that has his
    argument, Achilles.
NESTOR   All the better; their fraction is more our wish
    than their faction. But it was a strong composure a
    fool could disunite.
ULYSSES   The amity that wisdom knits not, folly may
    easily untie.

Enter Patroclus.

Here comes Patroclus.
NESTOR   No Achilles with him?
ULYSSES
    The elephant has joints, but none for courtesy.
    His legs are legs for necessity, not for bending.
PATROCLUS
    Achilles bids me say, he is much sorry
    If anything more than your sport and pleasure
    Did move your greatness and this noble state
    To call upon him. He hopes it is no other
    But, for your health and your digestion sake,
    An after-dinner's breath.
AGAMEMNON   Hear you, Patroclus.
    We are too well acquainted with these answers;
    But his evasion, winged thus swift with scorn,
    Cannot outfly our apprehensiòns.
    Much attribute he has, and much the reason
    Why we ascribe it to him; yet all his virtues,
    Not virtuously on his own part beheld,
    Do in our eyes begin to lose their gloss—
    Yea, like fair fruit in an unwholesome dish—
    Are like to rot untasted. Go and tell him,
    We come to speak with him; and you shall not sin
    If you do say we think him over-proud
    And under-honest, in self-assumption greater
    Than in the note of judgment. And worthier than
        himself
    Here attend the savage strangeness he puts on,
    Disguise the holy strength of their command,
    And underwrite in an observing kind
    His humorous predominance—yea, watch
    His pettish moods, his ebbs and flows, as if
    The passage and whole carriage of this action
    Rode on his tide. Go tell him this, and add
    That, if he overholds his price so much,
    We'll none of him. But let him, like an engine

Not portable, lie under this report:
'Bring action hither, this cannot go to war.'
A stirring dwarf we do allowance give
Before a sleeping giant. Tell him so.

PATROCLUS
I shall, and bring his answer presently.   *Exit.*

AGAMEMNON
In second voice we'll not be satisfied;
We come to speak with him. Ulysses, enter you.
                                                      Exit Ulysses.

AJAX   What is he more than another?

AGAMEMNON   No question.

AJAX   Will you subscribe his thought, and say he is?

AGAMEMNON   No, noble Ajax; you are as strong, as
valiant, as wise, no less noble, much more gentle, and
altogether more tractable.

AJAX   Why should a man be proud? How does pride
grow? I know not what pride is.

AGAMEMNON   Your mind is the clearer and your virtues
the fairer. He that is proud eats up himself. Pride is his
own glass, his own trumpet, his own chronicle; and
whatever praises itself but in the deed devours the
deed in the praise.

AJAX   I do hate a proud man as I do hate the engendering
of toads.

NESTOR   *[aside]* And yet he loves himself. Is it not
strange;

        Enter Ulysses.

ULYSSES
Achilles will not to the field to-morrow.

AGAMEMNON
What's his excuse?

ULYSSES   He does rely on none,
But carries on the stream of his dispose
Without observance or respect of any,
In will peculiar and in self-admission.

AGAMEMNON
  Why will he not upon our fair request
  Untent his person and share the air with us?
ULYSSES
  Things small as nothing, for request's sake only,
  He makes important. Possessed he is with greatness,
  And speaks not to himself but with a pride
  That quarrels at self-breath. Imagined worth
  Holds in his blood such swollen and hot discourse
  That between his mental and his active parts
  Kingdomed Achilles in commotion rages
  And batters down himself. What should I say?
  He is so plaguy proud that the death-tokens of it
  Cry 'No recovery.'
AGAMEMNON   Let Ajax go to him.
  Dear lord, go you and greet him in his tent:
  It is said he holds you well, and will be led
  At your request a little from himself.
ULYSSES
  O Agamemnon, let it not be so!
  We'll consecrate the steps that Ajax makes
  When they go from Achilles. Shall the proud lord
  That bastes his arrogance with his own fat,
  And never suffers matter of the world
  Enter his thoughts, save such as does revolve
  And ruminate himself—shall he be worshipped
  Of that we hold an idol more than he?
  No, this thrice-worthy and right valiant lord
  Shall not so stale his palm, nobly acquired,
  Nor, by my will, so subjugate his merit,
  As amply titled as Achilles' is,
  By going to Achilles.
  That were to enlard his fat-already pride,
  And add more coals to Cancer when he burns
  With entertaining great Hyperion.
  This lord go to him! Jupiter forbid,
  And say in thunder, 'Achilles, go to him.'

NESTOR   *[aside]*
  O, this is well. He rubs the vein of him.
DIOMEDES   *[aside]*
  And how his silence drinks up his applause!
AJAX
  If I go to him, with my armèd fist
  I'll bash him over the face.
AGAMEMNON
  O, no! you shall not go.
AJAX
  If he is proud with me, I'll settle his pride.
  Let me go to him.
ULYSSES
  Not for the worth that hangs upon our quarrel.
AJAX   A paltry, insolent fellow!
NESTOR   *[aside]* How he describes himself!
AJAX   Can he not be sociable?
ULYSSES   *[aside]* The raven chides blackness.
AJAX   I'll let his humorous blood.
AGAMEMNON   *[aside]* He will be the physician that
  should be the patient.
AJAX   If all men were of my mind—
ULYSSES   *[aside]* Wit would be out of fashion.
AJAX   He should not bear it so, he should eat swords
  first. Shall pride carry it?
NESTOR   *[aside]* If it would, you'd carry half.
ULYSSES   *[aside]* He would have ten shares.
AJAX   I will knead him; I'll make him supple.
NESTOR   *[aside]* He's not yet thoroughly warm. Force
  him with praises; pour in, pour in; his ambition is dry.
ULYSSES   *[to Agamemnon]*
  My lord, you feed too much on this dislike.
NESTOR
  Our noble general, do not do so.
DIOMEDES
  You must prepare to fight without Achilles.
ULYSSES
  Why, it is this naming of him does him harm.
  Here is a man—but it is before his face;
  I will be silent.
NESTOR   Wherefore should you so?
  He is not emulous, as Achilles is.

ULYSSES
 Know the whole world, he is as valiant—
AJAX
 A filthy dog, that shall palter with us thus!
 Would he were a Trojan!
NESTOR What a vice were it in Ajax now—
ULYSSES If he were proud—
DIOMEDES Or covetous of praise—
ULYSSES Ay, or surly borne—
DIOMEDES Or strange, or self-affected!
ULYSSES
 Thank the heavens, lord, you are of sweet composure;
 Praise him that got you, she that gave you suck;
 Famed be your tutor, and your parts of nature
 Thrice-famed beyond all eruditiòn.
 But he that disciplined your arms to fight,
 Let Mars divide eternity in twain
 And give him half; and, for your vigor,
 Bull-bearing Milo his addition yield
 To sinewy Ajax. I will not praise your wisdom,
 Which, like a bourn, a pale, a shore, confines
 Your spacious and dilated parts. Here's Nestor,
 Instructed by the antiquary times,
 He must, he is, he cannot but be wise.
 But pardon, father Nestor, were your days
 As green as Ajax, and your brain so tempered,
 You should not have the eminence of him,
 But be as Ajax.
AJAX   Shall I call you father?
NESTOR
 Ay, my good son.
DIOMEDES   Be ruled by him, Lord Ajax.
ULYSSES
 There is no tarrying here; the hart Achilles
 Keeps thicket. Please it our great general
 To call together all his state of war;
 Fresh kings are come to Troy. To-morrow,

We must with all our main of power stand fast.
And here's a lord—come knights from east to west,
And cull their flower, Ajax shall cope the best.

AGAMEMNON
Go we to council. Let Achilles sleep:
Light boats sail swift, though greater hulks draw
deep.

Exeunt.

Act III

SCENE I
Troy. Priam's palace.

Music sounds within. Enter Pandarus and a Servant.

PANDARUS   Friend you, pray you a word. Do you not follow the young Lord Paris?

SERVANT   Ay, sir, when he goes before me.

PANDARUS   You depend upon him, I mean.

SERVANT   Sir, I do depend upon the Lord.

PANDARUS   You depend upon a noble gentleman; I must needs praise him.

SERVANT   The Lord be praised!

PANDARUS   You know me, do you not?

SERVANT   Faith, sir, superficially.

PANDARUS   Friend, know me better. I am the Lord Pandarus.

SERVANT   I hope I shall know your honor better.

PANDARUS   I do desire it.

SERVANT   You are in the state of grace.

PANDARUS   Grace? Not so, friend. Honor and lordship are my titles. What music is this?

SERVANT   I do but partly know, sir. It is music in parts.

PANDARUS   Know you the musicians?

SERVANT   Wholly, sir.

PANDARUS   Whom play they to?

SERVANT   To the hearers, sir.

PANDARUS   At whose pleasure, friend?

SERVANT   At mine, sir, and theirs that love music.

PANDARUS   Command, I mean, friend.

SERVANT   Whom shall I command, sir?

PANDARUS   Friend, we understand not one another. I am
   too courtly, and you too cunning. At whose request do
   these men play?
SERVANT   That's to it, indeed, sir. Certainly, sir, at the
   request of Paris, my lord, who is there in person; with
   him the mortal Venus, the heart-blood of beauty,
   love's invisible soul.
PANDARUS   Who? My niece Cressida?
SERVANT   No, sir, Helen. Could you not find out that by
   her attributes?
PANDARUS   It should seem, fellow, that you have not
   seen the Lady Cressida. I come to speak with Paris
   from the Prince Troilus. I will make a complimental
   assault upon him, for my business seethes.
SERVANT   Sodden business! There's a stewed phrase, indeed.

   Enter Paris and Helen.

PANDARUS   Fair be to you, my lord, and to all this fair
   company. Fair desires in all fair measure fairly guide
   them. Especially to you, fair queen, fair thoughts be
   your fair pillow.
HELEN   Dear lord, you are full of fair words.
PANDARUS   You speak your fair pleasure, sweet queen.
   Fair prince, here is good broken music.
PARIS   You have broken it, cousin; and, by my life, you
   shall make it whole again; you shall piece it out with
   a piece of your performance. Nell, he is full of har-
   mony.
PANDARUS   Truly, lady, no.
HELEN   O, sir!
PANDARUS   Rude, in truth; in good truth, very rude.
PARIS   Well said, my lord. Well, you say so in parts.
PANDARUS   I have business to my lord, dear queen. My
   lord, will you permit me a word?
HELEN   Nay, this shall not hedge us out. We'll hear you
   sing, certainly.

PANDARUS Well, sweet queen, you are pleasant with me. But, indeed, thus, my lord: my dear lord and most esteemed friend, your brother Troilus—

HELEN My Lord Pandarus, honey-sweet lord—

PANDARUS Go to, sweet queen, go to—commends himself most affectionately to you.

HELEN You shall not bob us out of our melody. If you do, our melancholy upon your head!

PANDARUS Sweet queen, sweet queen; that's a sweet queen, in faith.

HELEN And to make a sweet lady sad is a sour offense.

PANDARUS Nay, that shall not serve your turn; that shall it not, in truth, la. Nay, I care not for such words; no, no. And, my lord, he desires you that, if the king calls for him at supper, you will make his excuse.

HELEN My Lord Pandarus—

PANDARUS What says my sweet queen, my very, very sweet queen?

PARIS What exploit is in hand? Where sups he to-night?

HELEN Nay, but my lord—

PANDARUS What says my sweet queen? My cousin will fall out with you.

HELEN You must not know where he sups.

PARIS I'll lay my life, with my disposer Cressida.

PANDARUS No, no; no such matter; you are wide. Come, your disposer is sick.

PARIS Well, I'll make excuse.

PANDARUS Ay, good my lord. Why should you say Cressida? No, your poor disposer's sick.

PARIS I spy.

PANDARUS You spy? What do you spy? Come, give me an instrument now, sweet queen.

HELEN Why, this is kindly done.

PANDARUS My niece is horribly in love with a thing you have, sweet queen.

HELEN She shall have it, my lord, if it is not my Lord Paris.

.

PANDARUS   He? No, she'll none of him; they two are
twain.

HELEN   Falling in, after falling out, may make them
three.

PANDARUS   Come, come, I'll hear no more of this. I'll
sing you a song now.

HELEN   Ay, ay, pray do. Now by my word, sweet lord, you
have a fine forehead.

PANDARUS   Ay, you may, you may.

HELEN   Let your song be love. This love will undo us all.
O Cupid, Cupid, Cupid!

PANDARUS   Love! ay, that it shall, in faith.

PARIS   Ay, good, now 'Love, love, nothing but love.'

PANDARUS   In good truth, it begins so:
     [Sings.]
Love, love, nothing but love, still love still more!
For, O, love's bow shoots buck and doe.
The shaft confounds not that it wounds,
But tickles still the sore.[1]
These lovers cry, O ho! they die!
Yet that which seems the wound to kill
Does turn O ho! to Ha, ha, he!
So dying love lives still.
O ho! a while, but Ha, ha, ha!
O ho! groans out for Ha, ha, ha!—Heigh ho!

HELEN   In love, in faith, to the very tip of the nose.

PARIS   He eats nothing but doves, love, and that breeds
hot blood, and hot blood begets hot thoughts, and hot
thoughts beget hot deeds, and hot deeds is love.

PANDARUS   Is this the generation of love—hot blood, hot
thoughts, and hot deeds? Why, they are vipers. Is love
a generation of vipers? Sweet lord, who is a-field to-
day?

PARIS   Hector, Deiphobus, Helenus, Antenor, and all the
gallantry of Troy. I would fain have armed to-day, but

_____

[1]Bawdy double-entendre—meaning both the wound and a
fourth-year buck.

my Nell would not have it so. How chances it my
brother Troilus went not?

HELEN   He hangs the lip at something. You know all,
Lord Pandarus.

PANDARUS   Not I, honey-sweet queen. I long to hear how
they sped to-day. You will remember your brother's
excuse?

PARIS   To a hair.

PANDARUS   Farewell, sweet queen.

HELEN   Commend me to your niece.

PANDARUS   I will, sweet queen. *[Exit.] Sound a retreat.*

PARIS

They're come from the field. Let us to Priam's hall
To greet the warriors. Sweet Helen, I must woo you
To help unarm our Hector. His stubborn buckles,
With these your white enchanting fingers touched,
Shall more obey than to the edge of steel
Or force of Greekish sinews. You shall do more
Than all the island kings—disarm great Hector.

HELEN

It will make us proud to be his servant, Paris;
Yea, what he shall receive of us in duty
Gives us more palm in beauty than we have,
Yea, overshines ourself.

PARIS

Sweet, above thought I love you.   *Exeunt.*

SCENE II
Pandarus' orchard.

Enter Pandarus and Troilus' Servant.

PANDARUS   How now, where's your master? At my niece
Cressida's?

SERVANT   No, sir; he stays for you to conduct him
thither.

Enter Troilus.

PANDARUS   O, here he comes. How now, how now?
TROILUS   Fellow, walk off.   *Exit Servant.*
PANDARUS   Have you seen my niece?
TROILUS
No, Pandarus. I stalk about her door
Like a strange soul upon the Stygian banks
Staying for waftage. O, be you my Charon,
And give me swift transportance to those fields
Where I may wallow in the lily-beds
Proposed for the deserver. O gentle Pandar,
From Cupid's shoulder pluck his painted wings,
And fly with me to Cressida.
PANDARUS
Walk here in the orchard. I'll bring her straight.
                                                Exit.
TROILUS
I am giddy; expectation whirls me round.
The imaginary relish is so sweet
That it enchants my sense. What will it be
When soon the watery palates taste indeed
Love's thrice-repurèd nectar? Death, I fear me,
Swooning destruction, or some joy too fine,
Too subtle, potent, turned too sharp in sweetness
For the capacity of my ruder powers.
I fear it much; and I do fear besides
Lest I lose discrimination in my joys,
As does an army, when they charge on heaps
The enemy flying.

Enter Pandarus.

PANDARUS   She's making her ready; she'll come straight;
you must be careful now. She does so blush, and
fetches her wind so short as if she were frighted by a
spirit. I'll fetch her. It is the prettiest villain; she
fetches her breath as short as a new-taken sparrow.
                                                Exit.

TROILUS
  Even such a passion does embrace my bosom.
  My heart beats thicker than a feverish pulse,
  And all my powers do their bestowing lose,
  Like vassalage at unawares encountering
  The eye of majesty.

Enter Pandarus and Cressida.

PANDARUS   Come, come, what need you blush? Shame
  is a baby. Here she is now; swear the oaths now to her
  that you have sworn to me. What! are you gone
  again? You must be watched ere you be made tame,
  must you? Come your ways, come your ways; if you
  draw backward, we'll put you in the shafts. Why do
  you not speak to her? Come, draw this curtain, and
  let's see your picture. Alas the day, how loath you are
  to offend daylight! If it were dark, you'd close sooner.
  So, so; rub on, and kiss the mistress. How now, a kiss
  in fee-farm!² Build there, carpenter; the air is sweet.
  Nay, you shall fight your hearts out ere I part you.
  The falcon as the tercel, for all the ducks in the river.
  Go to, go to.
TROILUS   You have bereft me of all words, lady.
PANDARUS   Words pay no debts, give her deeds; but
  she'll bereave you of the deeds too if she calls your
  activity in question. What, billing again? Here's 'In
  witness whereof the parties interchangeably'³ Come
  in, come in. I'll go get a fire.   *Exit.*
CRESSIDA   Will you walk in, my lord?
TROILUS   O Cressida, how often have I wished me thus!
CRESSIDA   Wished, my lord? The gods grant—O my
  lord!
TROILUS   What should they grant? What makes this
  pretty interruption? What too curious dreg espies my
  sweet lady in the fountain of our love?

---

²For good.
³The legal formula is completed by 'have set their hands and
seals.'

CRESSIDA   More dregs than water, if my fears have eyes.

TROILUS   Fears make devils of cherubins; they never see truly.

CRESSIDA   Blind fear, that seeing reason leads, finds safer footing than blind reason stumbling without fear. To fear the worst oft cures the worst.

TROILUS   O, let my lady apprehend no fear. In all Cupid's pageant there is presented no monster.

CRESSIDA   And nothing monstrous either?

TROILUS   Nothing but our undertakings when we vow to weep seas, live in fire, eat rocks, tame tigers, thinking it harder for our mistress to devise imposition enough than for us to undergo any difficulty imposed. This is the monstruosity in love, lady, that the will is infinite and the execution confined; that the desire is boundless and the act a slave to limit.

CRESSIDA   They say all lovers swear more performance than they are able, and yet reserve an ability that they never perform: vowing more than the perfection of ten and discharging less than the tenth part of one. They that have the voice of lions and the act of hares, are they not monsters?

TROILUS   Are there such? Such are not we. Praise us as we are tasted, allow us as we prove; our head shall go bare till merit crowns it. No perfection in reversion shall have a praise in present; we will not name desert before its birth and, being born, its addition shall be humble. Few words to fair faith. Troilus shall be such to Cressida, as what envy can say worst shall be a mock for his truth, and what truth can speak truest not truer than Troilus.

CRESSIDA   Will you walk in, my lord?

Enter Pandarus.

PANDARUS   What, blushing still: Have you not done talking yet?

CRESSIDA   Well, uncle, what folly I commit, I dedicate to
    you.
PANDARUS   I thank you for that. If my lord gets a boy of
    you, you'll give him me. Be true to my lord; if he
    flinches, chide me for it.
TROILUS   You know now your hostages, your uncle's
    word and my firm faith.
PANDARUS   Nay, I'll give my word for her too. Our kin-
    dred, though they are long ere they be wooed, they are
    constant being won. They are burrs, I can tell you;
    they will stick where they are thrown.
CRESSIDA
    Boldness comes to me now and brings me heart.
    Prince Troilus, I have loved you night and day
    For many weary months.
TROILUS
    Why was my Cressida then so hard to win?
CRESSIDA
    Hard to seem won; but I was won, my lord,
    With the first glance that ever—pardon me:
    If I confess much you will play the tyrant.
    I love you now, but not till now, so much
    But I might master it. In faith, I lie;
    My thoughts were like unbridled children grown
    Too headstrong for their mother. See, we fools!
    Why have I blabbed? Who shall be true to us
    When we are so unsecret to ourselves?
    But, though I loved you well, I wooed you not;
    And yet, good faith, I wished myself a man,
    Or that we women had men's privilege
    Of speaking first. Sweet, bid me hold my tongue,
    For in this rapture I shall surely speak
    The thing I shall repent. See, see! your silence,
    Cunning in dumbness, from my weakness draws
    My very soul of counsel. Stop my mouth.
TROILUS
    And shall, albeit sweet music issues thence.
PANDARUS   Pretty, in faith.

CRESSIDA
My lord, I do beseech you, pardon me;
It was not my purpose thus to beg a kiss.
I am ashamed. O heavens, what have I done?
For this time will I take my leave, my lord.

TROILUS
Your leave, sweet Cressida?

PANDARUS   Leave! If you take leave till to-morrow
morning—

CRESSIDA
Pray you, content you.

TROILUS   What offends you, lady?

CRESSIDA
Sir, my own company.

TROILUS
You cannot shun yourself.

CRESSIDA
Let me go and try.
I have a kind of self resides with you;
But an unkind self, that itself will leave
To be another's fool. I would be gone.
Where is my wit? I know not what I speak.

TROILUS
Well know they what they speak that speak so wisely.

CRESSIDA
Perchance, my lord, I show more craft than love,
And fell so roundly to a large confession
To angle for your thoughts. But you are wise,
Or else you love not, for to be wise and love
Exceeds man's might; that dwells with gods above.

TROILUS
O! that I thought it could be in a woman—
As, if it can, I will presume in you—
To feed for aye her lamp and flames of love;
To keep her constancy in plight and youth,
Outliving beauty's outward, with a mind
That does renew swifter than blood decays!
Or that persuasion could but thus convince me

That my integrity and truth to you
Might be affronted with the match and weight—
Of such a winnowed purity in love—
How were I then uplifted! But, alas,
I am as true as truth's simplicity,
And simpler than the infancy of truth.

CRESSIDA
In that I'll war with you.

TROILUS   O virtuous fight,
When right with right wars who shall be most right!
True swains in love shall in the world to come
Approve their truth by Troilus. When their rhymes,
Full of protest, of oath, and big compare,
Want similes, truth tired with iteration—
'As true as steel, as plantage to the moon,
As sun to day, as turtle to her mate,
As iron to adamant, as earth to the centre'—
Yet, after all comparisons of truth,
As truth's authentic author to be cited,
'As true as Troilus' shall crown up the verse
And sanctify the numbers.

CRESSIDA   Prophet may you be!
If I am false or swerve a hair from truth,
When time is old and has forgotten itself,
When waterdrops have worn the stones of Troy,
And blind oblivion swallowed cities up,
And mighty states characterless are grated
To dusty nothing, yet let memory,
From false to false among false maids in love,
Upbraid my falsehood! When they have said, 'as false
As air, as water, wind or sandy earth,
As fox to lamb, as wolf to heifer's calf,
Panther to hind, or stepdame to her son'—
Yea, let them say, to stick the heart of falsehood,
'As false as Cressida.'

PANDARUS   Go to, a bargain made; seal it; I'll be the witness. Here I hold your hand, here my niece's. If ever
you prove false one to another, since I have taken such

pains to bring you together, let all pitiful goers-
between be called to the world's end after my name.
Call them all Pandars; let all constant men be
Troiluses, all false women Cressidas, and all brokers-
between Pandars! Say, 'Amen.'

TROILUS Amen.

CRESSIDA Amen.

PANDARUS Amen. Whereupon I will show you a
chamber with bed, which—because it shall not speak
of your pretty encounters—press it to death. Away!
                              Exeunt Troilus and Cressida.
And Cupid grant all tongue-tied maidens here
Bed, chamber, Pandar to provide this gear!   *Exit.*

SCENE III
The Greek camp. Before Achilles' tent.

Flourish of trumpets. Enter Ulysses,
Diomedes, Nestor, Agamemnon,
Menelaus, Ajax, and Calchas.

CALCHAS
  Now, princes, for the sevice I have done,
  The advantage of the time prompts me aloud
  To call for recompense. Appear it to mind
  That through the sight I bear in things to come,
  I have abandoned Troy, left my possession,
  Incurred a traitor's name, exposed myself,
  From certain and possessed conveniences,
  To doubtful fortunes; sequestering from me all
  That time, acquaintance, custom, and condition
  Made tame and most familiar to my nature.
  And here, to do you service, am become
  As new into the world, strange, unacquainted.
  I do beseech you, as in way of taste,
  To give me now a little benefit

Out of those many registered in promise,
Who, you say, live to come in my behalf.

AGAMEMNON
What would you of us, Trojan? Make demand.

CALCHAS
You have a Trojan prisoner, called Antenor,
Yesterday taken, Troy holds him very dear.
Oft have you—often have you thanks therefor—
Desired my Cressida in right great exchange,
Whom Troy has ever denied. But this Antenor
I know is such a key in their affairs
That their negotiations all must slack,
Wanting his management; and they will almost
Give us a price of blood, a son of Priam,
In change of him. Let him be sent, great princes,
And he shall buy my daughter; and her presence
Shall quite strike off all service I have done
In most accepted pain.

AGAMEMNON   Let Diomedes bear him,
And bring us Cressida hither. Calchas shall have
What he requests of us. Good Diomedes,
Furnish you fairly for his interchange.
With that bring word if Hector will to-morrow
Be answered in his challenge. Ajax is ready.

DIOMEDES
This shall I undertake, it is a burden
Which I am proud to bear.   *Exit with Calchas.*
            Achilles and Patroclus stand in their tent.

ULYSSES
Achilles stands in the entrance of his tent.
Please it our general to pass strangely by him,
As if he were forgotten; and, princes all,
Lay negligent and loose regard upon him
I will come last. Likely he'll question me
Why disapproving eyes are bent, why turned, on him.
If so, I have derision medicinal
To use between your strangeness and his pride,
Which his own will shall have desire to drink.

It may do good; pride has no other glass
To show itself but pride, for supple knees
Feed arrogance and are the proud man's fees.

AGAMEMNON
We'll execute your purpose, and put on
A form of strangeness as we pass along.
So do each lord, and either greet him not
Or else disdainfully, which shall shake him more
Than if not looked on. I will lead the way.

ACHILLES
What comes the general to speak with me?
You know my mind; I'll fight no more against Troy.

AGAMEMNON
What says Achilles? Would he aught with us?

NESTOR
Would you, my lord, aught with the general?

ACHILLES   No.

NESTOR   Nothing, my lord.

AGAMEMNON   The better.

ACHILLES   Good day, good day.

MENELAUS   How do you? How do you?

ACHILLES   What, does the cuckold scorn me?

AJAX   How now, Patroclus?

ACHILLES   Good morrow, Ajax.

AJAX   Ha?

ACHILLES   Good morrow.

AJAX   Ay, and good next day too.   *Exeunt.*

ACHILLES
What mean these fellows? Know they not Achilles?

PATROCLUS
They pass by strangely. They were used to bend,
To send their smiles before them to Achilles,
To come as humbly as they used to creep
To holy altars.

ACHILLES   What, am I poor of late?
'Tis certain, greatness, once fallen out with fortune,
Must fall out with men too. What the declined is

He shall as soon read in the eyes of others
As feel in his own fall. For men, like butterflies,
Show not their dusty wings but to the summer;
And not a man, for being simply man,
Has any honor, but honor for those honors
That are without him—as place, riches, and favor,
Prizes of accident as oft as merit!
Who when they fall, as being slippery standers,
The love that leaned on them as slippery too,
Does one pluck down another, and together
Die in the fall. But it is not so with me;
Fortune and I are friends. I do enjoy
At ample point all that I did possess,
Save these men's looks; who do, it seems, find out
Something not worth in me such rich beholding
As they have often given. Here is Ulysses;
I'll interrupt his reading.
How now, Ulysses.

ULYSSES   Now, great Thetis' son.

ACHILLES
What are you reading?

ULYSSES   A strange fellow here
Writes me that man, how dear so ever his parts,
How much in having, either without or in,
Cannot make boast to have that which he has,
Nor feels what he owns but by reflection;
As when his virtues aiming upon others
Heat them, and they retort that heat again
To the first giver.

ACHILLES   This is not strange, Ulysses.
The beauty that is borne here in the face
The bearer knows not, but commends itself
To others' eyes. Nor does the eye itself,
That most pure spirit of sense, behold itself,
Not going from itself; but eye to eye opposed
Salutes each other with each other's form!
For speculation turns not to itself
Till it has travelled and is married there

Where it may see itself. This is not strange at all.

ULYSSES

I do no strain at the positiòn,
It is familiar, but at the author's drift;
Who in his circumstance expressly proves
That no man is the lord of anything—
Though in and of him there is much consisting—
Till he beholds them formed in the applause
Nor does he of himself know them for aught
Till he beholds them formèd in the applause
Where they are extended. Which, like an arch,
    reverberates
The voice again, or, like a gate of steel
Fronting the sun, receives and renders back
Its figure and its heat. I was much rapt in this,
And apprehended here immediately
The unknown Ajax.
Heavens, what a man is there! A very horse,
That has he knows not what. Nature, what things
    there are
Most abject in regard and dear in the esteem
And poor in worth! Now shall we see to-morrow,
An act that very chance does throw upon him,
Ajax renowned. O heavens, what some men do,
While some men leave to do!
How some men creep in skittish Fortune's hall,
While others play the idiots in her eyes!
How one man eats into another's pride,
While pride is fasting in its wantonness!
To see these Grecian lords—why, even already
They clap the lubber Ajax on the shoulder,
As if his foot were on brave Hector's breast,
And great Troy shrinking.

ACHILLES

I do believe it; for they passed by me
As misers do by beggars, neither gave to me
Good word nor look. What, are my deeds forgotten?

ULYSSES
    Time has, my lord, a wallet at his back,
    Wherein he puts alms for oblivion,
    A great-sized monster of ingratitudes.
    Those scraps are good deeds past, which are devoured
    As fast as they are made, forgotten as soon
    As done. Persèverance, dear my lord,
    Keeps honor bright; to have done, is to hang
    Quite out of fashion, like a rusty mail
    In monumental mockery. Take the instant way;
    For honor travels in a strait so narrow
    Where one but goes abreast. Keep, then, the path;
    For emulation has a thousand sons
    That one by one pursue. If you give way,
    Or hedge aside from the direct forthright,
    Like to an entered tide they all rush by
    And leave you hindmost;
    Or, like a gallant horse fallen in first rank,
    Lie there for pavement to the abject rear,
    O'errun and trampled on. What they do in present,
    Though less than yours in past, must o'ertop yours;
    For time is like a fashionable host,
    That slightly shakes his parting guest by the hand
    And, with his arms outstretched as he would fly,
    Grasps in the comer. The welcome ever smiles,
    And farewell goes out sighing. Let not virtue seek
    Remuneration for the thing it was. For beauty, wit,
    High birth, vigor of bone, desert in service,
    Love, friendship, charity, are subjects all
    To envious and calumniating time.
    One touch of nature makes the whole world kin,
    That all with one consent praise new-born trifles,
    Though they are made and moulded of things past,
    And give to dust that is a little gilt
    More laud than gilt o'er-dusted.
    The present eye praises the present object.
    Then marvel not, you great and complete man,
    That all the Greeks begin to worship Ajax;

Since things in motion sooner catch the eye
Than what not stirs. The cry went once on you,
And still it might, and yet it may again,
If you would not entomb yourself alive
And case your reputation in your tent;
Whose glorious deeds, but in these fields of late,
Made emulous missions among the gods themselves
And drove great Mars to faction.

ACHILLES   Of this my privacy
I have strong reasons.

ULYSSES   But against your privacy
The reasons are more potent and heroical.
It is known, Achilles, that you are in love
With one of Priam's daughters.

ACHILLES   Ha! known!

ULYSSES

Is that a wonder?
The providence that's in a watchful state
Knows almost every grain of Plutus' gold,
Finds bottom in the uncomprehensive deeps,
Keeps place with thought, and almost, like the gods,
Does thoughts unveil in their dumb cradles.
There is a mystery—with whom relation
Durst never meddle—in the soul of state,
Which has an operation more divine
Than breath or pen can give expression to.
All the commerce that you have had with Troy
As perfectly is ours as yours, my lord;
And better would it fit Achilles much
To throw down Hector than Polyxena.
But it must grieve young Pyrrhus now at home,
When fame shall in our islands sound its trump,
And all the Greekish girls shall tripping sing,
'Great Hector's sister did Achilles win,
But our great Ajax bravely beat down him.'
Farewell, my lord; I as your lover speak;
The fool slides over the ice that you should break.
                                                                Exit.

PATROCLUS
  To this effect, Achilles, have I moved you.
  A woman impudent and mannish grown
  Is not more loathed than an effeminate man
  In time of action. I stand condemned for this.
  They think my little stomach to the war
  And your great love to me restrains you thus.
  Sweet, rouse yourself; and the weak wanton Cupid
  Shall from your neck unloose his amorous fold
  And, like a dew-drop from the lion's mane,
  Be shaken to air.
ACHILLES   Shall Ajax fight with Hector?
PATROCLUS
  Ay, and perhaps receive much honor by him.
ACHILLES
  I see my reputation is at stake;
  My fame is shrewdly gored.
PATROCLUS   O, then, beware!
  Those wounds heal ill that men do give themselves.
  Omission to do what is necessary
  Seals a commission to a blank of danger;
  And danger, like an ague, subtly taints
  Even then when we sit idly in the sun.
ACHILLES
  Go call Thersites hither, sweet Patroclus.
  I'll send the fool to Ajax and desire him
  To invite the Trojan lords after the combat
  To see great Hector in his dress of peace,
  To talk with him and to behold his visage,
  Even to my full of view. A labor saved!

       Enter Thersites.

THERSITES   A wonder!
ACHILLES   What?
THERSITES   Ajax goes up and down the field, asking for
  himself.
ACHILLES   How so?

THERSITES   He must fight singly to-morrow with Hector, and is so prophetically proud of an heroical cud-
gelling that he raves in saying nothing.

ACHILLES   How can that be?

THERSITES   Why, he stalks up and down like a
peacock—a stride and a stand; ruminates like an
hostess that has no arithmetic but her brain to set
down her reckoning; bites his lip with a politic
regard, as who should say, 'There were wit in this
head if it would out'. And so there is, but it lies as
coldly in him as fire in a flint, which will not show
without knocking. The man is undone for ever, for if
Hector breaks not his neck in the combat, he'll break
it himself in vainglory. He knows not me. I said,
'Good morrow, Ajax'; and he replies, 'Thanks,
Agamemnon.' What think you of this man that takes
me for the general? He's grown a very land-fish, lan-
guageless, a monster. A plague of opinion! A man may
wear it on both sides like a leather jerkin.

ACHILLES   You must be my ambassador to him,
Thersites.

THERSITES   Who, I? Why, he'll answer nobody; he
professes not answering. Speaking is for beggars; he
wears his tongue in his arms. I will put on his presence; let Patroclus make demands to me, you shall see
the pageant of Ajax.

ACHILLES   To him, Patroclus. Tell him I humbly desire
the valiant Ajax to invite the most valorous Hector to
come unarmed to my tent, and to procure safe-
conduct for his person of the magnanimous and most
illustrious,   six-or-seven-times-honored   captain-
general of the Grecian army, Agamemnon, et caetera.
Do this.

PATROCLUS   Jove bless great Ajax!

THERSITES   Hum!

PATROCLUS   I come from the worthy Achilles—

THERSITES   Ha!

PATROCLUS   Who must humbly desires you to invite
  Hector to his tent—
THERSITES   Hum!
PATROCLUS   And   to   procure   safe-conduct   from
  Agamemnon.
THERSITES   Agamemnon?
PATROCLUS   Ay, my lord.
THERSITES   Ha!
PATROCLUS   What say you to it?
THERSITES   God be with you, with all my heart.
PATROCLUS   Your answer, sir.
THERSITES   If to-morrow is a fair day, by eleven of the
  clock it will be one way or other; howsoever, he shall
  pay for me ere he has me.
PATROCLUS   Your answer, sir.
THERSITES   Fare you well, with all my heart.
ACHILLES   Why, but he is not in this tune, is he?
THERSITES   No, but out of tune thus. What music will be
  in him when Hector has knocked out his brains, I
  know not; but I am sure none, unless the fiddler
  Apollo gets his sinews to make catgut of.
ACHILLES   Come, you shall bear a letter to him straight.
THERSITES   Let me bear another to his horse, for that is
  the more capable creature.
ACHILLES
  My mind is troubled, like a fountain stirred;
  And I myself see not the bottom of it.
                     Exeunt Achilles and Patroclus.
THERSITES   Would the fountain of your mind were clear
  again, that I might water an ass at it! I had rather be a
  tick in a sheep than such a valiant ignorance.
                                                Exit.

Act IV

SCENE I
Troy. A street.

Enter, at one door, Aeneas with a torch; at another, Paris, Deiphobus, Antenor, Diomedes the Grecian, and others, with torches.

PARIS
See, ho! who is that there?
DEIPHOBUS   It is the Lord Aeneas.
AENEAS
Is the prince there in person?
Had I so good occasion to lie long
As you, Prince Paris, nothing but heavenly business
Should rob my bed-mate of my company.
DIOMEDES
That's my mind too. Good morrow, Lord Aeneas.
PARIS
A valiant Greek, Aeneas; take his hand.
Witness the process of your speech, wherein
You told how Diomed, a whole week by days,
Did haunt you in the field.
AENEAS   Health to you, valiant sir,
During all question of the gentle truce;
But when I meet you armed, as black defiance
As heart can think or courage execute.
DIOMEDES
The one and other Diomed embraces.
Our bloods are now in calm and, so long, health!
But when contention and occasion meet,
By Jove, I'll play the hunter for your life
With all my force, pursuit, and policy.

449

AENEAS
    And you shall hunt a lion that will fly
    With his face backward. In humane gentleness,
    Welcome to Troy! Now, by Anchises' life,
    Welcome indeed! By Venus' hand I swear,
    No man alive can love in such a sort
    The thing he means to kill more excellently.
DIOMEDES
    We sympathize. Jove, let Aeneas live,
    If to my sword his fate is not the glory,
    A thousand complete courses of the sun!
    But, in my emulous honor, let him die
    With every joint a wound, and that to-morrow!
AENEAS
    We know each other well.
DIOMEDES
    We do, and long to know each other worse.
PARIS
    This is the most despiteful gentle greeting,
    The noblest hateful love, that ever I heard of.
    What business, lord, so early?
AENEAS
    I was sent for to the king; but why, I know not.
PARIS
    His purpose meets you; it was to bring this Greek
    To Calchas' house, and there to render him,
    For the enfreed Antenor, the fair Cressida.
    Let's have your company; or, if you please,
    Haste there before us. I constantly do think—
    Or rather call my thought a certain knowledge—
    My brother Troilus lodges there to-night.
    Rouse him and give him note of our approach,
    With the whole quality wherefore. I fear
    We shall be much unwelcome.
AENEAS   That I assure you.
    Troilus had rather Troy were borne to Greece
    Than Cressida borne from Troy.
PARIS   There is no help.

The bitter disposition of the time
Will have it so. On, lord; we'll follow you.

AENEAS

Good morrow, all.   *Exit Aeneas.*

PARIS

And tell me, noble Diomed; faith, tell me true,
Even in the soul of sound good-fellowship,
Who, in your thoughts, deserves fair Helen best,
Myself or Menelaus?

DIOMEDES   Both alike.

He merits well to have her that does seek her,
Not making any scruple of her soilure,
With such a hell of pain and world of charge;
And you as well to keep her that defend her,
Not palating the taste of her dishonor,
With such a costly loss of wealth and friends.
He, like a puling cuckold, would drink up
The lees and dregs of a flat tamèd piece;
You, like a lecher, out of whorish loins
Are pleased to breed out your inheritors.
Both merits poised, each weighs nor less nor more;
But he as he, the heavier for a whore.

PARIS

You are too bitter to your countrywoman.

DIOMEDES

She's bitter to her country. Hear me, Paris:
For every false drop in her bawdy veins
A Grecian's life has sunk; for every scruple
Of her contaminated carrion weight
A Trojan has been slain. Since she could speak,
She has not given so many good words breath
As for her Greeks and Trojans suffered death.

PARIS

Fair Diomed, you do as chapmen do,
Dispraise the thing that you desire to buy;
But we in silence hold this virtue well,
We'll not commend what we intend to sell.
Here lies our way.   *Exeunt.*

SCENE II
Pandarus' house.

Enter Troilus and Cressida.

TROILUS
Dear, trouble not yourself; the morn is cold.
CRESSIDA
Then, sweet my lord, I'll call my uncle down;
He shall unbolt the gates.
TROILUS   Trouble him not;
To bed, to bed. Sleep kill those pretty eyes,
And give as soft attachment to your senses
As infants' empty of all thought!
CRESSIDA   Good morrow then.
TROILUS
I pray you now, to bed.
CRESSIDA   Are you aweary of me?
TROILUS
O Cressida, but that the busy day,
Waked by the lark, has roused the ribald crows,
And dreaming night will hide our joys no longer,
I would not from you.
CRESSIDA   Night has been too brief.
TROILUS
Curse the witch! with venomous wights she stays
As tediously as hell, but flies the grasps of love
With wings more momentary-swift than thought.
You will catch cold and curse me.
CRESSIDA   Pray you, tarry;
You men will never tarry.
O foolish Cressida! I might have still held off,
And then you would have tarried. Hark, there's one
    up.
PANDARUS *[within]* What's all the doors open here?
TROILUS   It is your uncle.

CRESSIDA   A pestilence on him! Now will he be mocking.
I shall have such a life.

Enter Pandarus.

PANDARUS   How now, how now! How go maidenheads?
Here, you maid, where's my niece Cressida?
CRESSIDA
Go hang yourself, you naughty mocking uncle.
You bring me to do—and then you flout me too.
PANDARUS   To do what? To do what? Let her say what.
What have I brought you to do?
CRESSIDA
Come, come; bless your heart! You'll never be good,
Nor suffer others.
PANDARUS   Ha, ha! Alas, poor wretch! A poor
simpleton! Not slept to-night? Would he not, a
naughty man, let it sleep? A bugbear take him!
CRESSIDA
Did not I tell you? Would he were knocked in the
head!

One knocks.

Who's that at door? Good uncle, go and see.
My lord, come you again into my chamber.
You smile and mock me, as if I meant naughtily.
TROILUS   Ha, ha!
CRESSIDA
Come, you are deceived, I think of no such thing.

Knock.

How earnestly they knock! Pray you, come in.
I would not for half Troy have you seen here.
                         Exeunt Troilus and Cressida.
PANDARUS   Who's there? What's the matter? Will you
beat down the door? How now, what's the matter?

Enter Aeneas.

AENEAS
Good morrow, lord, good morrow.

PANDARUS   Who's there? My Lord Aeneas! By my word,
I knew you not. What news with you so early?

AENEAS
Is not Prince Troilus here?

PANDARUS   Here? What should he do here?

AENEAS
Come, he is here, my lord. Do not deny him.
It does import him much to speak with me.

PANDARUS   Is he here, say you? 'Tis more than I know,
I'll be sworn. For my own part, I came in late. What
should he do here?

AENEAS   Who! nay, then. Come, come, you'll do him
wrong ere you are aware. You'll be so true to him, to be
false to him. Do not you know of him, but yet go fetch
him hither; go.

Enter Troilus.

TROILUS   How now, what's the matter?

AENEAS
My lord, I scarce have leisure to salute you,
My matter is so rash. There are at hand
Paris your brother, and Deiphobus,
The Grecian Diomed, and our Antenor
Delivered to us. And for him forthwith,
Ere the first sacrifice, within this hour,
We must give up to Diomedes' hand
The Lady Cressida.

TROILUS   Is it concluded so?

AENEAS
By Priam, and the general state of Troy.
They are at hand and ready to effect it.

TROILUS
How my achievements mock me!

I will go meet them. And, my Lord Aeneas,
We met by chance; you did not find me here.

AENEAS

Good, good, my lord; the secrets of nature
Have not more gift in taciturnity.

> *Exeunt Troilus and Aeneas.*

PANDARUS   Is it possible? No sooner got but lost? The
devil take Antenor! The young prince will go mad. A
plague upon Antenor! I would they had broken his
neck!

Enter Cressida.

CRESSIDA

How now? What's the matter? Who was here?

PANDARUS   Ah, ah!

CRESSIDA

Why sigh you so profoundly? Where's my lord?
Gone? Tell me, sweet uncle, what's the matter?

PANDARUS   Would I were as deep under the earth as I
am above!

CRESSIDA   O the gods! what's the matter?

PANDARUS   Pray you, get you in. Would you had never
been born! I knew you would be his death. O poor
gentleman! A plague upon Antenor!

CRESSIDA   Good uncle, I beseech you on my knees, what
is the matter?

PANDARUS   You must be gone, wench, you must be gone;
you are changed for Antenor. You must to your father
and be gone from Troilus. It will be his death; it will
be his end; he cannot bear it.

CRESSIDA

O you immortal gods! I will not go.

PANDARUS   You must.

CRESSIDA

I will not, uncle. I have forgotten my father;
I know no touch of consanguinity—

No kin, no love, no blood, no soul so near me
As the sweet Troilus. O you gods divine,
Make Cressida's name the very crown of falsehood
If ever she leaves Troilus! Time, force, and death,
Do to this body what extremes you can;
But the strong base and building of my love
Is as the very centre of the earth,
Drawing all things to it. I'll go in and weep.

PANDARUS   Do, do.

CRESSIDA
Tear my bright hair, and scratch my praisèd cheeks,
Crack my clear voice with sobs, and break my heart
With sounding Troilus. I will not go from Troy.

Exeunt.

SCENE III
Before Pandarus' house.

*Enter Paris, Troilus, Aeneas, Deiphobus, Antenor,
Diomedes.*

PARIS
It is great morning, and the hour prefixed
For her delivery to this valiant Greek
Comes fast upon. Good my brother Troilus,
Tell you the lady what she is to do,
And haste her to the purpose.

TROILUS   Walk into her house.
I'll bring her to the Grecian presently;
And to his hand when I deliver her,
Think it an altar, and your brother Troilus
A priest there offering to it his own heart.

PARIS
I know what it is to love;
And would, as I shall pity, I could help!
Please you walk in, my lords.   *Exeunt.*

SCENE IV
Pandarus' house.

Enter Pandarus and Cressida.

PANDARUS   Be moderate, be moderate.
CRESSIDA
  Why tell you me of moderation?
  The grief is fine, full, perfect, that I taste,
  And is as violent in a sense as strong
  As that which causes it. How can I moderate it?
  If I could temporize with my affections,
  Or brew it to a weak and colder palate,
  The like abatement could I give my grief.
  My love admits no qualifying dross;
  No more my grief, in such a precious loss.

  Enter Troilus.

PANDARUS   Here, here, here he comes. Ah, sweet ducks!
CRESSIDA   *[embracing him]* O Troilus! Troilus!
PANDARUS   What a pair of spectacles is here! Let me em-
  brace too. 'O heart,' as the goodly saying is—
          O heart, heavy heart,
          Why sigh you without breaking?
  where he answers again,
          Because you cannot ease your smart
          By friendship nor by speaking.
  There was never a truer rhyme. Let us cast away noth-
  ing, for we may live to have need of such a verse. We
  see it, we see it. How now, lambs!
TROILUS
  Cressida, I love you in so strained a purity,
  That the blest gods, as angry with my fancy,
  More bright in zeal than the devotion which
  Cold lips blow to their deities, take you from me.

CRESSIDA   Have the gods envy?

PANDARUS   Ay, ay, ay, ay; it is too plain a case.

CRESSIDA

And is it true that I must go from Troy?

TROILUS

A hateful truth.

CRESSIDA   What, and from Troilus too?

TROILUS

From Troy and Troilus.

CRESSIDA   Is it possible?

TROILUS

And suddenly, where injury of chance
Puts back leave-taking, jostles roughly by
All time of pause, rudely beguiles our lips
Of all rejoining, forcibly prevents
Our locked embraces, strangles our dear vows
Even in the birth of our own laboring breath.
We two, that with so many thousand sighs
Did buy each other, must poorly sell ourselves
With the rude brevity and discharge of one.
Injurious time now with a robber's haste
Crams his rich thievery up, he knows not how.
As many farewells as have stars in heaven,
With distinct breath and consigned kisses to them,
He fumbles up into a loose adieu,
And scants us with a single famished kiss,
Distasted with the salt of broken tears.

AENEAS   *(within)* My lord, is the lady ready?

TROILUS

Hark! you are called. Some say the Genius
Cries so to him that instantly must die.
Bid them have patience; she shall come anon.

PANDARUS   Where are my tears? Rain, to lay this wind,
or my heart will be blown up by the root!   *Exit.*

CRESSIDA

I must, then, to the Grecians?

TROILUS   No remedy.

CRESSIDA

A woeful Cressida among the merry Greeks!
When shall we see again?

TROILUS

Hear me, love. Be you but true of heart—

CRESSIDA

I true! How now! What wicked thought is this?

TROILUS

Nay, we must use expostulation kindly,
For it is parting from us.
I speak not 'be you true' as fearing you,
For I will throw my glove to Death himself
That there is no impunity in your heart;
But 'be you true,' say I, to fashion in
My sequent protestation; be you true,
And I will see you.

CRESSIDA

O, you shall be exposed, my lord, to dangers
As infinite as imminent; but I'll be true.

TROILUS

And I'll grow friend with danger. Wear this sleeve.

CRESSIDA

And you this glove. When shall I see you?

TROILUS

I will corrupt the Grecian sentinels,
To give you nightly visitation.
But yet, be true.

CRESSIDA   O heavens! 'be true' again!

TROILUS

Hear why I speak it, love.
The Grecian youths are full of quality;
Their loving, well composed, with gift of nature,
And swelling over with arts and exercise.
How novelty may move, and parts with person,
Alas! a kind of godly jealousy—
Which, I beseech you, call a virtuous sin—
Makes me afraid.

CRESSIDA   O heavens, you love me not!

TROILUS

Die I a villain, then!
In this I do not call your faith in question
So mainly as my merit. I cannot sing,
Nor heel the leaping dance, nor sweeten talk,
Nor play at subtle games—fair virtues all,
To which the Grecians are most prompt and
     pregnant;
But I can tell that in each grace of these
There lurks a still and dumb-discursive devil
That tempts most cunningly. But be not tempted.

CRESSIDA   Do you think I will?

TROILUS   No.

But something may be done that we will not;
And sometimes we are devils to ourselves
When we will tempt the frailty of our powers,
Presuming on their changeful potency.

AENEAS   *(within)*

Nay, good my lord!

TROILUS   Come, kiss; and let us part.

PARIS   *(within)*

Brother Troilus!

TROILUS   Good brother, come you hither;
And bring Aeneas and the Grecian with you.

CRESSIDA

My lord, will you be true?

TROILUS

Who? I? Alas, it is my vice, my fault.
While others fish with craft for reputation,
I with great truth catch mere simplicity;
While some with cunning gild their copper crowns,
With truth and plainness I do wear mine bare.
Fear not my truth; the moral of my wit
Is 'plain and true'; there's all the reach of it.

*Enter Aeneas, Paris, Antenor, Deiphobus, and
Diomedes.*

Welcome, Sir Diomed. Here is the lady
Which for Antenor we deliver you.
At the gate, lord, I'll give her to your hand,
And by the way inform you what she is.
Entreat her fair; and, by my soul, fair Greek,
If ever you stand at mercy of my sword,
Name Cressida, and your life shall be as safe
As Priam is in Ilion.

DIOMEDES   Fair Lady Cressida,
So please you, save the thanks this prince expects.
The lustre in your eye, heaven in your cheek,
Pleads your fair usage; and to Diomed
You shall be mistress, and command him wholly.

TROILUS
Grecian, you do not use me courteously,
To shame the seal of my petition to you
In praising her. I tell you, lord of Greece,
She is as far high-soaring o'er your praises
As you unworthy to be called her servant.
I charge you use her well, even for my charge;
For, by the dreadful Pluto, if you do not,
Though the great bulk Achilles is your guard,
I'll cut your throat.

DIOMEDES   O, be not moved, Prince Troilus.
Let me be privileged by my place and message
To be a speaker free. When I am hence,
I'll answer to my liking; and know you, lord,
I'll nothing do on charge. To her own worth
She shall be prized; but that you say 'be it so,'
I'll speak it in my spirit and honor, 'no.'

TROILUS
Come, to the gate. I'll tell you, Diomed,
This boast shall oft make you to hide your head.
Lady, give me your hand and, as we walk,
To our own selves bend we our needful talk.

                    Exeunt Troilus, Cressida, and Diomedes.
          Sound trumpet.

PARIS

Hark! Hector's trumpet.

AENEAS   How have we spent this morning!

The prince must think me tardy and remiss,

That swore to ride before him to the field.

PARIS

It is Troilus' fault. Come, come, to field with him.

DEIPHOBUS

Let us make ready straight.

AENEAS

Yea, with a bridegroom's fresh alacrity,

Let us address to tend on Hector's heels.

The glory of our Troy does this day lie

On his fair worth and single chivalry.   *Exeunt.*

SCENE V
The Greek camp.

Enter Ajax, armed; Achilles, Patroclus,
Agamemnon, Menelaus, Ulysses, Nestor,
Calchas, etc.

AGAMEMNON

Here are you in appointment fresh and fair,

Anticipating time. With starting courage,

Give with your trumpet a loud note to Troy,

You dreadful Ajax, that the appallèd air

May pierce the head of the great combatant

And hale him hither.

AJAX   You, trumpet, there's my purse.

Now crack your lungs, and split your brazen pipe.

Blow, villain, till your spherèd bias cheek

Outswell the colic of puffed Aquilon.

Come, stretch your chest, and let your eyes spout
    blood;

You blow for Hector.

Trumpet sounds.

ULYSSES
No trumpet answers.
ACHILLES   It is but early days.
AGAMEMNON
Is not yon Diomed with Calchas' daughter?
ULYSSES
It is he, I ken the manner of his gait;
He rises on the toe. That spirit of his
In aspiration lifts him from the earth.

Enter Diomedes, with Cressida.

AGAMEMNON
Is this the Lady Cressida?
DIOMEDES   Even she.
AGAMEMNON
Most dearly welcome to the Greeks, sweet lady.
NESTOR
Our general does salute you with a kiss.
ULYSSES
Yet is the kindness but particular.
'Twere better she were kissed in general.
NESTOR
And very courtly counsel. I'll begin.
So much for Nestor.
ACHILLES
I'll take that winter from your lips, fair lady.
Achilles bids you welcome.
MENELAUS
I had good argument for kissing once.
PATROCLUS
But that's no argument for kissing now;
For thus popped Paris in his hardiment,
And parted thus you and your argument.
ULYSSES
O, deadly gall, and theme of all our scorns

For which we lose our heads to gild his horns.
PATROCLUS
     The first was Menelaus' kiss; this, mine:
     Patroclus kisses you.
MENELAUS   O, this is trim.
PATROCLUS
     Paris and I kiss evermore for him.
MENELAUS
     I'll have my kiss, sir. Lady, by your leave.
CRESSIDA
     In kissing, do you render or receive?
PATROCLUS
     Both take and give.
CRESSIDA   I'll make my match to live,
     The kiss you take is better than you give;
     Therefore no kiss.
MENELAUS
     I'll give you odds; I'll give you three for one.
CRESSIDA
     You are an odd man; give even, or give none.
MENELAUS
     An odd man, lady? Every man is odd.
CRESSIDA
     No, Paris is not, for you know 'tis true
     That you are odd and he is even with you.
MENELAUS
     You fillip me on the head.
CRESSIDA   No, I'll be sworn.
ULYSSES
     It were no match, your nail against his horn.
     May I, sweet lady, beg a kiss of you?
CRESSIDA
     You may.
ULYSSES   I do desire it.
CRESSIDA   Why, beg then.
ULYSSES
     Why, then, for Venus' sake, give me a kiss,
     When Helen is a maid again, and his—

CRESSIDA
 I am your debtor; claim it when it is due.
ULYSSES
 Never is my day, and then a kiss of you.
DIOMEDES
 Lady, a word. I'll bring you to your father.
                              Exeunt Diomedes and Cressida.
NESTOR
 A woman of quick sense.
ULYSSES   Fie, fie upon her!
 There's language in her eye, her cheek, her lip;
 Nay, her foot speaks. Her wanton spirits look out
 At every joint and motion of her body.
 O, these encounterers, so glib of tongue,
 That give a coasting welcome ere it comes,
 And wide unclasp the tables of their thoughts
 To every ticklish reader, set them down
 For sluttish spoils of opportunity
 And daughters of the game.

    Flourish. Enter Hector, Paris, Aeneas, Helenus,
    Troilus, and Attendants.

ALL
 The Trojans' trumpet.
AGAMEMNON   Yonder comes the troop.
AENEAS
 Hail, all the state of Greece. What shall be done
 To him that victory commands? Or do you purpose
 A victor shall be known? Will you the knights
 Shall to the edge of all extremity
 Pursue each other, or shall they be divided
 By any voice or order of the field?
 Hector bade ask.
AGAMEMNON   Which way would Hector have it?
AENEAS
 He cares not; he'll obey conditions.

ACHILLES
> 'Tis done like Hector; but securely done,
> A little proudly, and great deal misprising
> The knight opposed.
AENEAS   If not Achilles, sir,
> What is your name?
ACHILLES   If not Achilles, nothing.
AENEAS
> Therefore Achilles; but, whatever, know this:
> In the extremity of great and little,
> Valor and pride excel themselves in Hector:
> The one almost as infinite as all,
> The other blank as nothing. Weigh him well,
> And that which looks like pride is courtesy.
> This Ajax is half made of Hector's blood,
> In love whereof half Hector stays at home;
> Half heart, half hand, half Hector comes to seek
> This blended knight, half Trojan, and half Greek.
ACHILLES
> A maiden battle, then? O, I perceive you.

Enter Diomedes.

AGAMEMNON
> Here is Sir Diomed. Go, gentle knight,
> Stand by our Ajax. As you and Lord Aeneas
> Consent upon the order of their fight,
> So be it, either to the uttermost,
> Or else a breath. The combatants being kin
> Half stints their strife before their strokes begin.

Ajax and Hector enter the lists.

ULYSSES
> They are opposed already.
AGAMEMNON
> What Trojan is that same that looks so heavy?

ULYSSES
>The youngest son of Priam, a true knight,
>Not yet mature, yet matchless, firm of word,
>Speaking in deeds and deedless in his tongue,
>Not soon provoked, nor being provoked soon calmed.
>His heart and hand both open and both free,
>For what he has he gives, what thinks he shows;
>Yet gives he not till judgment guides his bounty,
>Nor dignifies an unfit thought with breath.
>Manly as Hector, but more dangerous;
>For Hector, in his blaze of wrath, subscribes
>To tender objects, but he in heat of action
>Is more vindictive than is jealous love.
>They call him Troilus, and on him erect
>A second hope as fairly built as Hector.
>Thus says Aeneas, one that knows the youth
>Even to his inches, and with private soul
>Did in great Ilion thus translate him to me.

>*Alarum. Hector and Ajax fight.*

AGAMEMNON
>They are in action.

NESTOR
>Now, Ajax, hold your own!

TROILUS   Hector, you sleep; awake you!

AGAMEMNON
>His blows are well disposed. There, Ajax!

DIOMEDES
>You must no more.

>*Trumpets cease.*

AENEAS   Princes, enough, so please you.

AJAX
>I am not warm yet; let us fight again.

DIOMEDES
>As Hector pleases.

HECTOR   Why, then will I no more.
  You are, great lord, my father's sister's son,
  A cousin-german to great Priam's seed;
  The obligation of our blood forbids
  A gory emulation between us twain.
  Were your own mixture Greek and Trojan so
  That you could say, 'This hand is Grecian all,
  And this is Trojan; the sinews of this leg
  All Greek, and this all Troy; my mother's blood
  Runs on the dexter cheek, and this sinister
  Bounds in my father's,' by Jove multipotent,
  You should not bear from me a Greekish member
  Wherein my sword had not impression made
  Of our rank feud. But the just gods gainsay
  That any drop you borrowed from your mother,
  My sacred aunt, should by my mortal sword
  Be drained! Let me embrace you, Ajax;
  By him that thunders, you have lusty arms;
  Hector would have them fall upon him thus.
  Cousin, all honor to you!
AJAX   I thank you, Hector.
  You are too gentle and too free a man.
  I came to kill you, cousin, and bear hence
  A great addition earnèd in your death.
HECTOR
  Not Neoptolemus so admired,
  On whose bright crest Fame with her loudest 'Oyes'[1]
  Cries, 'This is he!' could promise to himself
  A thought of added honor torn from Hector.
AENEAS
  There is expectance here from both the sides,
  What further you will do.
HECTOR   We'll answer it;
  The issue is embracement. Ajax, farewell.
AJAX
  If I might in entreaties find success—

---

[1] A town crier's 'O—yes.'

As seldom I have the chance—I would desire
My famous cousin to our Grecian tents.

DIOMEDES
It is Agamemnon's wish, and great Achilles
Does long to see unarmed the valiant Hector.

HECTOR
Aeneas, call my brother Troilus to me,
And signify this loving interview
To the expecters of our Trojan part.
Desire them home. Give me your hand, my cousin;
I will go eat with you and see your knights.

Agamemnon and the rest advance.

AJAX
Great Agamemnon comes to meet us here.

HECTOR
The worthiest of them tell me name by name;
But for Achilles, my own searching eyes
Shall find him by his large and portly size.

AGAMEMNON
Worthy all arms *[embraces him]*, as welcome as to
    one
That would be rid of such an enemy—
But that's no welcome. Understand more clear,
What's past and what's to come is strewed with husks
And formless ruin of oblivion;
But in this extant moment, faith and truth,
Strained purely from all hollow bias-drawing,
Bid you, with most divine integrity,
From heart of very heart, great Hector, welcome.

HECTOR
I thank you, most imperious Agamemnon.

AGAMEMNON   *[to Troilus]*
My well-famed lord of Troy, no less to you.

MENELAUS
Let me confirm my princely brother's greeting.
You brace of warlike brothers, welcome hither.

HECTOR
Who must we answer?

AENEAS   The noble Menelaus.

HECTOR
O, you, my lord? By Mars's gauntlet, thanks!
Mock not that I affect the untraded oath;
Your former wife swears still by Venus' glove.
She's well, but bade me not commend her to you.

MENELAUS
Name her not now, sir; she's a deadly theme.

HECTOR
O, pardon! I offend.

NESTOR
I have, you gallant Trojan, seen you oft,
Laboring for destiny, make cruel way
Through ranks of Greekish youth; and I have seen
    you,
As hot as Perseus, spur your Phrygian steed,
Despising many forfeits and subduements,
When you have hung your advancèd sword in the air,
Not letting it decline on the declined—
That I have said to some my standers-by,
'Lo, Jupiter is yonder, dealing life!'
And I have seen you pause and take your breath,
When a ring of Greeks have trapped you in,
Like an Olympian wrestling. This have I seen;
But this your countenance, ever locked in steel,
I never saw till now. I knew your grandsire,
And once fought with him. He was a soldier good;
But, by great Mars, the captain of us all,
Never like you. Let an old man embrace you;
And, worthy warrior, welcome to our tents.

AENEAS
It is the old Nestor.

HECTOR
Let me embrace you, good old chronicle,
That have so long walked hand in hand with time.
Most reverend Nestor, I am glad to clasp you.

NESTOR
  I would my arms could match you in contention,
  As they contend with you in courtesy.
HECTOR
  I would they could.
NESTOR
  Ha,
  By this white beard, I'd fight with you to-morrow.
  Well, welcome, welcome. I have seen the time—
ULYSSES
  I wonder now how yonder city stands,
  When we have here her base and pillar by us.
HECTOR
  I know your features, Lord Ulysses, well.
  Ah, sir, there's many a Greek and Trojan dead,
  Since first I saw yourself and Diomed
  In Ilion, on your Greekish embassy.
ULYSSES
  Sir, I foretold you then what would ensue.
  My prophecy is but half its journey yet,
  For yonder walls, that pertly front your town,
  Yon towers, whose wanton tops do buss the clouds,
  Must kiss their own feet.
HECTOR   I must not believe you.
  There they stand yet, and modestly I think,
  The fall of every Phrygian stone will cost
  A drop of Grecian blood. The end crowns all,
  And that old common arbitrator, Time,
  Will one day end it.
ULYSSES   So to him we leave it.
  Most gentle and most valiant Hector, welcome.
  After the general, I beseech you next
  To feast with me and see me at my tent.
ACHILLES
  I shall forestall you, Lord Ulysses, you!
  Now, Hector, I have fed my eyes on you;
  I have with exact view perused you, Hector,
  And noted joint by joint.

HECTOR   Is this Achilles?

ACHILLES

    I am Achilles.

HECTOR

    Stand fair, I pray you; let me look on you.

ACHILLES

    Behold your fill.   Nay, I have done already.

HECTOR

ACHILLES

    You are too brief. I will the second time,
    As I would buy you, view you limb by limb.

HECTOR

    O, like a book of sport you'll read me over;
    But there's more in me than you understand.
    Why do you so oppress me with your eye?

ACHILLES

    Tell me, you heavens, in which part of his body
    Shall I destroy him, whether there, or there, or there?
    That I may give the local wound a name,
    And make distinct the very breach whereout
    Hector's great spirit flew. Answer me, heavens!

HECTOR

    It would discredit the blessed gods, proud man,
    To answer such a question. Stand again.
    Think you to catch my life so pleasantly
    As to prenominate in nice conjecture
    Where you will hit me dead?

ACHILLES   I tell you, yea.

HECTOR

    Were you an oracle to tell me so,
    I'd not believe you. Henceforth guard you well,
    For I'll not kill you there, nor there, nor there;
    But, by the forge that stithied Mars's helm,
    I'll kill you everywhere, yea, over and over.
    You wisest Grecians, pardon me this brag.
    His insolence draws folly from my lips;
    But I'll endeavor deeds to match these words,
    Or may I never—

AJAX   Do not chafe you, cousin;
    And you, Achilles, let these threats alone,
    Till accident or purpose bring you to it.
    You may have every day enough of Hector,
    If you have stomach. The general state, I fear,
    Can scarce entreat you to be odd with him.
HECTOR
    I pray you, let us see you in the field.
    We have had paltry wars since you refused
    The Grecians' cause.
ACHILLES   Do you entreat me, Hector?
    To-morrow do I meet you, fierce as death;
    To-night all friends.
HECTOR   Your hand upon that match.
AGAMEMNON
    First, all you peers of Greece, go to my tent;
    There in the full convive we. Afterwards,
    As Hector's leisure and your bounties shall
    Concur together, each of you entreat him
    To taste your bounties. Let the trumpets blow,
    That this great soldier may his welcome know.
                    Exeunt all except Troilus and Ulysses.
TROILUS
    My Lord Ulysses, tell me, I beseech you,
    In what place of the field does Calchas keep?
ULYSSES
    At Menelaus' tent most princely Troilus.
    There Diomed does feast with him to-night;
    Who neither looks upon the heaven nor earth,
    But gives all gaze and bent of amorous view
    On the fair Cressida.
TROILUS
    Shall I, sweet lord, be bound to you so much,
    After we part from Agamemnon's tent,
    To bring me thither?
ULYSSES   You shall command me, sir.
    As gentle tell me, of what honor was
    This Cressida in Troy? Had she no lover there

That wails her absence?
TROILUS
    O, sir, to such as boasting show their scars
    A mock is due. Will you walk on, my lord?
    She was beloved, she loved; she is, and doth:
    But still sweet love is food for fortune's tooth.

                                              Exeunt.

Act V

SCENE I
The Greek camp. Before Achilles' tent.

Enter Achilles and Patroclus.

ACHILLES
I'll heat his blood with Greekish wine to-night,
Which with my scimitar I'll cool to-morrow.
Patroclus, let us feast him to the height.

PATROCLUS
Here comes Thersites.

Enter Thersites.

ACHILLES   How now, you core of envy!
You crusty batch of nature, what's the news?

THERSITES   Why, you picture of what you seem, and idol
of idiot-worshippers, here is a letter for you.

ACHILLES   From whence, fragment?

THERSITES   Why, you full dish of fool, from Troy.

PATROCLUS   Who keeps the tent now?

THERSITES   The surgeon's box or the patient's wound.

PATROCLUS   Well said, adversity, and what need these
tricks?

THERSITES   Pray, be silent, boy; I profit not by your talk.
You are said to be Achilles' male varlet.

PATROCLUS   Male varlet, you rogue! What's that?

THERSITES   Why, his masculine whore. Now, the rotten
diseases of the south, the guts-griping ruptures,
catarrhs, loads of gravel in the back, lethargies, cold
palsies, raw eyes, dirt-rotten livers, wheezing lungs,
bladders full of abscess, sciaticas, lime-kilns in the

palm, incurable bone-ache, and eruption on the skin,
and the like, take and take again such preposterous
discoveries!

PATROCLUS   Why, you damnable box of envy, you, what
mean you to curse thus?

THERSITES   Do I curse you?

PATROCLUS   Why, no, you ruinous butt, you blasted in-
distinguishable cur, no.

THERSITES   No? Why are you then exasperated, you idle
immaterial skein of sleave silk, you green satin flap
for a sore eye, you tassel of a prodigal's purse, you? Ah,
how the poor world is pestered with such waterflies,
diminutives of nature.

PATROCLUS   Out, gall!

THERSITES   Finch egg!

ACHILLES
My sweet Patroclus, I am thwarted quite
From my great purpose in to-morrow's battle.
Here is a letter from Queen Hecuba,
A token from her daughter, my fair love,
Both taxing me and gaging me to keep
An oath that I have sworn. I will not break it.
Fall Greeks, fail fame, honor or go to stay,
My major vow lies here; this I'll obey.
Come, come, Thersites, help to trim my tent;
This night in banqueting must all be spent.
Away, Patroclus!   *Exit with Patroclus.*

THERSITES   With too much blood and too little brain,
these two may run mad; but if with too much brain
and too little blood they do, I'll be a curer of madmen.
Here's Agamemnon, an honest fellow enough, and
one that loves quails, but he has not so much brain as
earwax; and the goodly transformation of Jupiter
there, his brother, the bull, the primitive statue and
oblique memorial of cuckolds; a thrifty shoeing-horn
in a chain, hanging at his brother's leg, to what form
but that he is should wit larded with malice and malice
forced with wit turn him to? To an ass, were nothing;

he is both ass and ox: to an ox, were nothing; he is
both ox and ass. To be a dog, a mule, a cat, a toad, a
lizard, an owl, a kite, or a herring without a roe, I
would not care; but to be Menelaus! I would conspire
against destiny. Ask me not what I would be, if I were
not Thersites, for I care not to be the louse of a leper,
so I were not Menelaus. Hey-day, spirits and fires!

*Enter Agamemnon, Ulysses, Nestor, Hector,
Ajax, Troilus, Menelaus, and Diomedes, with
lights.*

AGAMEMNON
We go wrong, we go wrong.
AJAX   No, yonder it is;
There, where we see the lights.
HECTOR   I trouble you.
AJAX
No, not a whit.
ULYSSES   Here comes himself to guide you.

Enter Achilles.

ACHILLES
Welcome, brave Hector; welcome, princes all.
AGAMEMNON
So now, fair prince of Troy, I bid good night.
Ajax commands the guard to attend on you.
HECTOR
Thanks and good night to the Greeks' general.
MENELAUS
Good night, my lord.
HECTOR
Good night, sweet Lord Menelaus.
THERSITES   Sweet privy! 'Sweet,' says he! Sweet sink,
sweet sewer.
ACHILLES
Good night and welcome both at once, to those
That go or tarry.

AGAMEMNON   Good night.
                    Exeunt Agamemnon and Menelaus.
ACHILLES
   Old Nestor tarries, and you too, Diomed,
   Keep Hector company an hour or two.
DIOMEDES
   I cannot, lord; I have important business,
   The tide whereof is now. Good night, great Hector.
HECTOR
   Give me your hand.
ULYSSES   *[aside to Troilus]* Follow his torch; he goes
   To Calchas' tent. I'll keep you company.
TROILUS
   Sweet sir, you honor me.
HECTOR   And so, good night.
                    Exeunt Diomedes, then Ulysses and Troilus.
ACHILLES
   Come, come, enter my tent.
                    Exeunt Achilles, Hector, Ajax, and Nestor.
THERSITES   That same Diomed is a false-hearted rogue, a
   most unjust knave; I will no more trust him when he
   leers than I will a serpent when it hisses. He will
   spend his mouth and promise like Brabbler the
   hound; but when he performs, astronomers foretell it,
   it is prodigious, there will come some change. The
   sun borrows of the moon when Diomed keeps his
   word. I will rather stop seeing Hector than not to dog
   him. They say he keeps a Trojan drab, and uses the
   traitor Calchas' tent. I'll after—nothing but lechery!
   All incontinent varlets!
                                                    Exit.

SCENE II
The Greek camp. Before Calchas' tent.

Enter Diomed.

DIOMEDES   What, are you up here, ho? Speak.

CALCHAS *[within]* Who calls?

DIOMEDES Diomed. Calchas, I think. Where's your daughter?

CALCHAS *[within]* She comes to you.

Enter Troilus and Ulysses; after them Thersites.

ULYSSES
Stand where the torch may not discover us.

Enter Cressida.

TROILUS
Cressida comes forth to him.

DIOMEDES   How now, my charge!

CRESSIDA
Now, my sweet guardian! Hark, a word with you.

Whispers.

TROILUS Yea, so familiar!

ULYSSES She will sing any man at first sight.

THERSITES And any man may sing her, if he can take her clef; she is well noted.

DIOMEDES Will you remember?

CRESSIDA Remember? Yes.

DIOMEDES Nay, but do, then;
And let your mind be coupled with your words.

TROILUS What shall she remember?

ULYSSES Listen!

CRESSIDA
Sweet honey Greek, tempt me no more to folly.

THERSITES Roguery!

DIOMEDES
Nay, then—

CRESSIDA I'll tell you what—

DIOMEDES
Foh, foh! come, tell a pin. You are forsworn.

CRESSIDA
   In faith, I cannot. What would you have me do?
THERSITES   A juggling trick—to be secretly open.
DIOMEDES
   What did you swear you would bestow on me?
CRESSIDA
   I pray you, do not hold me to my oath;
   Bid me do anything but that, sweet Greek.
DIOMEDES   Good night.
TROILUS   Hold, patience!
ULYSSES   How now, Trojan?
CRESSIDA   Diomed—
DIOMEDES
   No, no, good night; I'll be your fool no more.
TROILUS
   Your better must.
CRESSIDA   Hark, a word in your ear.
TROILUS
   O plague and madness!
ULYSSES
   You are movèd, prince; let us depart, I pray you,
   Lest your displeasure should enlarge itself
   To wrathful terms. This place is dangerous;
   The time right deadly. I beseech you, go.
TROILUS
   Behold, I pray you!
ULYSSES   Nay, good my lord, go off;
   You flow to great distraction; come, my lord.
TROILUS
   I pray you, stay.
ULYSSES   You have not patience; come.
TROILUS
   I pray you, stay. By hell, and all hell's torments,
   I will not speak a word!
DIOMEDES   And so, good night.
CRESSIDA
   Nay, but you part in anger.
TROILUS   Does that grieve you?

O withered truth!

ULYSSES   How now, my lord!

TROILUS   By Jove,
I will be patient.

CRESSIDA   Guardian! Why, Greek!

DIOMEDES
Foh, foh! adieu; you palter.

CRESSIDA
In faith, I do not, Come hither once again.

ULYSSES
You shake, my lord, at something. Will you go?
You will break out.

TROILUS   She strokes his cheek!

ULYSSES   Come, come.

TROILUS
Nay, stay; by Jove, I will not speak a word.
There is between my will and all offenses
A guard of patience. Stay a little while.

THERSITES   How the devil Lust, with his fat rump and
potato finger, tickles these together. Fry, lechery, fry!

DIOMEDES   But will you, then?

CRESSIDA
In faith, I will, la; never trust me else.

DIOMEDES
Give me some token for the surety of it.

CRESSIDA
I'll fetch you one.   *Exit.*

ULYSSES
You have sworn patience.

TROILUS   Fear me not, my lord;
I will not be myself, nor have cognition
Of what I feel. I am all patience.

Enter Cressida.

THERSITES   Now the pledge; now, now, now!

CRESSIDA   Here, Diomed, keep this sleeve.

TROILUS
  O beauty, where is your faith?
ULYSSES   My lord—
TROILUS
  I will be patient; outwardly I will.
CRESSIDA
  You look upon that sleeve; behold it well.
  He loved me—O false wench! Give it me again.
DIOMEDES
  Whose was it?
CRESSIDA   It is no matter, now I have it again.
  I will not meet with you to-morrow night.
  I pray you, Diomed, visit me no more.
THERSITES   Now she sharpens. Well said, whetstone!
DIOMEDES
  I shall have it.
CRESSIDA   What, this?
DIOMEDES   Ay, that.
CRESSIDA
  O, all you gods! O pretty, pretty pledge!
  Your master now lies thinking in his bed
  Of you and me, and sighs, and takes my glove,
  And gives memorial dainty kisses to it,
  As I kiss you. Nay, do not snatch it from me;
  He that takes that does take my heart with it.
DIOMEDES
  I had your heart before; this follows it.
TROILUS
  I did swear patience.
CRESSIDA
  You shall not have it, Diomed; faith, you shall not;
  I'll give you something else.
DIOMEDES
  I will have this. Whose was it?
CRESSIDA   It is no matter.
DIOMEDES
  Come, tell me whose it was.

CRESSIDA
 It was one's that loved me better than you will.
 But, now you have it, take it.
DIOMEDES   Whose was it?
CRESSIDA
 By all Diana's waiting-women yonder,
 And by herself, I will not tell you whose.
DIOMEDES
 To-morrow will I wear it on my helm,
 And grieve his spirit that dares not challenge it.
TROILUS
 Were you the devil, and wore it on your horn,
 It should be challenged.
CRESSIDA
 Well, well, 'tis done, 'tis past. And yet it is not;
 I will not keep my word.
DIOMEDES   Why then, farewell;
 You never shall mock Diomed again.
CRESSIDA
 You shall not go. One cannot speak a word
 But it straight starts you.
DIOMEDES   I do not like this fooling.
THERSITES   Nor I, by Pluto; but that that likes not you
 pleases me best.
DIOMEDES
 What, shall I come? The hour?
CRESSIDA   Ay, come—O Jove!—
 Do come—I shall be plagued.
DIOMEDES   Farewell till then.
CRESSIDA
 Good night. I pray you, come.   *Exit Diomedes.*
 Troilus, farewell. One eye yet looks on you,
 But with my heart the other eye does see.
 Ah, poor our sex! this fault in us I find,
 The error of our eye directs our mind.
 What error leads must err. O, then conclude
 Minds swayed by eyes are full of turpitude.   *Exit.*

THERSITES
  A proof of strength she could not publish more,
  Unless she says, 'My mind is now turned whore.'
ULYSSES
  All's done, my lord.
TROILUS   It is.
ULYSSES   Why stay we, then?
TROILUS
  To make a recordation to my soul
  Of every syllable that here was spoken.
  But if I tell how these two did co-act,
  Shall I not lie in publishing a truth?
  Since yet there is a credence in my heart,
  An esperance so obstinately strong,
  That does invert the attest of eyes and ears,
  As if those organs had deceptious functions,
  Created only to calumniate.
  Was Cressida here?
ULYSSES   I cannot conjure, Trojan.
TROILUS
  She was not, sure.
ULYSSES   Most sure she was.
TROILUS
  Why, my negation has no taste of madness.
ULYSSES
  Nor mine, my lord. Cressida was here but now.
TROILUS
  Let it not be believed for womanhood!
  Think we had mothers; do not give advantage
  To stubborn critics, apt, without a theme,
  For depravation, to square the general sex
  By Cressida's rule. Rather think this not Cressida.
ULYSSES
  What has she done, prince, that can soil our mothers?
TROILUS
  Nothing at all, unless that this were she.
THERSITES   Will he swagger himself out of his own eyes?

TROILUS

    This she? No, this is Diomed's Cressida.
    If beauty has a soul, this is not she;
    If souls guide vows, if vows are sanctimonies,
    If sanctimony is the gods' delight,
    If there is rule in unity itself,
    This was not she. O madness of discourse,
    That cause sets up with and against itself;
    Bi-fold authority, where reason can revolt
    Without perdition, and loss assume all reason
    Without revolt. This is, and is not, Cressida.
    Within my soul there does conduce a fight
    Of this strange nature that a thing inseparate
    Divides more widely than the sky and earth.
    And yet the spacious breadth of this division
    Admits no orifice for a point as subtle
    As Ariachne's broken web to enter.
    Evidence, evidence strong as Pluto's gates;
    Cressida is mine, tied with the bonds of heaven.
    Evidence, evidence strong as heaven itself;
    The bonds of heaven are slipped, dissolved, and
        loosed.
    And with another knot, five-finger-tied,
    The fractions of her faith, dross of her love,
    The fragments, scraps, the bits, and greasy relics
    Of her o'er-eaten faith, are bound to Diomed.

ULYSSES

    May worthy Troilus be half attached
    With that which here his passion does express?

TROILUS

    Ay, Greek; and that shall be divulgèd well
    In characters as red as Mars's heart
    Inflamed with Venus. Never did young man fancy
    With so eternal and so fixed a soul.
    Hark, Greek: as much as I do Cressid love,
    So much by weight hate I her Diomed;
    That sleeve is mine that he'll bear on his helm;

Were it a casque composed by Vulcan's skill,
My sword should bite it. Not the dreadful spout
Which shipmen do the hurricano call,
Built up in mass by the almighty sun,
Shall dizzy with more clamor Neptune's ear
In his descent than shall my prompted sword
Falling on Diomed.
THERSITES He'll tickle it for his concupiscence.
TROILUS
O Cressid! O false Cressid! false, false, false!
Let all untruths stand by your stainèd name,
And they'll seem glorious.
ULYSSES   O, contain yourself;
Your passion draws ears hither.

Enter Aeneas.

AENEAS
I have been seeking you this hour, my lord.
Hector, by this, is arming him in Troy;
Ajax, your guard, stays to conduct you home.
TROILUS
Have with you, prince. My courteous lord, adieu.
Farewell, revolted fair; and Diomed,
Stand fast, and wear a castle on your head!
ULYSSES
I'll bring you to the gates.
TROILUS
Accept distracted thanks.
                    Exeunt Troilus, Aeneas, and Ulysses.
THERSITES Would I could meet the rogue Diomed. I
would croak like a raven; I would bode, I would bode.
Patroclus will give me anything for the intelligence of
this whore. The parrot will not do more for an almond
than he for a commodious drab. Lechery, lechery; ever
wars and lechery; nothing else holds fashion. A burn-
ing devil take them!   *Exit.*

SCENE III
Troy: Before Priam's palace.

Enter Hector and Andromache.

ANDROMACHE
When was my lord so much ungently tempered,
To stop his ears against admonishment?
Unarm, unarm, and do not fight to-day.

HECTOR
You tempt me to offend you; get you in.
By all the everlasting gods, I'll go.

ANDROMACHE
My dreams will, sure, prove ominous to the day.

HECTOR
No more, I say.

Enter Cassandra.

CASSANDRA   Where is my brother Hector?

ANDROMACHE
Here, sister; armed and bloody in intent.
Consort with me in loud and dear petition;
Pursue we him on knees, for I have dreamed
Of bloody turbulence, and this whole night
Has nothing been but shapes and forms of slaughter.

CASSANDRA
O, 'tis true.

HECTOR   Ho, bid my trumpet sound.

CASSANDRA
No notes of sally, for the heavens, sweet brother.

HECTOR
Be gone, I say; the gods have heard me swear.

CASSANDRA
The gods are deaf to hot and peevish vows.
They are polluted offerings, more abhorred
Than spotted livers in the sacrifice.

ANDROMACHE

O, be persuaded! Do not count it holy
To hurt by being just. It is as lawful,
For we would give much, to use violent thefts,
And rob in the behalf of charity.

CASSANDRA

It is the purpose that makes strong the vow;
But vows to every purpose must not hold.
Unarm, sweet Hector.

HECTOR   Hold you still, I say;
My honor keeps the weather of my fate.
Life every man holds dear; but the dear man
Holds honor far more precious-dear than life.

Enter Troilus.

How now, young man; mean you to fight to-day?

ANDROMACHE

Cassandra, call my father to persuade.

                                    Exit Cassandra.

HECTOR

No, faith, young Troilus; doff your harness, youth;
I am to-day in the vein of chivalry.
Let grow your sinews till their knots be strong,
And tempt not yet the brushes of the war.
Unarm you, go, and doubt you not, brave boy,
I'll stand to-day for you and me and Troy.

TROILUS

Brother, you have a vice of mercy in you,
Which better fits a lion than a man.

HECTOR

What vice is that, good Troilus? Chide me for it.

TROILUS

When many times the captive Grecian falls,
Even in the fan and wind of your fair sword,
You bid them rise and live.

HECTOR

O, it is fair play.

TROILUS   Fool's play, by heaven, Hector.

HECTOR

How now, how now?

TROILUS   For the love of all the gods,

Let's leave the hermit pity with our mother,

And when we have our armors buckled on,

The venomed vengeance ride upon our swords,

Spur them to ruthful work, rein them from ruth.

HECTOR

Fie, savage, fie!

TROILUS   Hector, then 'tis wars.

HECTOR

Troilus, I would not have you fight to-day.

TROILUS

Who should withhold me?

Not fate, obedience, nor the hand of Mars

Beckoning with fiery truncheon my retire;

Not Priamus and Hecuba on knees,

Their eyes o'ergallèd with recourse of tears;

Nor you, my brother, with your true sword drawn,

Opposed to hinder me, should stop my way,

But by my ruin.

Enter Priam and Cassandra.

CASSANDRA

Lay hold upon him, Priam, hold him fast;

He is your crutch. Now if you lose your stay,

You on him leaning, and all Troy on you,

Fall all together.

PRIAM   Come, Hector, come; go back.

Your wife has dreamed, your mother has had visions,

Cassandra does foresee, and I myself

Am like a prophet suddenly enrapt

To tell you that this day is ominous:

Therefore, come back.

HECTOR   Aeneas is a-field;

And I do stand engaged to many Greeks,
Even in the faith of valor, to appear
This morning to them.
PRIAM   Ay, but you shall not go.
HECTOR
I must not break my faith.
You know me dutiful; therefore, dear sir,
Let me not shame respect, but give me leave
To take that course by your consent and voice,
Which you do here forbid me, royal Priam.
CASSANDRA
O Priam, yield not to him!
ANDROMACHE   Do not, dear father.
HECTOR
Andromache, I am offended with you.
Upon the love you bear me, get you in.
                                  Exit Andromache.
TROILUS
This foolish, dreaming, superstitious girl
Makes all these bodements.
CASSANDRA   O farewell, dear Hector!
Look, how you die; look, how your eye turns pale;
Look, how your wounds do bleed at many vents!
Hark, how Troy roars, how Hecuba cries out,
How poor Andromache shrills her dolors forth!
Behold, distraction, frenzy, and amazement,
Like witless loonies, one another meet,
And all cry Hector! Hector's dead! O Hector!
TROILUS
Away! Away!
CASSANDRA
Farewell. Yet, soft: Hector, I take my leave.
You do yourself and all our Troy deceive.   *Exit.*
HECTOR
You are amazed, my liege, at her exclaim.
Go in and cheer the town. We'll forth and fight;
Do deeds worth praise and tell you them at night.

PRIAM

Farewell. The gods with safety stand about you.

Exeunt Priam and Hector. Alarum.

TROILUS

They are at it, hark. Proud Diomed, believe,
I come to lose my arm, or win my sleeve.

Enter Pandar.

PANDARUS   Do you hear, my lord? Do you hear?

TROILUS   What now?

PANDARUS   Here's a letter come from yon poor girl.

TROILUS   Let me read.

PANDARUS   A blasted cough, a blasted rascally cough, so
troubles me, and the foolish fortune of this girl; and
what one thing, what another, that I shall leave you
one of these days; and I have a running in my eyes too,
and such an ache in my bones that, unless a man is
cursed, I cannot tell what to think of it. What says
she there?

TROILUS

Words, words, mere words, no matter from the heart;
The effect does operate another way.

Tearing the letter.

Go, wind to wind, there turn and change together.
My love with words and errors still she feeds,
But edifies another with her deeds.   *Exeunt.*

SCENE IV
Between Troy and the Greek camp.

Alarum. Excursions. Enter Thersites.

THERSITES   Now they are mauling one another; I'll go
look on. That dissembling abominable varlet,
Diomed, has got that same scurvy doting foolish

young knave's sleeve of Troy there in his helm. I
would fain see them meet, that that same young
Trojan ass, that loves the whore there, might send
that Greekish whore-masterly villain with the
sleeve back to the dissembling luxurious drab, of a
sleeveless errand. On the other side, the policy of
those crafty swearing rascals—that stale old mouse-
eaten dry cheese, Nestor, and that same dog-fox,
Ulysses—is not proved worth a blackberry. They set
me up, in policy, that mongrel cur, Ajax, against that
dog of as bad a kind, Achilles. And now is the cur Ajax
prouder than the cur Achilles, and will not arm to-
day. Whereupon the Grecians begin to proclaim
barbarism, and policy grows into an ill opinion.

Enter Diomedes and Troilus.

Soft! here comes sleeve, and the other one.
TROILUS
  Fly not; for should you take the river Styx,
  I would swim after.
DIOMEDES   You do miscall retire.
  I do not fly, but advantageous care
  Withdrew me from the odds of multitude.
  Have at you!
THERSITES   Hold your whore, Grecian! Now for your
  whore, Trojan! Now the sleeve, now the sleeve!
          Exeunt Troilus and Diomedes, fighting.

Enter Hector.

HECTOR
  What are you, Greek? Are you for Hector's match?
  Are you of blood and honor?
THERSITES   No, no. I am a rascal, a scurvy railing knave,
  a very filthy rogue.
HECTOR
  I do believe you; live.   *Exit.*

THERSITES   God-a-mercy, that you will believe me; but a
plague break your neck—for frightening me. What's
become of the wenching rogues? I think they have
swallowed one another. I would laugh at that
miracle—yet, in a sort, lechery eats itself. I'll seek
them.   *Exit.*

SCENE V
The same.

Enter Diomedes and Servant.

DIOMEDES
  Go, go, my servant, take you Troilus' horse;
  Present the fair steed to my Lady Cressida.
  Fellow, commend my service to her beauty;
  Tell her I have chastised the amorous Trojan,
  And am her knight by proof.
SERVANT   I go, my lord.   *Exit.*

Enter Agamemnon.

AGAMEMNON
  Renew, renew! The fierce Polỳdamas
  Has beaten down Menon; bastard Margarèlon
  Has Doreus prisoner,
  And stands colossus-wise, waving his lance,
  Upon the battered corpses of the kings
  Epìstrophus and Cedius. Polìxenes is slain,
  Amphìmachus and Thòas deadly hurt,
  Patròclus taken or slain, and Palamedes
  Sore hurt and bruised. The dreadful Sagittàry
  Appals our numbers. Haste we, Diomed,
  To reinforcement, or we perish all.

Enter Nestor.

NESTOR

Go, bear Patroclus' body to Achilles,
And bid the snail-paced Ajax arm for shame.
There are a thousand Hectors in the field.
Now here he fights on Galathe his horse,
And there lacks work; anon he's there afoot,
And there they fly or die, like scalèd schools
Before the belching whale. Then is he yonder,
And there the strawy Greeks, ripe for his edge,
Fall down before him, like a mower's swathe.
Here, there, and everywhere, he leaves and takes,
Dexterity so obeying appetite
That what he will he does, and does so much
That proof is called impossibility.

    Enter Ulysses.

ULYSSES

O, courage, courage, princes! Great Achilles
Is arming, weeping, cursing, vowing vengeance.
Patroclus' wounds have roused his drowsy blood,
Together with his mangled Myrmidons,
That noseless, handless, hacked and chipped, come to
    him,
Crying on Hector. Ajax has lost a friend,
And foams at mouth, and he is armed and at it,
Roaring for Troilus, who has done to-day
Mad and fantastic executiòn,
Engaging and redeeming of himself
With such a careless force and forceless care
As if luck should, in very spite of cunning,
Bade him win all.

    Enter Ajax.

AJAX

Troilus, you coward Troilus!   *Exit.*
DIOMEDES   Ay, there, there.

NESTOR
So, so, we draw together.   *Exit.*

Enter Achilles.

ACHILLES   Where is this Hector?
Come, come, you boy-killer, show your face;
Know what it is to meet Achilles angry.
Hector, where's Hector? I will none but Hector.
Exit.

SCENE VI
The same.

Enter Ajax.

AJAX
Troilus, you coward Troilus, show your head.

Enter Diomedes.

DIOMEDES
Troilus, I say, where's Troilus?
AJAX   What would you?
DIOMEDES
I would correct him.
AJAX
Were I the general, you should have my office
Ere that correction. Troilus, I say; what, Troilus!

Enter Troilus.

TROILUS
O traitor Diomed! Turn your false face, you traitor,
And pay your life you owe me for my horse.
DIOMEDES
Ha, are you there?

AJAX
　　I'll fight with him alone. Stand, Diomed.
DIOMEDES
　　He is my prize; I will not merely look.
TROILUS
　　Come, both you cheating Greeks; have at you both!
　　　　　　　　　　　　　　　　　　　　Exeunt, fighting.

　　　Enter Hector.

HECTOR
　　Yea, Troilus? O, well fought, my youngest brother!

　　　Enter Achilles.

ACHILLES
　　Now do I see you. Have at you, Hector!

　　　They fight.

HECTOR
　　Pause, if you will.
ACHILLES
　　I do disdain your courtesy, proud Trojan.
　　Be happy that my arms are out of use.
　　My rest and negligence befriend you now,
　　But you anon shall hear of me again;
　　Till when, go seek your fortune.   *Exit.*
HECTOR   Fare you well:
　　I would have been an even fresher man,
　　Had I expected you. How now, my brother!

　　　Enter Troilus.

TROILUS
　　Ajax has taken Aeneas! Shall it be?
　　No, by the flame of yonder glorious heaven,

He shall not carry him; I'll be taken too,
Or bring him off. Fate, hear me what I say!
I reck not though you end my life to-day.   *Exit.*

Enter one in armor.

HECTOR
Stand, stand, you Greek; you are a goodly mark.
No? Will you not? I like your armor well;
I'll smash it and unlock the rivets all,
But I'll be master of it. Will you not, beast, abide?
Why then, fly on, I'll hunt you for your hide.
                              Exit in pursuit.

SCENE VII
The same.

Enter Achilles with Myrmidons.

ACHILLES
Come here about me, you my Myrmidons;
Mark what I say. Attend me where I wheel;
Strike not a stroke, but keep yourselves in breath;
And when I have the bloody Hector found,
Fence him with your weapons round about;
In fiercest manner execute your arms.
Follow me, sirs, and my proceedings eye.
It is decreed, Hector the great must die.
                              Exit with Myrmidons.

*Enter Thersites, Menelaus, Paris the last two
fighting.*

THERSITES   The cuckold and the cuckold-maker are at it.
Now, bull! now, dog! 'Loo, Paris, 'loo! Now, my double—horned Spartan! 'Loo, Paris, 'loo! The bull has
the game; 'ware horns, ho!

Exeunt Paris and Menelaus.

Enter Bastard Margarelon.

MARGARELON   Turn, slave, and fight.

THERSITES   What are you?

MARGARELON   A bastard son of Priam's.

THERSITES   I am a bastard too; I love bastards. I am a
bastard begot, bastard instructed, bastard in mind,
bastard in valor, in everything illegitimate. One bear
will not bite another, and wherefore should one
bastard? Take heed, the quarrel's most ominous to us.
If the son of a whore fights for a whore, he tempts
judgment. Farewell, bastard.

MARGARELON   The devil take you, coward!   *Exit.*

SCENE VIII
The same.

Enter Hector.

HECTOR
Most putrefièd core, so fair without,
Your goodly armor thus has cost your life.
Now is my day's work done; I'll take my breath.
Rest, sword; you have your fill of blood and death.

*Puts off his helmet, and hangs his shield behind him.
Enter Achilles and his Myrmidons.*

ACHILLES
Look, Hector, how the sun begins to set,
How ugly night comes breathing at its heels.
Even with the cloud and darkening of the sun,
To close the day up, Hector's life is done.

HECTOR
I am unarmed; forgo this vantage, Greek.

ACHILLES
Strike, fellows, strike; this is the man I seek.

Hector falls.

So, Ilion, fall you next! Come, Troy, sink down!
Here lies your heart, your sinews, and your bone.
On, Myrmidons, and cry you all amain,
'Achilles has the mighty Hector slain!'

Retreat.

Hark, a retire upon our Grecian part.
GREEK
The Trojan trumpets sound the like, my lord.
ACHILLES
The dragon wing of night o'erspreads the earth,
And, stickler-like, the armies separate.
My half-supped sword, that frankly would have fed,
Pleased with this dainty bait, thus goes to bed.

Sheathes his sword.

Come, tie his body to my horse's tail;
Along the field I will the Trojan trail.　　　*Exeunt.*

SCENE IX
The same.

*Enter Agamemnon, Ajax, Menelaus, Nestor,
Diomedes, and the rest, marching. Sound
retreat. Shout.*

AGAMEMNON
Hark, hark, what shout is that?
NESTOR　　　　　　　　　　　　Peace drums!
SOLDIERS　*(within)*　　　　　　　　　　Achilles!
Achilles! Hector is slain! Achilles!
DIOMEDES
The noise is, Hector is slain, and by Achilles.

AJAX

   If it is so, yet bragless let it be;
   Great Hector was as good a man as he.

AGAMEMNON

   March patiently along. Let one be sent
   To pray Achilles see us at our tent.
   If in his death the gods have us befriended,
   Great Troy is ours, and our sharp wars are ended.

                                   Exeunt.

SCENE X
The same.

Enter Aeneas, Paris, Antenor, and Deiphobus.

AENEAS

   Stand, ho! yet are we masters of the field.
   Never go home; here starve we out the night.

   Enter Troilus.

TROILUS

   Hector is slain.

ALL   Hector! The gods forbid!

TROILUS

   He's dead and at the murderer's horse's tail,
   In beastly sort, dragged through the shameful field.
   Frown on, you heavens, effect your rage with speed;
   Sit, gods, upon your thrones, and smile at Troy.
   I say, at once let your brief plagues be mercy,
   And linger not our sure destructions on.

AENEAS

   My lord, you do discomfort all the host.

TROILUS

   You understand me not that tell me so.
   I do not speak of flight, of fear, of death,

But dare all imminence that gods and men
Address their dangers in. Hector is gone.
Who shall tell Priam so, or Hecuba?
Let him that will a screech-owl aye be called
Go in to Troy, and say there Hector's dead.
There is a word will Priam turn to stone,
Make wells and Niobes of the maids and wives,
Cold statues of the youth, and in a word
Scare Troy out of itself. But march away.
Hector is dead; there is no more to say.
Stay yet. You vile abominable tents,
Thus proudly pitched upon our Phrygian plains,
Let Titan rise as early as he dares,
I'll through and through you! And, you great-sized
   coward,
No space of earth shall sunder our two hates.
I'll haunt you like a wicked conscience ever,
That moulds goblins swift as frenzy's thoughts.
Strike a free march to Troy. With comfort go;
Hope of revenge shall hide our inward woe.

    Enter Pandarus.

PANDARUS
  But hear you, hear you!
TROILUS
  Hence, broker lackey! Ignominy in shame
  Pursue your life, and life aye with your name.
               Exeunt all but Pandarus.
PANDARUS A goodly medicine for my aching bones! O
world, world! thus is the poor agent despised. O
traitors and bawds, how earnestly are you set a-work,
and how ill requited! Why should our endeavor be so
loved, and the performance so loathed? What verse for
it? What instance for it? Let me see.
  Full merrily the humble-bee does sing,
  Till he has lost his honey and his sting;

And being once subdued in armèd tail,
Sweet honey and sweet notes together fail.
Good traders in the flesh, set this in your painted
    cloths:
'As many as are here of Pandar's hall,
Your eyes, half out, weep out at Pandar's fall;
Or if you cannot weep, yet give some groans,
Though not for me, yet for your aching bones.
Brethren and sisters of the hold-door trade,
Some two months hence my will shall here be made.
It should be now, but that my fear is this,
Some gallèd goose of Winchester would hiss.[1]
Till then I'll sweat and seek about for eases,
And at that time bequeath you my diseases.'   *Exit.*

---

[1] The South Bank stews were on land belonging to the see of
Winchester.

The Two Gentlemen of Verona

INTRODUCTION

T he *Two Gentlemen of Verona* is Shakespeare's first experiment in romantic comedy, but its prime interest is its autobiographical significance. He had already shown his range and accomplishment in chronicle plays with *Henry VI*, tragedy with *Titus Andronicus*, farce with *The Comedy of Errors*; throughout his career he was always ready to experiment, to respond to new challenges. Naturally to those of the theatre, but especially to those that chimed with personal experience.

Everything shows that the year is 1592, the first year of his momentous relationship with his young patron, and the theme of the play is the conflict between the claims of friendship and those of love—as in the Sonnets, with which we find revealing parallels of expression. So too with the experience that went into the play. It appears to have been written rapidly, perhaps for private performance, the end suddenly unravelled in a way that has dismayed critics.

The conclusion of the play has been generally regarded as improbable and unconvincing. Of the two gentlemen, Proteus deserts his own first love, for Valentine's Silvia, and betrays his friend to the Duke. On being exposed, he repents and asks for forgiveness; upon which Valentine says,

Who by repentance is not satisfied
Is nor of heaven nor earth, for these are pleased;
By penitence the Eternal's wrath's appeased.

> And, that my love may appear plain and free,
> All that was mine in Silvia I give thee.

Everybody finds it rather shocking, but this was precisely what happened between Shakespeare and his young friend and patron over the Dark Lady, Emilia Bassano, Mrs. Lanier. She made a pass at Southampton, who—though ambivalent and less vulnerable than his poet—was entangled, to Shakespeare's grief and alarm. The youth repented:

> Though thou repent, yet I have still the loss.

And Shakespeare concludes, like Valentine in the play:

> Take all my loves, my love; yea, take them all.

It is extraordinary that people have never perceived the autobiographical significance of this play, when it is written into the first scene. One friend says to the other:

> Yet writers say, as in the sweetest bud
> The eating canker dwells, so eating love
> Inhabits in the finest wits of all.

The other friend continues:

> And writers say, as the most forward bud
> Is eaten by the canker ere it blow,
> Even so by love the young and tender wit
> Is turned to folly.

Who are the writers who say this? Shakespeare is referring to himself. At this very moment in Sonnet 35, he is charging his friend and patron of betraying him with his dark young mistress, Emilia. Southampton repented of his betrayal of friendship:

No more be grieved at that which thou hast done,
Roses have thorns, and silver fountains mud. . .
And loathsome canker lives in sweetest bud.

Even more remarkable is the realisation of what
Shakespeare thought of himself in the give-away
phrase, 'the finest wits of all.' It bears out Robert
Greene's observation, in this same year, of the actor's
good opinion of himself, challenging the university wits
in turning to writing plays.

We hear that note in his reproach to the young woman
whose attitude to him is so ambivalent—'If I might
teach thee wit.' For she could not fully respond to the
older man's infatuation. The play at this same moment
corroborates the experience:

O,'tis the curse in love and still approved
  [ever proved]
When women cannot love where they're beloved.

Evidently his wit—Elizabethans meant by that intelligence, intellect—was a source of attraction in an
older man for her.

As for his young friend who has betrayed him, the
play closely repeats the experience recorded in the
Sonnets:

O, how this spring of love resembleth
  The uncertain glory of an April day,
Which now shows all the beauty of the sun,
  And by and by a cloud takes all away.

Sonnet 33 repeats just this:

Full many a glorious morning have I seen. . .
Anon permit the basest clouds to ride. . .
Even so, my sun one early morn did shine. . .
But out, alack, he was but one hour mine,
The region cloud hath masked him from me now.

Sonnet 34 goes on,

> Why didst thou promise such a beauteous day. . .
> To let base clouds o'ertake me in my way,
> 'Tis not enough that through the cloud thou
>   break
> To dry the rain on my storm-beaten-face.

Writers write out of their own experience: this was the experience at this time that went into the play.

In 1592 Marlowe was writing 'Hero and Leander' in rivalry with Shakespeare for the young patron's favour. There are even two references to it in the play. One friend says:

> Upon some book I love I'll pray for you.

The other replies:

> That's on some shallow story of deep love,
> How young Leander crossed the Hellespont.

And later, a rope of cords

> Would serve to scale another Hero's tower,
> So bold Leander would adventure it.

For want of combined historical and literary perception, scholars have been completely uncertain as to the dating of this play. Its date is 1592, in the earlier phase of the relationship with the friend and patron.

It is worth noting that, in this play, the importance of addressing sonnets to the lady of one's love is twice emphasised.

Something of the spirit of the age is evoked, when men

> Put forth their sons to seek preferment out:

> Some to the wars to try their fortune there;
> Some to discover islands far away;
> Some to the studious universities. . .

None of these had been his own route to fame and reputation, though something of a literary fashion of the time appears in the description of the Malcontent, with arms wreathed across breast. The musicality of the age comes through in references to popular songs like 'Light o' love', in the chaff about love in musical terms, as in the exquisite songs Shakespeare could always compose for his plays—in this, the beautiful

> Who is Silvia? What is she,
> That all our swains commend her?

(We are reminded that Shakespeare's own love, Emilia, was *musical*.)

What appeals most today are the realistic scenes drawn from lower-class life: Launce, with his dog Crab, who misconducts himself in the dining hall. 'Did I not tell you always mark me and do as I do? When did you see me heave up my leg and make water against a gentlewoman's farthingale?' From the very first, with the Jack Cade scenes in *Henry VI*, Shakespeare had shown his familiar observation of lower-class life and speech, its authenticity and realism. His social range was elastic and expansive—here his profession was such an advantage: it opened all doors to him. Launce and Speed enjoy a good deal of bawdy talk together, punning about 'standing', when the same puns occur contemporaneously in the Sonnets.

Since the text that has come down to us is a good one and offers few difficulties, we may note a few points where this modern text comes to the aid of the reader. For example, in the matter of accents to make the scansion clear:

Excuse it not, for I am pèremptòry...
And even in kind love I do conjùe you...
Are visibly charàctered and engraved.

A number of words of one syllable were in fact
pronounced as two: these I have marked with a diaeresis
or an accent, for example, fire, hoür, präyer, or hoùr.
One word which we pronounce as two syllables has to
be spoken as three—oceàn. Not many obsolete words
need replacing in this early play—inward for 'inly', for
example. Shakespeare's liking for recondite words and
indirection of phrase grew upon him, increasingly with
the middle and later plays, when the help of a modern
text becomes all the more urgent.

CHARACTERS

THE DUKE OF MILAN

SILVIA, his daughter, beloved of Valentine

THURIO, suitor for Silvia's hand

EGLAMOUR, Silvia's accomplice in her flight

PROTEUS
VALENTINE } the two gentlemen of Verona

JULIA, beloved of Proteus, later disguised as
  SEBASTIAN, a page

ANTONIO, father of Proteus

LUCETTA, waiting-woman of Julia

SPEED, servant of Valentine

LAUNCE, servant of Proteus

PANTHINO, servant of Antonio

Host of the Inn where Julia lodges in Milan

Outlaws, led by Valentine during his banishment, Servants, Musicians, Attendants

Act I

SCENE I
Verona. Before Julia's house.

Enter Valentine and Proteus

VALENTINE
Cease to persuade, my loving Proteus;
Home-keeping youth have ever homely wits.
Were it not affection chains your tender days
To the sweet glances of your honoured love,
I rather would entreat your company
To see the wonders of the world abroad
Than, living dully sluggardized at home,
Wear out your youth with shapeless idleness.
But, since you love, love still, and thrive therein,
Even as I would when I to love begin.

PROTEUS
Will you be gone? Sweet Valentine, adieu.
Think on your Proteus, when you haply see
Some rare noteworthy object in your travel.
Wish me partaker in your happiness,
When you do meet good hap; and in your danger—
If ever danger does environ you—
Commend your grievance to my holy prayers,
For I will be your petitioner, Valentine.

VALENTINE
And on a love-book pray for my success?

PROTEUS
Upon some book I love I'll pray for you.

VALENTINE
That's on some shallow story of deep love,
How young Leander crossed the Hellespont.

PROTEUS
That's a deep story of a deeper love,

For he was more than over-shoes in love.
VALENTINE
   It is true; for you are over-boots in love,
   And yet you never swam the Hellespont.
PROTEUS
   Over the boots? Nay, give me not the boots.[1]
VALENTINE
   No, I will not; for it boots [profits] you not.
PROTEUS   What?
VALENTINE
   To be in love, where scorn is bought with groans;
   Coy looks, with heart-sore sighs; one fading moment's
         mirth,
   With twenty, watchful, weary, tedious nights—
   If haply won, perhaps a hapless gain;
   If lost, why then a grievous labour won.
   However, but a folly bought with wit,
   Or else a wit by folly vanquishèd.
PROTEUS
   So, by your circumstance, you call me fool?
VALENTINE
   So, by your circumstance, I fear you'll prove.
PROTEUS
   It is Love you cavil at; I am not Love.
VALENTINE
   Love is your master, for he masters you;
   And he that is so yokèd by a fool,
   I think should not be chronicled for wise.
PROTEUS
   Yet writers say, as in the sweetest bud
   The eating canker dwells, so eating love
   Inhabits in the finest wits of all.
VALENTINE
   And writers say, as the most forward bud
   Is eaten by the canker ere it blows,
   Even so by love the young and tender wit
   Is turned to folly, blasting in the bud,

---

[1]Proverbial. Do not make a fool of me.

Losing his verdure even in the prime,
And all the fair effects of future hopes.
But wherefore waste I time to counsel you
That are a votary to fond desire?
Once more adieu. My father at the road
Expects my coming, there to see me shipped.

PROTEUS
And thither will I bring you, Valentine.

VALENTINE
Sweet Proteus, no; now let us take our leave.
To Milan let me hear from you by letters
Of your success in love, and what news else
Betides here in the absence of your friend;
And I likewise will visit you with mine.

PROTEUS
All happiness bechance to you in Milan.

VALENTINE
As much to you at home. And so farewell.   *Exit*

PROTEUS
He after honour hunts, I after love.
He leaves his friends to dignify them more;
I leave myself, my friends, and all for love.
You, Julia, you have metamorphosed me,
Made me neglect my studies, lose my time,
War with good counsel, set the world at naught;
Made wit with musing weak, heart sick with thought.

        Enter Speed

SPEED
Sir Proteus, God save you! Saw you my master?

PROTEUS
But now he parted hence to embark for Milan.

SPEED
Twenty to one then he is shipped already,
And I have played the sheep in losing him.

PROTEUS
Indeed, a sheep does very often stray,

If ever if the shepherd is a while away.

SPEED   You conclude that my master is a shepherd
then, and I a sheep?

PROTEUS   I do.

SPEED   Why then, my horns are his horns, whether I
wake or sleep.

PROTEUS   A silly answer, and fitting well a sheep.

SPEED   This proves me still a sheep.

PROTEUS   True; and your master a shepherd.

SPEED   Nay, that I can deny by a circumstance.

PROTEUS   It shall go hard but I'll prove it by another.

SPEED   The shepherd seeks the sheep, and not the sheep
the shepherd; but I seek my master, and my master
seeks not me. Therefore I am no sheep.

PROTEUS   The sheep for fodder follow the shepherd; the
shepherd for food follows not the sheep. You for wages
follow your master, your master for wages follows not
you. Therefore you are a sheep.

SPEED   Such another proof will make me cry, 'baa'.

PROTEUS   But do you hear? Gave you my letter to Julia?

SPEED   Ay, sir. I, a lost mutton, gave your letter to her, a
laced mutton,[2] and she, a laced mutton, gave me, a
lost mutton, nothing for my labour.

PROTEUS   Here's too small a pasture for such store of
muttons.

SPEED   If the ground is overcharged, you were best stick
her.

PROTEUS   Nay, in that you are astray; it were best
pound you.

SPEED   Nay, sir, less than a pound shall serve me for
carrying your letter.

PROTEUS   You mistake; I mean the pound—a pinfold.

SPEED

From a pound to a pin? Fold it over and over,
'Tis threefold too little for carrying a letter to your lover.

PROTEUS   But what said she?

---

[2]Bawdy, suggesting a prostitute.

Speed nods

A nod?

SPEED   Ay.

PROTEUS   Nod-ay? Why, that's noddy.

SPEED   You mistook, sir. I say she did nod; and you ask
me if she did nod, and I say 'Ay'.

PROTEUS   And that set together is 'noddy'.

SPEED   Now you have taken the pains to set it together,
take it for your pains.

PROTEUS   No, no; you shall have it for bearing the
letter.

SPEED   Well, I perceive I must be fain to bear with you.

PROTEUS   Why, sir, how do you bear with me?

SPEED   Sure, sir, the letter very orderly, having nothing
but the word 'noddy' for my pains.

PROTEUS   Bless me, but you have a quick wit.

SPEED   And yet it cannot overtake your slow purse.

PROTEUS   Come, come, open the matter in brief; what
said she?

SPEED   Open your purse, that the money and the matter
may be both at once delivered.

PROTEUS   Well, sir, here is for your pains.

He gives Speed money

What said she?

SPEED   Truly, sir, I think you'll hardly win her.

PROTEUS   Why? Could you perceive so much from her?

SPEED   Sir, I could perceive nothing at all from her; no,
not so much as a ducat for delivering your letter; and
being so hard to me that brought your mind, I fear
she'll prove as hard to you in telling your mind. Give
her no token but stones, for she's as hard as steel.

PROTEUS   What said she? Nothing?

SPEED   No, not so much as 'Take this for your pains'. To
testify your bounty, I thank you, you have given me
sixpence; in requital whereof, henceforth carry your

letters yourself. And so, sir, I'll commend you to my
master.   *Exit*

PROTEUS

Go, go, be gone, to save your ship from wreck,
Which cannot perish, having you aboard,
Being destined to a drier death on shore.
I must go send some better messenger.
I fear my Julia would not deign my lines,
Receiving them from such a worthless post.   *Exit*

SCENE II
Julia's house.

Enter Julia and Lucetta

JULIA

But say, Lucetta, now we are alone,
Would you then counsel me to fall in love?

LUCETTA

Ay, madam, so you stumble not unheedfully.

JULIA

Of all the fair resort of gentlemen
That every day with parley encounter me,
In your opinion which is worthiest love?

LUCETTA

Please you repeat their names, I'll show my mind
According to my shallow simple skill.

JULIA

What think you of the fair Sir Eglamour?

LUCETTA

As of a knight well-spoken, neat, and fine;
But, were I you, he never should be mine.

JULIA

What think you of the rich Mercutio?

LUCETTA

Well of his wealth; but of himself, so so.

JULIA
  What think you of the gentle Proteus?
LUCETTA
  Lord, lord, to see what folly reigns in us!
JULIA
  How now, what means this passion at his name?
LUCETTA
  Pardon, dear madam; it is a passing shame
  That I, unworthy body as I am,
  Should censure thus on lovely gentlemen.
JULIA
  Why not on Proteus, as of all the rest?
LUCETTA
  Then thus: of many good, I think him best.
JULIA
  Your reason?
LUCETTA
  I have no other but a woman's reason:
  I think him so, because I think him so.
JULIA
  And would you have me cast my love on him?
LUCETTA
  Ay, if you thought your love not cast away.
JULIA
  Why, he, of all the rest, has never moved me.
LUCETTA
  Yet he, of all the rest, I think best loves ye.
JULIA
  His little speaking shows his love but small.
LUCETTA
  Fire that's closest kept burns most of all.
JULIA
  They do not love that do not show their love.
LUCETTA
  O, they love least that let men know their love.
JULIA
  I would I knew his mind.
LUCETTA
  Peruse this paper, madam.

JULIA *(reads)*
> *To Julia.*—Say, from whom?

LUCETTA
> That the contents will show.

JULIA
> Say, say, who gave it you?

LUCETTA
> Sir Valentine's page; and sent, I think, from Proteus
> He would have given it you; but I, being in the way,
> Did in your name receive it; pardon the fault, I pray.

JULIA
> Now, by my modesty, a goodly broker!
> Dare you presume to harbour wanton lines?
> To whisper and conspire against my youth?
> Now, trust me, it is an office of great worth,
> And you an officer fit for the place.
> There take the paper. See it is returned,
> Or else return no more into my sight.

LUCETTA
> To plead for love deserves more fee than hate.

JULIA
> Will you be gone?

LUCETTA   That you may ruminate.   *Exit*

JULIA
> And yet I would I had o'erlooked the letter.
> It were a shame to call her back again,
> And pray her to a fault for which I chid her.
> What a fool is she, that knows I am a maid,
> And would not force the letter to my view,
> Since maids, in modesty, say no to that
> Which they would have the profferer cònstrue ay.
> Fie, fie! How wayward is this foolish love,
> That, like a testy babe, will scratch the nurse,
> And presently, all humbled, kiss the rod.
> How churlishly I chid Lucetta hence,
> When willingly I would have had her here.
> How angerly I taught my brow to frown,
> When inward joy enforced my heart to smile.

My penance is to call Lucetta back
And ask remission for my folly past.
What ho! Lucetta!

Enter Lucetta

LUCETTA   What would your ladyship?
JULIA
  Is it near dinner-time?
LUCETTA   I would it were,
  That you might kill your stomach on your meat,
  And not upon your maid.
JULIA
  What is it that you took up so gingerly?
LUCETTA
  Nothing.
JULIA
  Why did you stoop then?
LUCETTA
  To take a paper up that I let fall.
JULIA
  And is that paper nothing?
LUCETTA
  Nothing concerning me.
JULIA
  Then let it lie for those that it concerns.
LUCETTA
  Madam, it will not lie where it concerns,
  Unless it has a false interpreter.
JULIA
  Some love of yours has written to you in rhyme.
LUCETTA
  That I might sing it, madam, to a tune.
  Give me a note; your ladyship can set it.
JULIA
  As little by such toys as may be possible.
  Best sing it to the tune of 'Light o'love'.
LUCETTA
  It is too heavy for so light a tune.

JULIA

Heavy? Perhaps it has some burden then?

LUCETTA

Ay, and melodious were it, would you sing it.

JULIA

And why not you?

LUCETTA   I cannot reach so high.

JULIA

Let's see your song. How now, minion!

Julia snatches the letter

LUCETTA

Keep tune there still, so you will sing it out;
And yet I think I do not like this tune.

JULIA

You do not?

LUCETTA   No, madam; it is too sharp.

JULIA

You, minion, are too saucy.

LUCETTA

Nay, now you are too flat;
And mar the concord with too harsh a descant.
There wants a middle part to fill your song.

JULIA

The middle is drowned with your unruly bass.

LUCETTA

Indeed, I bid the bass for Proteus.[3]

JULIA

This babble shall not henceforth trouble me.
Here is a fuss with a declaration.

She tears the letter

Go, get you gone, and let the papers lie.
You would be fingering them, to anger me.

―――――――――
[3]i.e. challenge, from a contemporary game.

LUCETTA (*aside*)
　　She makes it strange, but she would be best pleased
　　To be so angered with another letter.   *Exit*
JULIA
　　Nay, would I were so angered with the same!
　　O, hateful hands, to tear such loving words.
　　Injurious wasps, to feed on such sweet honey,
　　And kill the bees that yield it with your stings.
　　I'll kiss each separate paper for amends.
　　Look, here is written *kind Julia*. Unkind Julia,
　　As in revenge of your ingratitude,
　　I throw your name against the bruising stones,
　　Trampling contemptuously on your disdain.
　　And here is written, *love-wounded Proteus*.
　　Poor wounded name, my bosom, as a bed,
　　Shall lodge you till your wound be thoroughly healed;
　　And thus I search it with a sovereign kiss.
　　But twice or thrice was Proteus written down.
　　Be calm, good wind, blow not a word away
　　Till I have found each letter in the letter,
　　Except my own name. That some whirlwind bear
　　Unto a ragged, fearful, hanging rock,
　　And throw it thence into the raging sea.
　　Lo, here in one line is his name twice written:
　　Poor, forlorn Proteus, passionate Proteus,
　　To the sweet Julia. That I'll tear away;
　　And yet I will not, since so prettily
　　He couples it to his complaining names.
　　Thus will I fold them one upon another.
　　Now kiss, embrace, contend, do what you will.

　　　　Enter Lucetta

LUCETTA
　　Madam,
　　Dinner is ready, and your father waits.
JULIA
　　Well, let us go.

LUCETTA
  What, shall these papers lie like tell-tales here?
JULIA
  If you respect them, best to take them up.
LUCETTA
  Nay, I was taken up for laying them down.
  Yet here they shall not lie for catching cold.
JULIA
  I see you have a great longing for them.
LUCETTA
  Ay, madam, you may say what sights you see;
  I see things too, although you judge I wink.
JULIA
  Come, come, will it please you go?   *Exeunt*

SCENE III
Antonio's house.

Enter Antonio and Panthino

ANTONIO
  Tell me, Panthino, what serious talk was that
  Wherewith my brother held you in the cloister?
PANTHINO
  It was of his nephew Proteus, your son.
ANTONIO
  Why, what of him?
PANTHINO   He wondered that your lordship
  Would suffer him to spend his youth at home,
  While other men, of slender reputation,
  Put forth their sons to seek preferment out:
  Some to the wars to try their fortune there;
  Some to discover islands far away;
  Some to the studious universities.
  For any or for all these exercises
  He said that Proteus your son was meet,
  And did request me to importune you

To let him spend his time no more at home—
Which would be great impeachment to his age,
In having known no travel in his youth.

ANTONIO

Nor need you much importune me to that
Whereon this month I have been hammering.
I have considered well his loss of time,
And how he cannot be a perfect man,
Not being tried and tutored in the world.
Experience is by industry achieved,
And perfected by the swift course of time.
Then tell me, whither were I best to send him?

PANTHINO

I think your lordship is not ignorant
How his companion, youthful Valentine,
Attends the Emperor in his royal Court.

ANTONIO

I know it well.

PANTHINO

'Twere good, I think, your lordship sent him thither.
There shall he practise tilts and tournaments,
Hear sweet discourse, converse with noblemen,
And be in eye of every exercise
Worthy his youth and nobleness of birth.

ANTONIO

I like your counsel; well have you advised;
And that you may perceive how well I like it,
The execution of it shall make known.
Even with the speediest expedition
I will dispatch him to the Emperor's court.

PANTHINO

Tomorrow, may it please you, Don Alphonso
With other gentlemen of good esteem
Are journeying to salute the Emperor,
And to commend their service to his will.

ANTONIO

Good company; with them shall Proteus go.

Enter Proteus

And in good time; now will we broach the matter.

PROTEUS *(aside)*

Sweet love, sweet lines, sweet life!
Here is her hand, the agent of her heart;
Here is her oath for love, her honour's pawn.
O, that our fathers would applaud our loves,
To seal our happiness with their consents!
O heavenly Julia!

ANTONIA

How now? What letter are you reading there?

PROTEUS

May it please your lordship, 'tis a word or two
Of commendations sent from Valentine,
Delivered by a friend that came from him.

ANTONIO

Lend me the letter. Let me see what news.

PROTEUS

There is no news, my lord, but that he writes
How happily he lives, how well beloved,
And daily gracèd by the Emperor;
Wishing me with him, partner of his fortune.

ANTONIO

And how stand you affected to his wish?

PROTEUS

As one relying on your lordship's will,
And not depending on his friendly wish.

ANTONIO

My will is somewhat in keeping with his wish.
Muse not that I thus suddenly proceed;
For what I will, I will, and there an end.
I am resolved that you shall spend some time
With Valentine in the Emperor's Court.
What maintenance he from his friends receives,
Like exhibition you shall have from me.
Tomorrow be in readiness to go.
Excuse it not, for I am pèremptòry.

PROTEUS
  My lord, I cannot be so soon provided.
  Please you deliberate a day or two.
ANTONIO
  Look what you want shall be sent after you.
  No more delay; tomorrow you must go.
  Come on, Panthino; you shall be employed
  To hasten on his expediti òn.
                 Exeunt Antonio and Panthino
PROTEUS
  Thus have I shunned the fire for fear of burning,
  And drenched me in the sea, where I am drowned.
  I feared to show my father Julia's letter,
  Lest he should take exception to my love,
  And with the vantage of my own excuse
  Has he excepted most against my love.
  O, how this spring of love resembles now
    The uncertain glory of an April day,
  Which now shows all the beauty of the sun,
    And by and by a cloud takes all away.

    Enter Panthino

PANTHINO
  Sir Proteus, your father calls for you.
    He is in haste; therefore, I pray you go.
PROTEUS
  Why, this it is; my heart accords thereto,
    And yet a thousand times it answers, 'No.'
                         Exeunt

Act II

SCENE I
Milan. Before the Duke's palace.

Enter Valentine and Speed

SPEED
Sir, your glove.

VALENTINE Not mine. My gloves are on.

SPEED
Why then, this may be yours, for this is but one.

VALENTINE
Ha! Let me see. Ay, give it me, it's mine.
Sweet ornament that decks a thing divine.
Ah, Silvia, Silvia!

SPEED Madam Silvia! Madam Silvia!

VALENTINE How now, fellow?

SPEED She is not within hearing, sir.

VALENTINE Why, sir, who bade you call her?

SPEED Your worship, sir, or else I mistook.

VALENTINE Well, you'll ever be too forward.

SPEED And yet I was last chidden for being too slow.

VALENTINE Go to, sir. Tell me, do you know Madam
Silvia?

SPEED She that your worship loves?

VALENTINE Why, how know you that I am in love?

SPEED Certain, by these special marks: first, you have
learned, like Sir Proteus, to wreathe your arms, like a
malcontent; to relish a love-song, like a robin-
redbreast; to walk alone, like one that had the
pestilence; to sigh, like a schoolboy that had lost
his ABC; to weep, like a young wench that had buried

her grandam; to fast, like one that takes diet; to watch, like one that fears robbing; to speak whining, like a begger at Hallowmas.[1] You were wont, when you laughed, to crow like a cock; when you walked, to walk like one of the lions; when you fasted, it was presently after dinner; when you looked sadly, it was for want of money. And now you are metamorphosed by a mistress, that, when I look on you, I can hardly think you my master.

VALENTINE   Are all these things perceived in me?

SPEED   They are all perceived without you.

VALENTINE   Without me? They cannot.

SPEED   Without you? Nay, that's certain; for without you were so simple, none else would. But you are so without these follies, that these follies are within you, and shine through you like the water in an urinal, that not an eye that sees you but is a physician to comment on your malady.

VALENTINE   But tell me, do you know my lady Silvia?

SPEED   She that you gaze on so, as she sits at supper?

VALENTINE   Have you observed that? Even she I mean.

SPEED   Why, sir, I know her not.

VALENTINE   Do you know her by my gazing on her, and yet know her not?

SPEED   Is she not hard-favoured, [ill-looking] sir?

VALENTINE   Not so fair, boy, as well-favoured.

SPEED   Sir, I know that well enough.

VALENTINE   What do you know?

SPEED   That she is not so fair as, of you, well favoured.

VALENTINE   I mean that her beauty is exquisite, but her favour infinite.

SPEED   That's because the one is painted, and the other out of all count.

VALENTINE   How painted? And how out of count?

SPEED   Sure, sir, so painted to make her fair, that no man counts of her beauty.

---

[1] All Saints tide.

VALENTINE . How esteem you me? I account of her
  beauty.

SPEED   You never saw her since she was deformed.

VALENTINE   How long has she been deformed?

SPEED   Ever since you loved her.

VALENTINE   I have loved her ever since I saw her, and still
  I see her beautiful.

SPEED   If you love her, you cannot see her.

VALENTINE   Why?

SPEED   Because Love is blind. O, that you had my eyes,
  or your own eyes had the lights they were wont to
  have, when you chid at Sir Proteus for going ungartered!

VALENTINE   What should I see then?

SPEED   Your own present folly, and her passing
  deformity; for he, being in love, could not see to garter
  his hose; and you, being in love, cannot see to put on
  your hose.

VALENTINE   Perhaps, boy, then you are in love; for last
  morning you could not see to wipe my shoes.

SPEED   True, sir; I was in love with my bed. I thank you,
  you beat me for my love, which makes me the bolder
  to chide you for yours.

VALENTINE   In conclusion, I stand affected to her.

SPEED   I would you were set, so your affection would
  cease.

VALENTINE   Last night she enjoined me to write some
  lines to one she loves.

SPEED   And have you?

VALENTINE   I have.

SPEED   Are they not lamely written?

VALENTINE   No, boy, but as well as I can do them. Peace,
  here she comes.

  Enter Silvia

SPEED   (*aside*) O excellent doll! O exceeding puppet!
  Now will he interpret to her.

VALENTINE   Madam and mistress, a thousand good
  morrows.

SPEED   (*aside*) O, give you good even! Here's a million of
    manners.
SILVIA   Sir Valentine and servant, to you two thousand.
SPEED   (*aside*) He should give her interest, and she gives
    it him.
VALENTINE
    As you enjoined me, I have written your letter
    Unto the secret nameless friend of yours;
    Which I was much unwilling to proceed in,
    But for my duty to your ladyship.
SILVIA   I thank you, gentle servant, it is very clerkly
    done.
VALENTINE
    Now trust me, madam, it came hard to write;
    For, being ignorant to whom it goes,
    I wrote at random, very doubtfully.
SILVIA
    Perchance you think too much of so much pains?
VALENTINE
    No, madam; so it serves you, I will write,
    Please you command, a thousand times as much;
    And yet—
SILVIA
    A pretty period! Well, I guess the sequel;
    And yet I will not name it; and yet I care not;
    And yet take this again; and yet I thank you,
    Meaning henceforth to trouble you no more.
SPEED   (*aside*)
    And yet you will; and yet, another 'yet'.
VALENTINE
    What means your ladyship? Do you not like it?
SILVIA
    Yes, yes; the lines are very quaintly written;
    But, since unwillingly, take them again.
    Nay, take them.
VALENTINE   Madam, they are for you.
SILVIA
    Ay, ay; you wrote them, sir, at my request,

But I will none of them; they are for you.
I would have had them written more movingly.
SILVIA

VALENTINE
Please you, I'll write your ladyship another.
SILVIA
And when it's written, for my sake read it over;
And if it pleases you, so; if not, why, so.
VALENTINE
If it pleases me, madam, what then?
SILVIA
Why, if it pleases you, take it for your labour.
And so, good morrow, servant.   *Exit*
SPEED (*aside*)
O jest unseen, inscrutable, invisible
As a nose on a man's face, or a weathercock on a steeple!
My master sues to her; and she has taught her suitor,
He being her pupil, to become her tutor.
O excellent device! Was there ever heard a better,
That my master, being scribe, to himself should
     write the letter?
VALENTINE   How now, sir? What are you reasoning with
   yourself?
SPEED   Nay, I was rhyming; 'tis you that have the reason.
VALENTINE   To do what?
SPEED   To be a spokesman from Madam Silvia.
VALENTINE   To whom?
SPEED   To yourself. Why, she woos you by a figure.
VALENTINE   What figure?
SPEED   By a letter, I should say.
VALENTINE   Why, she has not written to me.
SPEED   What need she, when she has made you write to
   yourself? Why, do you not perceive the jest?
VALENTINE   No, believe me.
SPEED   No believing you, indeed, sir. But did you
   perceive her earnest?
VALENTINE   She gave me none, except an angry word.
SPEED   Why, she has given you a letter.
VALENTINE   That's the letter I wrote to her friend.

SPEED   And that letter has she delivered, and there an
end.

VALENTINE   I would it were no worse.

SPEED   I'll warrant you, it is as well:

> For often have you written to her; and she, in
> modesty,
> Or else for want of idle time, could not again reply;
> Or fearing else some messenger, that might her
> mind discover,
> Herself has taught her love himself to write unto
> her lover.
> All this I speak in print, for in print I found it.
> Why muse you, sir? It is dinner-time.

VALENTINE   I have dined.

SPEED   Ay, but hearken, sir: though the chameleon Love
can feed on the air, I am one that am nourished by my
victuals, and would fain have meat. O, be not like
your mistress; be moved, be moved.   *Exeunt*

SCENE II
Verona. Julia's house.

Enter Proteus and Julia

PROTEUS

Have patience, gentle Julia.

JULIA

I must, where is no remedy.

PROTEUS

When possibly I can, I will return.

JULIA

If you turn not, you will return the sooner.
Keep this remembrance for your Julia's sake.

She gives him a ring

PROTEUS
Why, then, we'll make exchange; here, take you this.

He gives her a ring

JULIA
And seal the bargain with a holy kiss.
PROTEUS
Here is my hand for my true constancy;
And when that hour o'erslips me in the day
Wherein I sigh not, Julia, for your sake,
The next ensuing hour some foul mischance
Torment me for my love's forgetfulness!
My father awaits my coming. Answer not.
The tide is now—nay, not your tide of tears;
That tide will stay me longer than I should.
Julia, farewell. (*Exit Julia*) What, gone without a word?
Ay, so true love should do; it cannot speak,
For truth has better deeds then words to grace it.

Enter Panthino

PANTHINO
Sir Proteus, you are awaited.
PROTEUS   Go; I come.
(*Aside*) Alas, this parting strikes poor lovers dumb.
                                             Exeunt

Scene III
Verona. A street.

Enter Launce with his dog, Crab

LAUNCE Nay, it will be this hour ere I have done
weeping; all the kind of the Launces have this very
fault. I have received my proportion, like the prodigal
son, and am going with Sir Proteus to the Imperial's

court. I think Crab my dog is the sourest-natured dog that lives. My mother weeping, my father wailing, my sister crying, our maid howling, our cat wringing her hands, and all our house in a great perplexity; yet did not this cruel-hearted cur shed one tear. He is a stone, a very pebblestone, and has no more pity in him than a dog. A Jew would have wept to have seen our parting. Why, my grandam, having no eyes, look you, wept herself blind at my parting. Nay, I'll show you the manner of it. This shoe is my father. No, this left shoe is my father. No, no, this left shoe is my mother. Nay, that cannot be so either. Yes, it is so, it is so; it has the worse sole. This shoe with the hole in it is my mother, and this my father. A vengeance on it, there it is. Now, sir, this staff is my sister; for, look you, she is as white as a lily, and as small as a wand. This hat is Nan our maid. I am the dog. No, the dog is himself, and I am the dog. O, the dog is me, and I am myself. Ay, so, so. Now come I to my father: 'Father, your blessing.' Now should not the shoe speak a word for weeping. Now should I kiss my father; well, he weeps on. Now come I to my mother. O, that she could speak more like an old woman! Well, I kiss her. Why, there it is; here's my mother's breath up and down. Now come I to my sister. Mark the moan she makes. Now the dog all this while sheds not a tear, nor speaks a word; but see how I lay the dust with my tears.

Enter Panthino

PANTHINO   Launce, away, away! Aboard! Your master is shipped, and you are to post after with oars. What's the matter? Why weep you, man? Away, ass, you'll lose the tide, if you tarry any longer.

LAUNCE   It is no matter if the tied were lost, for it is the unkindest tied that ever any man tied.

PANTHINO   What's the unkindest tide?

LAUNCE   Why, he that's tied here, Crab, my dog.

PANTHINO   Tut, man, I mean you'll lose the flood; and in
losing the flood, lose your voyage; and, in losing your
voyage, lose your master; and, in losing your master,
lose your service; and in losing your service—Why
do you stop my mouth?

LAUNCE   For fear you should lose your tongue.

PANTHINO   Where should I lose my tongue?

LAUNCE   In your tale.

PANTHINO   In my tail!

LAUNCE   Lose the tide, and the voyage, and the master,
and the service, and the tied. Why, man, if the river
were dry, I am able to fill it with my tears. If the wind
were down, I could drive the boat with my sighs.

PANTHINO   Come, come away, man. I was sent to call
you.

LAUNCE   Sir, call me what you dare.

PANTHINO   Will you go?

LAUNCE   Well, I will go.   *Exeunt*

SCENE IV
Milan. The Duke's palace.

Enter Silvia, Thurio, Valentine, and Speed

SILVIA   Servant!

VALENTINE   Mistress?

SPEED   Master, Sir Thurio frowns on you.

VALENTINE   Ay, boy; it is for love.

SPEED   Not of you.

VALENTINE   Of my mistress, then.

SPEED   'Twere good you knocked him.   *Exit*

SILVIA   Servant, you are sad.

VALENTINE   Indeed, madam, I seem so.

THURIO   Seem you that you are not?

VALENTINE   Haply I do.

THURIO   So do counterfeits.

VALENTINE   So do you.

THURIO   What seem I that I am not?

VALENTINE   Wise.

THURIO   What instance of the contrary?

VALENTINE   Your folly.

THURIO   And how note you my folly?

VALENTINE   I note it in your jerkin.

THURIO   My jerkin is a doublet.

VALENTINE   Well, then, I'll double your folly.

THURIO   How?

SILVIA   What, angry, Sir Thurio? Do you change colour?

VALENTINE   Give him leave, madam; he is a kind of chameleon.

THURIO   That has more mind to feed on your blood than live in your air.

VALENTINE   You have spoken, sir.

THURIO   Ay, Sir, and done too, for this time.

VALENTINE   I know it well, sir; you always end ere you begin.

SILVIA   A fine volley of words, gentlemen, and quickly shot off.

VALENTINE   It is indeed, madam. We thank the giver.

SILVIA   Who is that, servant?

VALENTINE   Yourself, sweet lady; for you gave the fire. Sir Thurio borrows his wit from your ladyship's looks, and spends what he borrows kindly in your company.

THURIO   Sir, if you spend word for word with me, I shall make your wit bankrupt.

VALENTINE   I know it well, sir; you have exchequer of words and, I think, no other treasure to give your followers; for it appears by their bare liveries that they live by your bare words.

Enter the Duke of Milan

SILVIA   No more, gentlemen, no more! Here comes my father.

DUKE

Now, daughter Silvia, you are hard put to it.
Sir Valentine, your father is in good health.
What say you to a letter from your friends
Of much good news?

VALENTINE   My lord, I will be thankful
To any happy messenger from thence.

DUKE

Know you Don Antonio, your countryman?

VALENTINE

Ay, my good lord, I know the gentleman
To be of worth, and worthy estimation,
And not without desert so well reputed.

DUKE

Has he not a son?

VALENTINE

Ay, my good lord, a son that well deserves
The honour and regard of such a father.

DUKE

You know him well?

VALENTINE

I know him as myself; for from our infancy
We have conversed and spent our hours together;
And though myself have been an idle truant,
Omitting the sweet benefit of time
To clothe my age with angle-like perfection,
Yet has Sir Proteus—for that's his name—
Made use and fair advantage of his days.
His years but young, but his experience old;
His head unmellowed, but his judgement ripe;
And in a word, for far behind his worth
Come all the praises that I now bestow,
He is complete in feature and in mind,
With all good grace to grace a gentleman.

DUKE

Bless me, sir, but if he makes this good,
He is as worthy for an empress' love
As meet to be an emperor's counsellor.

Well, sir, this gentleman is come to me
With commendation from great potentates,
And here he means to spend his time awhile.
I think 'tis no unwelcome news to you.
VALENTINE
Should I have wished a thing, it had been he.
DUKE
Welcome him then according to his worth.
Silvia, I speak to you, and you, Sir Thurio;
For Valentine, I need not cite him to it.
I will send him hither to you presently.   *Exit*
VALENTINE
This is the gentleman I told your ladyship
Had come along with me but that his mistress
Did hold his eyes locked in her crystal looks.
SILVIA
Perhaps now she has enfranchised them
Upon some other pawn for loyalty.
VALENTINE
Nay, sure, I think she holds them prisoners still.
SILVIA
Nay, then, he should be blind; and, being blind,
How could he see his way to seek out you?
VALENTINE
Why, lady, Love has twenty pair of eyes.
THURIO
They say that Love has not an eye at all.
VALENTINE
To see such lovers, Thurio, as yourself;
Upon a homely object Love can wink.

        Enter Proteus

SILVIA
Have done, have done; here comes the gentleman.
VALENTINE
Welcome, dear Proteus! Mistress, I beseech you

Confirm his welcome with some special favour.

SILVIA

His worth is warrant for his welcome hither,
If this is he you oft have wished to hear from.

VALENTINE

Mistress, it is. Sweet lady, entertain him
To be my fellow-servant to your ladyship.

SILVIA

Too low a mistress for so high a servant.

PROTEUS

Not so, sweet lady; but too mean a servant
To have a look of such a worthy mistress.

VALENTINE

Leave off discourse of disability;
Sweet lady, entertain him for your servant.

PROTEUS

My duty will I boast of, nothing else.

SILIVA

And duty never yet did want reward.
Servant, you are welcome to a worthless mistress.

PROTEUS

I'll die on him that says so but yourself.

SILVIA

That you are welcome?

PROTEUS   That you are worthless.

Enter a Servant

SERVANT

Madam, my lord your father would speak with you.

SILVIA

I wait upon his pleasure. (*Exit Servant*) Come, Sir
    Thurio,
Go with me. Once more, new servant, welcome.
I'll leave you to confer of home affairs;
When you have done, we look to hear from you.

PROTEUS

We'll both attend upon your ladyship.

Exeunt Silvia and Thurio

VALENTINE

Now, tell me, how do all from whence you came?

PROTEUS

Your friends are well, and have them much
commmended.

VALENTINE

And how do yours?   I left them all in health.

PROTEUS

VALENTINE

How does your lady, and how thrives your love?

PROTEUS

My tales of love were wont to weary you;
I know you joy not in a love-discourse.

VALENTINE

Ay, Proteus, but that life is altered now;
I have done penance for contemning Love,
Whose high imperious thoughts have punished me
With bitter fasts, with penitential groans,
With nightly tears, and daily heart-sore sighs.
For, in revenge of my contempt of love,
Love has chased sleep from my enthrallèd eyes,
And made them watchers of my own heart's sorrow.
O gentle Proteus, Love's a mighty lord,
And has so humbled me as I confess
There is no woe to his correctiòn,
Nor to his service any such joy on earth.
Now no discourse, except it is of love;
Now can I break my fast, dine, sup, and sleep,
Upon the very naked name of love.

PROTEUS

Enough; I read your fortune in your eye.
Was this the idol that you worship so?

VALENTINE

Even she; and is she not a heavenly saint?

PROTEUS

No; but she is an earthly paragon.

VALENTINE
  Call her divine.
PROTEUS   I will not flatter her.
VALENTINE
  O, flatter me; for love delights in praises.
PROTEUS
  When I was sick, you gave me bitter pills,
  And I must minister the like to you.
VALENTINE
  Then speak the truth by her; if not divine,
  Yet let her be a principality,
  Sovereign to all the creatures on the earth.
PROTEUS
  Except my mistress.
VALENTINE   Sweet, except not any;
  Except you will except against my love.
PROTEUS
  Have I not reason to prefer my own?
VALENTINE
  And I will help you to prefer her too:
  She shall be dignified with this high honour—
  To bear my lady's train, lest the base earth
  Should from her vesture chance to steal a kiss;
  And, of so great a favour growing proud,
  Disdain to root the summer-swelling flower
  And make rough winter everlastingly.
PROTEUS
  Why, Valentine, what braggardism is this?
VALENTINE
  Pardon me, Proteus, all I can is nothing
  To her, whose worth makes other worthies nothing;
  She is alone.
PROTEUS   Then let her alone.
VALENTINE
  Not for the world! Why, man, she is my own;
  And I as rich in having such a jewel
  As twenty seas, if all their sand was pearl,
  The water nectar, and the rocks pure gold.

Forgive me, that I do not dream on you,
Because you see me dote upon my love.
My foolish rival, that her father likes
Only for his possessions are so huge,
Is gone with her along; and I must after,
For love, you know, is full of jealousy.

PROTEUS

But she loves you?

VALENTINE

Ay, and we are betrothed; nay more, our marriage-
  hour,
With all the cunning manner of our flight,
Determined of; how I must climb her window,
The ladder made of cords, and all the means
Plotted and agreed on for my happiness.
Good Proteus, go with me to my chamber,
In these affairs to aid me with your counsel.

PROTEUS

Go on before; I shall inquire after you.
I must unto the road to disembark
Some necessaries that I needs must use;
And then I'll presently attend you.

VALENTINE

Will you make haste?

PROTEUS

I will.   *Exit Valentine*
Even as one heat another heat expels,
Or as one nail by strength drives out another,
So the remembrance of my former love
Is by a newer object quite forgotten.
Is it my eye, or Valentine's praise,
Her true perfection, or my false transgression,
That makes me reasonless to reason thus?
She is fair; and so is Julia that I love—
That I did love, for now my love is thawed;
Which, like a waxen image against a fire,
Bears no impression of the thing it was.
I think my zeal to Valentine is cold,

And that I love him not as I was wont.
O, but I love his lady too too much!
And that is the reason I love him so little.
How shall I dote on her with more advice,
That thus without advice begin to love her!
It is but her picture I have yet beheld,
And that has dazzled now my reason's light;
But when I look on her perfectiòns,
There is no reason but I shall be blind.
If I can check my erring love, I will;
If not, to compass her I'll use my skill.   *Exit*

SCENE V
Milan. A street.

Enter Speed and Launce, meeting

SPEED   Launce! By my honesty, welcome to Milan.

LAUNCE   Mistake not yourself, sweet youth, for I am not welcome. I reckon this always, that a man is never undone till he is hanged, nor ever welcome to a place till some certain shot be paid, and the hostess says, 'Welcome.'

SPEED   Come on, you madcap; I'll to the alehouse with you presently; where, for one shot of five pence, you shall have five thousand welcomes. But, man, how did your master part with Madam Julia?

LAUNCE   Sure, after they closed in earnest, they parted very fairly in jest.

SPEED   But shall she marry him?

LAUNCE   No.

SPEED   How then? Shall he marry her?

LAUNCE   No; neither.

SPEED   What, are they broken?

LAUNCE   No, they are both as whole as a fish.

SPEED   Why then, how stands the matter with them?

LAUNCE   Sure, thus: when it stands well with him, it stands well with her.

SPEED   What an ass are you! I understand you not.

LAUNCE   What a block are you, that you can not! My staff understands me.

SPEED   What you say?

LAUNCE   Ay, and what I do too; look there, I'll but lean, and my staff understands me.

SPEED   It stands under you, indeed.

LAUNCE   Why, stand-under and under-stand is all one.

SPEED   But tell me true, will it be a match?

LAUNCE   Ask my dog. If he says ay, it will; if he says no, it will; if he shakes his tail and says nothing, it will.

SPEED   The conclusion is, then, that it will.

LAUNCE   You shall never get such a secret from me but by a parable.

SPEED   'Tis well that I get it so. But, Launce, how say you that my master is become a notable lover?

LAUNCE   I never knew him otherwise.

SPEED   Than how?

LAUNCE   A notable lubber, as you report him to be.

SPEED   Why, you silly ass, you mistake me.

LAUNCE   Why, fool, I meant not you, I meant your master.

SPEED   I tell you my master is become a hot lover.

LAUNCE   Why, I tell you, I care not though he burns himself in love. If you will, go with me to the alehouse; if not, you are an Hebrew, a Jew, and not worth the name of a Christian.

SPEED   Why?

LAUNCE   Because you have not so much charity in you as to go to the ale with a Christian. Will you go?

SPEED   At your service.   *Exeunt*

SCENE VI
The same.

Enter Proteus

PROTEUS

    To leave my Julia, shall I be forsworn;
    To love fair Silvia, shall I be forsworn;
    To wrong my friend, I shall be much forsworn.
    And even that power which gave me first my oath
    Provokes me to this threefold perjury:
    Love bade me swear, and Love bids me forswear.
    O sweet-suggesting Love, if you have sinned,
    Teach me, your tempted subject, to excuse it!
    At first I did adore a twinkling star,
    But now I worship a celestial sun.
    Unheedful vows may heedfully be broken;
    And he wants wit that wants resolvèd will
    To learn his wit to exchange the bad for better.
    Fie, fie, unreverend tongue, to call her bad
    Whose sovereignty so oft you have preferred
    With twenty thousand soul-confirming oaths!
    I cannot leave to love, and yet I do;
    But there I leave to love where I should love.
    Julia I lose, and Valentine I lose;
    If I keep them, I needs must lose myself;
    If I lose them, thus find I by their loss:
    For Valentine, myself; for Julia, Silvia.
    I to myself am dearer than a friend,
    For love is still most precious in itself;
    And Silvia—witness heaven, that made her fair!—
    Shows Julia but a swarthy Ethiope.
    I will forget that Julia is alive,
    Remembering that my love to her is dead;
    And Valentine I'll hold an enemy,
    Aiming at Silvia as a sweeter friend.
    I cannot now prove constant to myself

Without some treachery used to Valentine.
This night he means so with a corded ladder
To climb celestial Silvia's chamber-window,
Myself in counsel, his competitor.
Now presently I'll give her father notice
Of their disguising and intended flight,
Who, all enraged, will banish Valentine,
For Thurio he intends shall wed his daughter.
But Valentine being gone, I'll quickly cross
By some sly trick blunt Thurio's dull proceeding.
Love, lend me wings to make my purpose swift,
As you have lent me wit to plot this drift!   *Exit*

SCENE VII
Verona. Julia's house.

Enter Julia and Lucetta

JULIA
Counsel, Lucetta; gentle girl, assist me;
And, even in kind love, I do conjùre you,
Who are the table wherein all my thoughts
Are visibly charàctered and engraved,
To lesson me and tell me some good means
How, with my honour, I may undertake
A journey to my loving Proteus.

LUCETTA
Alas, the way is wearisome and long!

JULIA
A true-devoted pilgrim is not weary
To measure kingdoms with his feeble steps;
Much less shall she that has Love's wings to fly,
And when the flight is made to one so dear,
Of such divine perfection as Sir Proteus.

LUCETTA
Better forbear till Proteus makes return.

JULIA
  O, know you not his looks are my soul's food?
  Pity the dearth that I have pinèd in
  By longing for that food so long a time.
  Did you but know the inward touch of love,
  You would as soon go kindle fire with snow
  As seek to quench the fire of love with words.
LUCETTA
  I do not seek to quench your love's hot fire,
  But qualify the fire's extreme rage,
  Lest it should burn above the bounds of reason.
JULIA
  The more you dam it up, the more it burns.
  The current that with gentle murmur glides,
  You know, being stopped, impatiently does rage;
  But when his fair course is not hinderèd,
  He makes sweet music with the enamelled stones,
  Giving a gentle kiss to every sedge
  He overtakes thus in his pilgrimage;
  And so by many winding nooks he strays,
  With willing sport, to the wild oceàn.
  Then let me go, and hinder not my course.
  I'll be as patient as a gentle stream,
  And make a pastime of each weary step,
  Till the last step has brought me to my love;
  And there I'll rest as, after much turmoil,
  A blessèd soul does in Elysium.
LUCETTA
  But in what habit will you go along?
JULIA
  Not like a woman, for I would prevent
  The loose encounters of lascivious men.
  Gentle Lucetta, fit me with such clothes
  As may beseem some well-reputed page.
LUCETTA
  Why then, your ladyship must cut your hair.
JULIA
  No, girl, I'll knit it up in silken strings

With twenty odd fantastic true-love knots—
To be fantastic may become a youth
Of greater age than I shall show to be.

LUCETTA
What fashion, madam, shall I make your breeches?

JULIA
That fits as well as, 'Tell me, good my lord,
What compass will you wear your farthingale?'
Why even what fashion you best like, Lucetta.

LUCETTA
You must needs have them with a codpiece, madam.

JULIA
Out, out, Lucetta, that will be ill-looking.

LUCETTA
A round hose, madam, now is not worth a pin,
Unless you have a codpiece to stick pins on.

JULIA
Lucetta, as you love me, let me have
What you think meet, and is most mannerly.
But tell me, wench, how will the world repute me
For undertaking so unstaid a journey?
I fear me it will make me scandalized.

LUCETTA
If you think so, then stay at home and go not.

JULIA
Nay, that I will not.

LUCETTA
Then never dream on infamy, but go.
If Proteus likes your journey when you come,
No matter who's displeased when you are gone.
I fear me he will scarce be pleased with it.

JULIA
That is the least, Lucetta, of my fears:
A thousand oaths, an ocean of his tears,
And instances of infinite of love,
Warrant me welcome to my Proteus.

LUCETTA
All these are servants to deceitful men.

JULIA

> Base men, that use them to so base effect!
> But truer stars did govern Proteus' birth;
> His words are bonds, his oaths are oracles,
> His love sincere, his thoughts immaculate,
> His tears pure messengers sent from his heart,
> His heart as far from fraud as heaven from earth.

LUCETTA

> Pray heaven he proves so when you come to him!

JULIA

> Now, as you love me, do him not that wrong
> To bear a hard opinion of his truth;
> Only deserve my love by loving him.
> And presently go with me to my chamber,
> To take a note of what I stand in need of
> To furnish me upon my longing journey.
> All that is mine I leave at your dispose,
> My goods, my land, my reputation;
> Only, in lieu thereof, dispatch me hence.
> Come, answer not, but to it instantly;
> I am impatient of my tarrying.   *Exeunt*

Act III

SCENE I
Milan. Before the Duke's palace.

Enter the Duke, Thurio, and Proteus

DUKE

Sir Thurio, give us leave, I pray, awhile;
We have some secrets to confer about.   *Exit Thurio*
Now, tell me, Proteus, what is your will with me?

PROTEUS

My gracious lord, that which I would discover
The law of friendship bids me to conceal;
But when I call to mind your gracious favours
Done to me, undeserving as I am,
My duty pricks me on to utter that
Which else no worldly good should draw from me.
Know, worthy prince, Sir Valentine, my friend,
This night intends to steal away your daughter;
Myself am one made privy to the plot.
I know you have determined to bestow her
On Thurio, whom your gentle daughter hates;
And should she thus be stolen away from you,
It would be much vexation to your age.
Thus, for my duty's sake, I rather chose
To cross my friend in his intended drift
Than, by concealing it, heap on your head
A pack of sorrows which would press you down,
Being unprevented, to an untimely grave.

DUKE

Proteus, I thank you for your honest care,
Which to requite, command me while I live.
This love of theirs myself have often seen,

Haply when they have judged me fast asleep,
And oftentimes have purposed to forbid
Sir Valentine her company and my Court.
But, fearing lest my jealous aim might err,
And so, unworthily, disgrace the man—
A rashness that I ever yet have shunned—
I gave him gentle looks, thereby to find
That which yourself have now disclosed to me.
And, that you may perceive my fear of this,
Knowing that tender youth is soon led astray,
I nightly lodge her in an upper tower,
The key whereof myself have ever kept;
And thence she cannot be conveyed away.

PROTEUS

Know, noble lord, they have devised a means
How he her chamber-window will ascend
And with a corded ladder fetch her down;
For which the youthful lover now is gone,
And this way comes he with it now at once.
Where, if it please you, you may intercept him.
But, good my lord, do it so cunningly
That my discovery is not aimèd at.
For, love of you, not hate unto my friend,
Has made me publisher of this intent.

DUKE

Upon my honour, he shall never know
That I had any light from you of this.

PROTEUS

Adieu, my lord, Sir Valentine is coming.   *Exit*

          Enter Valentine

DUKE

Sir Valentine, whither away so fast?

VALENTINE

Please it your grace, there is a messenger
That stays to bear my letter to my friends,
And I am going to deliver them.

DUKE

Are they of much import?

VALENTINE

The tenor of them does but signify

My health and happy being at your Court.

DUKE

Nay then, no matter; stay with me awhile;

I am to break with you of some affairs

That touch me near, wherein you must be secret.

'Tis not unknown to you that I have sought

To match my friend Sir Thurio to my daughter.

VALENTINE

I know it well, my lord; and, sure, the match

Is rich and honourable; besides, the gentleman

Is full of virtue, bounty, worth, and qualities

Beseeming such a wife as your fair daughter.

Cannot your grace win her to fancy him?

DUKE

No, trust me; she is peevish, sullen, froward,

Proud, disobedient, stubborn, lacking duty;

Neither regarding that she is my child,

Nor fearing me as if I were her father.

And, may I say to you, this pride of hers,

Upon reflection, has drawn my love from her;

And where I thought the remnant of my age

Should have been cherished by her child-like duty,

I now am full resolved to take a wife

And turn her out to who will take her in.

Then let her beauty be her wedding-dower;

For me and my possessions she esteems not.

VALENTINE

What would your grace have me to do in this?

DUKE

There is a lady of Verona here

Whom I affect; but she is nice, and coy,

And naught esteems my agèd eloquence.

Now, therefore, would I have you to my tutor—

For long ago I have forgotten to court;

Besides, the fashion of the time is changed—
How and which way I may bestow myself
To be regarded in her sun-bright eye.

VALENTINE

Win her with gifts, if she respects not words;
Dumb jewels often in their silent kind
More than quick words do move a woman's mind.

DUKE

But she did scorn a present that I sent her.

VALENTINE

A woman sometime scorns what best contents her.
Send her another; never give her over;
For scorn at first makes after-love the more.
If she does frown, it is not in hate of you,
But rather to beget more love in you;
If she does chide, 'tis not to have you gone,
For why, the fools are mad if left alone.
Take no repulse, whatever she does say;
For 'Get you gone', she does not mean 'Away!'
Flatter and praise, commend, extol their graces;
Though never so black, say they have angels' faces.
That man that has a tongue, I say, is no man,
If with his tongue he cannot win a woman.

DUKE

But she I mean is promised by her friends
Unto a youthful gentleman of worth;
And kept severely from resort of men,
That no man has access by day to her.

VALENTINE

Why then, I would resort to her by night.

DUKE

Ay, but the doors are locked, and keys kept safe,
That no man has recourse to her by night.

VALENTINE

What else but one may enter at her window?

DUKE

Her chamber is aloft, far from the ground,
And built so shelving that one cannot climb it

Without apparent hazard of his life.
VALENTINE
  Why then, a ladder, deftly made of cords,
  To cast up with a pair of anchoring hooks,
  Would serve to scale another Hero's tower,
  So bold Leander would adventure it.
DUKE
  Now, as you are a gentleman of blood,
  Advise me where I may have such a ladder.
VALENTINE
  When would you use it? Pray, sir, tell me that.
DUKE
  This very night; for Love is like a child,
  That longs for every thing that he can come by.
VALENTINE
  By seven o'clock I'll get you such a ladder.
DUKE
  But, hark you; I will go to her alone;
  How shall I best convey the ladder thither?
VALENTINE
  It will be light, my lord, that you may bear it
  Under a cloak that is of any length.
DUKE
  A cloak as long as yours will serve the turn?
VALENTINE
  Ay, my good lord.
DUKE   Then let me see your cloak;
  I'll get me one of such another length
VALENTINE
  Why, any cloak will serve the turn, my lord.
DUKE
  How shall I fashion me to wear a cloak?
  I pray you, let me feel your cloak upon me.
  What letter is this same? What's here? *To Silvia!*
  And here an engine fit for my proceeding.
  I'll be so bold to break the seal for once.
    (*He reads*)
  My thoughts do harbour with my Silvia nightly,

And slaves they are to me, that send them flying.
O, could their master come and go as lightly,
  Himself would lodge where, senseless, they are lying!
My herald thoughts in your pure bosom rest them,
  While I, their king, that thither them importune,
Do curse the grace that with such grace has blessed them,
  Because myself do want my servants' fortune.
I curse myself, for they are sent by me,
  That they should harbour where their lord should be.
What's here?
Silvia, this night I will enfranchise thee.
'Tis so; and here's the ladder for the purpose.
Why, Phäethon—for you are Merops' son—
Will you aspire to guide the heavenly car,
And with your daring folly burn the world?
Will you reach stars, because they shine on you?
Go, base intruder, overweening slave,
Bestow your fawning smiles on equal mates;
And think my patience, more than your desert,
Is privilege for your departure hence.
Thank me for this more than for all the favours
Which, all too much, I have bestowed on you.
But if you linger in my territories
Longer than swiftest expedition
Will give you time to leave our royal Court,
By heaven, my wrath shall far exceed the love
I ever bore my daughter or yourself.
Be gone; I will not hear your vain excuse,
But, as you love your life, make speed from hence.

Exit

VALENTINE
  And why not death, rather than living torment?
  To die is to be banished from myself,
  And Silvia is myself; banished from her
  Is self from self—a deadly banishment.
  What light is light, if Silvia is not seen?
  What joy is joy, if Silvia is not by?
  Unless it is to think that she is by,

And feed upon the shadow of perfection.
Unless I am by Silvia in the night,
There is no music in the nightingale;
Unless I look on Silvia in the day,
There is no day for me to look upon.
She is my essence, and I cease to be,
If I am not by her fair influence
Fostered, illumined, cherished, kept alive.
I fly not death, to fly his deadly doom:
Tarry I here, I but attend on death;
But fly hence, I fly away from life.

Enter Proteus and Launce

PROTEUS Run, boy, run, run, and seek him out.
LAUNCE So-ho, so-ho!
PROTEUS What see you?
LAUNCE Him we go to find: there's not a hair on his head but 'tis a Valentine.
PROTEUS Valentine?
VALENTINE No.
PROTEUS Who then? His spirit?
VALENTINE Neither.
PROTEUS What then?
VALENTINE Nothing.
LAUNCE Can nothing speak? Master, shall I strike?
PROTEUS Whom would you strike?
LAUNCE Nothing.
PROTEUS Villain, forbear.
LAUNCE Why, sir, I'll strike nothing. I pray you—
PROTEUS
Fellow, I say forbear. Friend Valentine, a word.
VALENTINE
My ears are stopped and cannot hear good news,
So much of bad already has possessed them.
PROTEUS
Then in dumb silence will I bury mine,
For they are harsh, untuneable, and bad.

VALENTINE
Is Silvia dead?

PROTEUS
No, Valentine.

VALENTINE
No Valentine, indeed, for sacred Silvia.
Has she forsworn me?

PROTEUS
No, Valentine.

VALENTINE
No Valentine, if Silvia has forsworn me.
What is your news?

LAUNCE   Sir, there is a proclamation that you are
vanished.

PROTEUS
That you are banishèd—O, that's the news!—
From hence, from Silvia, and from me your friend.

VALENTINE
O, I have fed upon this woe already,
And now excess of it will make me surfeit.
Does Silvia know that I am banishèd?

PROTEUS
Ay, ay; and she has offered to the sentence—
Which, unreversed, stands in effectual force—
A sea of melting pearl, which some call tears;
Those at her father's churlish feet she tendered;
With them, upon her knees, her humble self,
Wringing her hands, whose whiteness so became them
As if but now they waxèd pale for woe.
But neither bended knees, pure hands held up,
Sad sighs, deep groans, nor silver-shedding tears,
Could penetrate her uncompassionate sire—
But Valentine, if he is taken, must die.
Besides, her intercession chafed him so,
When she for your recall was suppliant,
That to close prison he commanded her,
With many bitter threats of biding there.

VALENTINE

No more; unless the next word that you speak
Has some malignant power upon my life;
If so, I pray you breathe it in my ear,
As ending anthem of my endless dolour.

PROTEUS

Cease to lament for that you can not help,
And study help for that which you lament.
Time is the nurse and breeder of all good;
Here, if you stay, you can not see your love;
Besides, your staying will abridge your life.
Hope is a lover's staff; walk hence with that,
And manage it against despairing thoughts.
Your letters may be here, though you are hence,
Which, being written me, shall be delivered
Even in the milk-white bosom of your love.
The time now serves not to expostulate.
Come I'll convey you through the city gate;
And, ere I part with you, confer at large
Of all that may concern your love affairs.
As you love Silvia, though not for yourself,
Regard your danger, and along with me.

VALENTINE

I pray you, Launce, if you do see my boy,
Bid him make haste and meet me at the Northgate.

PROTEUS

Go, fellow, find him out. Come, Valentine.

VALENTINE

O my dear Silvia! Hapless Valentine!

Exeunt Valentine and Proteus

LAUNCE   I am but a fool, look you, and yet I have the wit
to think my master is a kind of a knave; but that's all
one if he is but one knave. He lives not now that
knows me to be in love; yet I am in love; but a team of
horse shall not pluck that from me; nor who 'tis I
love. And yet 'tis a woman; but what woman I will
not tell myself; and yet 'tis a milkmaid; yet 'tis not a
maid, for she has had boyfriends; yet 'tis a maid, for

she is her master's maid and serves for wages. She has more qualities than a water-spaniel—which is much in a bare Christian.

He pulls out a paper

Here is the catalog of her condition. *First: She can fetch and carry.* Why, a horse can do no more; nay, a horse cannot fetch, but only carry; therefore is she better than a jade. *Item: She can milk.* Look you, a sweet virtue in a maid with clean hands.

Enter Speed

SPEED How now, Signior Launce? What news with your mastership?
LAUNCE With my master's ship? Why, it is at sea.
SPEED Well, your old vice still: mistake the word. What news, then, in your paper?
LAUNCE The blackest news that ever you heard.
SPEED Why, man? How black?
LAUNCE Why, as black as ink.
SPEED Let me read them.
LAUNCE Fie on you, block-head; you can not read.
SPEED You lie; I can.
LAUNCE I will try you. Tell me this: who begot you?
SPEED Sure, the son of my grandfather.
LAUNCE O illiterate loiterer! It was the son of your grandmother. This proves that you can not read.
SPEED Come, fool, come; try me in your paper.
LAUNCE There; and Saint Nicholas speed you! Speed you!

Speed reads

SPEED *First: She can milk.*
LAUNCE Ay, that she can.
SPEED *Item: She brews good ale.*
LAUNCE And thereof comes the proverb: 'Blessing of your heart, you brew good ale.'

SPEED   *Item: She can sew.*

LAUNCE   That's as much as to say, 'Can she so?'

SPEED   *Item: She can knit.*

LAUNCE   What need a man care for a stock dowry with a wench, when she can knit him a stock?

SPEED   *Item: She can wash and scour.*

LAUNCE   A special virtue; for then she need not be washed and scoured.

SPEED   *Item: She can spin.*

LAUNCE   Then may I set the world on wheels, when she can spin for her living.

SPEED   *Item: She has many nameless virtues.*

LAUNCE   That's as much as to say, bastard virtues; that indeed know not their fathers, and therefore have no names.

SPEED   Here follow her vices.

LAUNCE   Close at the heels of her virtues.

SPEED   *Item: She is not to be kissed fasting, in respect of her breath.*

LAUNCE   Well, that fault may be mended with a break fast. Read on.

SPEED   *Item: She has a sweet mouth.*

LAUNCE   That makes amends for her sour breath.

SPEED   *Item: She does talk in her sleep.*

LAUNCE   It's no matter for that; so she sleep not in her talk.

SPEED   *Item: She is slow in words.*

LAUNCE   O villain, that set this down among her vices! To be slow in words is a woman's only virtue. I pray you, out with it, and place it for her chief virtue.

SPEED   *Item: She is proud.*

LAUNCE   Out with that too; it was Eve's legacy, and cannot be taken from her.

SPEED   *Item: She has no teeth.*

LAUNCE   I care not for that either, because I love crusts.

SPEED   *Item: She is curst.*

LAUNCE   Well, the best is, she has no teeth to bite.

SPEED   *Item: She will often praise her liquor.*

LAUNCE   If her liquor is good, she shall; if she will not, I will; for good things should be praised.

SPEED   *Item: She is too liberal.*

LAUNCE   Of her tongue she cannot, for that's written down she is slow of; of her purse, she shall not, for that I'll keep shut. Now, of another thing she may, and that cannot I help. Well, proceed.

SPEED   *Item: She has more hair than wit, and more faults than hairs, and more wealth than faults.*

LAUNCE   Stop there; I'll have her; she was mine and not mine twice or thrice in that last article. Rehearse that once more.

SPEED   *Item: She has more hair than wit—*

LAUNCE   More hair than wit? It may be I'll prove it: the cover of the salt hides the salt, and therefore it is more than the salt; the hair that covers the wit is more than the wit, for the greater hides the less. What's next?

SPEED   *And more faults than hairs—*

LAUNCE   That's monstrous. O, that that were out!

SPEED   *And more wealth than faults.*

LAUNCE   Why, that word makes the faults gracious. Well, I'll have her; if it is a match, as nothing is impossible—

SPEED   What then?

LAUNCE   Why, then will I tell you—that your master waits for you at the Northgate.

SPEED   For me?

LAUNCE   For you! Ay, who are you? He has waited for a better man than you.

SPEED   And must I go to him?

LAUNCE   You must run to him, you have stayed so long that going will scarce serve the turn.

SPEED   Why did you not tell me sooner? Pox of your love letters!   *Exit*

LAUNCE   Now will he be beaten for reading my letter. An unmannerly slave, that will thrust himself into secrets! I'll after, to rejoice in the boy's correction.

Exit

SCENE II
Milan. The Duke's palace.

Enter the Duke and Thurio

DUKE

  Sir Thurio, fear not but that she will love you
  Now Valentine is banished from her sight.

THURIO

  Since his exile she has despised me most,
  Forsworn my company, and railed at me,
  That I am desperate of obtaining her.

DUKE

  This weak impress of love is as a figure
  Trenchèd in ice, which with an hoür's heat
  Dissolves to water, and does lose its form.
  A little time will melt her frozen thoughts,
  And worthless Valentine shall be forgotten.

Enter Proteus

  How now, Sir Proteus? Is your countryman,
  According to our proclamation, gone?

PROTEUS

  Gone, my good lord.

DUKE

  My daughter takes his going grievously.

PROTEUS

  A little time, my lord, will kill that grief.

DUKE

  So I believe; but Thurio thinks not so.
  Proteus, the good opinion I hold of you—
  For you have shown some sign of good desert—
  Makes me the better to confer with you.

PROTEUS

  Longer than I prove loyal to your grace
  Let me not live to look upon your grace.

DUKE

You know how willingly I would effect
The match between Sir Thurio and my daughter?

PROTEUS

I do, my lord.

DUKE

And also, I think, you are not ignorant
How she opposes her against my will?

PROTEUS

She did, my lord, when Valentine was here.

DUKE

Ay, and perversely she persèvers so.
What might we do to make the girl forget
The love of Valentine, and love Sir Thurio?

PROTEUS

The best way is to slander Valentine,
With falsehood, cowardice, and poor descent—
Three things that women highly hold in hate.

DUKE

Ay, but she'll think that it is spoken in hate.

PROTEUS

Ay, if his enemy delivers it;
Therefore it must with circumstance be spoken
By one whom she esteems well as his friend.

DUKE

Then you must undertake to slander him.

PROTEUS

And that, my lord, I shall be loth to do:
It is an ill office for a gentleman,
Especially against his very friend.

DUKE

Where your good word cannot advantage him,
Your slander never can endamage him;
Therefore the office is indifferent,
Being entreated to it by your friend.

PROTEUS

You have prevailed, my lord; if I can do it
By aught that I can speak in his dispraise,

She shall not long continue love to him.
But say this weeds her love from Valentine,
It follows not that she will love Sir Thurio.

THURIO

Therefore, as you unwind her love from him,
Lest it should ravel and be good to none,
You must provide to wind it on to me;
Which must be done by praising me as much
As you in worth dispraise Sir Valentine.

DUKE

And, Proteus, we dare trust you in this kind,
Because we know, on Valentine's report,
You are already Love's firm votary,
And cannot soon revolt and change your mind.
Upon this warrant shall you have access
Where you with Silvia may confer at large—
For she is lumpish, heavy, melancholy,
And, for your friend's sake, will be glad of you—
Where you may temper her, by your persuasion,
To hate young Valentine and love my friend.

PROTEUS

As much as I can do I will effect.
But you, Sir Thurio, are not sharp enough;
You must lay lime to tangle her desires
By wailful sonnets, whose composèd rhymes
Should be full-fraught with serviceable vows.

DUKE

Ay,
Much is the force of heaven-bred poesy.

PROTEUS

Say that upon the altar of her beauty
You sacrifice your tears, sighs, your heart;
Write till your ink is dry, and with your tears
Moist it again, and frame some feeling line
That may discover such integrity.
For Orpheus' lute was strung with poets' sinews,
Whose golden touch could soften steel and stones,
Make tigers tame, and huge leviathans

Forsake unsounded deeps to dance on sands.
After your dire-lamenting elegies,
Visit by night your lady's chamber-window
With some sweet consort; to their instruments
Tune a deploring theme—the night's dead silence
Will well become such sweet complaining grievance.
This, or else nothing, will inherit her.

DUKE
This discipline shows you have been in love.

THURIO
And your advice this night I'll put in practice;
Therefore, sweet Proteus, my direction-giver,
Let us into the city immediately
To choose some gentlemen well skilled in music.
I have a sonnet that will serve the turn
To give the onset to your good advice.

DUKE
About it, gentlemen!

PROTEUS
We'll wait upon your grace till after supper,
And afterward determine our proceedings.

DUKE
Even now about it! I will pardon you.   *Exeunt*

Act IV

SCENE I
Near Milan. A forest.

Enter Outlaws

FIRST OUTLAW
Fellows, stand fast; I see a passenger.
SECOND OUTLAW
If there are ten, shrink not, but down with them.

Enter Valentine and Speed

THIRD OUTLAW
Stand, sir, and throw us that you have about you;
If not, we'll make you sit, and rifle you.
SPEED
Sir, we are undone; these are the villains
That all the travellers do fear so much.
VALENTINE
My friends—
FIRST OUTLAW
That's not so, sir; we are your enemies.
SECOND OUTLAW
Peace! We'll hear him.
THIRD OUTLAW
Ay, by my beard, will we; for he's a goodly man.
VALENTINE
Then know that I have little wealth to lose;
A man I am crossed with adversity;
My riches are these poor habiliments,
Of which, if you should here disfurnish me,
You take the sum and substance that I have.

SECOND OUTLAW
  Whither travel you?
VALENTINE
  To Verona
FIRST OUTLAW
  Whence came you?
VALENTINE
  From Milan.
THIRD OUTLAW   Have you long sojourned there?
VALENTINE
  Some sixteen months, and longer might have stayed,
  If crooked fortune had not thwarted me.
FIRST OUTLAW
  What, were you banished thence?
VALENTINE
  I was.
SECOND OUTLAW
  For what offence?
VALENTINE
  For that which now torments me to rehearse:
  I killed a man, whose death I much repent;
  But yet I slew him manfully in fight,
  Without false vantage or base treachery.
FIRST OUTLAW
  Why, never repent it, if it were done so.
  But were you banished for so small a fault?
VALENTINE
  I was, and held me glad of such a sentence.
SECOND OUTLAW
  Have you the tongues?
VALENTINE
  My youthful travel therein made me happy,
  Or else I often had been miserable.
THIRD OUTLAW
  By the bare scalp of Robin Hood's fat friar,
  This fellow were a king for our wild faction!
FIRST OUTLAW
  We'll have him. Sirs, a word.

SPEED   Master, be one of them; it's an honourable kind
of thievery.

VALENTINE
Peace, villain!

SECOND OUTLAW   Tell us this: have you anything to
take to?

VALENTINE
Nothing but my fortune.

THIRD OUTLAW
Know then that some of us are gentlemen,
Such as the fury of ungoverned youth
Thrust from the company of lawful men;
Myself was from Verona banishèd
For practising to steal away a lady,
An heir, and near allied unto the Duke.

SECOND OUTLAW
And I from Mantua, for a gentleman
Who, in my mood, I stabbed unto the heart.

FIRST OUTLAW
And I for such like petty crimes as these.
But to the purpose—for we cite our faults
That they may hold excused our lawless lives.
And partly, seeing you are beautified
With goodly shape, and by your own report
A linguist, and a man of such perfection
As we do in our quality much want—

SECOND OUTLAW
Indeed, because you are a banished man,
Therefore, above the rest, we parley to you.
Are you content to be our general—
To make a virtue of necessity,
And live as we do in this wilderness?

THIRD OUTLAW
What say you? Will you be of our consort?
Say 'ay', and be the captain of us all.
We'll do you homage, and be ruled by you,
Love you as our commander and our king.

FIRST OUTLAW
   But if you scorn our courtesy, you die.
SECOND OUTLAW
   You shall not live to brag what we have offered.
VALENTINE
   I take your offer, and will live with you,
   Provided that you do no outrages
   On simple women or poor passengers.
THIRD OUTLAW
   No, we detest such vile base practices.
   Come, go with us; we'll bring you to our crews,
   And show you all the treasure we have got;
   Which, with ourselves, all rest at your dispose.

Exeunt

SCENE II
Milan. The Duke's palace.

Enter Proteus

PROTEUS
   Already have I been false to Valentine,
   And now I must be as unjust to Thurio;
   Under the colour of commending him,
   I have access my own love to prefer;
   But Silvia is too fair, too true, too holy,
   To be corrupted with my worthless gifts.
   When I protest true loyalty to her,
   She twits me with my falsehood to my friend;
   When to her beauty I commend my vows,
   She bids me think how I have been forsworn
   In breaking faith with Julia, whom I loved.
   And notwithstanding all her sudden quips,
   The least whereof would quell a lover's hope,
   Yet spaniel-like, the more she spurns my love
   The more it grows and fawns more on her still.

Enter Thurio and Musicians

But here comes Thurio. Now must we to her window,
And give some evening music to her ear.
THURIO
How now, Sir Proteus, are you crept before us?
PROTEUS
Ay, gentle Thurio; for you know that love
Will creep in service where it cannot walk.
THURIO
Ay, but I hope, sir, that you love not here.
PROTEUS
Sir, but I do; or else I would be hence.
THURIO
Who? Silvia?
PROTEUS   Ay, Silvia—for your sake.
THURIO
I thank you for your own. Now, gentlemen,
Let's tune, and to it lustily awhile.

*Enter the Host of the Inn, and Julia disguised
as a page*

HOST   Now, my young guest, it seems you're allycholly
[melancholy];
I pray you, why is it?
JULIA   Well, mine host, because I cannot be merry.
HOST   Come, we'll have you merry; I'll bring you where
you shall hear music, and see the gentleman that you
asked for.
JULIA   But shall I hear him speak?
HOST   Ay, that you shall.
JULIA   That will be music.

The musicians play

HOST   Hark, hark!
JULIA   Is he among these?

HOST   Ay; but, peace! Let's hear them.

    Song

    Who is Silvia? What is she,
      That all our swains commend her?
    Holy, fair, and wise is she;
      The heaven such grace did lend her,
    That she might admirèd be.

    Is she kind as she is fair?
      For beauty lives with kindness.
    Love does to her eyes repair,
      To help him of his blindness;
    And, being helped, inhabits there.

    Then to Silvia let us sing
      That Silvia is excelling;
    She excels each mortal thing
      Upon the dull earth dwelling.
    To her let us garlands bring.

HOST   How now? Are you sadder than you were before?
  How do you, man? The music likes you not.
JULIA   You mistake; the musician likes me not.
HOST   Why, my pretty youth?
JULIA   He plays false, father.
HOST   How? Out of tune on the strings?
JULIA   Not so; but yet so false that he grieves my very
  heart-strings.
HOST   You have a quick ear.
JULIA   Ay, I would I were deaf; it makes me have a slow
  heart.
HOST   I perceive you delight not in music.
JULIA   Not a whit, when it jars so.
HOST   Hark, what fine change is in the music!
JULIA   Ay; that change is the spite.
HOST   You would have them always play but one thing?

JULIA

  I would always have one play but one thing.

  But, host, does this Sir Proteus, that we talk on,

  Often resort unto this gentlewoman?

HOST   I tell you what Launce, his man, told me: he

  loved her out of all reckoning.

JULIA   Where is Launce?

HOST   Gone to seek his dog, which tomorrow, by his

  master's command, he must carry for a present to his

  lady.

JULIA

  Peace! Stand aside; the company parts.

PROTEUS

  Sir Thurio, fear not you; I will so plead

  That you shall say my cunning drift excels.

THURIO

  Where meet we?

PROTEUS   Saint Gregory's Well.

THURIO   Farewell.

                Exeunt Thurio and Musicians

    Enter Silvia above

PROTEUS

  Madam, good even to your ladyship.

SILVIA

  I thank you for your music, gentlemen.

  Who is that that spoke?

PROTEUS

  One, lady, if you knew his pure heart's truth,

  You would quickly learn to know him by his voice.

SILVIA

  Sir Proteus, as I take it.

PROTEUS

  Sir Proteus, gentle lady, and your servant.

SILVIA

  What's your will?

PROTEUS   That I may compass yours.

SILVIA
    You have your wish; my will is even this,
    That instantly you hie you home to bed.
    You subtle, perjured, false, disloyal man,
    Think you I am shallow, or so thoughtless,
    To be seducèd by your flattery
    That have deceived so many with your vows?
    Return, return, and make your love amends.
    For me—by this pale queen of night I swear—
    I am so far from granting your request
    That I despise you for your wrongful suit;
    And by and by intend to chide myself
    Even for this time I spend in talking to you.
PROTEUS
    I grant, sweet love, that I did love a lady.
    But she is dead.
JULIA (aside)   'Tis false, if I should speak it;
    For I am sure she is not buried.
SILVIA
    Say that she is; yet Valentine your friend
    Survives, to whom, yourself are witness,
    I am betrothed; and are you not ashamed
    To wrong him with your importùnacy?
PROTEUS
    I likewise hear that Valentine is dead.
SILVIA
    And so suppose am I; for in his grave
    Assure yourself my love is buried.
PROTEUS
    Sweet lady, let me rake it from the earth.
SILVIA
    Go to your lady's grave and call hers thence;
    Or, at the least, in hers sepùlchre yours.
JULIA (aside)
    He heard not that.
PROTEUS
    Madam, if your heart is so obdùrate,
    Grant me yet your picture for my love,

The picture that is hanging in your chamber.
To that I'll speak, to that I'll sigh and weep;
For since the substance of your perfect self
Is else devoted, I am but a shadow;
And to your shadow will I make true love.

JULIA   *(aside)*
If though a substance, you would sure deceive it
And make it but a shadow, as I am.

SILVIA
I am very loth to be your idol, sir;
But since your falsehood shall become you well
To worship shadows and adore false shapes,
Send to me in the morning and I'll send it;
And so, good rest.

PROTEUS   As wretches have overnight
That wait for execution in the morn.

                              Exeunt Proteus and Silvia

JULIA   Host, will you go?
HOST   By my word, I was fast asleep.
JULIA   Pray you, where lies Sir Proteus?
HOST   Sure, at my house. Trust me, I think it is almost
    day.
JULIA
Not so; but it has been the longest night
That ever I watched, and the heaviest too.   *Exeunt*

SCENE III
The same.

Enter Eglamour

EGLAMOUR
This is the hour that Madam Silvia
Entreated me to call and know her mind;
There's some great matter she'd employ me in.
Madam, madam!

Enter Silvia at an upstairs window

SILVIA   Who calls?
EGLAMOUR   Your servant and your friend;
  One that attends your ladyship's command.
SILVIA
  Sir Eglamour, a thousand times good morrow.
EGLAMOUR
  As many, worthy lady, to yourself!
  According to your ladyships' command,
  I am thus early come, to know what service
  It is your pleasure to command me in.
SILVIA
  O Eglamour, you are a gentleman—
  Think not I flatter, for I swear I do not—
  Valiant, wise, remorseful, well-accomplished.
  You are not ignorant what dear good will
  I bear unto the banished Valentine;
  Nor how my father would enforce me marry
  Vain Thurio, whom my very soul abhors.
  Yourself have loved, and I have heard you say
  No grief did ever come so near your heart
  As when your lady and your true love died,
  Upon whose grave you vowed pure chastity.
  Sir Eglamour, I would to Valentine,
  To Mantua, where I hear he makes abode;
  Because the ways are dangerous to pass,
  I do desire your worthy company,
  Upon whose faith and honour I repose,
  Urge not my father's anger, Eglamour,
  But think upon my grief, a lady's grief,
  And on the justice of my flying hence,
  To keep me from a most unholy match,
  Which heaven and fortune do reward with plagues.
  I do desire you, even from a heart
  As full of sorrows as the sea of sands,
  To bear me company and go with me;
  If not, to hide what I have said to you,

That I may venture to depart alone.

EGLAMOUR

Madam, I pity much your grievances;
Which since I know they virtuously are placed,
I give consent to go along with you,
Recking as little what betides me now
As much I wish all good befortune you.
When will you go?

SILVIA   This evening coming.

EGLAMOUR

Where shall I meet you?

SILVIA   At Friar Patrick's cell,
Where I intend holy confessìon.

EGLAMOUR   I will not fail your ladyship. Good morrow,
gentle lady.

SILVIA   Good morrow, kind Sir Eglamour.   *Exeunt*

SCENE IV
The same.

Enter Launce, with his dog

LAUNCE   When a man's servant shall play the cur with
him, look you, it goes hard—one that I brought up of a
puppy; one that I saved from drowning, when three or
four of his blind brothers and sisters went to it. I have
taught him, even as one would say precisely, 'Thus I
would teach a dog.' I was sent to deliver him as a
present to Mistress Silvia from my master; and I
came no sooner into the dining-chamber, but he
steps to her trencher and steals her chicken's leg. O,
'tis a foul thing when a cur cannot keep himself in all
companies! I would have, as one should say, one that
takes upon him to be a dog indeed, to be, as it were, a
dog at all things. If I had not had more wit than he, to
take a fault upon me that he did, I think verily he had
been hanged for it sure as I live, he had suffered for it.

You shall judge. He thrusts himself into the company of three or four gentlemanlike dogs under the Duke's table; he had not been there, bless the mark, a pissing while but all the chamber smelt him. 'Out with the dog!' says one; 'What cur is that?' says another; 'Whip him out,' says the third; 'Hang him up,' says the Duke. I, having been acquainted with the smell before, knew it was Crab, and go to the fellow that whips the dogs. 'Friend,' said I, 'you mean to whip the dog?' 'Ay, sure, do I, ' said he. 'You do him the more wrong,' said I, 'it was I did the thing you know of.' He makes me no more ado, but whips me out of the chamber. How many masters would do this for his servant? Nay, I'll be sworn, I have sat in the stocks for puddings he has stolen, otherwise he had been executed; I have stood on the pillory for geese he has killed, otherwise he had suffered for it. You think not of this now. Nay, I remember the trick you served me when I took leave of Madam Silvia. Did not I bid you always mark me and do as I do? When did you see me heave up my leg and make water against a gentlewoman's farthingale? Did you ever see me do such a trick?

Enter Proteus, and Julia disguised

PROTEUS
Sebastian is your name? I like you well,
And will employ you in some service presently.
JULIA
In what you please; I will do what I can.
PROTEUS
I hope you will (*To Launce*) How now, you filthy
        peasant!
Where have you been these two days loitering?
LAUNCE   Sure sir, I carried Mistress Silvia the dog you
bade me.
PROTEUS   And what says she to my little jewel?

LAUNCE   Sure she says your dog was a cur, and tells you
  currish thanks are good enough for such a present.
PROTEUS   But she received my dog?
LAUNCE   No, indeed, did she not; here have I brought
  him back again.
PROTEUS   What, did you offer this from me?
LAUNCE   Ay, sir; the other squirrel was stolen from me
  by the hangman boys in the market-place; and then I
  offered her my own, which is a dog as big as ten of
  yours, and therefore the gift was greater.
PROTEUS
  Go get you hence and find my dog again,
  Or never return again into my sight.
  Away, I say! Stay you to vex me here?

                            Exit Launce

  A slave that continually turns me to shame!
  Sebastian, I have entertained you,
  Partly that I have need of such a youth
  That can with some discretion do my business,
  For 'tis no trusting to yon foolish lout;
  But chiefly for your face and your behavior.
  Which, if my augury deceives me not,
  Witness good bringing up, fortune, and truth;
  Therefore, know you, for this I entertain you.
  Go presently, and take this ring with you,
  Deliver it to Madam Silvia—
  She loved me well who delivered it to me.
JULIA
  It seems you loved not her, to leave her token.
  She is dead, perhaps.
PROTEUS   Not so; I think she lives.
JULIA
  Alas!
PROTEUS
  Why do you cry 'Alas'?
JULIA   I cannot choose
  But pity her.
PROTEUS   Wherefore should you pity her?

JULIA
  Because I think that she loved you as well
  As you do love your lady Silvia.
  She dreams on him that has forgot her love;
  You dote on her that cares not for your love;
  'Tis pity love should be so contrary;
  And thinking on it makes me cry 'Alas'!
PROTEUS
  Well, give her that ring, and therewith it
  This letter. That is her chamber. Tell my lady
  I claim the promise for her heavenly picture.
  Your message done, hie home unto my chamber,
  Where you shall find me sad and solitary.   *Exit*
JULIA
  How many women would do such a message?
  Alas, poor Proteus, you have entertained
  A fox to be the shepherd of your lambs.
  Alas, poor fool, why do I pity him
  That with his very heart despises me?
  Because he loves her, he despises me;
  Because I love him, I must pity him.
  This ring I gave him, when he parted from me,
  To bind him to remember my good will;
  And now am I, unhappy messenger,
  To plead for that which I would not obtain,
  To carry that which I would have refused,
  To praise his faith, which I would have dispraised.
  I am my master's true confirmèd love,
  But cannot be true servant to my master,
  Unless I prove false traitor to myself.
  Yet will I woo for him, but yet so coldly
  As, heaven it knows, I would not have him speed.

    Enter Silvia with Attendants

  Gentlewoman, good day! I pray you, be my means
  To bring me where to speak with Madam Silvia.

SILVIA

What would you with her, if then I am she?

JULIA

If you are she, I do entreat your patience
To hear me speak the message I am sent on.

SILVIA

From whom?

JULIA

From my master, Sir Proteus, madam.

SILVIA

O, he sends you for a picture.

JULIA

Ay, madam.

SYLVIA

Ursula, bring my picture there.
Go, give your master this. Tell him from me,
One Julia, that his changing thoughts forget,
Would better fit his chamber than this shadow.

JULIA

Madam, please you peruse this letter—
Pardon me, madam; I have unadvised
Delivered you a paper that I should not.

*Julia takes back the letter she offers and gives
Silvia another*

This is the letter to your ladyship.

SILVIA

I pray you let me look on that again.

JULIA

It may not be; good madam, pardon me.

SILVIA

There, hold!

She tears the letter

I will not look upon your master's lines.
I know they are stuffed with protestatiòns,

And full of new-found oaths, which he will break
As easily as I do tear his paper.

JULIA

Madam, he sends your ladyship this ring.

SILVIA

The more shame for him that he sends it me;
For I have heard him say a thousand times
His Julia gave it him, at his departure.
Though his false finger has profaned the ring,
Mine shall not do his Julia so much wrong.

JULIA

She thanks you.

SILVIA

What say you?

JULIA

I thank you, madam, that you consider her.
Poor gentlewoman! My master wrongs her much.

SILVIA

Do you know her?

JULIA

Almost as well as I do know myself.
To think upon her woes, I do protest
That I have wept a hundred separate times.

SILVIA

Perhaps she thinks that Proteus has forsaken her.

JULIA

I think she does, and that's her cause of sorrow.

SILVIA

Is she not passing fair?

JULIA

She has been fairer, madam, than she is.
When she did think my master loved her well,
She, in my judgement, was as fair as you.
But since she did neglect her looking-glass
And threw her sun-expelling mask away,
That air has starved the roses in her cheeks
And pinched the lily-tincture of her face,
That now she is become as black as I.

SILVIA
  How tall was she?
JULIA
  About my stature; for, at Pentecost,
  When all our pageants of delight were played,
  Our youth got me to play the woman's part
  And I was trimmed in Madam Julia's gown,
  Which servèd me as fit, by all men's judgements,
  As if the garment had been made for me;
  Therefore I know she is about my height.
  And at that time I made her weep agood,
  For I did play a lamentable part.
  Madam, 'twas Ariadne passioning
  For Theseus' perjury and unjust flight;
  Which I so lively acted with my tears
  That my poor mistress, movèd therewith it,
  Wept bitterly; and would I might be dead
  If I in thought felt not her very sorrow.
SILVIA
  She is beholding to you, gentle youth.
  Alas, poor lady, desolate and left!
  I weep myself, to think upon your words.
  Here, youth; there is my purse; I give you this
  For your sweet mistress' sake, because you love her.
  Farewell.
                        Exeunt Silvia and attendants
JULIA
  And she shall thank you for it, if ever you know her.
  A virtuous gentlewoman, mild, and beautiful!
  I hope my master's suit will be but cold,
  Since she respects my mistress' love so much.
  Alas, how love can trifle with itself!
  Here is her picture; let me see. I think
  If I had such attire this face of mine
  Were full as lovely as is this of hers;
  And yet the painter flattered her a little,
  Unless I flatter with myself too much.
  Her hair is auburn, mine is perfect yellow;

If that is all the difference in his love,
I'll get me such a coloured periwig.
Her eyes are grey as glass, and so are mine;
Ay, but her forehead's low, and mine's as high.
What should it be that he respects in her
But I can make respective in myself,
If this fond Love were not a blinded god?
Come, shadow, come and take this shadow up,
For 'tis your rival. O, you senseless form,
You shall be worshipped, kissed, loved, and adored!
And were there sense in his idolatry,
My substance should be statue in your stead.
I'll use you kindly for your mistress' sake,
That used me so; or else, by Jove I vow,
I should have scratched out your unseeing eyes,
To make my master out of love with you!   *Exit*

Act V

SCENE I
An abbey.

Enter Eglamour

EGLAMOUR
The sun begins to gild the western sky,
And now it is about the very hour
That Silvia at Friar Patrick's cell should meet me.
She will not fail, for lovers break not hours
Unless it is to come before their time,
So much they spur their expedition.

Enter Silvia

See where she comes. Lady, a happy evening!
SILVIA
Amen, amen! Go on, good Eglamour,
Out at the postern by the abbey wall;
I fear I am attended by some spies.
EGLAMOUR
Fear not. The forest is not three leagues off;
If we recover that, we are sure enough.   *Exeunt*

SCENE II
Milan. The Duke's palace.

Enter Thurio, Proteus, and Julia disguised

THURIO
Sir Proteus, what says Silvia to my suit?

PROTEUS
  O, sir, I find her milder than she was;
  And yet she takes exception at your person.
THURIO
  What? That my leg is too long?
PROTEUS
  No, that it is too little.
THURIO
  I'll wear a boot to make it somewhat rounder.
JULIA (*aside*)
  But love will not be spurred to what it loathes.
THURIO
  What says she to my face?
PROTEUS
  She says it is a fair one.
THURIO
  Nay then, the wanton lies; my face is black.
PROTEUS
  But pearls are fair; and the old saying is:
  Black men are pearls in beauteous ladies' eyes.
JULIA (*aside*)
  'Tis true, such pearls as put out ladies' eyes;
  For I had rather wink than look on them.
THURIO
  How likes she my discourse?
PROTEUS
  Ill, when you talk of war.
THURIO
  But well when I discourse of love and peace.
JULIA (*aside*)
  But better, indeed, when you hold your peace.
THURIO
  What says she to my valour?
PROTEUS
  O, sir, she makes no doubt of that.
JULIA (*aside*)
  She needs not, when she knows it cowardice.
THURIO
  What says she to my birth?

PROTEUS
  That you are well derived.
JULIA (*aside*)
  That such an ass should own them.
THURIO
  Considers she my possessions?
PROTEUS
  O, ay; and pities them.
THURIO
  Wherefore?
JULIA (*aside*)
  That such an ass should own them.
PROTEUS
  That they are out by lease.

  Enter the Duke

JULIA
  Here comes the Duke.
DUKE
  How now, Sir Proteus! How now, Thurio!
  Which of you saw Sir Eglamour of late?
THURIO
  Not I.
PROTEUS Nor I.
DUKE   Saw you my daughter?
PROTEUS   Neither.
DUKE
  Why then,
  She's fled unto that peasant Valentine;
  And Eglamour is in her company.
  'Tis true; for Friar Laurence met them both
  As he in penance wandered through the forest;
  Him he knew well, and guessed that it was she,
  But being masked, he was not sure of it.
  Besides, she did intend confessiòn
  At Patrick's cell this even; and there she was not.
  These likelihoods confirm her flight from hence;

Therefore, I pray you, stand not to discourse,
But mount you instantly, and meet with me
Upon rising of the mountain-foot
That leads toward Mantua, whither they are fled.
Dispatch, sweet gentlemen, and follow me.   *Exit*

THURIO
Why, this it is to be a peevish girl
That flies her fortune when it follows her.
I'll after, more to be revenged on Eglamour
Than for the love of reckless Silvia.   *Exit*

PROTEUS
And I will follow, more for Silvia's love
Than hate of Eglamour, that goes with her.   *Exit*

JULIA
And I will follow, more to cross that love
Than hate for Silvia, that is gone for love.   *Exit*

SCENE III
The forest.

Enter the Outlaws with Silvia captive

FIRST OUTLAW
Come, come,
Be patient; we must bring you to our captain.

SILVIA
A thousand more mischances than this one
Have taught me how to brook this patiently.

SECOND OUTLAW
Come, bring her away.

FIRST OUTLAW
Where is the gentleman that was with her?

THIRD OUTLAW
Being nimble-footed, he has outrun us,
But Moyses and Valerius follow him.
Go you with her to the west end of the wood;
There is our captain; we'll follow him that's fled.

The thicket is beset; he cannot escape.
FIRST OUTLAW
   Come, I must bring you to our captain's cave;
   Fear not; he bears an honourable mind,
   And will not use a woman lawlessly.
SILVIA
   O Valentine, this I endure for you.   *Exeunt*

SCENE IV
The same.

   Enter Valentine

VALENTINE
   How use does breed a habit in a man!
   This shadowy desert, unfrequented woods,
   I better brook than flourishing peopled towns.
   Here can I set alone, unseen of any,
   And to the nightingale's complaining notes
   Tune my distresses, and record my woes.
   O you that do inhabit in my breast,
   Leave not the mansion so long tenantless,
   Lest growing ruinous, the building falls
   And leaves no memory of what it was!
   Repair me with your presence, Silvia;
   You gentle nymph, cherish your forlorn swain.

      Noises within

   What halloing and what stir is this today?
   These are my mates, that make their wills their law,
   Have some unhappy passenger in chase.
   They love me well; yet I have much to do
   To keep them from uncivil outrages.
   Withdraw you, Valentine. Who's this comes here?

      He steps aside
      Enter Proteus, Silvia, and Julia disguised

PROTEUS

    Madam, this service I have done for you,

    Though you respect not aught your servant does,

    To hazard life, and rescue you from him

    That would have forced your honour and your love.

    Grant me, for my reward, but one fair look;

    A smaller boon than this I cannot beg,

    And less than this, I am sure, you cannot give.

VALENTINE *(aside)*

    How like a dream is this I see and hear!

    Love, lend me patience to forbear awhile.

SILVIA

    O miserable, unhappy that I am!

PROTEUS

    Unhappy were you, madam, ere I came;

    But by my coming I have made you happy.

SILVIA

    By your approach you make me most unhappy.

JULIA *(aside)*

    And me, when he approaches to your presence.

SILVIA

    Had I been seizèd by a hungry lion,

    I would have been a breakfast to the beast,

    Rather than have false Proteus rescue me.

    O, heaven be judge how I love Valentine,

    Whose life's as tender to me as my soul!

    And full as much, for more there cannot be,

    I do detest false perjured Proteus.

    Therefore be gone; solicit me no more.

PROTEUS

    What dangerous action, stood it next to death,

    Would I not undergo for one calm look?

    O, 'tis the curse in love, and ever approved,

    When women cannot love where they're beloved!

SILVIA

    When Proteus cannot love where he's beloved!

    Read over Julia's heart, your first best love,

    For whose dear sake you did then rend your faith

Into a thousand oaths; and all those oaths
Descended into perjury, to love me.
You have no faith left now, unless you've two,
And that's far worse than none; better have none
Than plural faith, which is too much by one.
You counterfeit to your true friend!

PROTEUS   In love,
Who respects friend?

SILVIA   All men but Proteus.

PROTEUS
Nay, if the gentle spirit of moving words
Can no way change you to a milder form,
I'll woo you like a soldier, at arms' end,
And love you against the nature of love—force you.

SILVIA
O heaven!

PROTEUS   I'll force you to yield to my desire.

Valentine steps forward

VALENTINE
Ruffian, let go that rude uncivil touch;
You friend of an ill fashion!

PROTEUS   Valentine!

VALENTINE
You common friend that's without faith or love—
For such is a friend now: treacherous man,
You have beguiled my hopes; naught but my eye
Could have persuaded me. Now I dare not say
I have one friend alive: You would disprove me.
Who should be trusted now, when one's right hand
Is perjured to the bosom? Proteus,
I am sorry I must never trust you more,
But count the world a stranger for your sake.
The private wound is deepest, O time most accurst!
Among all foes that a friend should be the worst!

PROTEUS
My shame and guilt confound me.

Forgive me, Valentine; if hearty sorrow
Is a sufficient ransom for offence,
I tender it here; I do as truly suffer
As ever I did commit.

VALENTINE   Then I am paid;
And once again I do receive you honest.
Who by repentance is not satisfied
Is nor of heaven nor earth, for these are pleased;
By penitence the Eternal's wrath's appeased.
And, that my love may appear plain and free,
All that was mine in Silvia I give thee.

JULIA   O me unhappy!

She swoons

PROTEUS   Look to the boy.

VALENTINE   Why, boy? Why, child, how now? What's
the matter? Look up; speak.

JULIA   O, good sir, my master charged me to deliver a
ring to Madam Silvia, which, out of my neglect, was
never done.

PROTEUS   Where is that ring, boy?

JULIA   Here it is; this is it.

She offers her own ring

PROTEUS   How? Let me see. Why, this is the ring I gave
to Julia.

JULIA
O, cry you mercy, sir, I have mistaken;
This is the ring you sent to Silvia.

She offers another ring

PROTEUS   But how came you by this ring? At my depart
I gave this unto Julia.

JULIA
And Julia herself did give it me;

And Julia herself has brought it hither.

PROTEUS

How? Julia?

JULIA

Behold her that gave aim to all your oaths,
And entertained them deeply in her heart.
How oft have you with perjury cleft the root!
O Proteus, let this habit make you blush!
Be you ashamed that I have taken upon me
Such an immodest raiment, if shame lives
In a disguise of love.
It is the lesser blot, modesty finds,
Women to change their shapes than men their minds.

PROTEUS

Than men their minds? 'Tis true. O heaven, were man
But constant, he were perfect! That one error
Fills him with faults; makes him run through all the
   sins:
Inconstancy falls off ere it begins.
What is in Silvia's face, but I may spy
More fresh in Julia's with a constant eye?

VALENTINE

Come, come, a hand from either.
Let me be blest to make this happy close;
'Twere pity two such friends should be long foes.

PROTEUS

Bear witness, heaven, I have my wish for ever.

JULIA

And I mine.

*Enter the Outlaw, with the Duke
and Thurio captives*

OUTLAWS

A prize, a prize, a prize!

VALENTINE   Forbear,
Forbear, I say! It is my lord the Duke.
Your grace is welcome to a man disgraced,
Banishèd Valentine.

DUKE   Sir Valentine?

THURIO

Yonder is Silvia; and Silvia's mine.

VALENTINE

Thurio, give back, or else embrace your death;
Come not within the measure of my wrath;
Do not name Silvia yours; if once again,
Verona shall not hold you. Here she stands;
Take but possession of her with a touch—
I dare you but to breathe upon my love.

THURIO

Sir Valentine, I care not for her, I:
I hold him but a fool that will endanger
His body for a girl that loves him not.
I claim her not and therefore she is yours.

DUKE

The more degenerate and base are you
To make such means for her as you have done,
And leave her on such slight conditiòns.
Now, by the honour of my ancestry,
I do applaud your spirit, Valentine,
And think you worthy of an empress' love.
Know, then, I here forget all former griefs,
Cancel all grudge, recall you home again,
Plead a new state in your unrivalled merit,
To which I thus subscribe: Sir Valentine.
You are a gentleman, and well derived;
Take you your Silvia, for you have deserved her.

VALENTINE

I thank your grace; the gift has made me happy.
I now beseech you, for your daughter's sake,
To grant one boon that I shall ask of you.

DUKE

I grant it, for your own, whatever it is.

VALENTINE

These banished men, that I have kept with here,
Are men endued with worthy qualities;
Forgive them what they have committed here,

And let them be recallèd from their exile.
They are reformèd, civil, full of good,
And fit for great employment, worthy lord.

DUKE

You have prevailed; I pardon them and you;
Dispose of them as you know their deserts.
Come, let us go; we will conclude all jars
With triumphs, mirth, and rare solemnity.

VALENTINE

And, as we walk along, I dare be bold
With our discoùrse to make your grace to smile.
What think you of this page, my lord?

DUKE

I think the boy has grace in him; he blushes.

VALENTINE

I warrant you, my lord—more grace than boy.

DUKE

What mean you by that saying?

VALENTINE

Please you, I'll tell you as we pass along,
That you will wonder what has fortunèd.
Come, Proteus it is your penance but to hear
The story of your loves discoverèd.
That done, our day of marriage shall be yours:
One feast, one house, one mutual happiness.

Exeunt